The
Vanishing
American
Jew

The Best Defense

Reversal of Fortune: Inside the von Bülow Case

Taking Liberties: A Decade of Hard Cases,
Bad Laws, and Bum Raps

Chutzpah

The Abuse Excuse: And Other Cop-Outs, Sob Stories,
and Evasions of Responsibility

Contrary to Popular Opinion

Reasonable Doubts

The Advocate's Devil

The Vanishing American Jew

In Search of Jewish Identity for the Next Century

Alan M. Dershowitz

A TOUCHSTONE BOOK
PUBLISHED BY SIMON & SCHUSTER

TOUCHSTONE
Rockefeller Center
1230 Avenue of the Americas
New York, NY 10020

First Touchstone Edition 1998
Published by arrangement with
Little, Brown & Company

Manufactured in the United States of America

1   3   5   7   9   10   8   6   4   2

Library of Congress Cataloging-in-Publication Data is
available upon request

ISBN 0-684-84898-8

To Lori, Lyle, Barbara, and Jamin,
New links in an old chain

Contents

VIII / *Contents*

Acknowledgments

ANY BOOK ABOUT Judaism is a book about family. My family reflects the wide panorama of the Jewish experience — from ultra-Orthodox to modern Orthodox to Conservative to secular to inter-married, from New York to Southern to Californian to Israeli. I have had loving, if sometimes contentious, input from my entire family. My special gratitude goes to those closest to me. My wife, Carolyn, has read and critiqued every draft. My daughter, Ella, has shared her Hebrew school experiences and suggested several titles. My sons, Elon and Jamin, read, argued, suggested, and helped me rethink. My mother, Claire, supported and encouraged, while disagreeing with much that I say. My "older" and wiser brother, Nathan (who was born four years after me), counseled and critiqued. My parents-in-law, Dutch and Mordechai Cohen, my sisters-in-law, Marilyn and Julie, and my brother-in-law, Marvin, read drafts, made valuable suggestions, and provided support. My daughter-in-law, Barbara, and my grandchildren, Lori and Lyle, were important inspirations for this book. My nephews and niece, Adam, Isaac, Jonah, and Rana, discussed drafts and provided ideas. Many other relatives, living and dead, inspired both my love for Judaism and my critical approach to thinking about religion, law, and life.

This book could not have been written without my students, who keep me current, challenge me at every turn, and know how to use all the fancy research machines that give me rashes even thinking about them. Special thanks to Wendy Amsellem, Jeremy Bash, Jeremy Blumenthal, Joshua Blumenthal, Ivan Deutsch, Daniel Eisenstadt, Robert Jancu, Daniel Libenson, Sharon Lisitzky, John Orsini, Jerrold Rapaport, Eli Schulman, and Adina Spiro.

Friends and colleagues also helped by reading drafts, giving me ideas, and telling me good jokes. Among them are Murray and Malkie Altman, Bernie and Judy Beck, Zolie and Katie Eisenstadt, Hal and Sandy Miller-Jacobs, Carl and Joan Meshenberg, Josh and Rachelle Wiesberger, Barry and Barbara Zimmerman, Joseph Weiler, Irwin Cotler, and Jeffrey Epstein. My assistant Gayle Muello oversaw the production of the book, with her usual professionalism and support. She was assisted by Lisa Green, Frances Justice, and John Orsini. Michael Schneider has been helpful in so many ways. My literary agent, Helen Rees, is a constant source of encouragement. And I value my editor, Fredrica Friedman, whose enthusiasm for this project, as for our first book together, *Chutzpah*, was unwavering, and whose counsel and judgment are part of these pages. My great appreciation also goes to Peggy Freudenthal, whose exceptionally able editing made the book better and whose pleasant manner made the process smoother.

I also want to thank my lecture audiences for the perceptive questions they ask, which I try to answer in this book.

The
Vanishing
American
Jew

Introduction

The *"Jewish Question"* for the Twenty-first Century: Can We Survive Our Success?

THE GOOD NEWS is that American Jews — as *individuals* — have never been more secure, more accepted, more affluent, and less victimized by discrimination or anti-Semitism. The bad news is that American Jews — as a *people* — have never been in greater danger of disappearing through assimilation, intermarriage, and low birthrates. The even worse news is that our very success as individuals contributes to our vulnerability as a people. The even better news is that we can overcome this new threat to the continuity of American Jewish life and emerge with a more positive Judaism for the twenty-first century — a Judaism that is less dependent on our enemies for its continuity, and that rests more securely on the considerable, but largely untapped, strengths of our own heritage.

American Jewish life is in danger of disappearing, just as most American Jews have achieved everything we ever wanted: acceptance, influence, affluence, equality. As the result of skyrocketing rates of intermarriage and assimilation, as well as "the lowest birth rate of any religious or ethnic community in the United States," the era of enormous Jewish influence on American life may soon be coming to an end.[1] Although Jews make up just over 2 percent of the population of the United States — approximately 5.5 million[2] out of 262 million — many Americans mistakenly believe that we constitute a full 20 percent of the American people, because of our disproportionate visibility, influence, and accomplishments.[3] But our numbers may soon be reduced to the point where our impact on American life will necessarily become marginalized. One Harvard study predicts that if current demographic trends continue, the American Jewish community is likely to number less than 1 million and conceivably as few as 10,000 by the time the United States celebrates its tricentennial in 2076.[4] Other projections suggest that early in the next century, American Jewish life as we know it will be a shadow of its current, vibrant self — consisting primarily of isolated pockets of ultra-Orthodox Hasidim.[5]

Jews have faced dangers in the past, but this time we may be unprepared to confront the newest threat to our survival *as a people*, because its principal cause is our own success *as individuals*. Our long history of victimization has prepared us to defend against those who would destroy us out of hatred; indeed, our history has forged a Jewish identity far too dependent on persecution and victimization by our enemies. But today's most serious threats come not from those who would persecute us, but from those who would, without any malice, kill us with kindness — by assimilating us, marrying us, and merging with us out of respect, admiration, and even love. The continuity of the most influential Jewish community in history is at imminent risk, unless we do something dramatic *now* to confront the quickly changing dangers.

This book is a call to action for all who refuse to accept our demographic demise as inevitable. It is a demand for a new Jewish state of mind capable of challenging the conventional wisdom that Judaism is more adaptive to persecution and discrimination than it is to an open, free, and welcoming society — that Jews paradoxically need enemies in order to survive, that anti-Semitism is what has kept Judaism alive. This age-old perspective on Jewish survival is illustrated by two tragic stories involving respected rabbinical leaders.

The first story takes place in 1812, when Napoleon was battling the czar for control of the Pale of Settlement (the western part of czarist Russia), where millions of Jews were forced to live in crowded poverty and under persecution and discrimination as second-class subjects. A victory for Napoleon held the promise of prosperity, first-class citizenship, freedom of movement, and an end to discrimination and persecution. A victory for the czar would keep the Jews impoverished and miserable. The great Hasidic rabbi Shneur Zalman — the founder of the Lubavitch dynasty — stood up in his synagogue on the first day of Rosh Hashanah to offer a prayer to God asking help for the leader whose victory would be good for the Jews. Everyone expected him to pray for Napoleon. But he prayed for the czar to defeat Napoleon. In explaining his counterintuitive choice, he said: "Should Bonaparte win, the wealth of the Jews will be increased and their [civic] position will be raised. At the same time their hearts will be estranged from our Heavenly Father. Should however our Czar Alexander win, the Jewish hearts will draw nearer to our Heavenly Father, though the poverty of Israel may become greater and his position lower."[6]

This remarkable story is all too typical of how so many Jewish leaders throughout our history have reasoned about Jewish survival. Without tsuris — troubles — we will cease to be Jewish. We *need* to be persecuted, impoverished, discriminated against, hated, and victimized in order for us to retain our Jewishness. The "chosen people" must be denied choices if Judaism is to survive. If Jews are given freedom, opportunity, and choice, they will choose to assimilate and disappear.

The story recurs, with even more tragic consequences, on the eve of the Holocaust. Another great Eastern European rabbi, Elchanan Wasserman — the dean of the Rabbinical College in Baranowitz, Poland — was invited to bring his entire student body and faculty to Yeshiva College in New York or to the Beis Medrish Letorah in Chicago, both distinguished Orthodox rabbinical colleges. He declined the invitations because "they are both places of spiritual danger, for they are run in a spirit of freethinking." The great rabbi reasoned, "What would one gain to escape physical danger in order to then confront spiritual danger?" Rabbi Wasserman, his family, his students, and their teachers remained in Poland, where they were murdered by the Nazis.*

I call the approach taken by these rabbis the Tsuris Theory of Jewish Survival. Under this theory, the Jews need external troubles to stay Jewish. Nor has this fearful, negative perspective on Jewish survival been limited to ultra-Orthodox rabbis. Many Jewish leaders, both religious and secular, have argued that Jews *need*

---

* As he was being taken to his death with his "head erect," Rabbi Wasserman reportedly said: "The fire which will consume our bodies will be the fire through which the people of Israel will arise to a new life." *Encyclopedia Judaica*, vol. 16 (Jerusalem: Ketet, 1972), p. 362.

enemies — that without anti-Semitism, Judaism cannot survive. Theodor Herzl, the founder of political Zionism and a secular Jew, believed that "our enemies have made us one . . . It is only pressure that forces us back to the parent stem."[7] In a prediction that reflects an approach to the survival of Judaism strikingly similar to that of the founder of the Lubavitch Hasidim, Herzl warned that if our "Christian hosts were to leave us in peace . . . for two generations," the Jewish people would "merge entirely into surrounding races."[8] Albert Einstein agreed: "It may be thanks to anti-Semitism that we are able to preserve our existence as a race; that at any rate is my belief."[9] Jean-Paul Sartre, a non-Jew, went even further, arguing that the "sole tie that binds [the Jewish people together] is the hostility and disdain of the societies which surround them." He believed that "it is the anti-Semite who makes the Jew."[10]*

If the Tsuris Theory of Jewish identity, survival, and unity is true, then Jews are doomed to live precariously on a pendulum perennially swinging in a wide arc between the extremes of persecution and assimilation. As the pendulum swings away from the Scylla of persecution, it inevitably moves toward the Charybdis of assimilation. In this reactive view, Jews have little power over their ultimate destiny. Our enemies always call the shots, either by persecuting us, in which case we fight back and remain Jewish, or by leaving us alone, in which case we assimilate. The only other alternative — the one proposed by Herzl — is for all Jews to move to Israel, where they control their own destiny. But most Jews will continue to ignore that option, certainly if our "hosts" continue to leave us in peace in our adopted homelands. In this respect, aliyah (emigration) to Israel has also been largely determined by our external enemies, since most Jews who have moved to the Jewish homeland have done so in reaction to anti-Semitism and persecution in their native countries.[11]

Historically, therefore, there has been some descriptive truth to this pendulum view of persecution alternating with assimilation. Jews have retained their Jewish identity, at least in part, because of tsuris. Our enemies herded us into ghettos, created pales of settlement, discriminated against us, excluded us from certain livelihoods

---

* The famed Russian writer Ilya Ehrenberg, an assimilated Jew who considered converting to Catholicism, insisted that he would remain a Jew "as long as there was a single anti-Semite left on earth." Joshua Rubenstein, *Tangled Loyalties* (New York: Basic Books, 1996), p. 13.

while pressing us into others.[12] We stuck together and remained Jews, resisting as best we could the persecution by our enemies.

But there is more — much more — to Jewish identity than collective self-defense. There is something important that is worth defending. After all, until anti-Semitism changed from religious bigotry to "racial" bigotry — roughly near the end of the nineteenth century — persecuted Jews generally had the option of conversion. Unlike Hitler, our religiously inspired persecutors — the Crusaders, the Inquisitors, Martin Luther, and the pogromists — did distinguish between Jews who converted to Christianity and Jews who did not.[13] Indeed, it was precisely their religious mission to convert the Jews, by whatever methods it took.

Many Jews did convert — some at knifepoint, others to advance themselves. The story about Professor Daniel Chwolson illustrates the latter phenomenon. Chwolson, a Russian intellectual of the nineteenth century, had converted from Judaism to Russian Orthodoxy as a young man, but he continued to fight against anti-Semitism. This led a Jewish friend to ask him why he had converted: "Out of conviction," the great man said. "What conviction?" his Jewish friend inquired. Chwolson responded: "Out of a firm conviction that it would be far better to be a professor in St. Petersburg than a Hebrew school teacher in Shklop." Yet despite the material advantages of conversion, most Jews resisted it. Clearly, those Jews — who sacrificed so much — remained Jewish not only in reaction to their enemies. More than our fabled "stiff-neckedness" was involved. There are substantive principles that Jews have been so stubborn about — that we have been willing to fight and even die for. For Jews who define their Jewishness in theological terms, it is easy to find that principle: It is God's will. For the large number of Jews who are skeptical about being God's "chosen people," the principle is more elusive, but it is palpable to most of us, though difficult to articulate. It is a disturbing reality, however, that for a great many Jews, their Jewish identity has been forged and nurtured by our external enemies who have defined *us* as victims of *their* persecution.

Now, after two millennia of persecution and victimization, we may well be moving into a new era of Jewish life during which we will not be persecuted or victimized. If this comes to pass, we will need to refocus our attention on defining the positive qualities of Jewish life that ought to make us want to remain Jews without "help" from our enemies. We must become positively Jewish instead of merely reacting to our enemies.

If Herzl's and Sartre's entirely negative view of the reason for Jewish survival were to persist even as we enter this new era of equality and acceptance, then Judaism would not deserve to endure. If Jewish life cannot thrive in an open environment of opportunity, choice, freethinking, affluence, success, and first-class status — if we really do need tsuris, czars, pogroms, poverty, insularity, closed minds, and anti-Semitism to keep us Jewish — then Jewish life as we know it will not, and should not, survive the first half of the twenty-first century. We have been persecuted long enough. The time has come to welcome the end of our victimization without fear that it will mean the end of our existence as a people. We must no longer pray for the czar's victory out of fear that the end of our collective tsuris and the success of individual Jews will mean the failure of Judaism.

I believe that Jewish life can thrive in the next century, not *despite* the end of institutional anti-Semitism, the end of Jewish persecution, and the end of Jewish victimization, but *because* of these positive developments. The ultimate good news may be that the denouement of negative Judaism — Jewish identification based largely on circling the wagons to fend off our enemies — compels us to refocus on a more positive and enduring Jewish identification, which will be more suitable to our current situation and the one we will likely be facing in the twenty-first century, when Jews will have the unconstrained choice whether to remain Jewish or to assimilate. We may be entering a true Jewish golden age, during which we will prove, once and for all, that Jews do not need enemies to survive. To the contrary: We can thrive best in an open society where we freely choose to be Jews because of the positive virtues of our 3,500-year-old civilization.

I say we *may* be entering this golden age; there are no guarantees. Many Jews believe that the end is near, because increasing rates of assimilation and intermarriage are propelling us toward a demographic Armageddon. A recent apocalyptic article in a Jewish journal concluded that "Kaddish time" is fast approaching for the American Jewish community. (Kaddish is the prayer for the dead.) But reports of the death of Judaism may be premature — *if* we can change the way we think, and act, about Jewish survival. If we refuse to change, if we accept the current demographic trends as intractable, then Jewish life in America may indeed be doomed.

The challenge is to move the Jewish state of mind beyond its past obsession with victimization, pain, and problems and point it in a new, more positive direction, capable of thriving in an open society. For unless we do, we may become the generation that witnesses the beginning of the end of one of the most influential civilizations in the history of our planet — a unique source of so much goodness, compassion, morality, creativity, and intelligence over the past several millennia. The demise of Jewish life as we have come to know it would be a tragedy not only for the Jewish people collectively, but also for most of us individually — and for the world at large.

The thesis of this book is that the long epoch of Jewish persecution is finally coming to an end and that a new age of internal dangers to the Jewish people is on the horizon. Institutional anti-Semitism is on its last legs as governments, churches, universities, and businesses embrace Jews. No Jew today needs to convert in order to become a professor, a banker, or a corporate CEO. Although anti-Semitism persists in many quarters, today's overt anti-Semites — the skinheads, militias, Holocaust deniers, and Farrakhan followers — have become marginalized. They continue to constitute a nuisance and pose a potential threat, but they do not have a significant day-to-day impact on the lives of most Jews, as anti-Semites in previous generations did. Today's marginalized anti-Semites do not decide which jobs we can hold, which universities we can attend, which neighborhoods we can live in, which clubs we can join, or even whom we can date and marry. We no longer look *up* to anti-Semites as the elites in our society who determine our fate. We look *down* on anti-Semites as the dregs of our society who make lots of noise but little difference.

As Jews and Israel become more secure against external threats, the internal threats are beginning to grow, as graphically illustrated by the recent assassination of an Israeli prime minister by a Jew, the growing conflict between fundamentalist Jews and more acculturated Jews, the increasing trends toward intermarriage and assimilation, and the decline of Jewish literacy.

For thousands of years, Jews have been embattled. Surrounded by enemies seeking to convert us, remove us, even exterminate us, we have developed collective defense mechanisms highly adaptive to combating persecution by anti-Semites. But we have not developed effective means of defending the Jewish future against our own actions and inactions. This is our urgent new challenge — to defend the Jewish future against voluntary self-destruction — and we must face it squarely, if we are to prevent the fulfillment of Isaiah's dire prophecy "Your destroyers will come from your own ranks."

We must take control of our own destiny by changing the nature of Jewish life in fundamental ways. The survival of the Jewish people is too important — to us and to the world at large — to be left in the hands of those ultra-Orthodox rabbis who would rather face Armageddon than change the religious status quo. Just as Jews of the past changed the nature of Jewish life in order to adapt to external necessities and to survive the ravages of their external enemies, so, too, must today's Jews change the nature of Jewish life to adapt to new internal necessities and to survive the demographic challenges of intermarriage, assimilation, low birthrates, and the breakdown of neighborhoods and communities.

A hundred years ago, Theodor Herzl identified the "Jewish question" of the twentieth century as the literal survival of Jews in the face of external enemies committed to our physical annihilation — Jew-haters in every nation where Jews lived as a minority. His solution — the creation of a secular Jewish state — was to change the nature of Jewish life in dramatic and unanticipated ways. A hundred years later, the "Jewish question" of the twenty-first century is survival in the face of our internal challenges. Herzl also anticipated that this new "Jewish question" might arise if and when our Christian hosts were to leave us in peace. This is now coming to pass. The solution to *this* Jewish question also requires the creation of yet another Jewish state: a new Jewish state *of mind!*

This book continues where *Chutzpah* (1991) left off, in exploring the larger issue of being Jewish today. In the concluding paragraphs of that book I issued the following challenge:

> We have learned — painfully and with difficulty — how to fight others. Can we develop Jewish techniques for defending against our own success?

Pogo once said: "We have [met] the enemy and he is us!" As Jews, we have not yet been given the luxury of seeing ourselves as the enemy. There are still too many external enemies who challenge the very physical survival of the Jewish people in Israel and throughout the world. But as we become stronger in the face of our external enemies, we must prepare to confront ourselves.

In confronting ourselves, we must face the reality that the generation of Jews I wrote about in *Chutzpah* — those of us who remember the Holocaust, the creation of Israel and the mortal threats to its survival, the movements to save Soviet, Syrian, and Ethiopian Jewry, the struggle against institutional anti-Semitism — is aging. Our children, who have no actual memory of embattled Judaism fighting for the life, liberty, and equality of endangered Jews, are now the crossroads generation that will determine what Jewish life in America and around the world will be in the coming century. It is to that younger generation of Jews, as well as to their parents, that I address this volume.

The last decade of the twentieth century has witnessed the end of state-sponsored and church-supported anti-Semitism. The fall of the Soviet Union, a nation that, since the time of Stalin, had been a major source of international anti-Semitism, had a domino effect on ending the state sponsorship of this oldest of bigotries. Other nations within the Soviet sphere of influence stopped espousing anti-Semitism as a matter of government policy. Even most Arab and Islamic countries dropped their overtly anti-Semitic policies. As a result, the United Nations has changed its tone, condemning anti-Semitism and reducing somewhat its pro-Arab and anti-Israel bias. Equally important, the Catholic church — the single institution most responsible for the persecution of Jews over the past two millennia — approved diplomatic relations with Israel, thus annulling its entrenched view that Jewish "homelessness . . . was the Divine judgment against Jews" for rejecting Jesus. The American Lutheran Church explicitly rejected Martin Luther's anti-Semitic teachings.

Bill Clinton's presidency marked the end of discrimination against Jews in the upper echelons of government. For the first time in American history, the fact that an aspirant for high appointive office was a Jew became irrelevant in his or her selection. President Clinton — our first president who grew up in an age when anti-

Semitism was unacceptable — selected several Jewish cabinet members, two Jewish Supreme Court justices, numerous Jewish ambassadors and other high-level executive and judicial officials. Nor, apparently, was Jewishness a bar to election to the United States Congress, which has ten Jewish senators and more than two dozen Jewish representatives, several from states with tiny Jewish populations.* Though we have still not had a Jew at the top of either party's ticket, it is fair to say that in today's America, a Jew can aspire to any office, any job, and any social status.

The wealth of individual Jews grew perceptibly during this decade, with 25 percent of America's richest people being of Jewish background. (If only earned, as distinguished from inherited, wealth is counted, the percentage would be even higher.)[14] An American Leadership study in 1971–72 found that Jews represented more than 10 percent of America's top "movers and shakers in business," a higher percentage than any other ethnic group.[15] Jews' per capita income is nearly double that of non-Jews. Twice the percentage of Jews as non-Jews earn more than $50,000 a year. And twice the percentage of non-Jews as Jews earn less than $20,000.[16] Jewish charitable giving has increased along with Jewish wealth. Jews are now among the largest contributors to universities, museums, hospitals, symphonies, opera, and other charities. "In 1991, the United Jewish Appeal raised more money than any other charity in America, including the Salvation Army, American Red Cross, Catholic Charities and the American Cancer Society."[17] Yet only one-tenth of Jewish philanthropists limit their giving to Jewish charities alone, while one-fourth give only to non-Jewish causes.[18]

A Jew today can live in any neighborhood, even those that were formerly "restricted." Jews live alongside white Anglo-Saxon Protestants in the most "exclusive" neighborhoods throughout the country — Grosse Pointe, Greenwich, Fifth Avenue, Beacon Hill. And they have been welcomed into the "best" families, including the Roosevelts, Kennedys, Cuomos, and Rockefellers. Economically, socially, and politically, we have become the new WASPs, as a perusal

---

* *The Daily Telegraph*, December 31, 1993. *Jewish Week*, Nov. 8, 1996, p. 11, puts the number of Jewish representatives at thirty-one, while the *Los Angeles Jewish Times* puts the number at twenty-five.

of the sponsor list of any major charitable or cultural event will show. Indeed, terms such as "J.A.S.P." (Jewish Anglo-Saxon Protestant) and "W.A.S.H." (White Anglo-Saxon Hebrew) have become current in some circles to denote the full social acceptance that Jews increasingly enjoy.[19]

Of America's Nobel Prize winners in science and economics, nearly 40 percent have been Jews.[20] Of America's 200 most influential intellectuals, half are full Jews, and 76 percent have at least one Jewish parent.[21] Jews attend Ivy League colleges at ten times their presence in the general population.[22] It is no wonder that so many non-Jews believe that we constitute so much higher a percentage of the American population than we actually do. Jews today are equal in virtually every way that matters. What could not have been said even at the end of the 1980s can be said today: American Jews are part of the American mainstream; we are truly victims no more.

Yet despite these enormous gains, many older Jews do not seem to be able to give up their anachronistic status as victims. A recent book on the American Jewish community notes: "[A]bout a third [of affiliated Jews in San Francisco said] that Jewish candidates could not be elected to Congress from San Francisco. Yet three out of four Congressional representatives . . . *were*, in fact, well identified Jews at the time the poll was conducted. And they had been elected by a population that was about 95 percent non-Jewish."[23]

Nor is this misperception limited to California. According to journalist J. J. Goldberg, "[T]he percentage of Jews who tell pollsters that anti-Semitism is a 'serious problem' in America nearly doubled during the course of the 1980s, from 45 percent in 1983 to almost 85 percent in 1990."[24] Yet by every objective assessment, the problem was less serious in 1990 than it was in 1983, and the trend has clearly been in the direction of improvement.

When I speak to older Jewish audiences, I am often accused, sometimes stridently, of minimizing anti-Semitism and am told that it is worse than ever. Social scientists call this dramatic disparity between the reality of declining anti-Semitism and the widespread belief that it is increasing a "perception gap" between what is actually happening and Jewish "sensibilities."[25] Some of the Jews who believe this are similar in this respect to some feminists and black activists I know, who insist that the plight of women and blacks is worse than it ever was.* These good and decent people, whose identities are so tied up with their victimization, are incapable of accepting the good news that their situation is improving. It is not even a matter of perceiving the glass as half full or half empty. They see the glass as broken, even though it is intact and quickly filling up. As the sociologist Marshall Sklare puts it: "American Jews respond more readily to bad news than to good news."[26]

I am reminded of the story of the two Jews reading their newspapers over a cup of coffee in a late-nineteenth-century Viennese café. Kurt is reading the liberal Yiddish-language newspaper and shaking his head from side to side, uttering soft moans of "Oy vey" and "Vey is meir." Shmulie is reading the right-wing, anti-Semitic German-language tabloid and smiling. Kurt, noticing what Shmulie is reading, shouts at his friend, "Why are you reading that garbage?" Shmulie responds, "When I used to take your newspaper, all I would ever read about was Dreyfus being falsely accused, the Jews of Russia being subjected to pogroms, anti-Semitic laws being enacted all over Europe, and the grinding poverty of the Jews in the Holy Land. Now, ever since I take this paper, I read about how the Jews control the banks, the press, the arts; how Jews hold all political power behind the scenes; and how we will soon take over the world. Wouldn't you rather read such good news than such bad news?"

With some of today's older Jews, it is exactly the opposite: they refuse to read the good news, even when it is demonstrably true. They insist on focusing on the "oys" rather than the joys of Judaism, as Rabbi Moshe Waldoks put it.[27] This is understandable, in light of the long history of persecution. Like an individual victim of a violent crime who sees his assailant around every corner, the Jewish people have been traumatized by our unrelenting victimization at the hands of Jew-haters. It is impossible for anyone who did not personally experience the Holocaust, or the other repeated assaults on Jewish life throughout our history, to comprehend what it must have been like to be victimized by unrelenting persecution based on primitive Jew-hating. We continue to see anti-Semitism even where it has ceased to exist, or we exaggerate it where it continues to exist in marginalized form. Indeed, some Jewish newspapers refuse to

---

* Among blacks and women, it tends to be members of the younger generation who believe that matters are worse than ever.

print, and some Jewish organizations refuse to acknowledge, the good news, lest they risk alienating their readerships or losing their membership. For example, in November of 1996 I saw a fundraising letter from a Jewish organization which claimed that "anti-Semitism . . . appears to be growing more robust, more strident, more vicious — *and* more 'respectable.'" Well-intentioned as this organization is, it seeks support by exaggerating the threats we currently face and by comparing them to those we faced during the Holocaust.

My students, my children, my friends' children — our next generation — understand our new status: they do not want to be regarded as victims. They do not feel persecuted, discriminated against, or powerless. They want to read the new good news, not the old bad news. A 1988 poll of Jewish students at Dartmouth College made the point compellingly: When asked whether they believed that their Jewishness would in any way hamper their future success, not a single student answered in the affirmative. That is the current reality, and it is different from the reality my parents faced — and even from the reality many of my generation perceived when we were in college or beginning our careers. The coming generation of Jewish adults will not remain Jews *because* of our enemies or because of our perceived status as victims.* They crave a more positive, affirmative, contemporary, and relevant Jewish identity. Unless we move beyond victimization and toward a new Jewish state of mind, many of them will abandon Judaism as not relevant to their current concerns.

If we are to counteract this trend, we must understand the dynamics of contemporary assimilation and not confuse them with past episodes of assimilation, which were based largely on the perceived need to escape from the "burdens" of Jewish identification. Today, there are no burdens from which to escape. Being Jewish is easy, at least in relation to external burdens. Jews today assimilate not because Christianity or Islam is "better" or "easier," but because Jewish life does not have a strong enough positive appeal to offset the inertial drift toward the common denominator. Jews do not convert to Christianity; they "convert" to mainstream Americanism,

---

* In response to this generational perception gap, one of my students suggested that I title this book *Ghetto-ver It!*

which is the American "religion" closest to Judaism. They see no reason not to follow their heart in marriage, their convenience in neighborhoods, their economic opportunities in jobs, their educational advantages in schools, their conscience in philosophy, and their preferences in lifestyle. Most Jews who assimilate do not feel that they are giving up anything by abandoning a Jewishness they know little about. They associate the Judaism they are abandoning with inconvenient rituals and rules that have no meaning to them. As one young woman remembers her Jewishness: "An old man saying no."[28]

We must recognize that many of the factors which have fueled current assimilation and intermarriage are *positive* developments for *individual* Jews: acceptance, wealth, opportunity. Most Jews do not want to impede these developments. Indeed, they want to encourage them. For that reason, we must accept the reality that many Jews will continue to marry non-Jews, but we should not regard it as inevitable that these marriages will necessarily lead to total assimilation. We can take positive steps to stem that tide — but it will take a change in attitude toward mixed marriages, and indeed toward the tribalism that has understandably characterized Jewish attitudes toward outsiders for so much of our history.

Why is this book different from other books about the Jewish future? Because its author does not have a religious or political agenda. This book is not a commercial for any particular brand of Judaism or Zionism. It does not begin with a priori assumptions about God, the survival of the Jewish people, the superiority of Orthodox, Conservative, Reform, or Reconstructionist Judaism, or the essential conservativism or liberalism of Judaism. I am neither a rabbi, a Jewish fund-raiser, a member of a Jewish studies faculty, an officer of any Jewish organization, nor an advocate for any particular Israeli party. Though I am essentially a secular Jew, I do belong to Orthodox, Conservative, Reform, and Reconstructionist congregations. Most of my family members are modern Orthodox, and a few are ultra-Orthodox. Some are completely secular. I have generally positive feelings about all Jewish denominations, as I do about the numerous Jewish political, educational, and philanthropic organizations to which I belong and contribute. I have no personal stake in any *particular* solution to the problem of Jewish survival. I just want American Jewish life to move from strength to strength. I love my Judaism and I feel passionately about its survival, but I do not believe in survival merely for survival's sake. Judaism should not be seen as a patient about to die a natural death, who is kept alive artificially on a respirator for as long as possible without regard to the quality of life. Our goal should be a self-sustaining Judaism that can thrive in the kind of open society in which most Jews want to spend their lives. I strongly believe that it is essential — both for Jews and for America — that the mainstream American Jewish community flourish. It would be a tragedy if the only forms of Judaism that made it past the twenty-first century were insular, ultra-Orthodox Judaism and Israeli Zionism. I hope that they, too, will continue to prosper, but I believe that a more diverse Jewish life has even more to contribute. If I have a bias, it is in favor of an eclectic, tolerant, many-branched menorah that is inclusive of all who wish to safeguard and share the future of the Jewish people.

I also bring to this book a unique perspective informed by my experiences growing out of the publication of *Chutzpah* five years ago. Since that time, I have spoken to well over 100,000 Jews in nearly every city with a significant Jewish population, not only in this country but throughout the world. The talk is usually preceded by a social hour and followed by a question period. I estimate that I have been asked more than a thousand questions by concerned Jews. I have received more than ten thousand letters and phone calls from Jewish men, women, and children. I have also been teaching young students, many of them Jewish, for a third of a century. I have served as faculty adviser to the Harvard Jewish Law Students Association, have been an active participant in Hillel, and have spoken to Jewish student groups at many colleges and universities around the world. Over these years, I have discussed virtually every Jewish issue — from God to intermarriage to Israel to anti-Semitism to Jewish feminism — with thousands of students. These questions, letters, calls, and discussions have given me an extraordinary window into the fears, hopes, and beliefs of a wide assortment of Jews. It has been quite an education. I think I understand what is on the minds and in the souls of many Jews, of all ages, and I try to address myself to these concerns in this book. I also have a unique window into the mind of the anti-Semite, since I continue to receive hundreds of anti-Semitic letters and calls each year, some quite lengthy and revealing.

Though I care deeply about the survival of the Jewish people, I do not believe that survival is assured by any biblical imperative or divine promise. I approach the issue of Jewish survival as I would any other important empirical challenge: with an open mind ready and willing to accept any pragmatic solution, or combination of solutions, that will work. I am committed to doing whatever is in my power to help ensure the Jewish future. I know that many Jews feel the same way.

I agree neither with those theologians who believe that Jewish survival is assured because God promised it nor with those demographers who believe that Jewish disappearance is inevitable because of forces beyond our control. I believe that our future as a people is largely in our own hands, and I want to help define and defend the new Jewish state of mind.

In the first chapter of this book, I focus on what is probably the most whispered-about subject among American Jews today: intermarriage and how to cope with this growing reality. I try to bring this controversial subject out of the closet in all its dimensions. I do not moan and groan and wring my hands. I do not present a religious agenda. I explore the issue from both a demographic and a personal perspective, in an effort to understand it and deal with it instructively and realistically. My analysis and conclusions will be controversial and will, I hope, stimulate a debate within the Jewish community and beyond. My goal is to ask all the hard questions, and to provide a wide variety of responses in addition to my own. I know that many readers will disagree with me, but I hope they will not be able to ignore the challenges I pose.

In chapters 2, 3, and 4, I develop my thesis that the nature of anti-Semitism is changing in fundamental and important ways: Mainstream anti-Semitism — as traditionally practiced by churches, states, corporations, universities, and other elite institutions — is coming to an end; today's Jew-haters are largely marginalized and powerless. This change means that although anti-Semitism persists and must continue to be monitored, it has far less daily impact on the lives of American Jews than in the past. Thus we must define our

Jewish identity in different and more positive ways than we did in the past.

In chapters 5, 6, and 7, I explore the most frequently proposed solutions to the problem of assimilation. To those who are sure that a return to religion is Judaism's *only* salvation, I say, Get as many to return as you can. Maybe you are right. But we cannot rely exclusively on your solution, because maybe you are wrong. Maybe not enough Jews will become religious. Maybe religion — at least as currently defined and practiced — is not the wave of the future for most young intellectuals. Maybe there is a strand of Judaism that can survive and thrive without exclusive dependence on theology and ritual. After all, the Yiddish secularism that flourished between the beginning of the Jewish Enlightenment (Haskalah) and the Second World War was an authentic Jewish culture, which was destroyed by external forces. Political Zionism, which grew largely out of that culture, remains an authentic Jewish civilization of enormous importance to the survival of Judaism. Today's influential American Jewish community is largely secular.

To those who look to Israel as Judaism's sole salvation, I say, Keep trying to get Jews from throughout the Diaspora to make aliyah. Maybe you are right. But we cannot count on Zionism and aliyah alone, because maybe you are wrong. Maybe most Jews will want to remain where they and their families have established a comfortable home. Maybe they will not come to Israel. Maybe Israel will not endure forever as a Jewish state. Maybe it will "normalize" — as Theodor Herzl put it — and become like most other states, which began as religious but became secular and multicultural over time.

To those who believe that an emphasis on Jewish ethics will be enough to transmit the essence of Judaism to our children, I say, Maybe you are right. Certainly many Jews, especially secular Jews, agree with you and *hope* you are right. But beyond broad generalities, it is difficult to distill from the highly diverse Jewish sources a few programmatic essences that are easily transmittable from generation to generation, without living the kind of Jewish lives that our grandparents lived.

To those who say that Jewish fund-raising, charity, and defense organizations are the answer, I say, Work on, raise money, build buildings, elect officers, bestow honors, monitor anti-Semitism, support Israel. But do not count on it to ensure the Jewish future, because maybe the next generation will not be as attracted to these institutions as the post-Holocaust generation was.

To those who say that Jewish education is the key to Jewish survival, I say, You are undoubtedly right. Whatever the essence or essences of Judaism may be, they are in large part, at least, to be discovered and rediscovered in our books, in our history, and in our approach to learning. But we cannot count on all Jews, so many of whom are busy with their successful careers, to become Jewishly educated, especially since Jewish education today is controlled almost entirely by the religious component of Jewish life and has been one of the great failures of the American Jewish community.

In the final chapter, I propose a series of steps that I believe we must take in order to safeguard the Jewish future. We must change the nature of American Jewish life in fundamental ways if we are to survive the new threats to our continuity as a people. These changes must make us more adaptive to the reality that we can no longer define ourselves — and our children — by reference to our past victimization and persecution. We must adopt a new, more positive, Jewish identity based on a 3,500-year-old tradition of education, scholarship, learning, creativity, justice, and compassion. But first we must figure out a way to make this diverse library of Jewish knowledge accessible and useful to generations of Jews who are abysmally ignorant of their remarkable tradition. The famed "Yiddisher cup" (*khop*) — Jewish head — is only half full: the typical Jewish college graduate is extraordinarily well educated about general subjects, but goes through life with a kindergarten understanding of Judaism. We must begin to fill the Yiddisher cup with the kind of useful Jewish knowledge that will assure both our success *and* our survival. To do this, we will have to loosen the monopolistic hold that rabbis now have over Jewish education, so that we can begin to compete effectively in the marketplace of ideas for the minds and hearts of our Jewish youth.* Unless we begin to make use of our competitive advantage — as teachers, communicators, scholars, advocates, and strategists — we will lose our children and grandchildren to the seductive drift toward assimilation and away from

---

* Rabbis must maintain their important role in Jewish education, but a little healthy competition from nonrabbinical Jewish scholars will improve Jewish education, as I show in Chapter 8.

Jewishness. The fundamental changes we must make will require a reordering of our priorities away from an almost exclusive focus on defending Jews against external enemies and toward new ways of defending ourselves and our children against self-destruction through assimilation. We will have to educate our children differently, allocate our charitable giving differently, select our leaders differently — even define our very Jewishness differently. Jewish life will have to become less tribal, more open, more accepting of outsiders, and less defensive.

When I describe some of the multiple roads we must take if we are to maximize our chances for survival, I think of a variation of the old story of the rabbinical judge who, after hearing a wife's complaints about her husband, says, "My daughter, you are right," and, after hearing the husband's complaints, says, "My son, you are right." When his student observes, "Rabbi, they can't both be right," he replies, "My son, you are right." Under my variation, the rabbi responds to his student, "No, you are wrong. They *can* both be right." To the differing and sometimes inconsistent approaches to Jewish survival, I would say, "You may *all* be right. Don't you dare tell each other that you are wrong. Nobody has a monopoly on the truth about the Jewish future. Everything that may work must be tried."

At the end of the last century, Theodor Herzl called for a new Jewish state. As we approach the close of this cataclysmic century, I believe we need a new Jewish state of mind if we are to define and ensure the Jewish future, not only for our sake but for the sake of all humankind.

PART I:

THE PROBLEM DEFINED

Chapter One

An America Without Jews

"There is no greater sin than to cause one's nation to disappear from the world."
— ISAAC BER LEVINSOHN (1853)

SICILIANO DESIRED by Jewess. Foreigner preferred . . . marriage-minded only, for provocative Jewish woman, 30's, 5'4", chocolate eyes, long black hair. Loves action.
— BOSTON PHOENIX personals section, July 19–25, 1996

IMAGINE AN AMERICA without Jews. By almost any measure, the size of the American Jewish community is in sharp decline while other segments of the U.S. population are growing.[1] In 1937, Jews made up nearly 4 percent of the U.S. population; today that figure has shrunk to just over 2 percent.[2] Within the Jewish community, differential birth and assimilation rates suggest that what remains of the Jewish community by the middle of the twenty-first century will consist primarily of ultra-Orthodox Jews, who have relatively little involvement in the general community. The significant Jewish contributions to the arts, sciences, education, politics, business, philanthropy, the media, medicine, law, and other important facets of life may well end. The Jewish community as we now know it — vibrant, involved, compassionate, influential — will disappear. Our great-grandchildren's world will be the poorer for it.

It may be difficult to contemplate a world without Jews — especially for those of us who are part of their long and productive history — but because of Hitler's genocide, such a world is no longer unimaginable. That indeed was the explicit goal of the Nazis, and they came perilously close to achieving it. Had they beaten the Allies in the close race to develop an atomic bomb, had they achieved a few more victories in crucial battles, had there been a failure of will by the Allies — any of these might well have produced not only a

Europe without Jews, but a Middle East and even an America where large Jewish populations would have ended up in death camps. A chilling chart produced at the Wannsee Conference that detailed the precise number of Jews in each country of Europe who would be included in the Final Solution makes it clear that if the Nazis had prevailed, the number of Jewish casualties could have reached 15 million — which would have been nearly 85 percent of the known Jewish population before World War II.[3] That level of destruction might well have marked the end of the Jewish people as history knows them.

Though entire Jewish communities, extended family trees, schools of thought, and civilizations were forever eradicated, the Jewish people ultimately survived and eventually thrived. Now a new threat to Jewish survival looms on the horizon, different from any previously faced. It is potentially more lethal precisely because our history of external persecution has left us unschooled in coping with this kind of internal threat of assimilation and voluntary demographic contraction. The upshot may be that where the Nazis failed in their nightmarish plan to eliminate Jews as a potent force in the world, we ourselves may succeed. This fear is reflected in the way the terms "another Holocaust," "silent Holocaust," and "spiritual Holocaust" are becoming a familiar part of American Jewish parlance.[4] I reject such analogies, because the Holocaust was genocide perpetrated by external enemies, whereas the situation we currently face is self-inflicted. It is like the difference between rape and seduction. We are far more responsible for that to which we have consented.

The Demographic Challenge:
How Many Jews Does It Take . . .

If trends continue apace, American Jewry — indeed, Diaspora Jewry — may virtually vanish by the third quarter of the twenty-first century.* In its stead, two categories of Jewry will remain. First, the

---

* A similar process will occur in other countries with significant Jewish populations — even, to some extent, in Israel, as the peace process opens borders and global Americanization increasingly homogenizes other cultures.

remnant of the currently vibrant and largely secular Jewish community will subsist as an attenuated collection of "partial Jews," "former Jews," "assimilated Jews," "people of Jewish background," and "Christian Jews."[5] In this respect, Jews will become more like other ethnic groups, with descendants proudly pointing to their partial Jewish heritage in the way that some Americans today identify themselves as part Scottish, part Irish, part Navajo, part French, and so on. Former White House chief of staff John Sununu, for example, boasted that his mixed Lebanese, El Salvadoran, and Greek ancestry makes him "the universal ethnic. It's a varied heritage and I'm proud of it."[6] The gradual demise of ethnicity in America, which has already diluted Italian, Irish, Greek, Polish, and other hyphenated Americans, will likewise emulsify secular American Jews whose identity is primarily ethnic.

The second type of Jew that will remain a half-century from now, and probably dominate the Jewish community in every way, is the "fundamentalist Jew," the "ultra-Orthodox right-wing Jew," the "Hasidic Jew," the "ba'al t'shuvah" (born-again Jew). There may also be modest communities of "modern Orthodox" Jews, and a smattering of Conservative, Reform, and Reconstructionist holdovers, but their numbers will be dramatically reduced.[7] The Jewish community of 2076 will bear little resemblance to the vibrant, influential, mainstream one of today.

The major factors fueling these trends are intermarriage, assimilation, and wildly disparate birthrates. The ultra-Orthodox (who constitute approximately one-fourth of the overall Orthodox population) average more than four children per couple. In very traditional neighborhoods, such as Borough Park in Brooklyn, families average close to six children. Nonobservant Jews, however, average between 1.5 and 1.6 children per couple, below the 2.1 "replacement level."[8] The biblical command to "be fruitful and multiply" is being ignored by most Jews.

The following chart, published in the October 1996 issue of *Moment* magazine, vividly projects the effects of disparate birth and intermarriage rates within the Jewish community. It suggests that by the fourth generation, two hundred current secular Jews will have produced ten Jewish great-grandchildren, and the same number of ultra-Orthodox Jews will have produced more than five thousand

WILL YOUR GRANDCHILD BE JEWISH ?

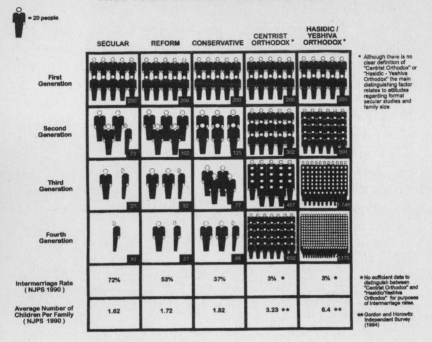

Based on current intermarriage rates and the average number of children per family, the chances of young contemporary Jews having Jewish grandchildren and great-grandchildren, with the exception of the Orthodox, are increasingly remote.

Jewish great-grandchildren. Even discounting substantially for statistical error and false assumptions, the point certainly must be taken seriously.

It has been widely reported that since 1988, more than half the marriages involving American Jews have been to non-Jews. If this data is accurate, more Jews now marry non-Jews than fellow Jews. The figure over the past several years has been estimated at between 53 percent and 58 percent (though it may be somewhat less).[9] What amazes me is not that 53 percent of Jews may be marrying non-Jews. In light of what I hear from my students, my children, and the current and upcoming generations of marriage-age Jews, what amazes me is that 47 percent of Jews *still* marry other Jews. After all, Jews comprise just slightly more than 2 percent of the U.S. population. Putting aside demography, propinquity, parental pressure, and religious commitment, the chances of a Jew marrying another Jew are considerably lower than 47 percent.[10] Some suggest that the "natural odds" of a mixed marriage for members of an ethnic group so tiny as American Jews is 95 percent.[11] Nevertheless, the four factors of demography, propinquity, parental pressure, and religious commitment responsible for maintaining the high degree of Jewish in-marriage will continue to diminish even in the near future, and certainly over the next several generations.

"Jewish neighborhoods" are becoming largely a thing of the past in many American cities, except for Hasidic and Orthodox enclaves which are geographically bound by the walking distance to a synagogue. The kind of Jewish neighborhood in which my friends and I grew up, where everyone knew each other's families, some from back in the old country, is disappearing. Our children and grandchildren are being raised in heterogeneous locations that hardly fit the description of "neighborhood" at all. Newlywed Jewish couples — even most of the 47 percent who marry each other and many of the smaller percentage who are affiliated with synagogues to which they drive — do not generally seek out religiously or ethnically homogeneous neighborhoods. Indeed, many deliberately resist the "gilded ghettos" of their parents' generation; others cannot afford them. Future generations of Jews are less likely to grow up in neighborhoods where meeting and marrying other Jews has been a natural function of propinquity. The rising age of first-time brides and grooms, combined with ever-increasing divorce and remarriage rates, also means that "neighborhood marriages" — which were almost never mixed marriages — will decrease markedly, since the older a person becomes, the more likely he or she is to move away from the possibly more homogeneous neighborhood of childhood.

Nor is propinquity found in college, professional school, or the workplace as much as it was in the days of religious exclusion, when ambitious Jews had to congregate in those few institutions that were open to them. Today there are few exclusions, and so Jews have spread out to all locations. Some elite universities and employers — prominent law firms, training hospitals, investment banks — still have a "disproportionately high" number of Jews, which helps to explain the artificially high percentage of Jewish marriage.* I call it ar-

* Others still appear to have a disproportionately *low* number of Jews, but that will inevitably change before long.

tificially high because I believe that a significant portion of the 47 percent of Jews who today marry fellow Jews do so largely *by accident*. What I mean is that many of these Jewish inmarriages are simply the result of a fortuitous propinquity: Jews *happening* to fall in love with Jews simply because they were in the same place at the same time by chance, *not* because they were religiously committed to marrying a fellow Jew. I call these marriages "accidental Jewish marriages."

Religious commitment to Jewish inmarriage is falling more quickly than Jewish inmarriage itself. Indeed, my discussions with young Jews convince me that with the exception of Orthodox Jews, an overwhelming majority of marriage-age and soon-to-be-marriage-age Jews — even relatively committed Jews — do not express or believe in a religious commitment to marry a fellow Jew.* Many regard it as *wrong* to take into account the religion of a prospective spouse. When I spoke recently to a group of Jewish college students, all of whom were members of Jewish organizations on campus, I asked for a show of hands as to how many preferred to marry a fellow Jew. The students looked at each other awkwardly and about half the hands went up. I then asked those who had raised their hands how many would be prepared to tell their dorm-mates of their preference. A small number of hands were raised. In the language of the day, it is "politically incorrect" to insist on marrying a coreligionist.[12] It is, however, perfectly correct to do so if it just happens that way. It will "just happen" that way with ever decreasing frequency.

Another powerful impetus toward Jewish marriage is also decreasing: parental (and even grandparental) pressure. It used to be virtually unthinkable for a Jew — even a secular Jew — to marry a non-Jew. To do so was the ultimate rejection of one's parents and other relatives. Some families would actually declare such a child to be dead and would sit shiva over the not-so-dear departed. The poignant refusal of Tevye to acknowledge his daughter Chava and her Christian husband was not a literary creation by Shalom Aleichem or his adapters in *Fiddler on the Roof*. It was the way things were, not only in the old country but also in America for much of

---

* A soon-to-be-published study finds that 65 percent of Conservative teens who had a bar or bat mitzvah said it was "OK for Jews to marry people of other religions" — as contrasted with 14 percent of their parents. (*Jewish Week*, December 13, 1996, p. 10)

this century. No self-respecting Jewish parent would attend the wedding of a child who was marrying "a shiksa" or "a shegetz" — the male equivalent of the far more common derogatory term *shiksa*. The female term was more common because far more Jewish men used to marry out than Jewish women did, another disparity that is now "normalizing." Indeed, the past phenomenon of Jewish men marrying non-Jewish women was part of a double inequity: it was primarily *men* who married *up* by marrying *out*. In today's more egalitarian world, neither of these inequities persists to the same degree. This new equality also serves to encourage intermarriage, by opening new options for Jewish women that were previously available only to Jewish men.

Today, such parental pressure (and the resulting guilt) is abating. This is not to say that many Jewish parents and grandparents are not as upset about intermarriage as their predecessors were, but it has become less socially acceptable — and hence less effective as a deterrent or preventive measure — to *show* that distress in such dramatic and guilt-producing ways.

We are thus witnessing a significant diminution in the external factors that have traditionally increased the percentage of Jewish inmarriage: Jewish neighborhoods, academic and professional contact, parental pressure. At the same time, we are experiencing a decline in other Jewish institutions that helped to foster propinquity, such as Jewish summer camps, Jewish country clubs, Jewish resorts, Jewish health clubs, and Jewish athletic clubs (such as the YMHA). To be sure, Jewish community centers may be increasing, but the total trend is clearly toward assimilated work and play. Indeed, many Jewish community centers are now open to non-Jews. The net result will be increasing assimilation at work, at play, in neighborhoods, and in families.

When I was growing up, virtually all summer camps were segregated by religion. I went to an assortment of Orthodox Jewish camps in the Catskill and Pocono Mountains, both as a camper and as a counselor. These camps were referred to as "shiddach" or "matchmaker" camps for Orthodox Jews, and they had an incredibly high success rate. Many of my friends married people they met at Camp Maple Lake, Camp Massad, and other such "marriage mills." I met my first wife and my brother met his wife at Camp Maple Lake in 1955. A few such camps still exist, catering primarily to

Orthodox and Conservative Jews, but many more Jewish kids go to nonsectarian camps.

In the future, Jewish marriages will thus fall into two categories: the decreasing, but persistent, number of accidental Jewish marriages (which, for a variety of reasons, will always exceed the simple arithmetical odds of one member of a group that constitutes 2 percent of the population marrying a member of that same group);* and the significant — but also decreasing — number of Jewish marriages based on religious commitment. The two categories are, of course, overlapping, since many apparently accidental Jewish marriages involve some degree of religious commitment — conscious, unconscious, or externally imposed — by at least one of the parties.

Accidental Jewish marriages will, of course, themselves produce an ever-increasing rate of mixed marriages among the future generations. Since accidental Jewish marriages are not based on religious or cultural commitment, their offspring will be more likely to marry non-Jews. Some accidental Jewish marriages do result in an after-the-fact religious or cultural commitment, which may be transmitted to the children. Even some religiously committed Jewish marriages will produce children who marry non-Jews. After all, virtually every mixed marriage involves children or grandchildren of a religiously committed Jewish marriage.

The net result of all these changes will be an America in which the vast majority of Jewish inmarriages will be among the ultra-Orthodox and Orthodox, and in which the vast majority of non-Orthodox Jews — who today comprise close to 90 percent of the total Jewish population[13] — will be marrying non-Jews at ever-increasing rates.

What, then, will become of the Jews who have non-Jewish spouses? What will become of their children? The answer to *those* questions will determine the future of American Jews as we now know them.

At present, the majority of mixed marriages end the Jewish identity of the family, both religiously and communally, if not immediately then in one or two generations. I do not, of course, include in the category of "mixed marriage" a marriage in which the non-

---

* Contrast Jewish inmarriage, for example, with the rates of inmarriage among left-handers, redheads, or type O blood types.

Jewish spouse converts to Judaism. It is reported that no more than 10 percent of the offspring of mixed marriages marry Jews,[14] and one Philadelphia study found that *none* of the grandchildren of mixed marriages surveyed married Jews.[15] Thus the old quip "What do you call the grandchildren of intermarried Jews? Christians" doesn't seem so funny anymore.*

Ironically, when the mixed marriage involves a Jewish man and a non-Jewish woman, the Jewish *identity* may sometimes persist a bit longer despite the Jewish religious law — observed by Orthodox and Conservative, but not by Reform, Jews — that the religion of the *mother* determines whether the children are Jewish. This is especially so when the Jewish man has an obviously Jewish last name, which he passes on to the children and which often carries with it a degree of Jewish identification. One striking example of this phenomenon is the publisher of the *New York Times*, Arthur Ochs Sulzberger, Jr., whose mother was Christian and who was himself baptized an Episcopalian. But because he carried the Sulzberger name, "ninety-nine people out of a hundred consider me Jewish," he told an interviewer. "How could a Sulzberger *not* be Jewish?"[16] We are also seeing an increase in the number of children with last names like O'Brien, McCauley, Famiglietti, and Johnson being bar and bat mitzvahed, as some Jewish women who married non-Jewish men bring up their children as Jews. But these are still the exceptions to a sociological rule — bolstered by some religious and tribal attitudes — that strongly pushes the children of mixed marriages away from Judaism and Jewish identity.

We do not yet have conclusive data on what happens to the children of marriages between a Jew and a non-Jew who converts to Judaism. On the one hand, the statistics are somewhat encouraging. The sociologist Egon Mayer observes that not only are the offspring of such unions "overwhelmingly raised as Jews," but also the religious "practices of such families are consistently more identifiably Jewish than is typical for American Jews in general."[17] On the other hand, some of these conversions have been overseen by Reform rabbis, and thus are not recognized by the Orthodox and Conservative Jewish communities. As a result, the offspring of these

---

* It is less clear, of course, that these grandchildren will be *Christians* than it is that they will not be Jews in any meaningful sense of that word.

couples will often be stigmatized as "non-Jewish" or "unmarriage-able" by many Jews.[18] They may not care — until they decide to marry an Orthodox or Conservative Jew and discover that they are not deemed "Jewish."

These, then, are the cold facts, but all the statistical and demographic information in the world concerning assimilation and inter-marriage does not come close to having the impact of a Jew's personal experience with a child or grandchild who marries a non-Jew. Almost all the Jews I know have had someone close to them marry a person from a different religious background. Wherever I lecture, several audience members come up to tell me — usually in an embarrassed whisper — about a child or grandchild of theirs who is "going with" a non-Jew. The pain on their faces is palpable. They know that friends and acquaintances are having similar experiences, but they are ashamed to talk to them. They love their child or grandchild, but they do not understand why he or she is "doing this to me." They feel helpless. They also feel that they are letting the Jewish people down. Nor are they helped by the smug and insensitive quips of those who now define a Jew as one whose "grandchildren will be Jewish," as if having grandchildren who are not considered to be Jewish by Orthodox or Conservative rules is a mark of personal failure. They want my guidance, as if somehow I can solve their problem. I tell them that I know precisely what it feels like, because I have experienced it myself.

The Personal Challenge: Will My Grandchildren Be Jewish?

When my son Jamin invited me to join him for dinner at a Chinese restaurant in February 1992 — "so we could talk about something" — I knew that I would finally have to deal with an issue that I had been grappling with but not confronting directly since he had started dating Barbara, who is of Irish Catholic ancestry, nearly ten years earlier. They had met in a Spanish class as undergraduates at the University of Pennsylvania and had dated, off and on but mostly on, since that time.

Jamin went on to Yale Law School, Barbara to Columbia Medical School. They spent almost every weekend together. After graduation, Jamin spent one year as a law clerk to a federal judge in Boston and then moved to New York, where he became a trial lawyer with the Legal Aid Society. He then joined me for a year in appealing Mike Tyson's rape conviction and thereafter became associate general counsel to the National Basketball Association. Barbara worked as an emergency room doctor at Columbia Presbyterian Hospital, where she now serves as an assistant clinical professor of medicine. Before long, Jamin and Barbara moved in together.

At dinner, Jamin told me what I knew he was going to: He and Barbara were getting engaged. Jamin was not planning to ask Barbara to convert to Judaism. Nor would Barbara ask Jamin to become Catholic. Their children — my grandchildren — would not be Jews, at least not under the Orthodox and Conservative religious definition of who is a Jew.

I congratulated my son on their decision, instinctively wishing him "Mazel tov." As I uttered those Hebrew words, I recalled a friend's description of his daughter's engagement to a non-Jew: "It was a 'Congratulations'-type engagement, not a 'Mazel tov.' " I was genuinely happy at Jamin's obvious joy and excitement over his forthcoming marriage, but happiness was not my only emotion.

"My children will be Jewish," Jamin assured me, even before I asked. "As long as they have me as their father and you as their grandfather, they *will* be Jewish," he insisted. "They will be as Jewish as I am," he continued, fully aware of the double meaning of his statement.

By current American standards, Jamin is a fairly committed Jew. He attends High Holiday services, fasts on Yom Kippur, attends the family Seders, refrains from eating bread products during Passover, participates in the festivities of Hanukkah, considers himself a Zionist and a supporter of Israel (though not of all its policies and governments), fights against anti-Semitism, supports the struggle for Russian Jewry, and believes that many of his liberal and egalitarian values derive from his Jewish heritage. On a trip we took together to Poland, Jamin was deeply moved by our visits to the abandoned shtetls of Galicia and to the stark horrors of Auschwitz. A piece of old rusted barbed wire that he took from Birkenau as a remembrance of that awful place hangs in his home.

But he is not a religious Jew. He does not think about God, theology, prayer, or Jewish Halakah (religious law). His observances, such as they are, tend to be traditional and familial. Judaism to Jamin is not a *faith*, it is a *heritage*.

Barbara's Irish Catholicism is similar for her, though no two heritages ever fill exactly the same role because of important differences in history. Barbara loves Christmas, not because of its theological significance to Christianity but rather because of its role in her family life. It is much like Thanksgiving to her. She, too, is not particularly religious. Her Catholicism is more a matter of heritage than theology.

When a friend described Jamin and Barbara's marriage as "interfaith," Jamin quickly corrected her: "It is an interfaith*less* marriage. Neither of us has much religious faith." Jamin likes to repeat the Woody Allen story of the Jewish atheist who married the Catholic atheist and fought over which religion their child should be taught to reject. He also tells the joke about the child of Catholic–Jewish parentage who never goes to confession without his lawyer. In our family, we often use humor to deal with conflict.*

I pressed Jamin as to what he meant when he said his children would be as Jewish as he is. His answer was descriptive. "They'll go to High Holiday services, Seders, and Hanukkah parties. You'll take them to Israel and Poland like you took me. They'll know they're Jewish, just like I know. And their name will be Dershowitz, which will guarantee they'll be Jewish, whether they want to or not!"

"Will they *also* be Irish Catholic?" I asked.

"They will have one Jewish parent and one Irish Catholic parent," Jamin replied. "And they will understand that they are a product of two different heritages. They'll go to Barbara's family home for Christmas and to your family home for the Jewish holidays."

"But what will they do in *your* home?" I asked.

"Barbara and I haven't really thought it through," Jamin acknowledged. "We don't have anything particularly religious in our apartment now. That's probably how it will be when we have kids. Maybe a tree and a menorah in December. We'll see how it feels to both of us."

As I sat there looking at my son, I realized that he could never understand — not as a rational matter, but as a matter of deep emo-

---

* Jamin once called to tell me that he was assigned to represent a woman who had shoplifted a copy of my book *Chutzpah*. I asked him what his defense would be, and he told me that under New York law, the prosecution had to prove that the stolen item was worth something!

tion — exactly how the news of his impending marriage affected me. He was trying very hard, and he probably believed he understood me. We are very close. Jamin understands a lot about me: what motivates me, what makes me happy and what makes me angry. But my feelings toward my Jewishness have always been something of a mystery to my children, especially to Jamin. Precisely because Jamin understands so much about me — we are very much alike in many important ways, even in physical appearance and in occupational choice — he is baffled by his inability to understand my Jewishness.

We have talked about God and theology and we tend to agree about such abstract matters. We both question and doubt everything, not only in matters of religion but in matters of science, politics, and other aspects of secular conventional wisdom. We reject certainty, authority, and schools of thought. We try to think everything through for ourselves. Because we are doubters, we could never be atheists; a firm belief in the *non*-existence of God would be far too certain for either of us. But we are borderline agnostic, and we act as if there probably is no God. Occasionally, however, I catch myself praying on Yom Kippur, especially at the final service just before God is supposed to close the book for next year, having written our future in indelible ink. Why take a chance? Maybe, just maybe . . . As W. C. Fields put it when asked why he was reading the Bible on his deathbed: "I'm looking for loopholes." Perhaps there are no atheists in foxholes, but there are plenty of skeptics in the Dershowitz household, and some would say that Jamin and I both make a living looking for "loopholes."

On a rational level, I am not a believer in Pascal's wager: the notion that faith is a worthwhile gamble, since we lose nothing if we believe and God doesn't exist, but we risk spending eternity in hell if we don't believe and God turns out to be real. On an emotional level, maybe, just maybe . . .

I have never seen Jamin praying, but prayer is not something that is easy to observe. It is not my episodic praying that baffles Jamin. He regards that as human weakness which comes with advancing age. He also notices that as I get older, I take my fortune cookies more seriously. He understands that it is not the occasional prayer that defines my deep Jewishness. It is something that is not only beyond his experience, it is something he will never be able to comprehend fully because it is a product of unique generational forces that permanently differentiate us.

I am the product of immigrant grandparents, and parents who came of age during the Great Depression; classmates who were survivors of the Holocaust; friends who made aliyah to Israel; clients — some now friends — who were imprisoned by the Soviets because they were Jewish dissidents; law firms that turned me down because I was Jewish; academic colleagues who urged me to tone down my Jewishness; and a university that tried to make me a second-class citizen when I began to teach there. I am also the product of a very positive Jewish neighborhood; a group of Jewish friends from that neighborhood who have remained close for more than half a century; an extensive, though flawed, Jewish education; a love for Israel, even with its imperfections; a pride in the spiritual, material, charitable, and progressive contributions of Jews to America and the world. Jamin was brought up in Cambridge, during the 1970s, when Israel was more secure and anti-Semitic discrimination had all but disappeared. He did not experience either the negative aspects of being an embattled Jew or the positive aspects of living in the kind of Jewish milieu in which I was raised.

Not only could I never have married a non-Jewish woman, I would never even have seriously considered it. It would have simply been unthinkable for me, not as a matter of rational decision-making but as a matter of emotional capacity. My Jewishness is just too important to me. Even if I — like some of my friends — had made the decision that my second marriage would be childless, I could not have married a non-Jew. It is not only a question of wanting my *children* to be Jewish: My own Jewishness is far too central to my life not to want to share it on a daily basis with a like-minded mate. I could have married a woman who had become a Jew by choice, but only if it were a *genuine choice*, not simply a willingness to convert in order to marry. Yet whenever I have tried to debate this issue with Jamin or with others of his generation, I lose the debate — if such debates can be judged on the logic and rationality of the argumentation.

I even lost a debate with the late Rabbi Meir Kahane over this issue. He asked me whether I wanted my children to marry Jews. Without hesitation, I said yes. Then he asked whether my desire was based on Halakah. I said no. "Then," he insisted, pointing a finger at me, "you are nothing but a racist." I was taken aback by this strident accusation, but Kahane explained: "There are plenty of wonderful non-Jewish people who would make marvelous spouses for your children. Why are you excluding them all, unless you are *obligated* to exclude them by religious law? If you are merely expressing an ethnic preference for one of your own kind, that is the essence of racism. It is just like an Aryan atheist in Germany forbidding children to marry people of Jewish backgrounds." Rabbi Kahane always did have a way of putting it to you in the most confrontational manner. (We learned our debating skills at the same yeshiva, where we were each captain of the debate team at different times.)

But how individuals define themselves — and how they wish their children and grandchildren to define themselves — is not merely a matter of debate or rationality. That is why it would be outrageous to prohibit "discrimination" in the selection of mates. Just as it is improper — and unconstitutional — for a state to prohibit a black person from marrying a white person, it would be equally wrong — and unconstitutional — to *require* intermarriage or to prohibit a person from selecting a spouse on racial, religious, ethnic, political, or any other grounds. The decision about whom to marry is simply too personal, too much a function of the history, psyche, and aspirations of the individual, to be anyone else's legitimate concern. Despite the logic of Kahane's argument, it is not racist for a deeply committed Jew to feel strongly about the continuity of the Jewish people, even if he rejects the strictures of the Halakah.

Jamin does not regard me as a racist because I want my children to marry Jews. (Neither, by the way, did Kahane; it was simply a debating point for him. After the debate, he urged me to insist that my children marry Jews for "whatever reason.") One reason Jamin does not take that position is because several of his black friends insist on marrying black spouses, and Jamin understands (without necessarily agreeing with) that preference. There, too, the issue of preserving a culture is the essence of the dispute. Jamin, trained as a lawyer, understands arguments from analogy. He *thinks* he understands my reasons because he thinks he understands the reasoning of his black friends. I think he does not fully understand either, because he has not lived our lives, and cannot. Nor can I fully understand Jamin's feelings regarding his marriage to Barbara, since I have not lived his life and experienced his emotions.

My Jewishness is not based on a belief in the details of Jewish theology or on compliance with the 613 commandments of the Torah — as evidenced by the fact that I was expressing my anguish about Jamin's decision while enjoying a meal in an unkosher Chinese restaurant. We both noticed the irony, but neither of us saw any inconsistency. Although Jamin may not understand my deep sense of Jewish identity, he knows that I have a sense of mission about the survival of the Jewish people. I am convinced that a world without Jews would be a much less noble place, a much poorer place in every way that matters. Jews and Jewishness add a palpably positive dimension to the places they inhabit. I do not believe we are a "chosen people" in the sense of any divine preference. But I do believe that our collective experiences, especially with persecution, have made many Jews especially sensitive to the suffering of others, to the need for equality for all, to the virtues of compassion toward those less fortunate, to the appreciation of creativity and education, and to other virtues that have been the hallmarks of the various Jewish civilizations over time and place.

The Jewish people are not alone, of course, in having experienced persecution and in having turned those collective experiences into positive survival traits. Nor have our experiences produced only positive characteristics. The consequences of any long historical journey — especially one as diverse as the Jews' — are inevitably a mixture of virtues, vices, and neutral attributes. I am not arguing that Jews have emerged from their ongoing history as better or more virtuous than non-Jews. I reject that sociological version of the "chosen people" concept as categorically as I reject its biblical counterpart. But I and my children are part of the Jewish historical experience. I do not want my grandchildren and great-grandchildren to break our link with Judaism. I do not want them to become the first non-Jews in our family history. I do not want them to assimilate, to melt into someone else's pot, to join a different religion, or to become part of another tradition or heritage. I do not want their Jewishness — however defined — to disappear in the next generation or the generation after that. I want them to stay Jewish, not because Jewish is better but because Jewish is what we have been for thousands of years, because my family has remained Jewish throughout that time despite incalculable external pressures, because Jewish values are generally very positive, because the Jewish presence in the world has contributed disproportionately to the welfare of society in relation to its meager numbers, because I love my Jewish heritage and believe that I have benefited enormously from it and want my progeny to experience its benefits as well.

If I were as sure as Jamin is that the Jewish heritage could be conveyed over the generations through its merger with other heritages, I would not be as troubled as I obviously am about the prospect of having grandchildren who are not Jewish or who are of mixed religious heritage. But the empirical evidence suggests that the children and grandchildren of mixed marriages in which neither party converts tend to abandon their Jewish heritage.[19] Jamin sees these statistics as a challenge, rather than a self-fulfilling prophecy. And I believe that Jamin will try very hard to preserve our Jewish heritage in his children. I will try to encourage that, without unduly interfering with the way Jamin and Barbara decide to raise their children.

When Jamin told my mother, who is strictly Orthodox, about his decision, she was devastated. She had suspected that Jamin was dating a non-Jewish woman, but she did not know for certain, and I did not want to tell her until Jamin and Barbara had made the decision to marry.

My mother's first reaction was to ask, "What did I do wrong?" I tried to explain that she had done nothing wrong, that Jamin is a wonderful young man with excellent values, that I would not want Jamin to have emerged with a different set of values, and that one of his values was to marry a woman he loved, not one he picked because she would make his parents and grandparents happy. "Why couldn't he have fallen in love with someone who would also make us happy?" my mother cried. I told her that Barbara does make me happy, because she is a wonderful person, because she makes Jamin happy, and because she will be a terrific mother to my grandchildren. I, too, wish that Barbara would choose to become Jewish, but I have no right — and no power — to dictate these existential matters to my adult children. I would certainly not want Barbara's parents to try to get Jamin to convert to *their* religion, which they have not done.

At first my mother considered staying away from the wedding —

and thus withholding her blessing on and approval of the marriage. Jamin told her how upsetting her absence would be to him and asked her please to come. She agreed to discuss the matter with a rabbi, if Jamin would attend the session as well. He agreed — not without some reluctance, since he did not want some stranger to try to talk him out of marrying the woman he loved. The rabbi, though an Orthodox Jew, did not try to dissuade Jamin from marrying Barbara. He did try to get Jamin to understand his grandmother's pain — and mine as well. He also asked Jamin to consider taking some concrete steps, such as Jewish education and summer camps, toward assuring that his children would be Jewish.

The discussion was quite emotional, with tears all around. My mother made it clear that she wanted to attend the wedding, but that she did not want to do the wrong thing or send the wrong message to her other grandchildren. She wanted the rabbi to "give her permission" to attend, but the rabbi said that it was not his role to give or deny permission. He saw himself simply as a facilitator, who could help Jamin discuss the issues meaningfully with his father and grandmother. The rabbi did say, at the end of the meeting, that it was clear to him that my mother's love for Jamin was too great for her to miss his wedding and that it would not be the "wrong thing" for her to follow her heart. But it was her decision to make, and not one mandated by any religious law.

My mother attended the wedding, as did Jamin's other grandparents and everyone else in our immediate family. It was a civil ceremony conducted by a judge — a "liberal" one, Jamin insisted — at Barbara's family home in Ridgewood, New Jersey.

The most memorable moment of the wedding came when my older son, Elon, who was the best man, gave the traditional toast. Before his toast, nobody mentioned what was obviously going through everyone's mind. We had all been told not to think about an elephant — so of course an elephant was on everyone's mind. Elon, as he always does, spoke directly to the issue of Jamin and Barbara's mixed marriage. He started by recognizing that some in attendance might wonder what Jamin and Barbara might have in common, considering their very different backgrounds. Then he related an incident that had occurred a year or so earlier, when Jamin was working in downtown Manhattan at the Legal Aid Society and Barbara was working uptown in the Columbia Presbyterian emergency room. After work one day, they met with Elon for dinner. As was typical, Jamin discussed his clients and Barbara her patients (while Elon, who makes movies, listened with an ear to whether there was a possible script in any of their stories). Jamin had spent the morning representing a homeless man afflicted with AIDS. Barbara had spent the afternoon treating a homeless man afflicted with AIDS. As they each related their experiences, it became apparent that they had both helped the *same* man — several hours and several miles apart. In a huge city with tens of thousands of sick and homeless people, a young lawyer and a young doctor who were soon to be married had ministered to the same sick and homeless person on the same day. Elon concluded his toast by declaring, "Let no one say that this is not a marriage between like-minded people with similar values. Let no one say that this is not a match made in heaven and blessed by destiny."

I now have two wonderful grandchildren from Jamin and Barbara's marriage. I do not — I cannot — see them any differently than I would if they had been born to two Jewish parents. I realize that their lives will probably not be very different from what they would have been had Barbara been a relatively irreligious Jew rather than a relatively irreligious Catholic. Jamin would not have raised his children religiously regardless of whom he married. And since I do not subscribe to the principle that Judaism, as a civilization, is matrilineal — or indeed any other kind of "lineal" or genetic — it should not matter all that much to me. But it still does concern me that Lori and Lyle may not be part of a tradition I love so much. I know they will be raised with Jamin and Barbara's values and heritages, and I hope that they turn out as great as their parents.

I never try to proselytize my grandchildren, because I believe that how to raise them is their parents' decision, but when Jamin and Barbara bring them to our home on Jewish holidays, I do try to make the occasions positive and memorable ones. My wife and I include Barbara, Lori, and Lyle in our Passover Seder, Hanukkah party, and other celebrations, emphasizing the ecumenical aspects of the holidays. I very much want my grandchildren to see the Jewish part of their heritage as something to be proud of and to enjoy. I regard Lori and Lyle not as the last links of an old chain, but rather the first links of a new and continuing chain. They are in the good company of many others who will determine their own destinies as part of the ever-changing panorama of Jewish history and civilization.

As to my audience members who seek advice about how to deal with an impending mixed marriage, my major suggestion is that when the decision to marry has already been made, *that* is precisely the *wrong* time to become involved, especially as a naysayer to a fait accompli. If you fail to dissuade your child, there will be continuing resentment. And if you succeed, there may be even greater resentment. The time to act is both well before any decision has been made and after the marriage has taken place.

A decision by a young Jewish man or woman to marry a non-Jew is generally a reflection of a well-established reality that their Jewishness is not all that central to their identity. This issue must be addressed much earlier than on the eve of the wedding. It is a lifelong process with no precise roadmap and absolutely no guarantee of success. But there are some steps that may change the odds, such as a positive Hebrew education, visits to Israel, and active involvement in synagogue life. (I address this issue more specifically in Part IV, which deals with my proposals for change.)

Once the decision has been made to marry, the non-Jewish spouse and the children must be welcomed with open arms and a full heart into the family, both because that is the right thing to do and because that will increase the likelihood that the children will see their Jewish heritage in a positive manner and be proud of it. Every family will deal with specific issues differently, such as religious observance, Jewish education, and participation in Jewish activities. But the spirit of acceptance must be communicated unambiguously to the non-Jewish spouse and the children. Treating one's children or grandchildren differently depending on whether they are "Jewish" is both wrong and self-defeating.

We must learn how to deal with the growing phenomenon of intermarriage. We cannot simply wring our hands and heave a collective "Oy vey." (In this regard, I am reminded of the three old Jewish women sitting on the boardwalk in Miami. The first moans, "Oy vey." The second groans, "Oy gevalt." The third one admonishes the others, "I thought we agreed not to talk about our children.") Nor can we devote all our energies to trying to prevent intermarriage. First of all, we will fail. Intermarriage is a fact of life that will not end, even if we can slow it down by imbuing our children with a more positive Judaism. Second, for some Jews a mixed marriage may be the right decision, which we are not entitled to second-guess. It is not as if all Jewish marriages are so great. Who are we to deny our children the happiness they believe will come only from marrying the spouse they love? We must recognize the inevitability and persistence of a significant amount of intermarriage and learn to deal with that reality in the most positive way.

Not all intermarriages are, of course, as "interfaithless" as Jamin and Barbara's is. My wife and I recently attended a dinner party at which the six other couples were all in mixed marriages. Five of the men were Jewish and their wives Christian, and one of the women was Jewish and her husband Christian.

Several of the Christian women had agreed, in deference to their husbands' strong feelings, to raise their children as Jews, but they explained that their husbands' definition of "Jewish" was entirely unspiritual and irreligious. It meant occasional visits to a synagogue, home celebrations such as Passover and Hanukkah, and not much else beyond the statement "They are Jewish, not Christian." Most of the women, even one who had nominally converted to Judaism, said that they missed the spirituality of their childhood religion and particularly their love for Jesus, which they felt uncomfortable expressing to their Jewish husbands and children. One of the women said that she felt totally comfortable during her occasional visits to her husband's synagogue — in fact, she loved it — but that her husband got sick to his stomach the few times she asked him to accompany her to church. She finally gave up trying. Another woman considered it unfair that she loved her husband's Judaism but that he wanted nothing to do with her Christianity, especially her love for Jesus. I tried to explain how the long history of Christian persecution of Jews made it difficult even for secular Jews to feel comfortable with Christianity. The women said that they understood rationally, but that it did not help them emotionally, since there is no persecution now.

One woman related how she was asked during her Reform Jewish conversion examination whether she renounced Jesus as the Messiah and she found that she had difficulty giving a straight answer. The rabbi then went on to the four other questions about raising her children to be Jewish, sharing the fate of the Jewish people, studying Jewish sources, and leading a Jewish life — all of which she answered perfectly. The rabbi approved her conversion, apparently on the theory that 80 percent is a passing grade, even though the one question she did not "get right" was her rejection of Jesus as Christ.

The dinner party became something of a catharsis for the Christian women, who had obviously had trouble discussing this issue with their very secular Jewish husbands, men who seemed to define their Judaism largely in negative terms: They were *not* Christians, and that was enough. They were the "un-cola" and proud of it.[20] For the spouses, the bargain they had struck seemed unfair: They were giving up their Christianity, but they were not getting any positive Judaism in return — merely a rejection of Christianity. Most of the Jewish men seemed bored or bemused by the conversation.

This brought to mind the joke about the Jewish businessman who warned his son against marrying a "shiksa." The son replied, "But she's converting to Judaism." "It doesn't matter," the old man said. "A shiksa will cause problems." After the wedding, the father called the son, who was in business with him, and asked him why he wasn't at work. "It's Shabbos," the son replied. The father was surprised: "But we always work on Saturday. It's our busiest day." "I won't work anymore on Saturday," the son insisted, "because my wife wants us to go to synagogue on Shabbos." "See," the father said. "I told you marrying a shiksa would cause problems."*

This dinner conversation with my friends, and discussions like it with many young Jews and Christian spouses of young Jews, have made it clear to me that there is a serious problem concerning how young, secular Jews define their Jewish identity. Many have no idea what it means to be Jewish, except that it distinguishes them from

---

* There is a reverse version of that joke, which does not resonate so much today because so few Jews formally convert to Catholicism: Patricia, a Catholic, and David, a Jew, were in love. But she refused to marry him unless he converted to Catholicism. He finally gave in and agreed to undertake the church's required course of study. He threw himself into his labors, poring over his books night and day, speaking with church officials, and asking profound questions of his instructors. Three months after David had begun his studies, Patricia went home to her parents, sobbing.

"What's the matter, dear?" asked her mother. "Why are you crying?"

"It's David," she wept. "He's decided to become a priest!"

Christians and other non-Jews. They know that they do not want their children to be Christians, but they don't know what they *do* want them to be — except something like what they are. They want them to be identified with Jewish causes (but perhaps not too identified); they want them to live Jewish lives (but not too Jewish); they want them to be a part of a long tradition (but not too bound by it); they want them to support Israel (but not too zealously); they want them to be compassionate, charitable, and concerned with human rights (without becoming extremists). But most of all, they do not want them to become Christian, because that would be an abandonment of something that is important, though hard to define.

A front-page story in the *New York Times* in 1996 described the growing trend toward interracial and interethnic marriages throughout the United States. Jews are not likely to be an exception to this phenomenon, which has been called the "end of ethnicity." Indeed, a subsequent article in the *New York Times Magazine* titled "Race Is Over" featured pictures of several partially Jewish children who shared Chinese, Puerto Rican, Dominican, African, and Irish heritages.[21] Nor is this prognostication limited to the children of interfaith — or interfaithless — marriages. Many children of Jewish couples will experience a drifting away. A friend of mine whose parents are Jewish was recently asked whether he was Jewish. He responded, "Only on my parents' side."

We must understand why so many of our children and grandchildren consider themselves Jewish only on their parents' side and are drifting away from a Jewish life that so many in my generation fought so hard to defend. We must ask ourselves whether we devoted so much of our energy and so many of our resources to the important battles *against* our external enemies — anti-Semitism and persecution — that we failed to reflect enough on what it is we were fighting *for*. We must now make sure that there is Jewish life after the death of anti-Semitism, and even in the face of the reality of increasing intermarriage.

The primary reason why so many Jews, especially young Jews, are marrying non-Jews and assimilating today is that they do not see any positive reasons for remaining Jewish. Jews today rarely "renounce" their Judaism, convert to Christianity, or even change their names, as many did during previous periods of assimilation — often without success. (The impossibility of assimilating in a world that hated Jews was a frequent subject of Jewish humor, as when financier Otto Kahn told a friend who was hunchbacked that he "*used to be* a Jew." The friend replied, "Yes, and I *used to be* a hunchback.") Today, young Jews simply stop — even that is too dramatic a word, because it suggests a particular point in time — being Jewish. The process tends to be gradual, passive, and often nonvolitional. There is rarely a definite decision to stop being Jewish. There is just no decision to continue being Jewish. Assimilation occurs today largely by inaction rather than by volition. In this regard, marriage to a non-Jew is *rarely the cause* of a young person's diminishing connection to Judaism; it is *more often a symptom* or an effect of an ongoing process that began much earlier.

When this reality of increasing intermarriage is combined with trends toward decreasing birthrates among non-Orthodox Jews, the future of American Jewry as we know it seems bleak.

The Ever-Dying People

But the future of Jews has seemed bleak before. Sometimes we have been able to reverse historical, demographic, and political trends. Other times, we have not. Our destiny is not in the heavens, "*lo B'shamayim*" — as the Talmud put it in a related context. Our destiny is, at least in part, in our hands. Even the most God-fearing Jews understand that matters cannot always be left to God, as the following story — which I was told by my Orthodox mother — illustrates. Yankel had never asked God for anything during his seventy-nine years of pious prayer. Finally, he pleaded with the Almighty to grant him one wish: "Before my eightieth birthday, God, please let me win the lottery." Weeks go by — nothing. Finally, on the eve of his eightieth birthday, Yankel rebukes God: "All these years I pray to you and ask for nothing for myself. Why couldn't you grant me my one small request?" A voice from heaven responds: "Yankel, help me out a little here — *buy a ticket!*" One of my mother's favorite aphorisms is "God helps those who help themselves."

In his stimulating essay titled "Israel: The Ever-Dying People," the historian Simon Rawidowicz rejects the self-imposed image of the Jewish people as "being constantly on the verge of . . . disappearing." He points out that "there was hardly a generation in the Diaspora that did not consider itself the final link in Israel's chain." After reviewing the long history of Jewish fears of disappearing, he concludes his essay on a triumphantly optimistic note: "There is no people more dying than Israel, yet none better equipped to resist disaster, to fight alone, always alone. . . . Let us prepare the ground for the last Jews who will come after us, and for the last Jews who will rise after them, and so on until the end of days."[22]

But despite the historic ability of the Jewish people to "resist disaster" in the past, the experience of the Holocaust should make it abundantly clear that we can't count on Providence to preserve us in the future. The historian Norman Cantor, in his provocative book *The Sacred Chain*, argues that "Jewish history as we have known it is approaching its end," that "the sacred chain is running through its last links." Citing the usual statistics about intermarriage, assimilation, and low birthrates, Cantor predicts the demographic disappearance of the Jewish community in America, and even — over a longer term — in the Middle East, after peace is achieved with the Palestinians. Nor does Professor Cantor necessarily bemoan this prospect. In his view, "The Jews have fulfilled their role in history." They have achieved their divine goal of being "a light to the world." They have given the world three great religions — Judaism, Christianity, and Islam — two of which dominate the world numerically. They have provided some of history's greatest thinkers, writers, artists, and scientists. "The Jews served their own purpose, and God's purpose, and mankind's purpose. Pragmatically, they are no longer very much needed as a distinct race. The Jewish heritage would endure if the Jews disappeared as a major group in the world in the twenty-first century."[23]

As a historian, Cantor should know better than to offer an essentially teleological justification for his predicted end of the Jewish people. Civilizations do not disappear because they have served some "purpose" — either earthly or heavenly. They disappear for empirical reasons: external destruction, geographic factors, assimilation, economic causes, and so on. Perhaps Cantor means something a bit different: namely, that even those who believe that the *empirical* trends toward Jewish disappearance will somehow be reversed by *divine* intervention should understand that the *divine* purpose of the Jewish people has been achieved.

I will not debate Professor Cantor on this theo-teleological plane. Nor do I necessarily disagree with his empirical data. I believe, however, that a people can control its own destiny — at least to a degree. There is no rule of historical inevitability that cannot be challenged by a determined counterforce. Perhaps Herzl overstated it when he proclaimed, "If you will it, it is no dream." Surely, the opposite is likely to be true: If we do nothing about it, the empirical trends will continue unabated. Indeed, I agree with another of Cantor's implicit conclusions: that the fate of the Jewish people should not be left in God's hands. We must take control of our own future, and we must not regard it as unthinkable that we, the Jewish people, may have no future unless we challenge what appears to be a historical inevitability. As Cantor cautions: "We must not think that it is either history's mandate or God's will that the Jews should continue to exist as an identifiable and distinctive group in any way near even their current modest numbers. Most Jewish communities disappeared before."[24]

It is, of course, true that previous Jewish communities disappeared. But in the past, they were replaced by new, often more vibrant ones. If the American Jewish community, as we know it, were to disappear, it, too, would probably be replaced by at least two distinct Jewish communities: an ultra-Orthodox community, which would have little impact on the outside world, and an Israeli Jewish community that would soon become divided between ultra-Orthodox and more secular Jews. These secular Israelis would probably retain their distinctively national Israeli Jewish character beyond the middle of the next century — but for how long, no one can predict.

I am not prepared, however, to concede the end of the non-Orthodox American Jewish community, though I recognize the uphill battle we face. Nor am I reassured by Rawidowicz's historical optimism. Even if Rawidowicz is correct in his assessment that no people "is better equipped to resist *disaster*, to fight alone, always alone," the question remains how well the Jewish people is equipped to resist *success*, especially when we are not *alone*, but rather in the company of *friends* — non-Jewish friends who do not want to destroy us out of hate, but rather to have us join with them out of mutual respect and even love. Rawidowicz argues that precisely because we always worry about being destroyed by our enemies, we have prevented such an end from occurring: "In anticipating the end, [the Jewish people] became its master. Thus no catastrophe could ever take this end-fearing people by surprise, so as to put it off balance, still less to obliterate it — as if its incessant preparation for the end made this very end impossible."[25]

But as much as the Jewish people has anticipated and prepared for an end brought about by external enemies, it has not anticipated and prepared for an end brought about by the voluntary decisions of large numbers of Jews to have so few children, to marry non-Jews, and to assimilate. Indeed, in a great many instances there is not even an explicit decision to assimilate; it occurs as the result of gradual inaction over time. Even Seymour Martin Lipset and Earl Raab, in a hard-hitting and unsentimental sociological analysis of "Jews and the New American Scene," are unwilling to face the prospect that the Jewish people as we know it may disappear. Their worst-case scenario appears to be a significant reduction in the size of the American Jewish community by the middle of the next century. But they appear confident, largely because of the "religion-connected aspect of Jewish life," that "it will not have disappeared and may even have reached some relatively stable plateau." Indeed, they claim that "no one is saying that American Jewry will vanish."[26] But that is exactly what historians like Norman Cantor and demographers like Elihu Bergman *are* saying. Cantor puts it most bluntly: "Saving an unforeseen reversal of current trends, it appears from present perspective that the history of the Jews as we have known it and them is probably approaching the end."[27]

Even this prophecy of doom does not mean that the small fraction of Jewry who live totally insulated lives — the ultra-Orthodox and Hasidim — will become extinct. But without the context of eclectic Jewry, as we now know it, these pockets of self-contained "extended families" will take on the aura of quaint little sects, akin to the Amish or the Shakers, which have absolutely no impact on American life or indeed life outside the "ghetto." The influential Jewish community will have disappeared, if Cantor's prediction comes to pass. An even smaller community than the ultra-Orthodox — namely, the "modern Orthodox" — may also persist for a considerable period of time. Modern Orthodox live mainstream American lives, attending college, working in large corporations and law firms, living in mixed neighborhoods, but they obey the basic commandments to observe the Sabbath, eat only kosher food, and pray three times a day. But this community (in which I have my roots) is being threatened from two flanks: Many of its children are moving to the right and becoming "ultra-Orthodox," while others are moving to the left and becoming what has now been called "Conservadox." It is unclear whether the modern Orthodox movement will thrive — or even survive — in the coming century. To the extent that its children live in the outside world, attend secular colleges, and so on, there will be *some* inter-marriage and assimilation, though far less than among more secular Jews. But all this means is that the trends toward assimilation may take several more generations, not that they are completely absent even among the modern Orthodox.

The first step toward preventing this tragedy from occurring is to recognize its possibility. As Rawidowicz put it: "In anticipating the end, [the Jewish people] became its master." We must now antici-pate the end of the Jewish people as we know it precisely to become the masters of our own destiny. The British historian Geoffrey Bar-raclough once said that "demography is destiny."[28] If we are to be-come the masters of our own destiny as a people, we must confront our mortality, painful as that is. We must imagine a world without Jews.

At one level, it is impossible to imagine a world without Jews. The history of Western society — which, for better or worse, *is* the dominant history of the world as most of us know it — is, in many ways, a *Jewish*-centered history. The major frame of reference of Western history is the story of this tiny tribe that has had such a dis-proportionate impact on the world. As the philosopher Ernest van den Haag has put it: "It is the Jews who have given the essential meaning to the last two thousand years of Western history."[29] Even Voltaire, who hated Judaism with a passion, berated Christian histo-rians for suggesting that "everything in the world" happens because of the Jews: "If God gave the Babylonians authority over Asia, He did so to punish the Jews; if God sent the Romans, He did so to pun-ish [the Jews] once more." Voltaire asked: "Why should the world be made to rotate around the insignificant pimple of Jewry?"[30] The answer is obvious. The Jews *wrote* the history, and history is always determined by the perspective of the narrator. The story of the Jews is the Bible, the most influential and widely read book of all time. Je-sus was a Jew. Mohammed believed in the Jewish Bible. Luther's early career was marked by a great affinity for Jews, since he believed that Christianity is incomprehensible without an appreciation of Judaism.[31] The world has always reacted to Jews — both positively and negatively. Wars have been fought against Jews, from the various conquests of Palestine to the Crusades to World War II and beyond. Western history — including Islamic and even much of North African history — has been largely Judeo-centric.

Even America, which has had a significant Jewish presence for only the last century, has been enormously influenced by Jews. The theater critic Walter Kerr, writing as early as 1968, demonstrated the integration of Jews into mainstream American life by describing not Jewish acculturation to gentile culture, but rather gentile adaptation to Jewish patterns of thought: "What has happened since World War II is that the American sensibility itself has become part Jewish, perhaps nearly as much Jewish as it is anything else. . . . The literate American mind has come in some measure to think Jewishly, to respond Jewishly. It has been taught to, and it was ready to. After the entertainers and novelists came the Jewish critics, politicians, theologians. Critics and politicians and theologians are by profession molders: they form ways of seeing."[32] Today this influence is even more apparent, as individual Jews dominate television, film, book publishing, newspapers, magazine advertising, public relations, and other opinion-shaping businesses. Professor Sylvia Barack Fishman of Brandeis University titled a November 1996 article "U.S. Culture Has Been Judaized, and Vice Versa."[33] She calls this process the "coalescence of two cultures."

All this does not, however, guarantee the continued centrality of Jews to our history, or even the continued survival of the Jews as a people. Other peoples and civilizations have made their mark on world history and then receded or disappeared. The Pharaonic dynasties of Egypt, the civilizations of the Sumerians, Assyrians, Babylonians, Phoenicians, and Romans have all vanished. Even peoples whose long-ago contributions to modern civilization remain relevant, such as the ancient Greeks, have undergone a near-total cultural, religious, and national discontinuity, to the extent that one cannot really speak of today's Greeks as the same people.

Mark Twain marveled at how "the Jew saw them all, beat them all, and is now what he always was."[34] He believed that "all things are mortal but the Jew; all other forces pass, but he remains." This was written in 1899. It was almost disproved between 1939 and 1945. It could not be written with such assurance in 1999.

Would We Be Missed?

That brings us back to the question of what a world without Jews would be like. Would it be a terrible thing for this people to pass into oblivion?

There are at least three perspectives from which this question can be addressed. The first is the perspective of the Jewish people. The second is the perspective of individual Jews. The third is the perspective of the non-Jewish world.

Asking this question from the perspective of the Jewish people is essentially tautological. Of course the demise of the Jewish people would be bad for the Jewish people. It's like asking a potential murder victim whether his death would be good for him! Unless he is suicidal, his answer will be a predictable no.

When this question is asked of *individual* Jews, however, the answer is neither tautological nor predictable. From the beginning of Jewish history, some individual Jews have believed that *they*, as individuals, would benefit from the disappearance of the Jewish people. Even Theodor Herzl flirted with this idea as an alternative to the establishment of a Jewish state. Hitler proved that individual intermarriage, assimilation, and even conversion are not always enough to exempt Jews from the burdens imposed on them by the existence of the Jewish people. But times have changed. Today, no individual Jew has *the right* to claim that the continued existence of the Jewish people will hurt him or her. Assimilation these days is so cost-free and easy that any Jew who does not want to belong to the Jewish people can resign with less hassle than it takes to get out of the Book-of-the-Month Club. Indeed, it takes no action at all, just inaction. I do not believe, therefore, that the question about the survival of the Jewish people asked of individual Jews who do not want to remain Jews raises any serious intellectual issues different from those raised when the question is addressed to the non-Jewish world.

To me, the *emotional* answer is clear: Of course it would be a terrible thing for the world at large if the Jewish people were to pass into oblivion. The world would be a much poorer place in every imaginable way and for every human being. But when I think about it *rationally* and try to come up with intelligent and persuasive *arguments* in support of my emotional response, the difficulty of the question becomes apparent.

Remember, the question is *not* whether the world would be better off had the Jewish people *never* existed. The answer to *that* question is demonstrably clear: The Jewish people has contributed enormously and disproportionately to the welfare of the world. Indeed, it is difficult to imagine the world as we know it without the positive contributions of Jews. There is a television commercial that tries to demonstrate what the world would look like without a certain company's products: suddenly, things we all need and take for granted — like electricity, medical equipment, car parts — begin to disappear before our very eyes. Try the same thing in relation to Jews: Much of what Western civilization today consists of — from Christianity to Islam to culture to economics to science to law to medicine — would look much different if we were to eliminate the contributions of Jews. No one is seeking to rewrite *past* history. The question is directed at the future. What would the world be like *from now on* if the Jewish people, which has *already* contributed so much, were to stop existing *from now on?*

Nor is the question whether the world would be better off if the Jews were to be destroyed by external enemies, such as the Nazis or Hamas. Our involuntary destruction would, of course, be a tragedy of enormous dimensions, as evidenced by the partial destruction brought about by the Holocaust. The question at hand — the one posed by historian Norman Cantor and political sociologist Charles Liebman and by the forces of history itself — is whether it would be so terrible if the vast majority of Jews, over time, decided to assimilate and this brought about the voluntary merger of the Jewish people into the general population. Nor is Liebman correct in arguing that "anyone who can seriously pose such a question to himself" — whether it was important for Judaism to survive — "is unlikely to answer that survival is worthwhile."[35] Posing that question is an essential first step to understanding what a world without Jews would be like and why we should care about current demographic trends. I pose the question precisely because I care deeply about Jewish survival.

A simpleminded answer could go something like this: Since it is incontestably true that the Jewish people contributed so much in the *past*, and are contributing so much in the *present*, it follows that they will contribute an equivalent amount — though its precise content cannot now be anticipated — in the *future*. But there are several problems with this line of argument.

First, to the extent that the major contributions of the Jewish people have been religious in nature — the Bible, monotheism, Jewish theology, the code of laws — these are unlikely to be recurring, or even continuing, contributions. Once made, they are there. There is no need for continued Jewish presence to improve upon them. Indeed, central to Jewish theology — especially to the traditional rabbinic Halakah — is the idea that the Jewish religion was established well in the past and must not be changed or even tampered with. Among Maimonides' thirteen fundamental principles of Judaism is that "no other Torah will come from God. One may not add to it nor delete from it, neither in the written nor the oral Torah."[36] Contemporary contributions to Jewish theology are, of course, being made by the Conservative, Reform, and Reconstructionist movements.[37] But it would be difficult to argue that, with a few notable exceptions such as Martin Buber, Gershom Scholem, Abraham Heschel, and Elie Wiesel, contemporary Jewish theologians are having a major impact on non-Jewish life.[38]

What, then, of the contributions of *individual* Jews to humankind? What would the world be like without a future Albert Einstein, Sigmund Freud, Franz Kafka, Isaiah Berlin, Yitzhak Perlman, Ludwig Wittgenstein, Jonas Salk, Heinrich Heine, George Gershwin, Louis Brandeis, Gertrude Stein, Simone Weil, Henri Bergson, Baruch Spinoza, Niels Bohr, Albert Sabin, Emma Goldman, Rosa Luxemburg, Marc Chagall, Camille Pissarro, Karl Marx, Nelly Sachs, Max Weber, Leonard Bernstein, Irving Berlin, Benjamin Disraeli, Emile Durkheim, Cesare Lombroso, Gustav Mahler, Arnold Schoenberg, Samuel Gompers, Marcel Proust, Claude Lévi-Strauss, the Marx Brothers, Barbra Streisand, Sarah Bernhardt, Nadine Gordimer, Louise Nevelson, Steven Spielberg, Marcel Marceau, Sam Goldwyn, or David Sarnoff?

This way of putting the question — with its emphasis on individuals of Jewish background — raises a fascinating, and rarely discussed, issue: How come so many of the Jews who contributed so much to the world were not *practicing* or *observant* Jews? How come so few of the most observant, ritualistic, and theological Jews have contributed as much as their more secular brothers and sisters? At one level, the question is somewhat tautological. If we measure contributions by reference to a secular standard, it will of course follow that those who have achieved the most, as measured by that secular standard, will be secular Jews. Religious Jews are more likely to make their contributions to the world of religion, because that is where their priorities lie. But there is more to it than this. If it is true that the *individual* Jews who have contributed the most to the world at large were those Jews who strayed from the core of religious Judaism, then it may not be *Judaism itself* that must survive if the intellectual and artistic successors to these gifted individual Jews are to continue to be produced. This suggests one of the great paradoxes of the Jewish people, which can be characterized as "the trickle-down theory of Judaism." Why has the Jewish *background* or *heritage* of so many individuals who have contributed so much to the world been so important to their success, while the core of Jewish *religious observance* has been relatively unimportant? Is it essential for religious Judaism to survive so that individual Jews may continue to *drift away from its core* and make great contributions to the world? Does the essence of what makes so many Jews so important to the world necessarily *trickle down* from the core of Judaism?

The Trickle-Down Theory of Jewish Success

The great paradox of Jewish life is that virtually all of the positive values we identify with Jews — compassion, creativity, contributions to the world at large, charity, a quest for education — seem more characteristic of Jews who are closer to the secular end of the Jewish continuum than to the ultra-Orthodox end. Put another way, the closer one lives to the religious core of Judaism, the further one is likely to be from the Jewish values so many of us cherish most. There are exceptions, of course, but as a general matter, it is difficult to quarrel with this empirical reality.[39] The opposite is not quite true: It is not true that the further one lives from the religious core, the greater the likelihood that one will embrace these values. There seems to be a delicate balance: Too close to the core creates insularity and parochialism; too far from the core dissipates the Jewish values. One possible explanation for this interesting paradox is that both ultra-Orthodox Jews and completely alienated, secular Jews live in only one world. The Jew who remains in touch with his or her Jewish tradition while living a full life in the general community must try to reconcile differing and often clashing worldviews. These conflicting views, and the need to reconcile them, stimulates the kind of creativity and imagination that is often lacking in those for whom there is no such clash.

Many Jewish parents seem instinctively to recognize this paradox, though I have never actually heard it articulated. They want their children to learn the core religious values and rituals of Judaism — the Sabbath, prayer, monotheism — and then to move away from strict adherence toward a more "reasonable" and "balanced" approach that does not inhibit their success in the outside world. They want their children to retain the "essence" of Judaism, without necessarily living under its constraints and burdens. They understand the need for *someone* to preserve the core of religious observance so that *their* children are able to benefit from its trickle-down values.

To put the issue of Jewish continuity more concretely: Why does anyone care whether, for example, Hasidic Jews, who by their own self-chosen insularity contribute little to the outside world, continue to perpetuate themselves? Pose that question to the secular Jewish Hollywood mogul or the Reform Jewish Denver businessman who contributes millions of dollars to the Lubavitch Hasidim, and you will get an interesting answer. The survival of "authentic," "traditional," "fundamentalist" Judaism of the sort practiced by the Hasidim is essential to the continuity of the kind of Judaism *he* would like to see in the future.

He will tell you that he would be appalled if his own children or grandchildren ever became Hasidim. (Indeed, I was once asked by a Reform Jewish woman to help "deprogram" her granddaughter who had been "kidnapped" by a Hasidic "cult.") But in order to ensure the perpetuation of *his* brand of watered-down Judaism — the occasional lighting of Friday-night candles, the half-dozen or so ritual observances, the Jewish "spirit" — there has to be a thick, rich core that *can* be watered down, and from which the essence that he wants so desperately to preserve can trickle down. He will tell you that the Hasidim practice a more "authentic" brand of Judaism than that practiced in his own Conservative or Reform temple, and that he wants to encourage such authenticity, without being burdened by it himself. He will also tell you that he wants the Jewish *people* to survive, and that the Jewish people cannot survive unless Jews marry each other. The Hasidim, who always marry each other, assure the continuation of the Jewish people — even if they are *a* Jewish people largely distinct from *the* Jewish people these secular Jews want to see preserved.*

This, then, is the paradox of Jewish survival. The world at large — and indeed, most Jews — could not care less if Hasidic and ultra-Orthodox Jewry were to disappear from the face of the earth (so long as it wasn't brought about by some external, involuntary cause, like Nazism). We don't really care about the insular and parochial values of these core groups. In fact, we affirmatively reject them. We do not want our children to be like them. They do not produce — at least not directly — the great scientists, artists, philanthropists of whom we are so proud. Yet we believe that *their* survival is essential to *our* Judaism since *they* do not marry non-Jews or assimilate. We need *them* to perpetuate *us*. But why should that be the case? Why can't we perpetuate *ourselves*, without the need for *them* as intermediaries? Why do we need a religious core from which the secular values can trickle down?

I believe we don't. Indeed, I believe that it is unhealthy for the survival of Jewish life to depend so heavily on minority groups of Jews who *themselves* have so little to do with the Jewish values the majority of us cherish most. I hope that ultra-Orthodox Judaism will thrive because it is good for ultra-Orthodox Jews. But more-secular Jews like me should not have to depend on ultra-Orthodox Jews to preserve *their* core from which *our* values can trickle down. We more-secular Jews must create a new Jewish state of mind — and way of life — that directly reflects the Jewish values we care about most and that is capable of perpetuating itself directly, without depending on these values' trickling down from an ultrareligious core. We must view our own Judaism as equally authentic to that of the ultra-Orthodox and become less defensive about our Jewish values.

---

* The joke goes: "Which religion in the world is closest to Judaism?" The answer: "Hasidism." In the beginning of the Hasidic era, this was no joke, since the more traditional Jews, called Mitnagdim, declared the Hasidim to be excommunicated from Judaism.

We must take control over our own destiny and not leave it in the hands of fundamentalists who have little sympathy for our desire to live full lives in both the secular and the Jewish worlds.

A related paradox is that as the power of individual Jews grows, the power of the Jewish community seems to diminish. The perverse promise of the Count de Clermont-Tonnerre, issued during the debate in the revolutionary French National Assembly over whether to extend civil rights to Jews, is in the process of being fulfilled: "To Jews as a people, nothing; to the Jews as individuals, everything."[40]

There are today more *individuals* of Jewish background in positions of power and authority in the United States than ever before. But it is questionable whether there is any more "Jewish power" — that is, power employed on behalf of the Jewish people — now than in the previous postwar decades. These individuals who have achieved success, prominence, and influence have done so as individuals, *not* as Jews. Although, as of this writing, there are ten Jewish senators and as many as thirty-one Jewish representatives in the U.S. Congress, few of these legislators think of themselves as representing Jewish constituents. The four Jewish cabinet members and two Supreme Court justices appointed by President Clinton during his first term were not appointed *because* they were Jewish. Most Jews at this level of government are so distant from their religion that it was quipped that the only member of the Clinton cabinet to go to High Holiday services was Clinton.

Since their Jewishness wasn't the reason these individuals of Jewish heritage were given their jobs, most of them feel no obligation to act Jewishly in their jobs or to represent "the Jewish point of view" — assuming there could even be one Jewish point of view on anything — and Jews don't expect them to. Contrast this with the anger many African-Americans feel toward Justice Clarence Thomas, who was clearly appointed because he was black, but who adamantly refuses to toe the politically correct line as mainstream blacks define it.

When anti-Semitic journals, such as *Spotlight* or *The Truth at Last*, compile lists of Jews in government, the media, academia, and corporations, they deliberately seek to convey the impression that these individuals are implementing "Jewish power" or "Jewish policy" in accord with some "master plan." For example, in 1995 and

1996 it became common in the hate media to point out that all the officials in Clinton's administration at that time who had power over the economy — the secretaries of the Treasury, Commerce, Labor, and Agriculture, as well as the chairman of the Federal Reserve Board — were Jews, as if to suggest some grand Jewish scheme to control the economy. The reality, of course, is that these individual Jews had little in common with one another and often disagreed quite sharply over economic policies. The fact that some Jewish individuals have achieved success disproportionate to their numbers in the general population tells us nothing about the power of the Jewish *people*. It may tell us something about a lowering of the barriers of discrimination, about the work ethic of many Jews, and about the American creed of meritocracy.

It may also tell us something quite important about the future of Jews in America. *As individuals*, Jews and people of Jewish heritage will continue to exercise considerable influence in the government, business, media, and academia of this nation. *As Jews*, these individuals will not be serving any particular religious or ethnic agenda. Indeed, Jewish *power* — as reflected in voting patterns, the influence of Jewish lobbying groups, and the magnitude of donations to election campaigns — will almost certainly diminish over the coming decades, as Jews disperse geographically, marry non-Jews, assimilate, and feel less defensive and in need of group power. On the eve of the 1996 election, an article was published in *Jewish Week* titled "The Incredible Shrinking Clout." It documented the movement of Jews out of crucial electoral states, the reduction in Jewish population, greater divisions within the Jewish community, and other factors that "are coming together to dilute the impact of the Jewish vote."[41] Yet, in the face of this decrease in Jewish power, individuals of Jewish background continue to thrive.

The Secret of Jewish Success

Why, then, do so many individuals of Jewish background achieve such great success? Throughout history, Jews and others have sought to discover the essence of what has been variously called the "Jewish mystique," "Jewish genius," or "Yiddisher cup" (or *khop*). The latter literally means "Jewish head," and refers to Jewish intelligence. Jokes abound, such as the one about Shloime who, victimized and discriminated against for seventy years, finally decides to convert to Episcopalianism. The morning after his conversion, his wife wakes up and sees him davening (praying) with his tallith and tefillin (prayer shawl and phylacteries). She says, "Shloime, why are you davening? You're an Episcopalian now!" Shloime hits himself on the head, exclaiming, "Oy, goyisher cup!" (i.e., "non-Jewish head").

Some contemporary writers have claimed that the secret of Jewish overachievement is as simple as *genetics*. The philosopher Ernest van den Haag argues that "to the extent that one can speak of a genotype, one can speak of a Jewish genotype, and one can say in comparative terms, it is remarkably pure." Writing in 1969, van den Haag pointed to Jews' relatively low rates of marriage to non-Jews, as well as to high IQ scores among Ashkenazi Jews and to studies conducted in Israel of blood type and fingerprint whorls which conclude that "Yemenite Jews, though separated from them for thousands of years, have more in common with German Jews than German Jews have in common with non-Jewish Germans or Yemenite Jews with non-Jewish Yemenites."[42] These kinds of studies, especially of IQ and "genotype," are disfavored today and their results considered suspect. But even contemporary scholars argue that the Jews are "a distinct genetic group . . . exhibiting an extraordinary creative behavior pattern."[43] Nor do they shy away from talking about "the genetic intellectual superiority of the Jews" and their "innate superior qualities."[44]

Van den Haag takes the pure genetic argument a step further and points to an acquired reproductive characteristic that has, in his view, widened the intellectual gap between Jews and Christians. Historically, the brightest Christians became priests, and until the advent of Protestantism, priests were celibate (at least in theory) and so did not procreate (at least very much). This "meant that the most intelligent portion of the population did not have offspring; their genes were siphoned off, generation after generation, into the church, and not returned into the world's . . . genetic supply. . . . The result," he claims, "was a reduction of the average intelligence level of the non-Jewish Western population to a level considerably below that which would have been achieved otherwise."[45]

In contrast, van den Haag points out, Jewish rabbis, whose stateless societies chose them as brightest among their group to fill the double role of religious and secular leader — were encouraged to marry the brightest women and have the most children. "Altogether if Jews had deliberately decided to breed children so as to maximize genetic intelligence, they could not have done much better." Van den Haag acknowledges that the Jews had "no such conscious purpose — any more than the Catholic rule of celibacy was intended to reduce the average intelligence of Christians." But the results, he argues, are the same: a significant differential between the average intelligence of Jews and Christians.[46]

This interesting observation, even if true, has no contemporary relevance. The differential pattern van den Haag described as characteristic of the procreative patterns of the Middle Ages is no longer in existence. Today's rabbis are not necessarily the smartest Jews, nor do they marry the most intelligent women or have the most children. Today's priests are not the same intellectual elite they once were, and non-Catholic priests and ministers marry and procreate. Thus, whatever differences may have been created by past patterns of procreation ceased to exist quite some time ago, even if it could be shown that they have left some continuing genetic residue.

Even if any or all of these claims were scientifically testable (which they are not) and true (which we have no way of knowing), they would not constitute a compelling argument for the preservation of the Jewish people. If the "Jewish mystique" is genetically based, why not spread the "superior" genes as widely as possible? If one wishes to procreate with the highest-IQ mate possible — a perverse form of eugenics[47] — then one should seek that mate without regard to religious background, since there are surely many non-Jews who are smarter than many Jews. In any event, the genetic and IQ arguments would hardly be worthy of a principled defense of the Jewish people. They certainly would not be very persuasive in convincing young Jews not to marry their very bright non-Jewish classmates and work associates.

Most commentators on the Jewish mystique point to the shared experiences of the Jewish people as the building blocks of that "something special" about the "Jewish character." Some focus on the long history of victimization and persecution as character building or as contributing to Jewish creativity. I have also heard a variation of Darwin's "survival of the fittest" according to which the persecution of the Jews resulted in the weeding out of the less intelligent. If it does indeed require persecution to produce genius, then the time has come for Jews to stop contributing so large a share to the genius quotient. It is far better that the persecution of Jews come to an end than that we continue to be persecuted into creativity.

Others argue that our collective history has created a unique will to succeed among Jews. For example, in an internal memorandum circulated to the Supreme Court in the *Bakke* case, Justice Harry Blackmun — who was generally supportive of Jewish causes — made the following observation about an argument against racial quotas that had been advanced by Professor Alexander Bickel:

> [Bickel's] position is — and I hope I offend no one, for I do not mean to do so — the "accepted" Jewish approach. It is to be noted that nearly all the responsible Jewish organizations who have filed amicus briefs here are on [one] side of the case. They understandably want "pure" equality and are willing to take their chances with it, knowing that they have the inherent ability to excel and to live with it successfully. Centuries of persecution and adversity and discrimination have given the Jewish people this great attribute to compete successfully and this remarkable fortitude.[48]

But this history seems to be wearing thin. It is no longer as true as it once may have been that Jews, as a people, have more drive, more fortitude than others. Even in my thirty-plus years of teaching at Harvard, I have seen a significant change: Jewish students are simply not as outstanding as they once seemed to be. As they have become more "normalized" — more accepted, less discriminated against — they have also become less driven, less creative, less obsessed with proving themselves. They are also less compassionate, less willing to identify with the downtrodden than they once seemed to be, although still apparently more than the average person is. Indeed, to the extent these special qualities are still discernible, they seem to be part of the trickle-down paradox. Most Jews who are closest to the "core" — the Hasidim and the ultra-Orthodox — appear to have *less* compassion for the non-Jewish downtrodden than many secular Jews do, at least as measured by voting patterns.[49] The more ultra-Orthodox a Jew, the more likely he or she is to vote *against* programs for the poor and the more likely to vote for selfish programs that help them but not others.[50]

If this is true — as it clearly seems to be — then we must again ask the difficult question: Is it the *core* practice of Judaism itself or is it the *falling away* from that core — the trickling down — that creates the "Jewish values" the majority of Jews admire most and want to preserve? And if it is this trickling down, can we in the majority create it *directly*, without needing to preserve the core from which it trickles down?

In Chapter 7, I pose the question, Is there indeed "an essence" of Judaism — such as a quest for justice, charitability, creativity — since each of these characteristics, individually, exists in other groups? To say it is the unique confluence of *all* of these characteristics that is the essence of the Jewish people is both wrong and reductionist. It is wrong because not all Jews — not even all Jews who have contributed greatly to the world — embodied *all* of these qualities. It is reductionist because it simply states that the whole is equal to the sum of its parts and that a group is the product of all of its experiences. But it is certainly true that the vast majority of Jews share a common history and that certain events — such as the Holocaust and the establishment of the State of Israel — have had a significant emotional impact on a great many contemporary Jews. Indeed, the Holocaust made it clear to all Jews that they may share a common destiny, without regard to the degree of their religious observance or self-identification as a Jew.

It is not surprising, therefore, that another argument frequently made for why the Jewish people must do everything in its power to survive is that the "Jew of today is forbidden to hand Hitler yet another, posthumous victory," as the theologian Emil Fackenheim put it in what he called the "614th Commandment."[51] To assimilate — even voluntarily — would, against the backdrop of "Hitler's victory at Auschwitz," achieve the goal of the Nazis.

This "Holocaust argument" for Jewish survival is very powerful — at least to the generation of Jews for whom Auschwitz and its immediate aftermath is an actual memory. But its emotional impact is not nearly as great on the younger generation, for whom the Holocaust is yet another in the long chain of historical tragedies that have befallen the Jewish people. The evil that the villains of history — from Haman to Hitler — tried to inflict on the Jewish people in the past is not a particularly compelling explanation to the young as to why *they* should not be afforded the choice to live their lives as they choose, even if that means intermarriage and assimilation.

When I try to persuade my children and my students with the Holocaust argument, it falls rather flat. My students often give me a variation of the response made by Professor Michael Wyschogrod to Emil Fackenheim. Wyschogrod hypothesized an evil tyrant who seeks to exterminate all the world's stamp collectors and, in fact, succeeds in murdering a significant proportion of them: "Does it not follow [according to Fackenheim] that subsequent to the tyrant's demise it becomes the duty of the remaining stamp collectors not to lose interest in their stamp collecting, so as not to hand the tyrant a posthumous victory?"[52]

Wyschogrod then asks whether it would indeed be a posthumous victory for the tyrant if stamp collecting were to disappear "as long as the disappearance is due, not to force, but to free choice?" He goes on to argue that he sees no obligation on behalf of secular Jews to preserve Judaism just because Hitler wanted to destroy it. His obligation, he says, "was to destroy Hitler, but once this is accomplished, the free choice of every individual is restored and no further Hitler-derived burdens rest on the non-believing Jew."

I am a bit troubled by Wyschogrod's analogy between the Jewish people and stamp collectors, but his point is well worth considering. Indeed, it raises the broader and more complex issue of the proper role that the memory of the Holocaust — and Jewish persecution in general — should play in contemporary Judaism. Perhaps a more apt — and more contemporary — analogy would be to a tyrant who denied all women the right to choose abortion. Surely the response to his demise would not be a call for all women to have more abortions. The victory over this tyrant was not a victory for abortions; it was a victory for choice. So long as women have the right to choose, there is no reason they have to choose abortion just because the tyrant opposed abortion. So, too, the victory over Hitler, it can be argued, was a victory for choice: Jews can now *choose* to remain or not to remain Jewish with no external consequences.* Thus, so long as this choice remains uninfluenced by external pressures, the content of the choice does not hand the tyrant a posthumous victory.

This debate over the role of the Holocaust in preserving Judaism is simply a microcosm of the much larger theme running through

---

* Even this analogy is far from perfect, since Hitler killed even those "Jews" who chose, or whose parents chose, not to remain Jewish.

the whole question of Jewish survival, which I address in the coming chapters: namely, how much *does* and *should* Jewish survival depend on our *external enemies*, and how much does and should it depend on *positive Jewish values?* This issue was brought home to me recently when I received a frantic call from the student head of the Jewish umbrella organization at a large university. She was desperate to have a Jewish speaker come to the university to help bring the Jewish students together. "Most of them don't even know they're Jews," she complained, asking me to come and give a talk that conveyed a positive Jewish message to the students. I agreed in principle, but told her that my schedule was full for the coming two months. When she called back a few weeks later, she was elated. "We don't need you anymore. Farrakhan is coming. The Black Student Organization invited him. This has united all the Jewish students against him. We're organizing protests, teach-ins, and leafleting. It's just great," she concluded almost breathlessly.

No, it's not! We depend far too heavily for our survival on two groups: our external enemies (the Hamans, Hitlers, and now Farrakhans) and our internal extremists (the Hasidim, the ultra-Orthodox). Neither group is particularly interested in the perpetuation of secular Jewry, yet we secular Jews rely so much on their existence and perceived influence. Perhaps one reason we rely so heavily on these two groups is that we know they will always be there. Whatever may happen to the Jewish community, we can be absolutely certain that there will be some fringe anti-Semites.

Judaism has proved its adaptability to external enmity, poverty, and political exclusion and discrimination. Now it must prove its adaptability to external friendship, affluence, political power, and inclusion. Just as the nature of Jewish life — indeed the nature of Judaism itself — changed repeatedly throughout history in order to meet the needs of past realities, so, too, it must change now in order to meet current challenges. We must rediscover, redefine, and reawaken Jewish values and approaches that are more suited to the dangers we face from our new friends than from our old enemies. We can accomplish this difficult task, but first we must be prepared to confront the myth that authentic Judaism cannot change.

The historical reality is that change has been a constant in Judaism, both in ritual and in theology. Our "traditions" are always evolving. The very nature of the Jewish belief system has undergone significant change since Abraham's first encounter with God, from the exodus of Moses to the teachings of the very diverse array of prophets, psalmists, and early rabbis to the current explosion of contrasting and competing Jewish philosophies of Hasidism, ultra-Orthodoxy, modern Orthodoxy, Conservativism, Reform, Reconstructionism, and all their variations and permutations. Judaism is a living civilization, and living organisms must change to survive. Today once again, the Jewish state of mind — and even the state of Jewish identity — must change in order to give the Jewish people a fighting chance to confront the new challenges its success has brought it. For unless we are prepared to make fundamental changes, we may lose that for which we fought so long and hard to make possible: a Jewish identity that is not so defined by our external enemies. I believe we can make the necessary changes, while preserving the best of our tradition. As the great Jewish writer Isaac Leib Peretz counseled a century ago: "We should leave the ghetto, but we should leave as Jews [carrying] our own spiritual treasures."[53]

PART II:

WHY SO MANY JEWS

ARE DRIFTING AWAY

Chapter Two

Will the End of Institutional Anti-Semitism Mean the End of the Jews?

WE HAVE MUCH to celebrate. Thanks to the determined efforts of Jewish individuals and organizations, anti-Semitism in America is at an all-time low. Even more important, the most dangerous form of the oldest bigotry — state-sponsored, church-supported, and institutionally implemented anti-Semitism — has virtually ended. Today's Jews have entered the mainstream in America and experience few constraints, either professional or personal, on their life choices. The fortunes of individual Jews are at an all-time high. Remaining pockets of anti-Semitism, such as the militias, the Holocaust deniers, the neo-Nazis, and the Nation of Islam, are well outside the mainstream, and the current crop of Jew-haters are, for the most part, marginalized, desperate, and generally impotent, certainly as compared to our state- and church-sponsored enemies of the past. In this chapter, I will document the decline of institutional and mainstream anti-Semitism. In the next two chapters, I will describe several new strains of the old virus, manifest in different forms.

There are those who argue, however, that this very decline and marginalization of anti-Semitism, which removes former limits on Jewish choices, may itself be a significant factor contributing to the increase in assimilation, especially among young Jews. This perspective — that Jews need enemies to keep them Jewish — is particularly frustrating for my generation of Jews, who fought so hard, and so successfully, against anti-Semitism at home and abroad, only to be told that it has been precisely our victory that has turned our children away from that which we have been striving to preserve. Perhaps that is why we find it is so hard to give up the ghosts of battles past and to let go of our identity as eternal victims of persecution.

My generation of Jews saw important reasons for remaining Jewish, even if we did not always practice the ritual or completely believe in the theology. As actual or vicarious survivors of the Holocaust, of Israel's defense against sworn enemies, and of the numerous assaults on Judaism and Zionism, we saw ourselves as having a vital — indeed, a sacred — mission: to protect embattled Jews against our external enemies. We were part of a long tradition of defending the Jewish barricades, which were always on the verge of being overrun by the pharaohs, the Amalekites, the Philistines, the Romans, the Crusaders, the Inquisitors, the pogromists, the Nazis, the Arabs, the religiously inspired Jew-haters, the racially motivated anti-Semites, and the assorted bigots and crazies who have persecuted us from the beginning of Jewish history.

But we have protected the barricades successfully, and while we still have a scattering of external enemies waiting for any sign of complacency or weakness, we also have many unemployed warriors who are finding it difficult to adjust to relatively peaceful conditions. As they scan the horizon in search of external enemies, they leave the most dangerous contemporary threats to Jewish survival inadequately addressed. The Chinese people have a folk curse: "May you live in interesting times." The analogous Jewish curse may well be "You should live in good times." We live in relatively good times — at least for most Jews as individuals. And these good times may mark the beginning of the end of Jewish life in America as we know it.

The projected disappearance, or at least significant shrinkage, of the Jewish presence in America is largely a function of the improving status of the Jew in the world today. In some respects, this "new" phenomenon is merely the culmination of a trend that began with the Jewish Enlightenment (the Haskalah) in the late eighteenth century, continued through the period of massive emigration from the shtetls of Europe to America (and other democracies), and would have accelerated by the 1950s had it not been for the Holocaust, the dangers to Israel, the struggle for Soviet Jewry, and other recent threats to Jews. This era, from the Holocaust through the present, has been aptly referred to as the "sacred survival" period. Jonathan Woocher, the expert on Jewish identity who coined the term, describes the period as one in which survival has been Jewry's consuming passion. "Since the Holocaust . . . physical survival of Jews and the Jewish people . . . [has been] our paramount concern."[1]

Sacred Survival

The pressing need for "sacred survival," following the near-destruction of European Jewry, postponed a process of assimilation that was well on its way by the time of the Holocaust, not only in the United States but also in Western Europe. Though America in the prewar period was rife with anti-Semitism, it was far different from the Eastern Europe of the pogroms. American anti-Semitism, even at its worst, was almost never a matter of life or death. With the striking exception of Leo Frank, American Jews were not lynched.* Occasionally they were beaten, sometimes tormented, and often suffered discrimination. But they were not forced to live in ghettos (though they were excluded from certain neighborhoods and voluntarily gathered in others), and they were legally free to marry whomever they wanted.† As early as 1913 — when the percentage of mixed marriages was in the low single digits in America — the Jewish sociologist Arthur Ruppin lamented the ironically deleterious effects of the liberalized attitudes in the West toward Jews: "The structure of Judaism, once so solid, is crumbling away before our very eyes. Conversion and intermarriage are thinning the ranks of Jews in every direction, and the loss is the heavier to bear, in that the great decrease in the Jewish birth-rate makes it more and more difficult to fill up the gaps in the natural way. . . . *We see in the assimilative movement the greatest danger that has assailed Judaism since the Dispersion.*"[2] Some ultra-Orthodox Jews referred to this country as "America ganif," meaning America the "thief" of traditional Jewish values.

---

* Frank, a Jew living in Georgia, was falsely convicted of murdering a young female employee and sentenced to death in 1913. When the governor commuted his sentence, he was taken out of prison by a lynch mob and hanged. Subsequent evidence established his complete innocence.

† They weren't free to marry "Negroes" in those states that had laws prohibiting "miscegenation," however.

After being interrupted by the Holocaust, the inevitable process of marginal first-generation assimilation, incremental second-generation assimilation, and increasing third-generation assimilation resumed in America, just as it had in Europe in previous eras. As Arthur Hertzberg notes: "A generational clock has ticked away over and over again in the open society. Whether in . . . Paris and Bordeaux in the 1850s, in Budapest around the turn of the century, in Berlin and Vienna in the 1920s, and now in the United States . . . it tells the same frightening time. The third generation in the open society intermarries and erodes out of Judaism at a rate of one in three."[3] Subsequent generations see an even markedly greater attrition. In 1840, Ben Levi wrote: "The grandfather believes, the son doubts, and the grandson denies. The grandfather prays in Hebrew, the father reads the prayer in French, and the son does not pray at all. The grandfather observes all festivals, the father observes Yom Kippur, the son does not observe any. The grandfather is still a Jew, the father has become an Israelite, and the son is simply a deist . . . unless he is an atheist, a Fourierist, or a Saint-Simonist."[4]

A contemporary version of this generational devolution focuses on Jewish dietary restrictions:

First Generation: Anything that isn't kosher.

Second Generation: Anything that isn't kosher except Chinese food.

Third Generation: Anything with cholesterol.

Fourth Generation: Anything with meat in it, and anything that wasn't organically grown.[5]

During the height of the "sacred survival" period, increasingly secular American Jews had a raison d'être for remaining Jewish despite these generational dilutions: to save other endangered Jews and prevent another Holocaust. In part, this was a reaction to the guilt and impotence felt by many American Jews for their failure to do more for the Jews of Europe.[6] Even among those Jews who married out during this period, many remained devoted to the cause of sacred survival. They stayed active in wonderful organizations like the Anti-Defamation League of B'nai B'rith (ADL), the American Israel Public Affairs Committee (AIPAC), and the United Jewish Appeal (UJA). Indeed, some of these Jews in mixed marriages who formally converted to Christianity did not seem so different from some of those who remained Jews and who defined their Judaism solely by their commitment to sacred survival. Neither group observed Jewish rituals, and both groups helped endangered Jews around the world.

The defense of endangered Jews and of embattled Israel became part of the "secular religion" of many nonobservant Jews. The Jewish "defense" organizations, such as the ADL, the American Jewish Congress, the American Jewish Committee, and AIPAC, became the secular shrines of many Jews who felt more comfortable defending Judaism than practicing it.

An apocryphal story, told by the Jewish labor organizer Paul Jacobs, captures the role of these organizations during this postwar period. A Jew goes to the men's room of a New York City bar and notices that someone has scrawled "Screw the Jews" on the wall of the toilet stall. He calls various Jewish organizations, which immediately snap into action. The ADL issues a press release adding this act of anti-Semitism to its list of anti-Semitic incidents and announcing that this proves that anti-Semitism is on the rise again and everyone should join the ADL. The American Jewish Congress files a lawsuit seeking to enjoin the sale of liquor to anti-Semites. The American Jewish Committee, after checking with the National Council of Churches, makes a large grant to Columbia University to study the effects of liquor on anti-Semitism and other forms of bigotry, urging everyone not to jump to any conclusions, since it is possible that an Eastern European Jewish immigrant might have scrawled the graffiti. The Jewish Defense League organizes a demonstration against the bar, breaking windows and yelling "You can't screw with this tough Jew" and "Every Jew and a .22." Finally, the American Zionist Council announces that this incident proves that the only place Jews can live safely is in Israel, where we will be able to write "Screw the Goyim" on our toilet walls. This spoof on the role of Jewish organizations will resonate with anyone who has observed each of these organizations struggling to define its unique role in the defense of Jewish interests during the period of sacred survival.

The era of sacred survival is finally coming to an end. This does not mean that there are no Jews in danger or that Israel's security is assured. It does mean that the primary concerns of the sacred survival period need no longer be at the top of the Jewish agenda. Anti-

Semitism in the United States (and in most countries around the world) has lessened considerably and has been marginalized. The Jews of the Soviet Union are now relatively free to leave for Israel. Anti-Zionism is less virulent and widespread than it was a generation ago. Israel is more secure, both militarily and economically, than it was in the last generation. And American Jews (along with Jews in most other countries) have never been more influential, affluent, and accepted than they are today.

For Jews, good news always seems to bring the possibility of bad news. My grandmother recognized this whenever she greeted good news with *"Kineahora"* — a plea to keep the evil eye away. Even modern Jews, who don't believe in evil eyes, worry about tempting fate, since our fate has generally been in the hands of those whose theology has mandated our persecution and who have thus had an interest in assuring that good news not last too long for us. Jews recognize this uncertainty when we break a glass at the most joyous of Jewish events, the wedding.* Not only are we remembering terrible days gone by, but we are also reminding ourselves that unbounded joy has rarely been a permanent condition for the Jewish people.

The crumbling of the Berlin Wall and the demise of Soviet tyranny brought joy to the world and to the Jews, but it was soon followed by an unleashing of hitherto suppressed grassroots anti-Semitism. Earlier in this century, the victory of America, England, and France over Germany in the First World War brought joy to most of the world, but it set the stage for the most destructive period in Jewish history barely twenty-five years later. In the late 1700s and early 1800s the Enlightenment opened the world to wonderful new ideas, liberties, and opportunities. But for many Jews it carried a mixed message of the breakup of Jewish communities, the beginning of the end of traditional rabbinic authority, and new challenges to the centrality of Orthodox religion to Jewish life. Indeed, a certain degree of assimilation was demanded as a precondition to the

---

* For those who believe that the birth of a son is the most joyous event, the ceremony honoring it has a good news–bad news quality, at least for the boy. A week after the birth, the boy is given a party, with herring, wine, cake. Then suddenly comes the bad news, as he realizes the purpose of the party! Maybe that's why Jews have traditionally had such an aversion to alcohol. But it doesn't explain our attraction to cake!

granting of civil rights to Jews. For instance, Napoleon convened a Sanhedrin of France's Jewish notables in 1806 in order that the rabbis declare Jews to be mere coreligionists rather than members of a discrete Jewish nation. The rabbis complied. One of the pettier preconditions of emancipation was that insisted on by Joseph II of Austria in 1782, whose Edict of Tolerance mandated that Jews cease speaking Yiddish.[7] It is small wonder that the emancipation of Jews in Europe has been called "a Faustian pact."[8]

In light of the long and pervasive history of Jew-hating, Jew-baiting, and Jew-killing, it would be foolhardy for the Jewish people to lower its guard against old, new, anticipated, and unexpected enemies. As a Passover song reminds us: "In every generation, new enemies rise up against us." So far, this maudlin prophecy has proved all too accurate. The likelihood is that some anti-Semitism, in one form or another, will be with us as long as Jews are with us (and perhaps even longer, since anti-Semitism persists in parts of the world where Jews no longer live, such as Poland, and even in places where they *never* lived, such as Japan.)[9] The truth is that we cannot be certain what the state of anti-Semitism will be in the twenty-first century, precisely because the phenomenon is so longstanding, so unpredictable, so subject to change, so dependent on unknowable variables. Despite some fairly clear trends over the past quarter-century, it would take a seer or a fool to try to predict whether these, or other, trends will carry through the next quarter- or half-century and beyond.

But it would be equally foolish to ignore recent trends and not to prepare for the welcome prospect that anti-Semitism, at least as we know it, may become in the twenty-first century a faint shadow of what it has been in the past two millennia. This process of marginalization of anti-Semitism has already begun, as younger Jews clearly recognize. It is likely to continue and to accelerate to the point where mainstream and institutional anti-Semitism, as we have known it throughout our history, may cease to exist. If we fail to plan for this scenario, we may be subjecting ourselves to a danger different in kind but as serious as the dangers of external enmity. For example, Rabbi Irving Greenberg has noted that "college is a disaster area for Judaism, Jewish loyalty, and Jewish identity" — not because of anti-Semitism, but because of the degree of *acceptance* by gentiles of Jews as academic peers, social friends, and romantic partners.[10] If we ignore these significant trends, we do so at our peril — and at peril to the survival of the Jewish people — since they have the greatest impact on precisely those Jews at greatest risk of intermarriage and assimilation, namely, the youngest Jews.

The nature of anti-Semitism has changed more dramatically in the past twenty-five years than in the previous two thousand. Unless we recognize this important change, we will be directing our attention to *past* threats that no longer pose the greatest dangers and ignoring the *new* threats that pose significant dangers against which we are inadequately prepared.

If the changes of the past twenty-five years persist — as they are likely, though not certain, to do — we may be experiencing one of the most important developments in Jewish history. Yet these changes have often been played down — perhaps because some Jewish and Zionist organizations have a stake both in *exaggerating* anti-Semitism and in responding as if it were *the same* as it has always been.

In order to understand the nature of these important changes, it is necessary to distinguish among different types of anti-Semitism, different kinds of anti-Semitic stereotypes, and different ways of measuring the complex phenomena known collectively as anti-Semitism.

The End of Institutional Anti-Semitism

First, there is the distinction between "abstract" anti-Semitism and "personalized" anti-Semitism.[11] For example, a person who believes that "the Jewish people" are socially inferior, religiously perverse, or morally corrupt is an abstract anti-Semite, while a person who discriminates against individual Jews in his personal interactions is guilty of personalized anti-Semitism. It is precisely this distinction that many of Patrick Buchanan's supporters fail to understand. Buchanan is not a personal anti-Semite. He has many Jewish friends, sees a Jewish doctor, and so on. But his statements about "the Jews" and Judaism qualify him as an abstract anti-Semite. The fact that many Jews understand this distinction is reflected in our reaction to the claim by an abstract anti-Semite that "some of my best friends are Jews." It is also illustrated by the old joke that asks the question "What is the difference between an anti-Semite and a Jew?" The answer: An anti-Semite will tell you that "the Jewish people are dishonest, untrustworthy, and moneygrubbing," but when you ask him about his neighbor Cohen, he will say, "Cohen's an exception, as honest as they come"; the Jew will praise the Jewish people as "the best, the most charitable, and the most honest people in the world," but when you ask him about his neighbor Levine, he will say, "That no-good crook, you can't trust him as far as you can throw him."

Another important distinction — perhaps the most important of all — is between institutional anti-Semitism and individual anti-Semitism. Institutional anti-Semitism is sponsored, supported, encouraged, or tolerated by powerful institutions such as the government, the church, universities, corporations, the media, or the power elite. Germany, Poland, the Catholic church, the Metropolitan Life Insurance Company, Wall Street law firms, the major oil companies, Harvard University under President A. Lawrence Lowell, the New York Athletic Club, all used to practice institutional anti-Semitism that directly limited the ability of Jews to live, work, be educated, and play freely. Individual anti-Semitism is practiced by ordinary people, without any support from, and indeed now over the opposition of, these important institutional power bases. My anti-Semitic hate mail comes from such people, most of whom are on the margins of society. Before the Second World War, anti-Semitism was both institutional and individual. Over the past half-century, and especially over the past twenty-five years, institutional anti-Semitism (which is easy to measure) has virtually disappeared, while individual anti-Semitism (which is harder to measure) has abated but persists, at least at the margins.

Yet another, related, distinction is between religious anti-Semitism and racial or ethnic anti-Semitism. For the first nineteen centuries of the contemporary era, virtually all anti-Semitism was religious and sponsored by the church ("The Jews killed Jesus"; "Jews must suffer God's wrath"). If a Jew converted to Christianity, he could often turn this form of Jew-hatred away from himself.[12] Between the end of the nineteenth century and the victory over Nazism, racial anti-Semitism took center stage ("Jews are bloodsucking vermin"; "Jews control the world"). Even conversion could not ameliorate this form of bigotry, since a Jew was born immutably tainted. It was this form of anti-Semitism that led to jokes about the Jewish physiognomy. An old anti-Semitic joke asks, "What happens to a Jew with an erection who walks into a wall?" The answer: "He breaks his nose."* In some places, especially Poland, a particularly vicious combination of both religious and racial anti-Semitism took root.

All forms of anti-Semitism share in common the stereotyping and scapegoating of Jews, but the nature of the stereotyping and scapegoating may differ from place to place. For example, Adam Michnick, the Jewish Solidarity leader in Poland, distinguishes between traditional anti-Semitic scapegoating and the uniquely Polish brand. Traditional anti-Semites believe that if someone is Jewish, he must be bad, whereas Polish anti-Semites believe that if anything bad has happened, it must be the work of Jews. Max Nordau, the great Zionist leader, put it differently: "The Jews are not hated because they have evil qualities; evil qualities are sought for in them, because they are hated."

Many anti-Semitic stereotypes come in pairs. What is ironic is that the paired images are generally inconsistent. Jews are both too strong and too weak; too liberal and too conservative; too Communist and too capitalist; too religious and too atheistic; too parochial and too universalistic; too extravagant and too cheap; too passive and too pushy; too glitzy and too conventional; too charitable and too selfish; too political and too isolated; too promiscuous and too repressed. The absurdity of such incompatible charges is highlighted by the events of the Russian Civil War (1918–1920). Bolshevik detachments and White Guards took turns massacring thousands of Jews — the Bolsheviks demonizing the Jews collectively as "capitalists," and the Guards hating them collectively as "Communists." Similarly, the nationalist White Guards accused the Jews they slaughtered of being too cosmopolitan, while the Red forces accused their Jewish victims of rejecting internationalism.[13] A variation on this theme of universal persecution of Jews appears in the following story:

Ignacy Paderewski, Poland's post–World War I prime minister,

---

* Many current "Jewish" jokes actually began as anti-Semitic jokes. I used to tell the story of the Jewish grandmother who was walking her six-year-old grandson on the beach when a gigantic wave swept the youngster into the water. A lifeguard heroically jumps in, braving the undercurrent, and miraculously saves the child from certain drowning. When the exhausted lifeguard returns the child, the grandmother complains, "He *had* a hat!" Recently, I saw a late-nineteenth-century anti-Semitic print, in which the grandmother, with caricatured Jewish features, makes this complaint in a thick Yiddish accent to a very gentile-looking lifeguard.

was discussing his country's problems with President Woodrow Wilson. "If our demands are not met at the conference table," Paderewski said, "I can foresee serious trouble in my country. Why, my people will be so irritated that many of them will go out and massacre the Jews."

"And what will happen if your demands are granted?" asked President Wilson.

"Why, my people will be so happy that they will get drunk and go out and massacre the Jews."

Jews are also the only group regularly criticized for their virtues: They are accused of being "too smart," "too well educated," "too successful," "too devoted to their children." As the novelist Theodore Dreiser once put it:

> The world's quarrel with the Jew is not that he is inferior, but that he is superior. He is uniformly altogether too successful in the professions, as well as in science, philosophy, education, trade, finance, religious theory, musicianship — also musical composition, painting, poetry, and the other arts. My real quarrel with the Jew is not that he is inefficient or ignorant or even unaesthetic. It is that he is really too clever and too dynamic in his personal and racial attack on all other types of persons and races.[14]

It is as if Jews are just too much. Or as the comedian Sam Levenson once put it, "Jews are just like everyone else, except more so!" It is the essence of stereotyping and scapegoating to find fault with virtually every characteristic or its opposite and to assign negative attributes to these characteristics when they are displayed by one group. Jews themselves mock this stereotyping by self-denigrating jokes, such as the one about the two Hasidim who see a sign outside a church, "$5,000 for any Jew who converts to Christianity." They agree that one will go inside and pretend to convert so that they can share the $5,000. An hour later the first emerges from the church with a glow on his face. The second asks, "So did you get the $5,000?" The first looks at the second contemptuously and sneers, "All you people think about is money."

In addition to these distinctions among different types of anti-Semitism, there are also different ways of measuring anti-Semitism. First, there is the superficial, and in my view misleading, measure sometimes employed by the Anti-Defamation League (an organization that was founded to combat anti-Semitism in the aftermath of the Leo Frank trial and that does much good) in its annual "Audit of Anti-Semitic Incidents" released to the press amid great fanfare and reported with little nuance by most media.

Although the audits, since 1980, organize the incidents into categories (for example, vandalism, harassment, threats, assaults), they also feature an overall *count* of the *number* of incidents that qualify as anti-Semitic. The media often give a warped impression of the state of anti-Semitism by seizing on this undifferentiated sum. Recent headlines reported, for example, "Anti-Semitic Hate Crimes Up 53%," "Anti-Semitic Incidents Up in '94, ADL Says; State's 20% Increase Mirrors National Trend," "NY Anti-Semitic Incidents Up 50%," "An Outbreak of Anti-Semitic Incidents."[15] There are also methodological problems. First, the 1994 audit conceded that the figures generally rise each year because techniques of "refining data collection" continually improve, and thus it is altogether possible that the actual number of anti-Semitic incidents remains stable or even decreases while the statistics swell.[16] Second, according to the 1995 audit, the number of anti-Semitic incidents declined for the first time in three years and by a greater amount than in any year over the last decade, which the audit's authors attributed in great part to the general reduction in all crime across the United States that year.[17] In other words, the rate of hate crimes against Jews might have as much to do with variation in general crime rates as it has to do with specific hatred of Jews. Finally, there is the problem of accurate reporting. For example, if I were to report all the vile, anti-Semitic hate mail and phone calls I receive — as many as thirty-five letters and fifty calls a week — each would qualify as an "anti-Semitic incident," and the overall count of national incidents would be three times as high! This problem cannot be remedied simply by refining data collection techniques, since the vast majority of anti-Semitic incidents will never be reported in the first place. For all these reasons, the numbers presented in these audits tell only a part of a much larger story of anti-Semitism in our nation — and the most obvious and visible part at that. Nor is it necessarily the most important part. For example, during the years when anti-Semitism in the marketplace was abating dramatically — when Jews were no longer systematically excluded from law, banking, and insurance firms — the number of swastika incidents may well have risen (perhaps even in response to our success). That would not necessarily mean that anti-Semitism as a whole was increasing. It would only mean that while anti-Semitism in the workplace was declining, other manifestations of anti-Jewish bigotry in certain neighborhoods were increasing. The total picture may have been one of decreasing anti-Semitism, but the focus on the increasing number of swastika incidents would distort that larger picture.

If a Martian were to come down to Earth and read only the publications of the Anti-Defamation League, he might conclude that anti-Semitism over the past few years was at an all-time high and that it was unsafe for any Jew to go near a synagogue. If the ADL were to describe the changing *quality* of anti-Semitism in America, as distinguished from the *quantity* of "incidents," many Jews then would conclude that their charitable contributions might be better allocated to other priorities. So we continue to be inundated with increasingly less relevant statistics about how many drunken teenagers have painted swastikas on how many synagogue walls, while playing down the increasingly more relevant actions of mainstream church and civic organizations in delegitimating the kind of anti-Semitism that really matters.

Why, then, does the ADL focus so heavily on swastika-type incidents? I think I know. There is rarely any ambiguity about the anti-Semitic nature of a swastika incident. The ADL does not want to be accused of crying anti-Semitism in questionable cases, lest it lose credibility. But this cautious attitude creates a dilemma not only for the ADL, but also for others who care deeply about anti-Semitism in America. The dilemma is this: Some of the most important manifestations of anti-Semitism — important in the sense of being mainstream, rather than lunatic fringe — are also among the most subtle.[18] The more mainstream a manifestation of anti-Semitism is, the less likely it will be as crude or obvious as a swastika.

A far more relevant measure than the ADL's swastika-counting would focus on the *source* of the expression and its *influence* on others. It would also try to measure the degree of public *acceptability* of overt or subtle anti-Semitic expression. The most elusive and difficult-to-measure aspect of anti-Semitism is the private, unexpressed feelings of non-Jews toward Jews and Judaism. Even public opinion polls are inconclusive: if it has become less acceptable to express anti-Semitic feelings in public, then many who harbor such feelings will be reluctant to express them even to pollsters. This very reluctance is itself a useful measure of the public acceptance, or lack thereof, of anti-Semitism.[19]

Viewed against this background, the most important changes in anti-Semitism experienced over the past quarter-century can be summarized as follows:

1. A qualitative reduction in *state*-sponsored, *church*-sponsored, and otherwise *officially* sanctioned *institutional* anti-Semitism almost everywhere in the world.

2. A sharp decrease in *openly acceptable* anti-Semitism, even among private individuals and groups in America and in many other parts of the world.

3. A meaningful change in the *social and economic status* of those who are willing to express anti-Semitism, reflected in the virtual elimination of publicly expressed anti-Semitism among the elite and the relegation of such expression to the lowest-status individuals and most marginalized groups in America and in most parts of the world.*

4. An incremental, though perceptible, reduction in institutional *anti-Zionism* in some parts of the world and among some journalists, academics, churches, and governments. It is as yet unclear whether this reduction merely reflects changes in Israeli policies or whether it is of a more enduring nature.†

That is the good news, and it is very good news indeed. There is an enormous difference between *officially* sanctioned, *officially* encour-

---

* As with all complex social phenomena, it is difficult to determine which is cause and which is effect. Does the reduction of these more public manifestations of anti-Semitism reflect decreasing anti-Semitic feelings on a widespread basis, or is it that changes among elite opinion makers filter down pervasively? Probably some of each.

† To the degree that some anti-Zionism has always been a disguised form of anti-Semitism, any reduction in anti-Semitism will have implications for anti-Zionism. To the degree that some anti-Zionism reflects objection to Israeli policies, any changes in policy will affect anti-Zionism. It is a complicated mix.

aged, and *officially* defended bigotry, on the one hand, and *individual* bigotry on the other, particularly if the individuals who express it are relatively powerless. This does not mean, of course, that if the individual bigotry becomes widespread, it will not have an influence on official attitudes and actions. But without the imprimatur of the state and the church, the bigot is relatively impotent. If the state and the church actively oppose anti-Semitism, the anti-Semite becomes even less of a threat.

Compare the situation faced by Jews in the 1930s with the current much-improved one of today. In the 1930s, anti-Semitism was the official policy of the Catholic church, many Lutheran churches, and numerous other Christian denominations.[20] Priests and ministers preached that "the Jews" killed Jesus and were being punished for their refusal to accept the true Messiah. Religious schools taught anti-Semitism, and the faithful practiced it with the blessing of their spiritual leaders. Jews were terrified of priests and were the frequent targets of physical abuse by parishioners. Anti-Semitism was also the official policy of many governments, certainly those allied with Nazi Germany and the Stalinist Soviet Union, but also of most Central European countries. Those nations that did not officially sponsor anti-Semitism certainly did little to oppose it among the large numbers of political parties, universities, and other institutions that practiced it openly. Even in the United States — historically among the least anti-Semitic nations in the world — the State Department was rife with anti-Semitism in the 1930s and 1940s, as our government's reaction to the Holocaust demonstrated.*[21] Many of the largest corporations, universities, and churches also practiced institutional anti-Semitism.

Among the non-Jewish population in the first decades of this century, anti-Semitism was, if not quite a badge of honor, certainly not a mark of shame. Many of "the best and the brightest" — such as H. L. Mencken, T. S. Eliot, Henry Adams, George Bernard Shaw, H. G. Wells, Theodore Dreiser, Thomas Edison — openly expressed it without fear of social ostracism.[22] Resort clubs, real estate agents, and banks boasted of their anti-Semitic policies. "No Jews

---

* Great Britain was even worse, as evidenced by its active suppression during the war of documented information about the Holocaust and its adamant refusal to open Palestine to Jewish immigration.

allowed" signs were pervasive. "Gentile-only" want ads were as common as "white-only" ads. Politicians were overtly anti-Semitic. Congressman John Rankin of Mississippi publicly called Jews "little kikes" in the 1940s and his voters loved him for it. Patriotic organizations such as the American Legion, the Veterans of Foreign Wars, and the Daughters of the American Revolution expressed anti-Semitic views.[23] The popular radio broadcasts of Father Charles E. Coughlin in the 1930s were patently anti-Semitic, as was the opposition to involvement in World War II of America's greatest hero, Charles Lindbergh, and its most influential industrialist, Henry Ford. It was to be expected, therefore, that even after the outbreak of the war, when Americans were asked who the "greatest menace to American society" was, they cited "the Jews" immediately after our declared enemies, the Germans and the Japanese.[24] More than half of American non-Jews polled expressed negative views toward "the Jews," whom they excluded from their clubs, corporations, university faculties — and indeed from the country itself, under the anti-Semitic immigration laws enacted two decades earlier that were expressly designed to end the influx of Jews from Eastern Europe.[25]

Jews, of course, created humor about the discrimination they suffered. An entire genre of jokes emerged out of the desire of some Jews to be accepted at "restricted" clubs and resorts. Perhaps the most famous quips were Groucho Marx's, asking whether his half-Jewish son could go into a restricted swimming pool "up to his waist," or his insistence that he would never join a club that would accept *him* as a member. There was also the story of a guy named Bernstein who was so determined to get into a restricted club that he changed his name, faked his educational background, and converted. When the membership committee asked his name, he replied "Belmont." When they asked his college, he said "Princeton." And when they inquired about his religion, he responded "Goy, of course."* Then there was Cohen, who, when he became wealthy, not only changed his name and religion but insisted on exchanging his painting by Rubens for a Goya.†

Though jokes of this type have become anachronistic, it is im-

---

* A variation on this joke has "Belmont" beginning his acceptance speech "Fellow goyim!"
† *Goya* is the Yiddish term for a female goy.

possible to know for certain how much change has taken place in the hearts and minds of Americans, since private attitudes cannot accurately be measured. I suspect the change has been considerable, especially since so many non-Jewish families now include a Jew or two as a result of increasing intermarriage.[26] Certainly a residue of bigotry remains within the private thoughts of many Americans, particularly older ones who were influenced by the officially approved attitudes of the past.

But it *is* possible to gauge, with a considerable degree of accuracy, changes in the *officially* declared positions of public institutions, such as governments, churches, corporations, universities, and the media. And these changes are of great importance in calculating the overall diminution in the impact of anti-Semitism on the Jewish people. It matters greatly whether bigotry may be expressed and practiced openly or whether it is obliged to remain under the rocks and in the closet. Even private bigotry is hurtful and dangerous, especially because if it becomes sufficiently widespread, it will eventually become public policy. But when the private anti-Semitism of individuals is backed up by the public power of the state, the church, and other important institutions, the dangers to Jews become qualitatively greater. (This has been especially true when the power of the church is enforced by the power of the state, as it has been throughout history and in most nations that do not separate church and state, as we do in this country.) Conversely, when the private anti-Semitism of individuals is actively opposed by the public power of the state, the church, and other important institutions, the dangers to Jews are considerably reduced, though certainly not eliminated. Imagine what a difference it would have made if the Catholic and Lutheran churches had actively opposed the Holocaust and if the Allied governments — especially the United States — had opened their doors to Jews, instead of deliberately sabotaging rescue efforts.

We have been witnessing, over the past twenty-five or thirty years, the virtual elimination of *institutional* anti-Semitism in most parts of the world. The Catholic church — which was, perhaps, the greatest source of institutional anti-Semitism between the writing of the New Testament and the publication of *Nostra Aetate* ("Our Age") in 1965 (Vatican II) — has now officially declared anti-Semitism to be "a great sin against humanity."[27] That is not to say that anti-Semitism is still not a powerful force among some Catholic clergy and laity in places like Poland and parts of South America, where individual clergymen, ranging from a cardinal to ordinary parish priests, continue to preach the sinful gospel of hate. But when they are *caught* and *publicly exposed* — as Cardinal Joseph Glemp of Poland, Abbé Pierre of France, and Father Henryk Jankowski of Poland recently have been — the church, the state, and the media can be counted on to take action against them.* This is a far cry from what happened in the 1930s and before. In 1996, the Polish government and the Catholic church officially apologized for the massacre of forty-two Jews in Kielce after the Second World War.[28] Contrast that apology with the official position of the Polish Catholic church at the time of that pogrom, when the Primate of Poland, Augustus Cardinal Hlond, essentially justified it, blaming it on "the Jews."[29] There was no criticism from the Vatican then. In 1995, the Catholic church officially sought forgiveness — *tshuva* was the Hebrew word used by the pope — for its long history of anti-Jewish teachings and actions.

In addition to the monumental changes within the Catholic church, there have been other significant shifts in the attitudes of other churches toward anti-Semitism.[30] A Lutheran minister named Richard Koenig spearheaded a successful effort to get the Evangelical Lutheran Church in America to condemn Luther's anti-Semitic teachings, and to "acknowledge the special burden felt by the Lutherans because of the Holocaust." I was proud to read that Reverend Koenig "became motivated in his undertaking after reading Alan Dershowitz's book *Chutzpah*, which takes on the Lutheran church for Luther's anti-Jewish diatribes."[31]

Other Protestant churches have also condemned anti-Semitism, as have many individual Christian theologians, who have led the way in reforming the attitudes of various denominations.[32] Even some Islamic religious leaders — many of whose laity still regard themselves as in a state of war with Israel — have softened their pro-

---

* Jankowski's case is quite interesting because he is much less well known than Glemp or Pierre, and yet the Vatican took the trouble to condemn him for a sermon in which he equated the Communist hammer and sickle, the Nazi swastika, and the Jewish Star of David, and blamed the outbreak of World War II partly on "Jewish greed." In a further development, President Clinton took Lech Walesa to task for failing to criticize Jankowski immediately (see "Priest in Poland Issues an Apology," *Boston Globe*, July 5, 1995).

nouncements toward Jews. As Egypt, and then Jordan, negotiated peace with Israel, political leaders successfully pressed some of their leading Muslim clerics to issue a religious decree legitimating peace with Israel. Previously, Muslim clerics had issued *fatwa* after *fatwa*, ruling that peace with Israel was Islamically impermissible.[33]

Governments too have been more sensitive to Jewish concerns. In 1995, following the election of Jacques Chirac as president, France officially accepted responsibility for its ignoble role in the Holocaust. It admitted to criminal complicity in the deportation and execution of 76,000 French and foreign Jews during the Nazi occupation. Chirac also condemned the anti-Semitism of the extreme right (while continuing to champion the Palestinian cause in a one-sided manner).[34]

Even the United Nations, which had become an international megaphone for state-sponsored anti-Semitism since 1967, has now, through its Human Rights Commission, condemned anti-Semitism (over the objection of Syria) as well as other forms of racism.[35] In December 1991, it also, finally, repealed its notorious 1975 resolution that had declared Zionism to be a form of racism. It is difficult today to find any *official* statements by any important institutions that deny Jews equal rights and that do not officially condemn anti-Semitism.

These and other similar actions in many parts of the world have sent a powerful message to political, economic, religious, and other leaders that anti-Semitism has become bad politics, bad business, bad morality, bad religion — and even bad form. The message of the post-Holocaust civil rights era — that bigotry is wrong — has finally been applied to the Jews. I am told by an old British friend that even in London's most "exclusive" clubs, anti-Semitic jokes — which used to be a staple — are no longer told out loud; now they must be whispered. In January 1992, when the Duchess of York gave a luncheon at the Everglades Club in Palm Beach — one of the last bastions of bigotry — her Jewish lawyer in London resigned as her solicitor. Even she had to pay a price for her complicity in bigotry. Clubs that continue to discriminate, as some still do, now must *deny* that they do so, in contrast with years past, when they could *boast* of their anti-Jewish membership policy. In 1995, when I visited Sydney, Australia, as a guest of the Jewish community, the Harvard Law School Society of Sydney asked me to address a luncheon group at the Australia Club.

After checking with Jewish leaders, I learned that the Australia Club had a sordid history of discrimination against Jews, women, and other groups. I advised the president of the Harvard Law School Society of what I had learned and of my policy against speaking at clubs that discriminate. He quickly admitted that the club did not allow *women* as members — boasting that it is a "gentlemen's club" — but he vehemently denied that it discriminated against *Jews*, pointing to one or two token Jews and claiming that few others had applied. The point is not so much whether there is current discrimination against Jews; the point is that discrimination against *Jews* — as distinguished from *women* — is no longer seen as in any way defensible. I refused to speak at the club, and the event was moved to a restaurant where women, Jews, and blacks felt welcome.

On talk shows, as well, anti-Semitism has become unacceptable. While some prominent hosts openly acknowledge their sexism, racism, and homophobia, I am aware of no mainstream host who will admit to being an anti-Semite. Anonymous callers still make overtly anti-Jewish comments, but they are almost always rebuffed by the hosts.*

No self-respecting, mainstream politician in most parts of the world would today *admit* that he or she was an anti-Semite. Even Patrick Buchanan, some of whose best friends acknowledge that his views are anti-Semitic, goes to great lengths to disavow any anti-Jewish feelings, claiming that others of his best friends are Jews.

Anti-Zionism, which reached its zenith with the UN resolution of 1975, has been diminishing as well in recent years. This carries with it a concomitant reduction in anti-Semitism, since much (though not all) anti-Zionism is a cover for anti-Semitism. The breakup of the Soviet Union, the beginning of a peace process with the Palestinians, and the Gulf War all contributed to a moderating of the rhetoric against Israel from many sources, at least publicly.[36] Anti-Zionism persists in many quarters, but this bias is no longer buttressed by as much institutional Israel-bashing as much of the left engaged in as recently as a decade ago. Indeed, it is fair to say that the strident, knee-jerk anti-Zionism that used to characterize

---

* A striking exception is some African-American talk radio in New York and Atlanta. In 1992, the ADL filed a formal complaint with the FCC with regard to this issue. See Chapter 3 for a more general discussion of black anti-Semitism.

much of the academic and media left has lost some of its cachet. It is no longer as "in" as it once was to be known as anti-Zionist or anti-Israel, though there remains an anti-Israel bias among some academics and media people on the extreme left.[37]

Oy Vey! What We Really Have to Worry About

The importance of this virtual elimination of *institutional* anti-Semitism and considerable reduction in institutional anti-Zionism must be appreciated by all who care about the Jewish future. Those Jewish and Zionist organizations that continue to act as if there have been no changes in the nature and degree of anti-Semitism do a tremendous disservice both to the continuing fight against the new forms of anti-Semitism and also to the struggle for Jewish continuity.

For purposes of assessing the impact of current anti-Semitism on Jewish continuity, the 1988 Dartmouth survey is far more telling than the catalog of swastika paintings annually released by the Anti-Defamation League. According to that survey, "not a single Jewish student thought that being Jewish made any difference in his or her future opportunities in America."[38] While this optimism may not be warranted by the continuing reality of some quotas and glass ceilings (high as they both may be in certain occupational choices), the perception of these students is *their* reality. Nor is this attitude limited to Dartmouth. I hear it among my students at Harvard and at other universities where I speak. The anger over anti-Semitism will simply not keep the current generation of students Jewish, because they simply do not see themselves as victims of contemporary persecution, despite efforts by some Jewish organizations to persuade them that they are. When the head of ADL comes to Harvard to talk about anti-Semitism, he barely gets a minyan (ten people). Many more Jewish students come out to hear about the current problems faced by gays, blacks, and women.

Despite the *objective* evidence that institutional anti-Semitism has virtually ended and that private anti-Semitism, although still prevalent, is no longer respectable in most parts of the world, Jews still remain worried about their external enemies. This is particularly the case among older Jews, whose memories of institutional anti-Semitism are still fresh. Whatever the perception of older Jews —

and whatever the well-intentioned motives of those Jewish and Zionist organizations that refuse to recognize the good news about the changing patterns of anti-Semitism — the perception among most young Jews is what matters most, and most young Jews recognize the important changes that have occurred during the past quarter-century. Indeed, some do not even see them as changes and find it difficult to believe it was ever as bad as older Jews say it was. The unwillingness of some older Jews to acknowledge the dramatic reduction in institutional anti-Semitism contributes to this credibility gap with younger Jews. This credibility gap causes some young Jews to underestimate the possibility that anti-Semitism may return and it causes some older Jews to overestimate the current levels of anti-Semitism. Both types of misperception can be dangerous.

My generation and those a bit older and younger vividly remember and can still feel the dangers of anti-Semitism and anti-Zionism. We remember the Holocaust, the displaced persons, the numbers on the wrists of our classmates. We remember the Nuremberg and Eichmann trials. We remember the establishment of Israel and its war of independence. We remember the sinking feeling in our stomachs when Nasser threatened to drive Israel into the sea. We remember the exhilaration of the Six-Day War and the fear of the Yom Kippur War. We participated in the struggle for Soviet Jewry: the defense of prisoners of conscience, the rescue of the refuseniks. We fought against the unthinking, knee-jerk anti-Zionism on campuses around the world.

But that is not how the younger generation sees things. To my children and my students, the Holocaust is the trial of stupid old men like John Demjanjuk (who may or may not have been "Ivan the Terrible" of Treblinka, but who certainly was a Nazi death camp collaborator). To the current generation of young Jews, Israel is the Intifada, the strutting General Ariel Sharon, and the always articulate Benjamin Netanyahu. To Jews in their twenties, a Soviet Jew is a rude cab driver at LaGuardia Airport. No one will convince *this* generation of what *our* generation needed no convincing of: that Jews are underdogs who need help. Their generational perception is different from ours, and their commitment to Judaism will inevitably be different from ours. It will be less defensive, less negative, less protective. If it is to survive, it will have to be more affirmative, more giving, more positive.

The time has come for a candid reassessment of the status of anti-Semitism in America and throughout the world. This reassessment cannot come from Jewish organizations, Jewish leaders, rabbis or scholars who have a stake in exaggerating (or minimizing) the phenomenon.[39] It must come from neutral, objective studies conducted by social scientists with no axe to grind.

A Personal Perspective

But sometimes perception can be influenced more by a single vivid experience than by volumes of poll data, annual audits, and scholarly tomes. In the case of my family and friends, that experience occurred on a September day in 1994. What we saw and heard that day said more to us about the changing attitudes toward Jews than anything I had previously read.

My family has a summer home on Martha's Vineyard. Since Rosh Hashanah fell around Labor Day in 1994, we decided to celebrate the Jewish New Year on the Vineyard and daven in its small synagogue. As it turned out, the president and Mrs. Clinton were on the Vineyard for Labor Day, and the rabbi suggested that I invite them to join us for services. I wrote the following letter:

Dear Mr. President:

It is my great honor to invite you on behalf of the Martha's Vineyard Hebrew Center (the only Jewish house of prayer on the Island) to attend one of our Rosh Hashanah (Jewish New Year) services. It is a part of the Jewish tradition for the congregation to bless the President of the United States and the great nation that has given us the freedom to practice our religion without prejudice or discrimination. Our congregation would love to extend that blessing personally to you and to invite you to respond with your own New Year's greeting or to accept our good wishes silently. We also extend this invitation to your family and to any members of your staff (Jewish or non-Jewish) who would like to join our services. In some countries in years gone by, Jewish congregants dreaded the prospect of government officials entering their sanctuary on the High Holidays. [Recall the rabbi's prayer in *Fiddler on the Roof*: "May God bless and keep the czar — far away from us!"] In this country we welcome our President with open arms.

The president immediately accepted, thus becoming, we are told by the eminent Jewish historian Jacob Marcus, the first American president ever to attend a Jewish High Holiday service. I sat next to him during the service and shared a mahzor (Holiday prayer book) with him for most of the davening, pointing out the prayers and whispering explanations of such concepts as "fringes" and "mitzvoth." We used a prayer book in which the Hebrew was transliterated for the parts that are chanted, and the president and Mrs. Clinton sang along in Hebrew. Then the president spoke briefly from the lectern, declaring his role in the Mideast peace process "one of the most rewarding things I've done," and then wishing the Jewish people a "Shana Tova."

As I watched the president, I thought of Jules Farber's quip: "The time is at hand when the wearing of prayer shawl and skullcap will not bar a man from the White House — unless, of course, the man is Jewish!" Perhaps the time will soon be at hand when even this barrier will fall. There is, naturally, a joke about the first Jewish president who invites his mother to the White House. As she is waiting in front of her house for the presidential limousine to pick her up, a neighbor asks where she is going. She replies, "You know my son the doctor? Well, I'm going to visit his brother."

After the service, Mr. Clinton invited my family to join him and the First Lady for dinner. When I thanked the president for appointing two Jews to the Supreme Court, he gave me a look that suggested that the religious background of his two appointees was not a relevant factor. This is quite a contrast to the days when Jewish nominees to the Supreme Court, such as Louis Brandeis, were openly opposed because of their religion, or when there was talk of "a Jewish seat."*[40]

At the end of the evening, President Clinton lifted a glass of champagne to toast the Jewish New Year. As I touched my glass to his, I said, "L'chaim." He responded, "This has been a really great

---

* When Justice Felix Frankfurter was being considered to replace Justice Benjamin Cardozo in 1939, *New York Times* publisher Arthur Hays Sulzberger reportedly implored President Roosevelt not to appoint Frankfurter to a Court that already included another Jew, Justice Louis Brandeis, lest it fuel anti-Semitism. Roosevelt rejected the advice.

evening." As I smiled back at President Clinton, I thought about how differently President Nixon had talked about Jews in the "privacy" of the Oval Office, counting (and exaggerating) the number of Jews among the notorious Chicago Seven, bemoaning Jewish "control" over the arts, and warning his daughter to "stay away" from Jews. (It seems that President Nixon's brand of anti-Semitism was more like the Polish strain of the virus, since he was assuming that the Chicago Seven must be Jewish because they were so bad.) Even his friend and admirer Henry Kissinger told a journalist during the Nixon presidency, "You can't believe how much anti-Semitism there is at the top of this government — and I mean at the top." There does not appear to be any anti-Semitism at or near the top today.

Another epiphany that brought home to me how different it is for Jews in America today took place in June 1996, when the International Association of Jewish Jurists bestowed its "Pursuit of Justice" Award on Justice Stephen Breyer. Justice Breyer has been a close family friend and professional colleague since we both clerked for Justice Arthur Goldberg, and so I was asked to present the award. The ceremony took place in an elegant courtroom of the Supreme Court, with its high marble pillars and immense mahogany bench. Hebrew words filled the courtroom as Justice Breyer, Nathan Lewin (president of the Association), and I spoke proudly of the long Jewish tradition of justice, legal commentary, and learning. Following the formal presentation, a *glatt* kosher buffet was served in the elegant West Conference Room of the high court. As I was finishing my chicken, Nathan Lewin's wife, Ricky, tapped my shoulder and said, "Nat needs you for a minyan, since he has to say Kaddish for his father, who died recently." I knew Nat's father — a great Yiddish scholar and teacher — and instantly agreed, of course, to participate, asking her at which synagogue the minyan was to be held. She pointed to the adjoining East Conference Room, whose mahogany walls were covered with portraits of Supreme Court justices from the eighteenth and nineteenth centuries, and said, "Right there."

My first reaction was, "I can't daven in the Supreme Court!" I have devoted my entire adult life to fighting for the separation of church and state, even opposing the opening of court sessions with a prayer for God to "save this honorable court." Turning the East Conference Room of our nation's highest court into a shul, in which Jewish men would put on yarmulkes, daven minhah, exclude women, and praise God for making us different from the other nations of the world would make me uncomfortable as a civil libertarian.

I expressed my discomfort to Ricky — whom I've known for forty years and whose father was my Talmud teacher in high school — but she immediately resolved any doubts by insisting, "Nat *needs* you for a minyan." I put on a yarmulke and joined the others in prayer. When I reached the part of the eighteen blessings (the Sh'mona Esrai) in which God's attributes are catalogued, I lingered longest on the words *matir assurim* — redeemer of the imprisoned — in the hope that perhaps this relatively conservative court, especially when it came to the rights of *assurim* (the imprisoned), might improve their record as *matirim* (redeemers). By emphasizing this relevant prayer, I was hoping to alleviate some of my own ambivalence about davening in the Supreme Court so that an old friend could say Kaddish for his recently departed father. I placed friendship — and respect for the memory of a great man — before principle, though this breach in the wall of separation was minimal. The prayer service was not officially approved by the Supreme Court. I doubt they even knew it was taking place. We had just borrowed a room for fifteen minutes. The Court had not given its imprimatur to our prayers. It had not "established" Judaism — or religion — even during that brief period. It would have been no different if a group of atheists had spontaneously gathered in a corner of the Supreme Court building to confirm their disbelief in God.

The important fact was not my personal ambivalence about the principle. It was how comfortable we all felt davening so publicly in so American a place. There was not an iota of embarrassment as Nat chanted, as some of the congregants swayed back and forth in the Orthodox style of praying, as one Hasid placed his *gartel* (religious sash) around his waist, or as non-Jewish clerks and staff observed these odd goings-on in a place generally reserved for secular legal events. None of us felt like second-class citizens. It was our Supreme Court as much as anyone else's.

Things certainly have changed. Standing next to the president of the United States and listening to him sing "Sh'ma Yisrael" along with the Jewish congregants, davening minhah in the Supreme Court, seeing students in my classes comfortably wearing yarmulkes — all this brought it home to me more powerfully than any statistic: Jews have come a long way since 1930 — even since 1990 — and we are no longer subject to the dangers of state- and church-sponsored anti-Semitism that led to the Crusades, the Inquisition, the pogroms, and eventually the Holocaust. Nor are we currently subject to the kind of institutional anti-Semitism that made it impossible for Jews to achieve equality and success in their host countries. Put most bluntly, we are no longer second-class citizens in America, and we must stop behaving as if we were. I'm reminded of the story of the Jewish salesman from Minsk who always traveled second-class to Pinsk. This time there were no more second-class rail tickets and he had an important customer waiting, so he splurged on a first-class ticket. As he entered the first-class compartment, he saw noblemen, ladies, and army officers with drinks in their hands, speaking with upper-class accents. Frightened, the Jewish salesman cowered in a corner. The conductor took one look at him and said, "You don't belong here — get back to the second-class compartment." The Jew sheepishly showed the conductor his first-class ticket. The conductor looked at the ticket, then he looked at the cowering Jew and said, "You do have a first-class ticket. Why don't you behave like a first-class passenger?"

Younger Jews do not perceive themselves as second-class Americans. They do not view anti-Semitism as a significant barrier to their lives and liberties, as the studies show and as my own experiences with several generations of Harvard students confirm. Today's Jewish law students would not spend an instant worrying that a law firm might turn someone down because of his or her religion. Thirty-five years ago, religion was *the* dominant factor in law firms' hiring decisions. Today it is not even a consideration. For the future generations of Jews, the cement of anti-Semitism and anti-Zionism will not be enough to keep us together, even if Farrakhan pays an occasional visit to a college campus. We will need a more positive, a more affirmative Judaism if we are to survive without the help of our enemies. We must teach our children what it is that we fought so long and hard to preserve. But first, we must learn it ourselves.

Chapter Three

Anti-Semitism in the Twenty-first Century: Changing to Adapt to the New Realities

IN EVERY AGE, the oldest bigotry takes new forms, reacting to changing realities, perceptions, and fears. As we approach the twenty-first century, the outlines of these developing forms of anti-Semitism are beginning to take shape. Some may be transient, others more enduring. All seem to be adaptive to the new reality that American Jews are now mainstream and that our enemies are marginalized.

Among the most perceptible manifestations of the new anti-Semitism is the growth, both in size and danger, of the so-called militia movements. Although the militias and their offshoots target mainly government agencies, and although they are concentrated in areas of the country where few Jews live, some of the most radical and violent militias subscribe to conspiracy theories about Jewish world domination. A related form of anti-Semitism, especially targeted at students, is Holocaust denial, which essentially accuses the Jewish people of perpetrating a fraud on the world by claiming that millions of Jews were systematically murdered by the Nazis. Holocaust deniers also accuse the Jews of controlling the media and preventing their story from being heard. Another significant source of anti-Semitism in the twenty-first century is likely to be the Nation of Islam, which is growing in influence, especially among young blacks. Its leader, Louis Farrakhan, was listed by *Time* magazine as among the twenty-five most influential people in America in 1996.[1]

Its members, too, scapegoat Jews as their enslavers and as part of the establishment that is persecuting them. Then there is the violent terrorism of some Middle Eastern Islamic fundamentalist groups, which is directed as much against American targets as it is against Israel and Jews. Indeed, these terrorists regard America as a surrogate for "Zionist interests." Finally, there is the lingering plague of primitive Jew-hating in Eastern Europe, which seems resistant to changes in governments and in church policy.

Let there be no mistake that these forms of anti-Semitism pose significant threats that may increase as we approach the millennium.* Institutions eventually respond to grassroots pressures, and if marginalized anti-Semitism in this country were ever to gather popular support, as it has in Russia and other countries, some institutions might go along with such a mandate. But let there also be no mistake that at least for the foreseeable future, these groups of current anti-Semites are well outside the mainstream, and — with the exception of Islamic terrorism — have no significant support from powerful states, churches, and other influential institutions, which plainly distinguishes them from previous persecutors. The anti-Semitism of the twenty-first century will reflect the new reality that Jews have become mainstream and our enemies have become marginalized. Indeed, twenty-first-century anti-Semitism will be directed at Jews *as members of the establishment*, rather than as marginal deviants.

Anti-Semitism has always focused on *both* the power*less*ness and the power*ful*ness of Jews, generally exaggerating each. Even when most Jews were poor, weak, excluded, and discriminated against, classic anti-Semitism portrayed "the Jew" as powerful, wealthy, and bent on world domination. The lowliest shtetl dweller was in league with Rothschild. They worked together to control the world, as "revealed" in *The Protocols of the Elders of Zion*.† And even the Rothschilds

---

* Professor Richard Landes of Boston University, who directs a center for millennial studies, is concerned about increasing anti-Semitism as we approach the year 2000.

† According to the *Protocols*, the Jewish elites have used the poor, toiling masses "to annihilate the aristocracy," and when the "universal economic crisis" comes to a head, these same masses "will rush delightedly to shed the blood of those whom, in the simplicity of their ignorance, they have envied from their cradles, and whose

were "dirty," "dishonest," "cheap," "perverted," and "parochial." All Jews were, of course, "Christ-killers" and "bloodsuckers."

This cross-eyed vision of the Jew was a perversion of the historical reality of times past. The vast majority of Jews were forced by discrimination and exclusion to underachieve, while a tiny but highly visible number of Jews would overcome these barriers and overachieve. Those who underachieved were despised as "dirty Jews." Those who overachieved were feared as "predators."

The one thing few Jews were ever accused of was being part of any "establishment." Those who became part of the establishment, such as Benjamin Disraeli, had generally abandoned their Judaism. Indeed, when Queen Victoria asked her prime minister, who had formally converted to Christianity, what he was, Disraeli replied: "In the King James Bible, there is a blank page separating the Old and New Testaments. I am that page." Jews were, in the apt words of Hannah Arendt, either "pariahs" or "parvenus."[2] They were always outsiders, never part of the mainstream. And the anti-Semitism that was directed at them was directed at them *as* outsiders, whether they were the poor outsiders of the shtetl or the rich outsiders of the Rothschild family.

Today's anti-Semitism is also a perversion of the very different historical reality of our time. Individual Jews are quite successful, powerful, and part of many establishments. Individual Jews have enormous influence in the media, in finance, in education, in government, and in the arts. They comprise 26 percent of the members of the elite media, 59 percent of the writers, producers, and directors of Hollywood's most popular films, 40 percent of the premier lawyers in New York and Washington, 13 percent of business executives younger than forty, and contribute approximately 30 percent of the campaign funds of the major parties.[3] The power of individual Jews does not, however, translate into "Jewish power" or "Jewish control," as the anti-Semite would have one believe, because "those Jews who gravitate toward the media tend to come overwhelmingly from the most assimilated quarters of the Jewish community" and do not make "a high priority of Jewish concerns."[4]

---

properties they will then be able to loot" (*World Conquest Through World Government: The Protocols of the Learned Elders of Zion*, trans. Victor E. Marsden [London: Britons, 1920], pp. 30–31).

Current anti-Semites — from those in the militia to followers of Farrakhan to Holocaust deniers to Islamic terrorists — all target "Jewish power" and "Zionist control" over the government, the media, and other important institutions, pointing to the number of individual Jews who are in positions of influence. One rarely hears any more of the "dirty" Jew, the "cheap" Jew, or the "outsider Jew." Today's "villain" is the establishment Jew, who — along with other members of the power elite — is "controlling," "persecuting," "silencing," and "disempowering" those at the margins of society. Jews are no longer excluded because of anti-Semitism. Instead, today's anti-Semites accuse them of excluding others and denying them their birthright, their proper place, or their version of the truth.

This is an important change in the nature of anti-Semitism, reflecting the important change in the status of Jews. Until we recognize this change, we will remain unprepared to confront it differently from the anti-Semitism of the past, as we must do.

The Growth of Militias and Its Implications for the Jews

While the militia movement is directed primarily at the federal government, and particularly at the government's power over weapons, and while there are some militia leaders and members who are not focused on "the Jews," there are dangerously anti-Semitic overtones in much of the militia rhetoric. There are also many overt anti-Semites and neo-Nazis in the militias, some in leadership roles.

Although the militias consist predominantly of marginalized ne'er-do-wells, there is cause for concern because of the potentially lethal combination of massive weaponry, neo-Nazi rhetoric, and a perverted white Christian theology that warns of Jewish world domination and Apocalypse.

No one knows for certain how many militia members there are in the United States, how many of them are anti-Semites or associated with neo-Nazi groups, how many weapons, and of what sort, they are hiding. Both the militias and their critics have a stake in exaggerating their numbers, and since the militias are, by their nature, secretive and isolated, little reliable data is available. Estimates range from ten thousand to forty thousand persons actively involved in the armed militia movement, with as many as 5 million people being "influenced" by the rhetoric of the "Patriot Movement,"[5] which is a broad umbrella term for groups that employ nativist themes and hark back to the "good old days" when all Americans were white and Protestant.* Indeed, it is the very absence of hard information about these groups that makes them even more dangerous. But we do know from the bombing of the Oklahoma City federal building that no more than a handful of determined mass murderers, with some easily accessible chemicals, can do devastating damage.

We also know that one of the bibles of the militia extremists is *The Turner Diaries*, a fictional account of an underground militia group that takes power in America by bombing the FBI building, the Capitol, and various communication centers. The new regime then launches a military attack against Israel and sets out to finish Hitler's work by killing all the world's remaining Jews. The book's author, Dr. William Pierce, acknowledges that his "blueprint" might have been the "inspiration" for Oklahoma City and predicted that "one day, there will be real organized terrorism," as outlined in *The Turner Diaries*, which is "aimed at bringing down the government." Even before a major publisher reissued the book in 1996 — so that the public would know what the extremists were reading — there were more than 185,000 copies in circulation around the United States.[6]

There have always been small pockets of anti-Semitic extremists in the so-called Patriot Movement, especially since the rebirth of the Ku Klux Klan during the post–World War II civil rights era. Organizations like the Minutemen, which formed in the early 1960s, stockpiled weapons in order to make war against "subversives." They were allied with the Klan, the Liberty Lobby, and other anti-Semitic groups. In the 1970s, Aryan Nation emerged out of an ersatz Christian church which preached that the Jews were "children of Satan" and had to be destroyed "like a virus that attacks our racial body to destroy our Aryan culture and purity of our race." Also around that time, a fundamentalist minister named James Ellison founded "The Covenant, the Sword, and the Arm of the Lord" as a

---

* It is pathetically ironic that Patrick Buchanan, a practicing Catholic, employed the traditional rhetoric of nativist movements — referring to his followers as "peasants with pitchforks," "farmers with muskets" — when he ran for president in 1996 and tried to appeal to the Patriot Movement. The nativist movements were historically as anti-Catholic as they were anti-Jewish and anti-black.

"church" whose mission was to persuade all Christians that the "Jews of today are an anti-Christ race, whose purpose it is to destroy God's people and Christianity through Talmudic teaching,* forced inter-racial mixings and perversions."[7] The church runs a "survival" school, and in 1995, FBI agents found quantities of cyanide there that were apparently intended to poison the water supply of a large city. Among the "holy" books used by the church are *Who's Who in the Zionist Conspiracy*, *A Straight Look at the Third Reich*, and, of course, *The Protocols of the Elders of Zion*. Finally, there was "the Order" (also known as "Bruders Schweigen" — silent brothers), which in 1984 murdered Jewish talk show host Alan Berg in Denver, bombed an Idaho synagogue, and robbed a Brink's truck of $3.6 million.[8]

Dangerous as these groups were, they tended to be isolated and disconnected — until the mid-1990s, when federal actions at Ruby Ridge and Waco unified many right-wing extremist groups under the banner of the "militia movement." One reason the movement has grown so quickly and has organized so effectively is that its members have learned how to use the information superhighway, including computer networks, fax transmissions, and shortwave radio broadcasting. As one observer recently put it, "It is arguably the first U.S. social movement to be organized primarily through nontraditional electronic media such as the Internet."[9] Before the advent of such rapid communication, the various right-wing "patriot" and "neo-Nazi" groups — which are spread out over large, isolated geographic areas — had little ability to organize, except on a local basis. But now they can quickly communicate with one another nationally, and even internationally.

One of the basic organizing themes of the militia movement is a paranoid fear of the "new world order," which would establish a "Godless, socialist, worldwide totalitarian government." Their literature commonly refers to the United States and other Western democracies as the ZOGs — Zionist Occupational Governments. Jews *are* the government, according to literature circulated widely

---

* The Christians would have nothing to worry about if the Jews set out to destroy them through "Talmudic teaching," since hardly any Jews today have an inkling of what is in the Talmud!

over the Internet. Lists of prominent Jewish names — often accurate, sometimes not — are popular. And the government is the enemy. In a recent television interview with Dan Rather, an imprisoned militia leader told America that 95 percent of the people who control the "world government" are Jews.

Not all the messages are overtly anti-Semitic, but the implicit message is that Jews are in control of the institutions that the militias despise most. When this message is received by an audience that is already predisposed to accept it, there is no need for direct scapegoating of Jews.

Morris Dees, the head of the Southern Poverty Law Center, which monitors hate groups, sees "Christian Identity" ideology as central to much of the militia movement. That ideology is explicitly anti-Semitic and racist, viewing Jews and blacks as "the children of Satan." According to Dees, "Christian Identity adherents believe Jews have usurped the God-given religious-politico order in the United States." They advocate that "war must be waged against federal authorities" — which they characterize as the "ZOG."[10] Dale Jacobi of the Montana Freemen added an ironic twist, claiming that Jews brought the blacks into this country to destroy the United States. He thus agrees with Louis Farrakhan's canard that Jews were central to the slave trade.

Another experienced militia watcher has argued that anti-Semitism is "essential" to the movement in four ways. The first is that many of its leaders, such as Bo Gritz, John Trochman, and Pete Peters, are notorious anti-Semites. Gritz, who claims that the Star of David is the symbol of the Antichrist, argues that "eight Jewish families virtually control the entire FED [Federal Reserve system] — only three are American Jews." Trochman blames the nation's problems on the "banking elite" and the "shadow government," which are euphemisms for "the Jews" and believes that Jews should not be "sovereign citizens." Peters, a spokesman for the Christian Identity movement, uses *The Protocols of the Elders of Zion* to prove that "the anti-Christ forces have had a monopoly on the media."[11]

The second way anti-Semitism is central to the militia movement is that the literature distributed at its gatherings and even over the Internet is the standard literature of anti-Semitism: *The Protocols of the Elders of Zion*, *Spotlight*, and Holocaust-denial tracts. Third is the

Posse Comitatus theory of county government, which is a cover for giving authority over law enforcement to "white, Christian males," who make up the posses.[12] Fourth, and most important, is that the movement's crucial conspiracy theories are rooted in *The Protocols of the Elders of Zion* and other canards that place "the Jews" or "Jewish bankers" at the center of the "One World Government" and other international plots "to subvert American interests to foreign domination." A related claim of some militias is that Jewish banks are foreclosing on Christian farmers because Jews, "incapable of farming, had to control the world's monetary system in order to control the global food supply."[13]

These and other conspiracy theories take advantage of the generally accurate perception that *individual* Jews are disproportionately influential in banking, the media, and government. They then falsely imply that these individual Jews have somehow conspired to control the world as part of some grand Jewish plan.

As another observer of the militia movements put it: "Even when conspiracy theories do not center on Jews or people of color, they create an environment where racism and anti-Semitism flourish." He argues that the "scapegoating conspiracy theories on the right have a greater audience than many believe," and that particularly during periods of economic or social crisis, "some people persuaded by these scapegoating arguments conclude that the swiftest solution is to eliminate the scapegoat."[14] Jews do not need to be reminded of this dynamic. That is why we must keep tabs on the emerging militia movement and understand that it *could* become the vanguard of a dangerous know-nothing populism that blames "the Jews" for the problems of America; at the same time, we must recognize that it is still a marginal phenomenon which today does not have any discernible impact on the daily lives of individual Jews or pose a significant danger to the Jewish people.

The militia movement, as it now exists, has virtually no presence on college campuses. It appeals largely to the uneducated and fringe elements in our society, though it also has a certain appeal to some who spend their waking hours on the information superhighway. We must neither understate nor overstate its potential danger. For the present, the best response is careful monitoring and effective law enforcement whenever rhetoric crosses the line into violence.

Holocaust Denial in the Twenty-first Century

Holocaust denial takes many forms, some more subtle than others. But at bottom they are all anti-Semitic in nature, intent, and effect. The most obvious form is that employed by the neo-Nazis, the militias, and other groups which do not even make a pretense of seeking the truth. This type of Holocaust denial has no real chance of persuading anyone but the most rabid anti-Semite. A far more dangerous form is that currently directed at college students, because it is slick, sophisticated, and couched in the language of the young. It is dangerous precisely because it plays in to other problems of continuity faced by young Jews in college today and in the years to come. By the beginning of the twenty-first century, nearly all the perpetrators, survivors, and witnesses of the Holocaust will be gone. That is when Holocaust denial may begin to move from the margins and toward the center.

In one regard, Holocaust denial is the other side of a good-news coin, because it reflects — albeit in a perverse and dangerous way — the freedom we now have to think the unthinkable, to imagine the unimaginable, and to publish what used to be the unpublishable. Among some naive students, it also reflects the well-intentioned belief that all suffering is comparable, that we ought not to have a Euro-centric, Judeo-centric, Caucasio-centric, or any other self-centric view of the world. But the bad news of Holocaust denial so outweighs any good news that it must be exposed for the deliberately anti-Semitic lie that it is.

Let there be no mistake about the reality that Holocaust denial *is* anti-Semitic in nature, intent, and effect. Professor Noam Chomsky has argued that there is not even an "anti-Semitic implication" or "hint" of one in denial of the Holocaust.[15] In defense of his views — which have been cited by some who would bring Holocaust denial to campuses — Chomsky makes the naive claim that a purported statement of *fact*, whether true or false, cannot have *normative* anti-Semitic implications. Under this misunderstanding of the naturalistic fallacy,[16] there would also be no anti-Semitic implications to advocating the truth of *The Protocols of the Elders of Zion*, the blood libel, and other "facts" that make the Jews out to be baby-killers and world dominators. What Chomsky fails — or refuses — to understand is that the *history* of anti-Semitism has been a history of *false factual claims*, from the killing of Jesus to the blood libel to the *Protocols* and now to the claim that "the Jews" are perpetrating an "enormous political and financial fraud" on the world by circulating the "massive lie" that millions of them were the victims of a nonexistent Holocaust, nonexistent gas chambers, nonexistent death camps. Holocaust denial is core, classic Jew-hatred, expressed primarily by known anti-Semites in order to further anti-Semitic agendas. It has also been borrowed by some anti-Zionists determined to use any lie in their efforts to delegitimate Israel by arguing that the Jewish state was established by a guilt-ridden world that had been hoodwinked into believing that millions of Jews were murdered by the Nazis (who were, not so coincidentally, supported by many Palestinian, Arab, and Muslim leaders). Recently, Holocaust denial has even become a staple of the black anti-Semitism preached by the Nation of Islam.

The anti-Semitic nature, content, and effect of Holocaust denial can best be understood when this modern-day phenomenon is seen as part of a long and *successful* history of pernicious lies directed against the Jewish people. Throughout history, Jews have been the object of demonstrably false charges, which, despite their absurdity, were *believed* by large numbers of people.

The blood libel — the claim that Jews ritually murdered Christian children in order to use their blood in the baking of matzos for Passover — and its many variations was a staple of anti-Jewish propaganda for centuries. In our home we have a framed poster printed in 1490 in Nuremberg portraying the Jew Thobias in the act of bleeding a terrified Christian child. We keep this as a reminder that just thirty-seven years after the invention of the movable printing press by Gutenberg, among the first uses to which this technology was put was to promote the blood libel.

Jews have also been falsely accused of poisoning wells, causing famines, and spreading the black plague. In a particularly nasty contemporary version of the plague libel, the Nation of Islam recently distributed tapes alleging that Jewish doctors have injected the AIDS virus into African-American children in order to spread *that* plague. The group has also distributed literature blaming "the Jews" for the African slave trade and for the current status of blacks in America.

Another big lie that has been widely credited is *The Protocols of the*

Elders of Zion, a nineteenth-century forgery concocted by the czarist secret police that purports to be the minutes of a secret meeting of Jewish leaders planning to take over the world. Despite its evident spuriousness, the *Protocols* has been widely printed and distributed to millions of avid readers. Even in the United States, which has generally been less susceptible to blatant anti-Semitic falsehoods, Henry Ford distributed hundreds of thousands of copies of his *Dearborn Independent* newspaper that carried the text of the *Protocols* during the second decade of the twentieth century. Ford's book *The International Jew: The World's Foremost Problem*, a compilation of articles published in his newspaper in 1920 and 1921, became a bestseller, with over half a million American readers and numerous others in the sixteen foreign languages into which it was translated.

The lesson learned by Holocaust deniers from the success of these and other lies is that there is no "fact" about Jews that is too preposterous, no claim about Jewish power too incredible, no allegation of Jewish evil too bizarre to be believed by large numbers of bigots ready and willing to hear the worst about a group that has been vilified throughout history. As the German historian Theodor Mommsen recognized many years ago, reason alone is rarely enough to counter the lies of the anti-Semite. "You are mistaken," he wrote, "if you believe that anything at all can be achieved by reason [when it comes to anti-Semitism]. In years past I thought so myself and kept protesting against the monstrous infamy that is anti-Semitism. But it is useless, completely useless."[17] Sartre made a similar point: "Let us recall that anti-Semitism is a conception of the ... primitive world. ... We have seen that it is not a matter of isolated opinion, but of the total choice that a man in a situation makes of himself and of the meaning of the universe. ... If we wish to make such a choice impossible, it will not be enough to address ourselves by propaganda, education, and legal interdictions against the liberty of the anti-Semite."[18]

I do not believe this is true for most people of good will, but it has surely been a historical reality that for many anti-Semites, reason alone — even when buttressed by indisputable fact — has not been enough to alter their misconceptions.

It should not be surprising, therefore, that the most preposterous and bizarre of all lies ever told about the Jews — namely, that the systematic murder of millions of them by the Nazis did not happen — has a receptive audience among a significant number of anti-Semites, anti-Zionists, conspiracy nuts, fools, and other assorted knaves and naifs.

The lie of Holocaust denial is not singular. It is multifaceted and layered. At the bottom are the outright deniers, an assorted group of haters who have several characteristics in common: None is a recognized historian (they include engineers, politicians, high school teachers, and — in one ironic case — a professional photo retoucher); most were bigots before they became deniers; all routinely speak to groups of other haters, including anti-black, anti-Semitic, and anti-immigrant bigots; all "love Hitler" and argue that the Nazis were merely defending themselves against "the Jews." This claim, made primarily by avowed Nazis and Jew-haters, is that there was no genocidal plan directed against the Jews, that no Jews were systematically murdered either in gas chambers or by *Einsatzgruppen*, that the Holocaust is a "swindle," a "Zionist lie," a "fraud" perpetrated on the world by "the Jews." There is little subtlety to this position. It is not targeted toward thinking people. It is patent anti-Semitism, anti-history. The evidence against these claims is overwhelming and indisputable. It includes the records of the *Einsatzgruppen* themselves, the eyewitness accounts of death camp commandants, guards, victims, townsfolk, and liberators, as well as the recorded speeches of Hitler and his disciples. There is also corroborated forensic and physical evidence, including canisters of the deadly gas used to murder the babies, women, and men, as well as photographs of the mass shootings taken by the perpetrators themselves. It is as clear that the Holocaust occurred as that slavery existed, that Japanese-Americans were interned during World War II, that the government of Japan bombed Pearl Harbor, that the United States dropped atomic bombs on Hiroshima and Nagasaki. No reasonable person can consider this issue any more debatable than whether the earth is round and revolves around the sun. If there is any such concept as epistemological certainty, then the basic facts of the Nazi genocide against the Jews sets that standard.

The *details* of the Holocaust are, of course, subject to reasonable debate. We will never know the precise number of Jews murdered: Was it 6.2 million, as many historians estimate, or was it 5.8 million, as others have suggested?[19]* Did some Nazis make soap, lamp-shades, and other objects out of Jewish corpses, as some have as-serted and others have denied? Was John Demjanjuk *the* Ivan the Terrible of Treblinka, or just another terrible Ivan who was trained to murder Jews at Trawniki and then murdered them at Sobibor? Have some victims misremembered certain events, as many wit-nesses to tragedy sometimes do?

In assessing the evidence that establishes the basic facts and spe-cific details of the Holocaust, we must always keep the scale of the genocide in mind. Entire villages and extended families were wiped out, leaving no survivors to document the carnage. The retreating Nazis made desperate efforts to cover their tracks, murdering the remaining death camp inmates before blowing up the gas chambers and crematoria. In light of these realities, it is remarkable how well historians have been able to triangulate sources to arrive at indis-putable conclusions. This process involves the matching of eyewit-ness testimony with independently researched documentation and physical evidence. Given the accepted canons of historical research, there is no respectable historian who would question the basic facts of the Holocaust.

Slightly above the outright deniers — above only in the sense of slicker and more polished — are those who admit that a significant number of Jews were killed during the war, but who deny that it was part of any genocidal plan. The Jews, they claim, died along with many other groups, from disease, famine, crossfire, and other causes. If any Jews were executed, it was because they were spies, traitors, enemies, or "hostages" who were killed in lawful retaliation against the acts of other Jews.

---

* Recently declassified German cables and British intelligence reports concerning the murder of Russian Jews in 1941 have caused still other historians to revise these estimates *upward:* "Historians who have worked on the Russian materials say that the total number of Holocaust victims may have to be revised up from the six mil-lion to seven million Jews." One of the declassified cables shows a British diplomat arguing against the publicizing of the Holocaust as late as September 1944 on the grounds that it would compel officials to "waste a disproportionate amount of their time dealing with wailing Jews." (*International Herald Tribune*, Nov. 11, 1996, pp. 1, 12)

The evidence against this variation on the denial theme is equally overwhelming and indisputable. While it is, of course, true that thousands of Jews were executed — along with others — as spies and such, it is also true that millions of babies, women, and noncombatant men were ingathered from throughout the areas of Europe under German control and executed simply because they were Jews. No group other than the Romanies, or Gypsies, as they are often referred to, was targeted in this way for genetic uprooting and extermination — for genocide. Approximately 220,000 Gypsies were murdered by the Nazis — a much smaller percentage than that of the European Jews.[20]

Another subtle variation on this theme is the minimization or relativization of the Holocaust. Yes, Jews were targeted for extermination, say these distorters, but no more so than the Poles or other groups. The *Post Eagle*, a bigoted rag published by an anti-Semite in Clifton, New Jersey, calls the Holocaust the "Policaust" and claims that not only have the Jews deliberately overstated the number of Jews killed by sevenfold (his numbers always vary), they have understated the number of Polish people killed by the Nazis. He also denies that any Poles killed Jews after the Nazis left. Even though current Polish political and religious leaders have acknowledged these crimes, a recent report by a group calling itself the "Polish Historical Society" claims that the documented massacre of forty-two Jews in Kielce by Polish Catholics in 1946 was "staged" and that "live extras" were "hired to play the dead and wounded."[21] Other minimizers and relativists seek to deny the uniqueness of the Jewish experience by comparing it to other wartime atrocities that were either on a much smaller scale or not targeted toward an entire people.

Then there are the comparativists, who acknowledge the Holocaust but argue that it was no worse than the "slaughter of 6 million babies" by abortionists (sometimes *Jewish* is inserted before *abortionists*), or other particular events they feel strongly about. It is more difficult to refute these claims, since they are more normative than factual. But they, too, must be answered, if the factual uniqueness of the Holocaust is to be preserved.[22]

Supporting these Holocaust deniers, minimizers, relativists, and comparativists are fellow travelers such as Patrick Buchanan, who has become a sounding board, mail drop, and mouthpiece for these haters.[23] As Charles R. Allen, Jr., a leading authority on Nazi war criminals, wrote in the Winter 1996 issue of *Reform Judaism*, "In his unwavering and passionate defense of Nazi war criminals, since the late 1970s, Patrick Buchanan has introduced revisionist themes into the mainstream media and, in so doing, has become the most effective Nazi war criminal apologist and Holocaust denier in America." The conservative columnist George Will accused Buchanan of employing falsehoods to abet "the principal neo-Nazi obsession — Holocaust denial."[24]

Although the most extreme Holocaust deniers still remain at the fringe and have not yet achieved any real acceptance in the mainstream, they should be a significant cause for concern for several reasons. First, as Professor Deborah Lipstadt of Emory University has correctly observed: "[T]he deniers may have an impact on truth and memory in [a] less tangible but potentially more insidious way. Extremists of any kind pull the center of a debate to a more radical position. They can create — and, in the case of the Holocaust, have already created — a situation whereby added latitude may be given to ideas that would once have been summarily dismissed as historically fallacious."[25] Second, and even more important, is the *locus* of the Holocaust-denial controversy: namely, college and even high school campuses. There can be no dispute that the primary target of the deniers and their ilk is the young and impressionable, who have no memory of the Holocaust. The assault on the Holocaust is a not-too-subtle assault on the Jewish future.

The primary purveyor of Holocaust denial to colleges is a Californian named Bradley Smith, who has long been associated with denial groups, but who is more adept than the others at appealing to the minds of students. His avowed goal is to "plant seeds" for future generations by bringing Holocaust denial onto the campus now. He has a two-step plan: The first step is making the existence or nonexistence of the Holocaust a *debatable issue* on college campuses *today*. He doesn't expect to win that debate now. But his second step is to win that debate for the deniers *in the next generation*, after all the survivors, perpetrators, and witnesses are dead. The means he has selected to achieve the first step is the publication of slick full-page Holocaust-denial ads in every major college newspaper.

For Smith, this tactic entails no risks; it is a no-lose proposition. If the ad is accepted, he gets his message across. If it is rejected, he screams censorship and gets his message across that way. The ad speaks in the language of academe. It invokes political correctness, "thought police," "free inquiry," "intellectual taboos," and a litany of other catchphrases likely to attract the attention of students. This packaging is wrapped around the typical Holocaust denial that is the essence of the ad's message: The gas chambers didn't exist, the photographic evidence has been doctored, the numbers of dead exaggerated, and the entire notion of Nazi genocide is "anti-German hate propaganda."

By submitting these ads to college newspapers around the country, Smith has been able to generate *two* debates, one of which he has won, the other of which he has lost — at least for now. The first debate was over whether college newspapers should publish the ads. Many did — either as paid ads or as free op-ed articles. Among the colleges whose papers published Smith's message were Arizona, Cornell, Duke, Georgia, Howard, Illinois, Louisiana State, Michigan, Montana, Northwestern, Ohio State, Rutgers, Vanderbilt, Washington University, and the University of Washington. Virtually all of these newspapers have policies rejecting ads that are racist, sexist, homophobic, or offensive. One student editor who decided to run the Holocaust-denial ad said his paper would refuse to run a beer ad with a woman holding a beer bottle between her breasts! Several others have declined ads for *Playboy*, for X-rated movies, and for cigarettes.

Many college papers, after spirited debate, exercised their own editorial judgment — and their own freedom of the press — by rejecting the ad. These included Berkeley, Brown, Santa Barbara, Chicago, Dartmouth, Emory, Georgetown, Harvard, Minnesota, North Carolina, Penn, Purdue, Rice, Southern California, Tennessee, Texas, UCLA, Virginia, Wisconsin, and Yale.

Despite the quantitative and (at least to this biased observer) qualitative victory for those who declined publication, Smith won the debate over censorship, since he was on the side of those who appeared to take the high moral ground of the open marketplace of ideas. The *Washington Post* and the *New York Times* both editorialized in favor of publishing the Smith propaganda.

During this controversy, I was called by the editors of several college newspapers and asked for my advice — as both a committed Jew and a committed civil libertarian — on whether they should publish the ad. I explained that it was entirely a matter of their editorial judgment, since freedom of the press gives the publisher, rather than the government, the right *to publish* or *not to publish* as he or she sees fit. I recommended that they look to their existing policy: If it required them to publish *all* submitted ads regardless of content, then they should not make an exception for this one. But if their policy banned racist, sexist, or otherwise false or offensive ads, they should ban *this* one. I told them the one tack they could not take was to maintain their policy against racist, sexist, false, or otherwise offensive ads and find that *this* one did not belong to that category. But that is precisely what some newspapers — the *Michigan Daily* and the *Duke Chronicle* among them — did: They sought to distinguish between Smith's ad and other offensive ads on the grounds that Smith's ad was not anti-Semitic. That decision reflects ignorance not only of the First Amendment but also of the history of anti-Semitism and Holocaust denial.

All in all, the debate over whether to publish the ad demonstrated an appalling lack of sensitivity among many editors, students, faculty, and administrators about how newspapers should deal with Holocaust denial. In assessing the impact of Smith's provocation on colleges around the country, Deborah Lipstadt concluded that "this failure suggests that correctly cast and properly camouflaged, Holocaust denial has a good chance of finding a foothold among coming generations."[26]

Even the debate that Smith lost — over the *merits* of his Holocaust-denial claims — he really won, since his goal was to make the very existence of the Holocaust a *debatable issue* on college campuses. Those newspapers that ran the ad as an op-ed piece, surrounded by opposing points of view, as the Rutgers *Targum* did, also gave Smith his victory. He became part of a debate, even if he was on the losing side — this time.

I became involved in the matter in a more personal way. During the college-ad controversy, Smith wrote me a letter challenging me to debate him — on any university campus — about whether the Holocaust had happened. I have a policy of refusing to debate crackpots on crackpot ideas, lest I help legitimate their nonsense, so my first instinct was to decline. But then it occurred to me that this slick ad-monger would take out ads in every college newspaper declaring that "Alan Dershowitz, who seems willing to debate anybody on anything, is unwilling to debate me on the Holocaust, because he knows he can't win." For a moment, I considered changing my principle and agreeing to debate him. Then I realized that if I did agree to debate him, he would immediately take out ads in every college newspaper declaring that "Even Alan Dershowitz, who claims that relatives of his were killed in the so-called Holocaust, agrees that the Holocaust is a debatable issue." Catch-22!

So I decided on the following response. I agreed to the debate, but only on one condition: that it be part of a four-part debate, the other three parts of which would be "(1) that slavery did not exist in America; (2) that Elvis Presley is still alive; and (3) that the earth is flat." I concluded my letter to him by saying that this "is the company of crackpot 'ideas' into which Holocaust denial comfortably fits." Needless to say, he did not take out an ad to publish my letter, nor have I heard from him since.

But neither Bradley Smith nor the anti-Semitism he represents will go away. We must figure out a way to respond to the Holocaust deniers on college campuses and elsewhere. At the end of this section, I will present what I believe is the best approach. But first let me dismiss as the *worst* approach the one accepted by several other democratic countries and advocated by many Jews (and others) in this country: namely, government censorship enforced through the courts.

Whenever one is defamed by a blatant and malicious lie, the temptation is great to "sue the bastard." "I'll see you in court" is as American as "Take me out to the ballgame." In fact, we Americans sue one another more frequently and for more money than any other people do. Nor is this a recent phenomenon. When Alexis de Tocqueville chronicled the United States in the nineteenth century, he observed that we take all our great issues to the courts. In light of this penchant for suing thy neighbor, it may be surprising to some that ours is one of the few democracies in which there is no legal prohibition, either civil or criminal, against *group* defamation. Under our First Amendment, anyone can say anything he or she chooses about any *group* — as distinguished from any *individual*.[27] In other Western democracies, such as Canada, Australia, France, and Israel, a bigot can be punished or sued for defaming Jews, or blacks, or other groups. He can also be punished for spreading lies about groups, and in some European countries it is specifically prohibited to deny the truth of the Holocaust. But not in the United States — and thank God for that.

Putting aside the constitutional barriers to placing the Holocaust on trial, there are important reasons of policy for keeping the Holocaust out of the courts, as evidenced by the disastrous consequences experienced by well-intentioned Canadian Holocaust survivors who tried to silence a particularly nasty Canadian neo-Nazi denier named Ernst Zundel.

Zundel — a professional photo retoucher, adept at changing reality — has written a book titled *The Hitler We Loved and Why*. Not surprisingly, he has also written a book about UFOs, claiming that Nazi UFOs — Hitler's secret weapons — are "actually still in use at bases in the Antarctic beneath the earth's surface."[28] Normally it would be best to ignore such a nutcase and let people laugh at his ridiculous claims. But in addition to publishing his own self-ridiculing books, Zundel also began to publish a wide array of Holocaust-denial books and other neo-Nazi material by other authors, which he distributed throughout Canada, the United States, and Germany. Zundel is also an accomplished showman (some might say clown) who is adept at attracting media attention to himself and his outrageous claims by pulling off headline-grabbing stunts, such as applying for the job of director of the Canadian Jewish Congress's Holocaust Documentation Bank Project and sending Jewish New Year cards to Holocaust survivors. Because of these and other gambits, he has earned the title "the P. T. Barnum of Holocaust denial." But to Holocaust survivors, Zundel is no joke. He has described his "Aryan" mission as destroying the "monstrous lie that is the Holocaust."[29]

To Sabrina Citron, a Holocaust survivor, this was all too much. In 1985 she filed a legal action against Zundel and, with the help of the Canadian Holocaust Remembrance Association, persuaded the Canadian government to charge the neo-Nazi with an assortment of crimes, including "willfully publishing news that he knows is false and that causes or is likely to cause injury or mischief to a public interest."

Inevitably, such a charge puts the truth of the Holocaust on trial and pits the Holocaust against freedom of speech. It also gives the defendant a free forum for spreading his lies. And Zundel knew how to make the most of this opportunity. He arrived at court dressed in a bulletproof vest and hardhat and carried an eleven-foot cross with the words "freedom of speech" emblazoned across it. His lawyer, a fellow traveler, called the survivor witnesses "liars" and had his witnesses testify that Auschwitz was a recreational facility equipped with a dance hall, sauna, and swimming pool for the enjoyment of its "guests."

Although the jury ruled in favor of the survivors, Zundel claimed victory, boasting that he "got a million dollars' worth of publicity for my cause." Moreover, he eventually won the appeal on the grounds that the "false news" statute was unconstitutional. The trial — really trials, because he was tried twice — of Ernst Zundel proved to be a total victory for Holocaust deniers and a total disaster for Holocaust survivors and the Jewish people. Though other trials have produced convictions and even jail terms for other deniers, those deniers too have always claimed victory. A trial is simply the wrong vehicle for educating the public about the truth of the Holocaust, because "truth" is never the issue in such a trial. The issue is always freedom of speech. The defendant becomes the free-speech martyr, and his free speech gets free and often sympathetic press coverage from a media that is sensitive to any threats to its own freedom of expression.

On the basis of my experience with Holocaust deniers, I believe the best approach to the problem is multifaceted.

1. Never sue, prosecute, or debate the deniers themselves. They should be either ignored or ridiculed. If *they* want to sue for defamation as a result of the ridicule, welcome such a suit, because it pits *them* against freedom of speech and exposes their hypocrisy. Moreover, a suit by them does not put the *truth* of the Holocaust on trial.

2. Every time a denier gets any attention — through ads or other media — *use* that attention as an occasion to *educate* the general public, and particularly the young, about the truth of the Holocaust. But do not specifically respond to, or even acknowledge, the deniers themselves, except in a ridiculing manner. Their claims do not deserve serious attention, and we should not dignify them by responding.

3. Assemble a simple multimedia package setting out in understandable terms the overwhelming evidence in support of the historical truth of the Holocaust. This package should consist of a twenty-five- or thirty-page pamphlet with photographs of the *Einsatzgruppen* and the death camps, the charts prepared by the Nazis documenting the killings, the confessions of the death camp commandants and guards, the text of the Wannsee Conference at which the genocide was planned, eyewitness accounts by survivors, and judicial pronouncements confirming the Holocaust by courts around the world. It should also include statements by the world's most renowned historians of every nationality and background — professors whose names are familiar to college students — confirming that there is no possible historical dispute about the basic facts of the Holocaust. The pamphlet should be accompanied by a professionally produced videotape, including motion picture and still archival pictures of the *Einsatzgruppen*, death camps, trials, and survivors. The purpose of this package is to lay to rest any question that the public in general, and students in particular, may have about the truth of the Holocaust — without dignifying the deniers. Obviously, a package of this kind cannot be prepared by individual communities. It must be done on a national or international level by an organization or group with considerable resources.

4. Make the videotape available to every cable TV station, since Holocaust deniers are now demanding, and obtaining, airtime on public access TV. No attempt should be made either to censor them or to debate them, but *their* exercise of freedom of speech should be turned to *our* advantage — and to the advantage of truth — by using it to educate the public about the indisputable truths of the Holocaust.

5. Continue efforts to document and archive every aspect of the Holocaust through survivor testimony, document collection, and other evidence gathering. New sources, such as the files of the former Soviet Union, should be triangulated with existing sources. We must be prepared for a time — in the not

so distant future — when there will be no eyewitnesses left alive and when the deniers will begin the second stage in their campaign: to try to *win* the debate they are now trying to start about whether the Holocaust ever occurred. As time passes, we can expect the claims of the deniers to become increasingly extreme.

6. Continue to develop curricular material for inclusion in courses throughout the country, so that students will learn about the Holocaust in the same manner, and with the same degree of historical certainty, as they learn about other incontrovertible events.

7. Continue to challenge all *comparisons* to the Holocaust, especially when they come from mainstream sources, and explain its uniqueness in modern history by focusing on its unique characteristics, such as the *ingathering* of Jews for execution from throughout Europe and the deliberate murder of a million *babies and young children* in an effort to eliminate the Jewish people by literal genocide.

8. In addition to ridiculing the deniers, emphasize their bigoted backgrounds — many of them are anti-black as well — and the anti-Semitic intentions and effects of denial. But in doing so, we must not engage in substantive debate with them, or legitimate them in any way. By ridiculing them and disclosing their racist background and agenda, we delegitimate them and make it more difficult for the media and young people to take them seriously, or to want to be associated with them.

9. Never *use* the Holocaust as a *justification* for Jews doing anything wrong. The "Holocaust mentality" should not serve as an "abuse excuse" for actions that cannot be justified on other grounds.[30] The experience of the Holocaust may *explain* certain Jewish (or Israeli) attitudes, fears, concerns, or even paranoia, but it cannot justify them, lest the memory of the Holocaust be denigrated by becoming part of a political debate over current actions.

10. Finally, never put any Jew on the *defensive* when it comes to the Holocaust. We have the moral high ground, and we should insist on maintaining that moral authority.

The Rise of Anti-Semitism Among Some African-Americans

If there is any lingering doubt that anti-Semitism is at the very core of Holocaust denial, this doubt is plainly resolved by observing how some African-American anti-Semites have woven Holocaust denial into the fabric of their anti-Jewish bigotry. These African-American Holocaust deniers obtain their hate material directly from white neo-Nazi Holocaust deniers who hate blacks but who share a common enemy, namely the Jews.

It is crucial not to exaggerate the influence of African-American anti-Semitism or to generalize about "all blacks." Despite its recent increase among some students, African-American anti-Semitism is still relatively marginal in American society at large and of uncertain influence within the African-American community. Its voice is loud and shrill on some college campuses, but there are countervailing voices of reason and accommodation. Our goal must be to marginalize the bigots without ignoring the real dangers they may pose, especially to the future of Jewish–black relations. It is with this goal in mind that I recount the mixture of bad news and good news about recent conflicts between African-Americans and Jews.

A group of radical black bigots has established an organization called the Black African Holocaust Council, headed by Eric Muhammad, a Black Muslim activist, whose mailing address is the same as the one used by the Nation of Islam for its anti-Semitic publication *Blacks and Jews News*.[31]

The usual assortment of black bigots have been associated with the Black African Holocaust Council and its anti-Semitic agenda. These include Steve Cokely, who claims that Jewish doctors are injecting the AIDS virus into black children; Khalid Muhammad, who claims that Hitler was merely defending himself against the Jews; Leonard Jeffries, who blames Russian Jews for "the destruction of black people"; and Tony Martin, who tells his Wellesley College students that Jews controlled the slave trade.[32]

These racist hatemongers berate Holocaust victims, denigrate the suffering of Jews, and argue that the Jewish Holocaust was trivial compared to the "Holocaust" directed against blacks by Jews.* They also distribute Holocaust-denial books and videotapes and sponsor talks by deniers. For example, a video titled *The Myths of the Jewish Holocaust* was shown at an event sponsored by the Black African Holocaust Council at which Leonard Jeffries spoke,[33] and Arthur Butz, a well-known white Holocaust denier, was a speaker at the Nation of Islam's Savior Day rally in Chicago.

On April 15, 1994, a night-long rally directed to "Documenting the Black Holocaust" was held at Howard University in front of two thousand students, community people, and others. The event was characterized as "the Woodstock of anti-Semitism." Khalid Muhammad, a featured speaker, addressed himself specifically to Jewish Holocaust survivors: "You make me sick — always got some old crinkly, wrinkled cracker that you bring up, talking about 'this is one of the Holocaust victims.' Goddamn it! I'm looking at a whole audience full of Holocaust victims. [Your] Holocaust lasted 10 years; ours lasted 500. How can you compare, buddy? You are so arrogant."[34] He then went on to blame the Holocaust on the Jews: "Nobody wants to talk about what the Jews did; they always are talking about what Hitler did to the Jews, but what did the Jews do to Hitler?" On other occasions, Khalid Muhammad has "questioned" whether Hitler actually killed 6 million Jews in the "so-called Jew Holocaust," and has referred to *Schindler's List* as "Swindler's List."[35]

Leonard Jeffries, who also spoke at the Howard hatefest, dismissed the Jewish Holocaust as "irrelevant," and asked the world to focus instead on "the most devastating Holocaust ever conceived," namely black slavery. Tony Martin's contribution to the night's anti-Semitism menu was his charge that Zionist Jews "collaborated with the Nazis" during the Second World War.[36]

One of the most disturbing — and for blacks, self-destructive — aspects of these lies about the Holocaust is the close relationship between these black bigots and the white bigots who hate Jews and also hate blacks. Indeed, black Holocaust denial has come to depend almost exclusively on the published lies of white neo-Nazis and

---

* Some African-Americans argue that they cannot be racist, since racism is institutional. This is a semantic point. Certainly individuals can be racists without regard to their own minority status. In any event, if Farrakhan and his ilk prefer to be called bigots, so be it.

other anti-black bigots. The common bond of Jew-hating and Jew-baiting seems to overcome the mutual hatred between black bigots and white bigots. As Robert Brock, a well-known black bigot and mentor to Khalid Muhammad, put it: "There may be more in common between David Duke and Louis Farrakhan than meets the eye."[37] In January 1994, the Long Island chapter of the neo-Nazi SS Action Group praised Khalid Muhammad for his attack on the Jews and proclaimed that "we must work together to eliminate the Jew." Tom Metzger, the founder of White Aryan Resistance, told the *Washington Post* that Farrakhan's Nation of Islam is "the black counterpart of us." Not surprisingly, therefore, the Anti-Defamation League has been able to trace most of the Holocaust-denial material issued by black anti-Semites to white racist sources.[38]

African-American anti-Semites have linked together three big lies: that the Holocaust against the Jews is a fraud (or at least an exaggeration); that Jews played a disproportionate role in the "Holocaust" against blacks; and that Jews today continue to play a disproportionate role in exploiting blacks. Each of the three lies is easily disproved, but they persist within some bigoted elements of the African-American community. In a 1992 national survey, 37 percent of the African-Americans polled held "strongly anti-Semitic views," as compared to 20 percent of the general population.[39] This disturbing fact is true despite the reality that, according to the ADL, "between half and three-quarters of the contributions to the NAACP, SCLC, SNCC, and CORE [in the 1960s] came from Jewish givers. Similarly, more than half the white freedom riders were Jews, as were nearly two-thirds of the white participants in 1964's Freedom Summer."[40] Even today, Jews contribute more to black causes than any other nonblacks do. What Martin Luther King, Jr., asked in 1965 could still be asked today:

> How could there be anti-Semitism among Negroes when our Jewish friends have demonstrated their commitment to the principle of tolerance and brotherhood not only in the form of sizable contributions, but in many other tangible ways, and often at great personal sacrifice? Can we ever express our appreciation to the rabbis who chose to give moral witness with us in St. Augustine during our recent protest against segregation in that unhappy city? Need I remind anyone of the awful beating suffered by

Rabbi Arthur Lelyveld of Cleveland when he joined the civil rights workers there in Hattiesburg, Mississippi? And who can ever forget the sacrifice of two Jewish lives, Andrew Goodman and Michael Schwerner, in the swamps of Mississippi? It would be impossible to record the contribution that the Jewish people have made toward the Negro's struggle for freedom — it has been so great.[41]

Some argue that the relatively higher level of anti-Semitism within the African-American community exists not *despite* Jewish involvement in the civil rights movement but *because* of it. But history does not support this conclusion. Anti-Semitism existed within radical elements of the black community well before the 1960s. Marcus Garvey's "back to Africa" movement in the 1920s was laced with anti-Semitic rhetoric, as were the Harlem riots of the 1930s.[42] Most African-Americans have always eschewed anti-Semitism and embraced Jewish support, but a strain of Jew-hatred has long been associated with some black radicals.

There has also been a strain of religiously inspired anti-Semitism within some black churches. As Richard Wright wrote of his youth in the South:

All of us Black people hated Jews, not because they exploited us but because we had been taught at home and in Sunday School that Jews were Christ killers. A Black jingle went this way:

> Virgin Mary had one son
> The cruel Jews had him hung
> Bloody Christ killer
> Never trust a Jew
> Bloody Christ killer
> What won't a Jew do?[43]

In any event, to an anti-Semite, nothing done *by* Jews changes the bigotry. If Jews had *not* been involved in the civil rights movement, *that* would be the excuse for anti-Semitism.

The double-bind role of Jewish actions and attitudes in contributing to black anti-Semitism is well illustrated by the currently voguish lie making the rounds among some African-American college students: namely, that Jews played a disproportionate role in the slave trade. The most extreme version of this canard has been expressed by the most influential of the black bigots, Louis Farrakhan, the leader of the Nation of Islam. Farrakhan and Khalid Muhammad have both said that "75% of the slaves owned in the South were owned by Jewish slaveholders."[44]

That would indeed be a remarkable statistic, if it were true, since Jews constituted less than one-fifth of 1 percent of the population of the slave states before the Civil War. The Farrakhan number is, of course, totally made up. Jews owned considerably less than 1 percent of the slaves. Indeed, both blacks and Muslims were more extensively involved in the slave trade than Jews.[45] Yet this phony 75 percent figure has become a staple of the bigoted rhetoric of the Nation of Islam.

Why would Farrakhan and his "information ministers" want to exaggerate the Jewish ownership of slaves by more than a hundredfold? The answer to that question is as old as the history of classic anti-Semitism. Farrakhan's purpose is to single out and scapegoat Jews for all the problems, historical and contemporary, faced by African-Americans. That is why it has also become a staple of the Nation of Islam's rhetoric that Jewish doctors deliberately injected the AIDS virus into black babies as part of some genocidal master plan. That is why classic anti-Semitic forgeries, such as *The Protocols of the Elders of Zion*, are on sale at Nation of Islam bookstores, along with copies of *The Jewish Onslaught* by Tony Martin and the Nation's own anonymously written collection of half-truths, *The Secret Relationship Between Blacks and Jews*, whose thesis is that Jews played a disproportionate role in the slave trade. And that is why the Nation of Islam's newspaper, *Blacks and Jews News*, an anti-Semitic screed that would have made Joseph Goebbels beam, is being widely circulated around college campuses.

These speeches and publications exaggerating the tiny role of some individual Jews in the slave trade are part of a well-orchestrated campaign by the Nation of Islam and other black racist groups to focus black anger and frustration on the historic target of scapegoating, namely "the Jews." As Professor David Brion Davis, the leading authority on slavery, has put it: "[A] selective search for Jewish slave traders becomes inherently anti-Semitic unless one keeps in view the larger context and the very marginal place of Jews in the history of the overall system."[46]

Despite this history of anti-Jewish bigotry, the Congressional Black Caucus, then headed by Congressman Kweisi Mfume (D-Md.), who is now head of the NAACP, entered into a "covenant" in September 1993 to work with Farrakhan and his Black Muslim group on legislative concerns, thereby legitimating this controversial group and including it among other respected black groups who work side by side with the Caucus. In announcing this new arrangement, Congressman Mfume stated, "No longer will we allow people to divide us" — an obvious reference to Jews. The Black Caucus entered into this covenant in the face of the Black Muslims' long history of rabid anti-white bigotry in general and anti-Semitism in particular. The hope expressed was that by making this agreement, the members of Congress might encourage Farrakhan and his followers to pull away from the divisive rhetoric that has alienated them from mainstream Americans.

This hope was dashed on November 29, 1993, when Khalid Muhammad, at that time the national spokesman for the Nation of Islam, delivered a speech at Kean College in Union, New Jersey, in which he accused the Jews of controlling the slave trade, and accused victims of the Holocaust of bringing genocide on themselves because they "went in there, in Germany, the way they do everywhere they go, and they supplanted, they usurped, they turned around and a German, in his own country, would almost have to go to a Jew to get money. They had undermined the very fabric of the society." Muhammad accused Jews of controlling the media, finance, and politics in the United States, and of conspiring to keep black people down by being the "bloodsuckers of the black nation and the black community." And he employed crude anti-Semitic references such as "Columbia Jew-niversity and "Jew York City."[47]

Although much of Muhammad's speech was devoted to preaching this all-too-familiar brand of anti-Semitic rhetoric, he did not hesitate to attack other groups, including whites, homosexuals, Catholics, and even other black Americans. Muhammad suggested at one point that somebody "[g]o to the Vatican in Rome. When the old, no-good Pope, you know that cracker. Somebody need [sic] to raise that dress up and see what's really under there." His prescription for white South Africans is genocide: "We kill the women, we kill the children, we kill the babies . . . we kill the blind . . . the crippled. We kill the faggot, we kill the lesbian. We kill 'em all."

As if Muhammad's bigoted comments were not bad enough, Dr. Jay L. Spaulding, a history professor and an African specialist at Kean, also observed that during the course of Muhammad's lecture, "the leading Kean College faculty and student exponents of Afro-centricity sat in the front row cheering . . ."

Following the appearance of news reports about the speech and a full-page advertisement by the Anti-Defamation League, virtually all responsible black leaders condemned Muhammad's ravings. Among them were Benjamin Chavis, then executive director of the NAACP, William H. Gray III, president of the United Negro College Fund, the Reverend Jesse Jackson, and Congressman Mfume.

On January 24, 1994, Mfume wrote a letter to Farrakhan urging him to disassociate himself and the Black Muslims from the statements made at Kean College by Khalid Muhammad. As Mfume said, "What concerned me was that reports were identifying him as the national spokesperson of the Nation of Islam . . . , which would be a concern to all of us who have reached out to find ways to bring about unity among different groups." The following day, Farrakhan responded to Mfume's letter in a speech to an audience of ten thousand in Harlem. Explicitly refusing to disassociate himself from Khalid Muhammad's bigotry, Farrakhan said: "They're trying to use my brother Khalid's words against me to divide the house." Referring specifically to the Jewish community, Farrakhan said: "They don't want Farrakhan to do what he's doing. They're plotting as we speak."

In light of this sharp rebuke by Reverend Farrakhan, many Americans — black and white — called on Congressman Mfume to sever all relationships between the Black Caucus and Farrakhan, formally and unequivocally. I wrote a column in which I argued that "to continue a covenant with such hate mongers is to become complicitous in the bigotry of Mr. Farrakhan and his henchman Mr. Muhammad. The time has come — indeed it is long past — for responsible Black leaders to disassociate themselves and their decent organizations from all Black bigotry, whether it emanates from Farrakhan's thugs or from those university professors and students who applaud their divisive messages of hate."

Several other columnists criticized Jewish leaders for "overreacting" to the bigoted words of Khalid Muhammad "before 100 students at Kean College."[48] That misses the point. Muhammad often speaks at two or three colleges in a single day, drawing more than a thousand to a single speech. According to the respected *Chronicle of Higher Education*, Khalid Muhammad is very popular among many black college students, who refer to him as "the new Malcolm X." This comparison is an insult to the memory of Malcolm X. Over dinner a few weeks before his assassination by Nation of Islam killers, he told me he was becoming more open to cooperation with Jews. His murder was applauded by Louis Farrakhan, who is Khalid Muhammad's mentor.

Nor are Farrakhan and his Nation of Islam trivial figures in the black community. If they were, Mfume's Caucus would not have established a "sacred covenant" with them — a covenant it finally broke following Farrakhan's refusal to disavow the content of Khalid Muhammad's notorious speech.

The NAACP, on the other hand, stated that it was "satisfied" with Farrakhan's statements about Khalid Muhammad and was "prepared to believe Minister Farrakhan's statement that he is neither anti-Semitic nor racist." When asked about Farrakhan's claim that Jews owned 75 percent of the slaves, the NAACP's director of communications said that Farrakhan "may have exaggerated the historical fact [but] that is a matter for academics to debate." He concluded that Farrakhan's possible exaggeration "should not be a yardstick upon which he or anyone else should be condemned as anti-Semitic."[49] I respectfully disagree. Exaggerating the role of a small number of individual Jews by more than a hundredfold in order to scapegoat "the Jews" for the horrors of slavery is a proper yardstick by which to measure and condemn for anti-Semitism.

Some defenders of the NAACP's soft line on Farrakhan point to the fact that the Nation of Islam does some good in its fight against drugs and its emphasis on black pride. This rationale was cited by many centrist blacks who participated in Farrakhan's Million Man March in 1995. But it is precisely the "good" works of the Nation of Islam that make its pervasive scapegoating of the Jews so dangerous. Its "good" works give its "bad" speech credibility among elements of the black community. If it did no good, few would be listening to its divisive message of hate. For bigotry to succeed, the negative message *must* be attached to something positive. Bigotry alone rarely has an audience. In Germany the message of the Nazi Party was twofold: German pride must be restored, and the Jews are to blame for most of Germany's problems. In the pre–civil rights South, the message of the Ku Klux Klan was also twofold: White Protestant pride and economic power must be restored, and the blacks, Jews, and Catholics are to blame for most of the problems.

It should be neither surprising nor exculpatory that the Nation of Islam has learned from past bigots that for its scapegoating message to be heard, it must be accompanied by the positive work the group is now doing. But if it is to retain its soul, the NAACP cannot make a pact with the devil.

After it recovers from recent leadership crises and financial scandals, it is possible that the NAACP will return to its traditional alliance with Jewish civil rights organizations and individuals, but it is too early to tell. Whatever the NAACP does will likely have limited influence, however, on college campuses, where the problem of anti-Semitism is being fueled by the three big lies of Holocaust denial, exaggerating the role of the Jews in slavery, and blaming the Jews for the current problems of the African-American community. Indeed, one of the reasons the NAACP, traditionally a centrist, mainline organization, moved toward an unholy alliance with radical anti-Semitic elements was to have an increased voice and increased relevance on campuses.[50] If it were to move back to the center, it would risk alienating, or simply being ignored by, black campus radicals.

It is impossible to know for certain what percentage of African-American students are influenced by the racist rhetoric of the Khalid Muhammads and Louis Farrakhans versus how many listen to the reasoned voices of such eminent African-American scholars as Henry Louis Gates, Cornel West, John Hope Franklin, Charles Ogletree, Randy Kennedy, Kwame Anthony Appiah, Manning Marable, Stephen Carter, and Patricia Williams. It is impossible to know, for example, how many African-American students have read the following words by Harvard professor Henry Louis Gates:

> The Secret Relationship [Between Blacks and Jews] itself is an invidious document of anti-Semitism; that is, it's hard to think of any historical motivation for it other than the fomenting of hostility toward Jews and as a defense for anti-Semitic rhetoric. Unfortu-

nately, its "scholarly apparatus" is likely to impress lay persons who aren't familiar with the relevant historiography. . . .

Now, nobody who is familiar with the vast body of archival material on slavery is likely to be impressed by the book's approach. Typically, the authors list the names of 11 Jewish Confederate Navy officers, or the number of Jewish soldiers in the Confederate Army in each state. But the paltriness of the numbers is disguised by the book's failure to supply the obvious comparison figures: how large was the army and navy? Ironically, it appears that more blacks participated in the Confederate Army than Jews! But that's how this book works: the accretion of anecdotes, with no honest attempt to place them in an historical or demographic perspective. . . . And the generalizations it makes are unsupported by the "evidence" it provides.

Using this technique, you could easily produce a book about the special culpability of left-handed people, one that adduced example after example of left-handed malfeasance. Now, since left-handers make up about 8% of the population, there should be an ample supply of material; and if you didn't know better, the book might make rousing reading. . . .

[T]he net involvement of all Jewish merchants in the slave trade would not equal the level of participation of any *one* of the largest Christian-owned trading firms. Being implicated in the tragic history of America's racial drama doesn't distinguish Jewish Americans from other white Americans. In contrast, the active role of American Jews in the struggles of the Civil Rights era *does* so distinguish them. Why elevate the former over the latter? The "Historical Research Department" of the Nation of Islam is not known for its disinterested pursuit of knowledge for its own sake, after all. So, again, the issue of motivation — and therefore the issue of anti-Semitism — can't be avoided.[51]

Nor do we know how many African-Americans read the following words by Coretta Scott King:

Jewish Americans provided strong support and often encouraged sacrifices for the cause of racial equality. . . . They suffered threats, beatings, and jailings along side their black brothers and sisters. . . .

Any African-American who betrays this noble heritage of solidarity to wallow in the vile shadows of anti-Semitism is a puppet of the Klan and other hate groups.[52]

Even Jesse Jackson's recent condemnations of anti-Semitism have been spoken largely to Jewish audiences and published widely in the Jewish press.

Several summers ago, I was asked to discuss Jewish–black issues with Professor Gates at the Whaling Church on Martha's Vineyard. The house was packed — primarily with Jews, who gave Gates an appropriately enthusiastic welcome. There were very few blacks, even though Martha's Vineyard has a large black summer population. The problem of the Jewish–black relationship seems to be more of a concern to the Jewish community than to the black community, though many prominent black leaders are trying to focus on it.

A far more serious problem than the occasional visiting speaker like Khalid Muhammad or Louis Farrakhan is the permanent presence on some faculties of anti-Semitic black professors such as Leonard Jeffries and Tony Martin, who attract huge numbers of students — most of them black — to their classes, where they miseducate generations of future leaders with paranoid "Afro-centric" lies about whites in general and Jews in particular.

In 1994, a reporter for *Time* magazine attended one of Jeffries's classes at City College. The professor sauntered in "fully an hour late" and made a lame excuse about the laundry (the teacher's version of the old student excuse "The dog ate my homework"). The forty students — thirty-nine blacks and one Asian — listened as Jeffries lectured about "sun people" and "ice people." Sun people have more melanin than ice people, which makes them less exploitative and "allows [them] to negotiate the vibrations of the universe." He drew a triangle with "RNA" and "DNA" and "melanin" at the corners and explained: "[This is] the aspect of the internal-external, the aspect of systems analysis." When asked for a clarification, he responded, "You want to have the duality-polarity in life. There is a mix of DNA, RNA and there's a not-too-understood question of melanin, the organized molecule. . . . And this is the relationship that produces the processes of life, the multiplicity of cells."[53]

This "lecture" sounds like some of the mail I receive daily from inmates of mental institutions. It is word salad, utter nonsense, an embarrassment to any university. No student could possibly get anything but a few big words out of it. It is not scholarship. It is not even propaganda. It is educational malpractice. The primary victims are not those who are the targets of Jeffries's attacks — ice people, Jews, Catholics. The real victims are the students whom Jeffries defrauds of their time and tuition on a daily basis.

I have challenged Professor Jeffries to a debate on *his* theories before *his* students in *his* classroom. He has declined this opportunity, as he has declined every opportunity to publish his theories in journals or books where they can be reviewed and criticized by real experts. "We don't have time to write," says this ersatz scholar. "We're making history." He is the David Koresh of black studies, preaching racial Armageddon to a captive audience of students who expect to be rewarded for parroting Jeffries's racial gobbledygook.

Jeffries accuses his critics — including me — of wanting to deny him freedom of speech and academic freedom. There is, of course, no truth to this accusation. I have defended Jeffries's right to speak and teach his nonsense. But I insist that it be exposed in the marketplace of ideas, where it can be challenged, debated, and demolished. Jeffries has no respect for freedom of speech, as evidenced both by his refusal to expose his ideas in the marketplace and by the threats of violence he has directed against his critics.

A striking example of these threats took place when an African-American Harvard College student named Jonathan Morgan sought to interview Jeffries for the *Harvard Crimson* in October 1991. During the interview, Jeffries criticized professors Henry Gates and Shelby Steele. At some point, Jeffries apparently learned that Morgan was not "a brother representing the black students at Harvard," but rather a black Jew who wrote for the university newspaper. He immediately accused the student — whom I did not even know — of having been "sent by Dershowitz" to set him up. (I guess he believes, like most anti-Semites, that all Jews know each other and work together in the same conspiracy.) Jeffries then ordered one of his bodyguards to grab Morgan's tape recorder and threatened him: "If I hear this again, I'll kill you." When Morgan left, one of Jeffries's bodyguards followed him and also threatened to kill him if he disclosed what Jeffries had said. So much for freedom of expression!

Though Jeffries is no longer chairman of the Black Studies

Department at New York's City College — that department has now been disbanded and its faculty dispersed among other departments — he continues to miseducate students, preparing them for a life of separatist paranoid hatred, rather than for a twenty-first-century career in a world built on coalition and civil rights.

Also miseducating students is Professor Tony Martin of Wellesley College, who assigns his students *The Secret Relationship Between Blacks and Jews*. Employing pseudoscholarship and quoting extensively (but out of context) from Jewish sources, the book has been used by its publishers, the Nation of Islam, to spread the lie that 75 percent of the slaves owned in the South were owned by Jewish slaveholders. I have already demonstrated the absurdity of this bigoted statement and the falsity of the book, *The Secret Relationship Between Blacks and Jews*, on which it purports — erroneously but quite deliberately — to be based. Professor Martin himself insists that "Jews were an integral part of the slave trade." He also insists that he is among Wellesley's most popular teachers and that he has the support of the black students for his rantings and ravings.[54] In a recent book that he published, entitled *The Jewish Onslaught*, he refers to Henry Gates as "African America's most notorious Judeophile," to college Hillel chapters as "shock troops in the ongoing Jewish onslaught against black progress," and to B'nai B'rith as "stable mates of the Anti-Defamation League."[55] Typical of anti-Semites, he accuses "the Jews" of controlling the media, including the Associated Press, public radio, and the *Boston Globe* (even though the latter two take a distinctly critical approach to Israel).[56] He characterizes other African-Americans who disagree with him as "Jewish spokes[men]." All this is part of a paranoid fantasy that runs through Martin's writing suggesting that "the Jews" constitute a monolithically powerful anti-black conspiracy of which he is an important target. Even the anonymous hate mail he receives — much of which sounds like it comes from the same anti-black and anti-Jewish crazies who write to me — Martin attributes to Jews!

Martin's assault on Jews knows few bounds. He attacks the Torah, the Talmud, virtually every Jewish organization, and even Jewish songwriters like Oscar Hammerstein for writing "Old Man River" and *making* Paul Robeson sing it (thousands of times, all around the world). He demands that "the Jews" pay reparations to the blacks for the Torah, which contains "their invention of the Hamitic myth, which killed many millions more than all the anti-Jewish pogroms and holocausts."[57]

No wonder his African-American Wellesley colleague Professor Marcellus Andrews has called Martin a "racist Pied Piper" and has wondered "how and why this person has gained a following on campus." But regardless of how and why, the fact remains that ignorant bigots like Jeffries and Martin, who specialize in Jew-baiting and Jew-hating, do have a considerable following among many African-American students on campuses around the country. Fortunately, they are often criticized by other African-American teachers and students who reject their conspiratorial paranoia and who seek to build bridges of trust and cooperation. Still others simply ignore their racism as a diversion from the real issues, or are embarrassed by their stupidity. It is impossible to discern the extent of the influence — current and future — of these ridiculous figures on African-American students.

There are two competing views of what the future holds for Jewish–black relations. The pessimistic view focuses on the fact that the highest levels of black anti-Semitism (and anti-Zionism) appear to be among the young, the best educated, and the future leaders. This would suggest a bleak future. But appearances may be misleading. In my experience, at Harvard and other universities where I have lectured, the highest levels of black anti-Semitism may be limited to some of the most radical and therefore most visible activists among black student and faculty leaders. There may well be a "silent majority" who do not share these views, but are less expressive about the views they do hold. It is not voguish these days on college campuses for black students to be too close to — and thus seen as co-opted by — their Jewish classmates and teachers. Nor is it as "in" to support the moderate black voices on campus, such as those of professors Gates, West, Ogletree, and Kennedy, as it is to attend the raucous rallies of Khalid Muhammad, Tony Martin, or Louis Farrakhan. The most prestigious African-American studies program is located at Harvard.[58] It will be training many of the nation's future academics who specialize in this and related areas. There is no evidence of any tolerance for anti-Semitism within this distinguished department.

No one can chart with confidence the future direction of Jewish–black relations. It is important to remember that neither the black nor the Jewish community is monolithic. Indeed, it is the essence of prejudice to lump all Jews together or to blame all Jews for the failings of some, as Farrakhan and his ilk do. It is equally prejudiced to lump all African-Americans together or to blame all blacks for Farrakhan and those who parrot or applaud his views. We make a terrible mistake when we try to change the minds of strident anti-Semites, whether black or white. The struggle is for the minds and souls of the vast majority of young African-American students and future leaders who have an open attitude about black–Jewish relations. These students and future leaders are exposed to a multiplicity of conflicting views, including anti-Semitism, philo-Semitism, and much in between. We must develop a strategy for increasing the odds (and that is all we can ever do) that a significant number of young African-Americans will reject the anti-Semitism of the extremists and listen to the more accommodating voices of the moderates. We must not remain passive in the face of anti-Semitism. But neither should we exaggerate the importance of the extremists and fanatics.

I have been at the center of black–Jewish dialogue, conflict, friendship, and tension at Harvard and in the general community for a quarter of a century. During that time, I have observed much change — some for the better, some for the worse. It is not a monolithic or static issue. It is always in flux. As a result of my experiences, I have been asked advice by many Jewish groups at universities and other settings around the country as to how to deal with this divisive and emotional issue. My suggestions are as follows:

1. Do *not* treat African-American bigots, such as Farrakhan, Muhammad, Jeffries, and Martin, exactly like neo-Nazi Holocaust deniers should be treated. These black bigots have significant constituencies on and off campus, who support them, identify with them, and believe in them. They cannot simply be ignored or mocked. There is no constituency for neo-Nazi Holocaust deniers on campuses or other important institutions today, though there is a constituency for their freedom of speech.

2. Try to arrange a debate between these extremists and more moderate African-American voices. The best possible opponent is a popular African-American professor or leader who is

an expert on the issues. If no such opponent is willing to debate, try to find a popular teacher or other figure, regardless of race, who has a history of involvement in civil rights. Do *not* make it a debate between "the Jews" and "the blacks," and do not expect to "win," at least as measured by comparative applause. The goal is to *educate* for the future, to open minds, to plant seeds, to raise doubts about the views of the bigots.

3. Publicize the debate invitation. It is unlikely that the bigots will accept, because they know they cannot defend their views against real experts. If they refuse, publicize the rejection and then *repeat* the offer. Keep it open-ended. If there is no debate, print up *factual* leaflets, with quotes from prominent experts of all races and backgrounds, and distribute them widely around the campus or other avenues of dialogue.

4. Try to get prominent professors and leaders from all races and backgrounds to assist you in the distribution of the leaflets or to join you in conducting an *informational* picket, specifically rebutting the claims about Jewish "control" of the slave trade and other canards. Do *not* urge students to boycott the anti-Semitic lecture. But do urge them to read your literature and signs. When one of these bigots came to speak at Harvard a few years ago, Professor Randy Kennedy — a prominent black teacher — and I stood silently at the back of the room holding informational signs. It had a real impact on the audience, as reflected in the critical questions put to the speaker by some of the African-American audience members.

5. Organize a countertalk or teach-in, but *not* for the same time the bigot is speaking. If it is at the same time, you will be preaching to the converted. Invite those who go to the bigoted speech to attend your event as well — in fairness and as part of the open marketplace of ideas.

6. Do not, under any circumstances, try to stop the bigoted event, censor the speaker, or criticize the institution for "allowing" him a forum. That argument always backfires and gives the bigot the high ground on freedom of speech.

7. Do not *single out* moderate black leaders by demanding that *they* always condemn every statement by every black racist. All good people, regardless of race, should condemn all bigots, regardless of race. But if a given black moderate, such as Kweisi Mfume, embraces or joins forces with a black bigot, demand that *he* condemn the bigot and disassociate himself from the bigotry.

8. Try to understand what may motivate good people — some even your friends — to want to hear such bigoted drivel. To understand is not to justify, but it is important to understand in order to mount the most effective response.

9. Unlike Holocaust denial, which is totally false, black bigotry sometimes contains a kernel of truth about *individual* Jews.[59] Do not destroy your credibility by defending *every* Jew or *every* decision made by every Jewish organization or Israel. But do not hesitate to label negative generalizations or selective half-truths about Jews as anti-Semitism.

10. Do not turn *general campus or community controversies* — over such issues as affirmative action, speech codes, multiculturalism — into Jew-versus-black issues. There is no single Jewish view on these issues. Regardless of where you stand on such an issue, create coalitions; work with others; make it clear that it is not only a Jewish issue. Even anti-Semitism should be seen as an issue of concern to *all* students, faculty, administrators, and citizens.

11. Encourage students and other citizens to work closely with faculty, administration, and community groups. Most professors, administrators, and political leaders are, by nature, cowards. They are conflict averse, want to be loved by everyone, and are afraid of being seen as controversial. Challenge them to speak their minds. Remind them that tenure and position carry some responsibilities, including speaking one's mind. Do not let them sit on the sidelines, especially if you know they support your positions. Remind them of what Ed-

mund Burke said: "The only thing necessary for the triumph of evil is for good [people] to do nothing."

12. Always remember that the vast majority of Jews have nothing to be ashamed of, or defensive about, concerning our relationship with African-Americans. We were disproportionately involved in every phase of the civil rights movement, and even today more Jews support affirmative action than any other white group does.* For example, many Jews were at the forefront in opposing California's Proposition 209, which outlawed many forms of race-based affirmative action programs. The proposition was approved in November 1996 and is now being challenged by several Jewish lawyers.† We must maintain the moral high ground and never sink to the level of those bigots who scapegoat us. If the marketplace of ideas is kept open, our views will be heard and will prevail with fair-minded people, regardless of race.

Islamic Fundamentalist Terrorism and Anti-Semitism

Although the Mideast peace process initiated by Israel's late Prime Minister Yitzhak Rabin and former Prime Minister Shimon Peres has brought about a reduction in mainstream state-sponsored Islamic anti-Semitism by nations such as Saudi Arabia, Egypt, and Jordan, Islamic extremists continue to employ the rhetoric of classic anti-Semitism and to direct their terrorism against Israelis, American Jews, and others. Let there be no mistake about the anti-Semitic nature of much of Islamic fundamentalism, especially in its most violent incarnation. As Martin Kramer, a scholar at Tel Aviv University, wrote in a recent issue of *Commentary*, violent Islamic fundamentalism "could eclipse all other forms of anti-Semitism over the next decade."[60] These extremists target Jews, since they believe that the Jews are the enemy of Islam, indeed "the enemy of the entire human race."[61] As the leading spokesman for Hamas put it:

---

* 74 percent of Jewish voters surveyed in northern and southern California voted against Proposition 209 — which passed overwhelmingly, ending most forms of affirmative action in California. See *Los Angeles Jewish Times*, November 22, 1996, p. 9.
† Ironically, the leading proponent of the proposition was an African-American educator.

"We think the conflict between the Arabs and the Jews, between the Muslims and the Jews, is a cultural conflict that will continue to rage throughout all time."[62] This conflict cannot end, according to Islamic jihad, "until Israel ceases to exist and the last Jew in the world has been eliminated."[63] The Hamas covenant, published in 1988, characterizes the Arab–Israeli conflict as an irreconcilable one between Muslims and Jews and between Islam and Judaism. It quotes the following Islamic prophecy: "The time will not come until Muslims fight the Jews and the rocks and the trees cry, 'Oh, Muslim, there is a Jew hiding behind me. Come and kill him.' "[*64]

The language of genocide against Jews is common in radical Islamic literature. The Islamic Salvation Front, for example, declared during a 1995 demonstration in support of Iraq that "we are here to drink the blood of Jews."[65] Nor has the call for genocide been limited to literature. The alliance between the Grand Mufti of Jerusalem and Hitler during the Second World War was an attempt to implement the Nazi call for genocide.

Islamic anti-Semitism borrows heavily from the European genre, invoking the stereotypes common in Christian anti-Semitism. Hamas pamphlets describe Jews as "bloodsuckers" who "poison the waters, kill infants," as "thieves and usurers" who "manipulate the world economies."[66] Holocaust denial is also common among the most extreme elements, but even "moderate" Arab governments found excuses to ban the film *Schindler's List*.

As with the militia groups in America, the worst dangers come not from the rhetoric, but rather from the ability of small numbers of extremists to wreak havoc through acts of terrorism. Since 1990, Islamic terrorists have caused the explosion at New York's World Trade Center, conspired to destroy commuter tunnels in the New York area, planned to blow up twelve commercial airliners, killed and wounded hundreds of American soldiers in attacks on military barracks in Lebanon and Saudi Arabia, murdered nearly a hundred civilians in the bombing of the Jewish Communal Building in Buenos Aires, and killed scores of women, children, and men in assorted terrorist attacks throughout Israel and the world.

The State Department's report "Patterns of Global Terrorism, 1995" reveals that while "[l]ethal acts of international terrorism and

---

* In a December 1996 rally in Gaza, a large Hamas sign in English read, "We worship God by Killing the Jews." (*Boston Globe*, December 14, 1996, p. A4)

the number of deaths declined in 1995, . . . terrorism by extremist individuals or groups claiming to act for religious motives continued to
dominate international terrorism in 1995," and that Islamic terrorism
is on the upswing.[67] The report found that 45.2 percent of all "significant acts of international terror" had been committed by Islamic extremists, up from 31.5 percent the previous year.[68]

It must be emphasized, however, that Islamic terrorism, deadly as
it is, remains a marginal phenomenon. Although much of it *is* state-
sponsored, the states that sponsor it have themselves been marginalized by the international community, and even by most Arab and
Islamic nations. It is also church-supported, in the sense that important Islamic religious leaders are behind it, but these leaders
most directly involved in terrorism (and anti-Semitism) are also
marginalized.

There are, of course, several important exceptions. Syria is trying
to have it both ways. While sponsoring terrorist groups, President
Hafez al-Assad is also courting the West and seeking to become part
of the mainstream. Iraq, Iran, and Libya, on the other hand, remain
international outlaw states.

Perhaps the most frightening dangers lie in the possibility of fundamentalist takeovers in currently moderate countries, such as
Egypt and Saudi Arabia, which have powerful fundamentalist un-
dergrounds. Egypt's pervasive poverty makes it a more likely target
for a Khomeini-type "revolution," but Saudi Arabia's royal family
may also be in danger of losing the tight grip it has long held over
its subjects, despite the country's immense wealth. At this writing,
Turkey has an Islamic prime minister who was elected by a minority
of the voters, Afghanistan is in the midst of an Islamic revolution,
and Pakistan is undergoing some religiously inspired instability.
Again, the distinction between state- and church-sponsored terrorism and anti-Semitism and marginal, though dangerous, terrorism
and anti-Semitism must be kept in mind as we approach the twenty-
first century. (In Chapter 6, I discuss the dangers of Jewish fundamentalist extremism.)

Though American academia rarely tries to justify Islamic terrorism, widespread support for the Palestinian cause and considerable
opposition to Israel can be found there — especially when the right-
wing Likud Party is in control in Israel. There is also deep division
among Jewish students and faculty members over the best road to
peace. The emphasis should, in my view, continue to be on building

a consensus against terrorism, against efforts to deligitimate Israel, and in favor of factually accurate reporting on the Middle East, without trying to muzzle conflicting views on the peace process. We must also continue to condemn all manifestations of anti-Jewish views in the ongoing debate.

The Resurgence of Primitive Anti-Semitism in Russia and Other Eastern European Countries

Eastern European anti-Semitism seems to be the most enduring, resilient, and pervasive, at least at the grassroots level. Although dramatic changes in the nature of state and church sponsorship of anti-Semitism in Russia, Poland, Hungary, Slovakia, Romania, and other recently liberated nations have taken place, Jew-hating remains acceptable at even some of the highest levels. Undercurrents of anti-Semitism run through political campaigns, with candidates often pandering — sometimes subtly, other times overtly — to the old bigotry. For example, anti-Semitism has emerged as a potent force in recent Polish elections, as candidates accused each other of being a Jew. Aleksander Kwasniewski, a candidate for president in 1995, was targeted for this accusation.[69] In the minds of some Polish voters, when someone calls Kwasniewski a Jew, "he is calling him a thief or somebody who can't be trusted," said Kazimierz Bujak, professor of political sociology at Krakow's Jagiellonian University.[70]

"Anti-Semitism has always been a part of Poland's national tradition," says Konstanty Gebert, an expert on Polish–Jewish relations. "It surfaced in 1989, and there were anti-Semitic slurs in the presidential election in 1990 and the parliamentary elections of 1991 and 1993."[71] In 1990, presidential candidate and then–prime minister Tadeusz Mazowiecki was given a Jewish label that still follows him today. In 1990 then–president Lech Walesa told voters that he was a "real Polish man" — which was understood to mean a non-Jew — thus boosting his ratings.[72]

Similarly, in the Russian elections of 1996, anti-Semitic diatribes came from all points on the political spectrum, including the left-wing candidate of the Communist Party, Gennady Zyuganov, the right-wing nationalist Vladimir Zhirinovsky, and "centrist" Boris Yeltsin's former vice president, Alexander Lebed. *Newsweek* magazine reported:

According to Zyuganov, the real tragedy of the Soviet Union was that Joseph Stalin died too soon. In a 1995 book called "I Believe in Russia," he praised Stalin for abandoning a strict Marxist course in World War II in favor of "an ideology of patriotism," combining communism with Russian nationalism and Orthodox Christianity. "He needed another five to seven years to make his 'ideological perestroika' irreversible," Zyuganov writes. If the dictator had lived longer, Zyuganov contends, he would have "restored Russia and saved it from the cosmopolitans." That refers to the Jews. Although anti-Semitism is implicit in his campaign, Zyuganov seldom mentions the Jews openly these days. But in another book called "Beyond the Horizon," he claims that before World War II, Jews owned a "controlling interest in the entire economic system of Western civilization."[73]

Lebed made a number of statements during his campaign that appeared to reveal a deep-seated anti-Semitism. It was widely reported that "[a]t a meeting with supporters in Moscow . . . [w]hen a Cossack stood up and began to speak apologetically, Mr. Lebed stopped him [and said,] 'You say you are a Cossack. . . . Why do you speak like a Jew?'" It was also reported that Lebed publicly stated that "Russia has three 'established, traditional religions' — Orthodox Christianity, Islam and Buddhism — pointedly excluding the faith of the country's 650,000 Jews, who have endured fierce anti-Semitism here for centuries."[74]

Although news reports have suggested that the ultranationalist Zhirinovsky was himself half-Jewish, and although he has denied being anti-Semitic, he has repeatedly made statements with anti-Semitic overtones, like his recent attack on the NATO Partnership for Peace program as a "pro-American, pro-Israel, pro-Zionist" plot.[75] And during the 1996 U.S. presidential campaign, Zhirinovsky offered to cooperate with Republican candidate Pat Buchanan in deporting Jews from Russia and America, an offer that even Buchanan had to reject.[76]

In Hungary, recent elections have been marked by an outpouring of anti-Semitic graffiti and hate mail.[77] In the national elections of 1990, Jewish leaders of the progressive Free Democrats "were regularly described by their arch nationalist opponents, the Democratic Forum, as 'rootless cosmopolitans' — an old anti-Jewish hate phrase that attempts to paint Jews as people without national allegiances."[78] And in the 1994 elections, posters began appearing in Budapest depicting "an unshaven Jewish banker, ears pointed and nose hooked, with a Star of David on each shoulder ... hovering over a map of Hungary bound by a dollar-sign-emblazoned ball and chain" and announcing that Hungary was an "Interest Colony" of foreign Jewish banking circles.[79] In Romania, the parliament in 1991 "rose for a silent tribute to Ion Antonescu, who was executed after World War II for his role in the deaths of 250,000 Jews."[80] In Lithuania, the Nazi former chief of the Lithuanian security police, who was personally responsible for ordering the murder of thousands of Vilna's Jews during the war, was given a hero's welcome in November 1996, after he was deported from the United States as a war criminal.[81]

Now that the lid of the pressure cooker has been removed throughout the former Soviet Empire, private bigotry has been boiling over. Whether this proves to be a short-term reactive phenomenon or a permanent and pervasive return to the bad old days remains to be seen. What is clear is that without the support of the state, the party, the churches, and other important institutions, private anti-Semitism in the former Soviet Union and its satellites has been frightening but relatively toothless — at least so far. In 1993, a Russian judge ruled that *The Protocols of the Elders of Zion* was a forgery and that its publication by the ultranationalist Russian organization Pamyat was an act of anti-Semitism.[82] This influential fraud, which has been circulated in virtually every country of the world, has certainly come full circle, having originally been concocted by the czarist secret police and now being officially exposed as a forgery by the Russian courts.

Some church leaders, such as the Primate of Poland, Cardinal Joseph Glemp, are open about their primitive Jew-hating. Jews continue to be scapegoated for the transitional problems being experienced by countries trying to move from Communism to democratic governance and free market economies. But the absence of officially state-sponsored anti-Semitism has made at least one major difference: Jews are free, at least for now, to leave these countries, and many are doing so in response to the persistence of grassroots anti-Semitism. It has also become clear that anti-Semitism is not good for international business, and this new reality is creating an incentive for government and business leaders to do more to control the grassroots anti-Jewish feelings that seem pervasive throughout Eastern Europe.

Just about every European country has its own far-right party whose members hold seats in government, and even the European Parliament includes neo-Fascist representatives from Belgium's Vlaams Blok, Greece's National Political Union, Spain's National Front, Italy's Social Movement, and France's National Front.[83]

Again, we must monitor European anti-Semitism and insist that it not be legitimated by church, state, or other mainstream institutions. When a representative of any such institution — a priest, a government official, a business leader — is caught expressing anti-Semitic views, we should demand that the anti-Semite be condemned by the institution. Most important, we must remain vigilant that grassroots anti-Semitism never again become sufficiently popular, so that the churches and governments begin to support and promote it, as they did in the past.

In sum, there has been a significant improvement even in the bad news about the newly emerging forms of this oldest of bigotries. Most anti-Semitism today, as contrasted with the past, is not state- or church-sponsored; it is marginalized; it is directed at Jews because of our perceived influence as part of the establishment; and it is waning. Anti-Semitism is no longer directed against Jews from above — from the government, employers, universities, and other powerful institutions. Jews no longer must *apply to* anti-Semites and to *depend on* them for their employment, admission to college, or anything else of importance. This is in sharp contrast to former times, when Jews were beholden to anti-Semites who made some of the most important decisions affecting their lives. Today the occasional anti-Semite who is in a position of authority and who acts on his bigotry is the exception to a rule that can even be enforced legally in the United States and several other countries. Today's anti-Semitism comes from below — from those on the margins of society who have no real impact on the lives of Jews. We no longer need to look up to anti-Semites who wield power. Now we look down on anti-Semites who are powerless and marginalized. These ne'er-do-well bigots can be annoying and even frightening, but, at least at the present time, they are relatively toothless. This important change — from the elite and institutional anti-Semitism from above that affected the jobs, education, and daily lives of past generations of Jews to the marginalized anti-Semitism from below that has no such effect on today's Jews — explains the negative responses of the Dartmouth students to the poll question about whether current anti-Semitism will limit their life choices.

While anti-Semitism still remains a danger, especially if economic or political circumstances should deteriorate, our external enemies are weaker than they have ever been, and we are stronger than we have ever been. When I made this point recently to a friend, he reminded me that the Cossacks were peasants too. But the Cossack pogroms were *initiated* by the state and the church, whereas today's "Cossacks" are *opposed* by these powerful institutions. I am also frequently reminded of how successful some individual Jews were in Weimar Germany and France in the period between the world wars. But institutionalized anti-Semitism was still rampant in the church, the state, corporations, and universities in those days. That simply does not exist today. To ignore the lessons of the past is to invite their repetition, but to assume that everything that happened before will inevitably recur is to fail to understand that some things really do change for the better.

This important change in the nature and sources of anti-Semitism is the *reality*, and — perhaps even more important to the survival of Jewish life — this is the *perception* of young Jews today. They will not be frightened into remaining Jews by exaggerated accounts of our current victimization. They will doubt claims, such as those recently made by the Simon Wiesenthal Center in a fund-raising letter, that anti-Semitism is growing "more respectable," more "mainstream," and more attributable to "haters whose positions in society lend authority to their messages of hate."* Young Jews do not experience this kind of "respectable" anti-Semitism. They will not be recruited into the Jewish army that has forever manned the barricades against our powerful enemies, because they don't see any. They will remain Jews not to defend against persecution they have not experienced, but because, and only because, they choose to be part of a tradition and civilization with positive values that are meaningful to them and to their children. That is the Jewish challenge of the twenty-first century.

---

* The Simon Wiesenthal Center does wonderful work, especially with young children in California.

Chapter Four

The Dangers of the Christian Right — and Their Jewish Allies

IN ADDITION TO the continuing threats from our marginalized enemies old and new, there is one external danger that cannot fairly be characterized as anti-Semitic. Nor is its source necessarily an enemy, in the sense of someone who hates us. I am talking about the Christian right and its efforts — abetted by some Jews — to lower the wall of separation between church and state, to Christianize America, and, ultimately, to convert the Jews to Christianity. Like the other dangers we face, this one is directed at "the Jews" precisely because individual Jews have become so successful, influential, and mainstream.

My grandparents, all of whom emigrated to the United States from Poland, were very patriotic toward their adopted home. "America has been wonderful to the Jews" was the common refrain. Indeed, America has been far better to its Jewish population than any other host country in which the Jewish people has ever lived. This is not merely a reflection of who the American people are. The U.S. population, after all, consists of émigrés from many of the same countries where Jews have been long persecuted. For example, more Americans claim roots in Germany than in any other foreign country.[1]

There are three essential reasons, in my view, why America has been different from other nations that we emigrated to in the past. We must understand these reasons so that we can try to preserve them. This is especially important now, because each of these factors that have figured so heavily in why "America has been so good to the Jews" is being challenged.

The first reason is that America, unlike the other nations to which we emigrated in large numbers, does not have a *native* population — other than the one we tragically decimated and put on reservations. There are no *real* Americans as opposed to *others* who just live here. We are *all* real Americans, of differing religious and ethnic backgrounds. Contrast this attitude with those of the Polish, the German, the French, the British, the Ukrainian, the Russian, and the other hosts of the Jews throughout history. Jews lived in Poland for eight hundred years, but they were never regarded as *Poles*. Even today, Lech Walesa calls them the "Jewish nation" living side by side with the "Polish nation." Jews were never part of the German "volk"; they were never quite British, nor Ukrainian, nor Russian. But America is a nation of immigrants, and the recency of Jewish immigration is only a matter of degree and becoming even less important as time passes. (This "nation of immigrants" phenomenon also helps to explain the great successes, though on a smaller scale, of the Canadian, Australian, and New Zealand Jewish communities.) A very large percentage of all Americans have at least one grandparent or great-grandparent who emigrated to this country near the end of the nineteenth or early in the twentieth century. Whether one's ancestors came over on a boat called the *Mayflower* or one called the SS *Hamburg* may matter to stuffy old elitists who proudly display their "Mayflower descendants" wall plaques, but most contemporary Americans, especially young ones, couldn't care less.* A boat's a boat, and an American is an American.

The second factor, which is being directly challenged today, is that America, unlike every other country to which Jews emigrated, has no *established* church, no *official* religion. Judaism, therefore, is not merely *tolerated*; it has *equal* status — at least in theory. President George Washington assured the tiny Jewish community in Newport, Rhode Island, "It is now no more that toleration is spoken

---

* I also proudly display a certificate from the "General Society of Mayflower Descendants" on my wall. I bought it at a flea market for five dollars, and I have crossed out *Mayflower* and substituted the name of the boat on which one of my grandparents came over.

of as if it was by the indulgence of one class of people, that another enjoyed the exercise of their inherent natural rights." Jews were the equal of any other religious group under American law. It may have taken an additional two hundred years for the seeds of constitutional equality to blossom into the flower of real equality, but Jews were always better off here than in other host countries, where the power of the established church was enforced by the imprimatur of the state, and the Jew was by definition a second-class citizen *because* he was not a member of the state's official church.

The separation of church and state — which, in my view, has been the single most important reason for the success of the American Jewish community — is now being challenged by the Christian right as well as by the *Jewish right*. This challenge poses the single greatest external danger to the equality and first-class status of the Jewish community in America today.

The third reason America has been so good for the Jews is that American politics has always been *centrist*. Americans have generally eschewed the extremes of right and left and have gravitated toward the middle. This is not because there are no extremists among the American population. There have always been, and still are, fanatics of the right and the left. But the *structure* of the U.S. political system has marginalized the extremists, as contrasted with countries whose political systems have *magnified* their extremists. (Israel is a perfect example of the latter.)

The United States does not have proportional representation, multiparty politics, a parliamentary system. Instead, it has a winner-take-all, two-party, majority-rule system, with an electoral college, a Supreme Court with the power of judicial review, and other mechanisms for stabilizing the government, for marginalizing the extremes, and for moving our politics toward the center.

This system has been good for America, and it has been especially good for the Jews of America. History has demonstrated that although some individual Jews are always attracted to the extremes, extremism in politics has not been good for the Jews. We have too often been crushed between the red and the black.[2] Extremist left-wing politics tends toward anti-Zionism, religious intolerance, and denial of basic liberties. Extremist right-wing politics tends toward nationalism, anti-Semitism, and denial of basic liberties. The extreme left tends to demonize Jews as capitalists, rootless cosmopolitans, and tribal. The extreme right tends to demonize Jews as alien, radical, and un-American. Both extremes need scapegoats, and Jews have historically served in that capacity whenever politics has moved toward either or both extremes. Theodor Herzl recognized that when he observed:

> Is it not true, that the passions of the mob are incited against our wealthy people? Is it not true, that our poor endure greater sufferings than any other proletariat? I think that this external pressure makes itself felt everywhere. In our economically upper classes it causes discomfort, in our middle classes continual and grave anxieties, in our lower classes absolute despair. Everything tends, in fact, to one and the same conclusion, which is clearly enunciated in that classic Berlin phrase: *"Juden Rouse!"* (Out with the Jews!). [W]e are certain to suffer very severely in the struggle between classes, because we stand in the most exposed position in the camps of both Socialists and Capitalists.[3]

The traditional centrism of the United States is currently being challenged by some on the extreme right, as well as on the extreme left. The right-wing challenge comes from those on the Christian right who would move our political system away from the centrist influences of federalism and toward the devisive influences of *local* power. The more local the power — local school boards, town councils, and so on — the more insular and extremist the politics, since it is not subjected to the leavening and leveling influences of a larger and more heterogeneous community. That is one of the reasons the militia movement, with its emphasis on local institutions, including the Posse Comitatus, is so dangerous. Small towns that have few non-whites and non-Protestants will be less sympathetic to the feelings of Jewish schoolchildren forced to choose between participating in Christian prayer or removing themselves from their peers. A larger political power base, with a more diverse constituency, will be more sympathetic on this and other issues of importance to the Jewish community.

The Christian right has learned that competing for *national* office under our current political system was a losing proposition. Even if Pat Robertson (or Buchanan) could garner 25 percent of the vote, that would make him a loser in America. In a country with proportional representation and a multiparty parliamentary system, 25 percent would have made him a potential prime minister (or at least prime-minister *maker* or *breaker*).

The extreme left understands this as well. Jesse Jackson cannot win a majority of voters in a single state, either as a senatorial or as a presidential candidate. But he could probably win close to 20 percent of the national vote. In the United States, that makes him an "also-ran." In many countries with different political systems, 20 percent would make him a realistic candidate.

When Lani Guinier was nominated by President Clinton in 1993 to become the assistant attorney general for civil rights, this issue came to a head, since Professor Guinier had written articles proposing changes in our political system that would have brought it closer to those systems in which extremists enjoy enhanced power.[4] Many Jews were instinctively troubled by her proposals, though not all of them quite understood why. Their instincts were right on target. Guinier's proposals were good neither for America nor for American Jews, because they would have enhanced the power of both extremes in our political system. We are doing what is best for America *and* what is best for Jews when we seek to preserve our present centrist political system, which requires candidates to build broad-based coalitions, rather than to appeal to extremist elements within particular religious, racial, or other groups.* Were we to change our political system so as to magnify the power of extremists, the secure position of American Jews might well be endangered. We would see the strengthening of extremist figures such as Farrakhan, Duke, Robertson, and Buchanan. The greatest dangers would come from the Christian right.

I have deliberately *not* included the Christian right in my chapters on anti-Semitism, since I do not believe that most of its leaders are *motivated* by *hatred* of Jews. Many of them are stridently pro-Israel (sometimes for theological reasons) and sensitive to the history of Jewish persecution. They aggressively seek support from politically conservative Jews, and employ people of Jewish background as lobbyists, publicists, and lawyers. There is no question that *some* within the Christian right are classic anti-Semites, or that much of the

---

* I also believe the Guinier proposals would not be good for African-Americans, certainly not for the large majority of moderates within that community.

group's agenda is dangerous to the position of Jews in America. But that is different from calling it anti-Semitic.[5]

I believe that most of the leaders and grassroots members of the Christian right are not *anti*-Semitic or *anti*-Jewish so much as they are *pro*-Christian. Their pro-Christianity can often be quite parochial, intolerant, xenophobic, selfish, and unthinking. But we risk misdiagnosing the danger they pose if we lump them together with the primitive, Jew-hating anti-Semites of old, or with their contemporary cousins.

The stories of primitive anti-Semitism go so far back that several of them appear in the Talmud, such as the one about the second-century Roman emperor Hadrian:

A certain Jew happened to be walking in the street when the emperor rode by. The Jew greeted him.

"Who are you?" asked Hadrian.

"I am a Jew," answered the man.

The emperor flew into a rage. "How dare a Jew greet me! Let him be executed for his impudence."

The next day, another Jew chanced to be walking as the emperor went by. The man had learned of the fate of the first Jew and did not dare greet the emperor. Hadrian again showed his anger. "Who are you?" he demanded.

The man did not answer.

Hadrian then shouted: "What impudence of this fellow to walk past me and not acknowledge me. Let him be executed for his disrespect."

His counselors then said: "Sire, we do not understand your policy; yesterday a man was executed for greeting you and today another man is executed for not greeting you."

Hadrian replied, "Why do you try to teach me how to behave toward the Jews? Whatever they do is wrong" (Lamentations Rabbah 3:41).

Most of the Christian right cannot be accused of this kind of Jew-hatred.

Moreover, critics of the "Christian right" must recognize the catchall nature of this grouping. It includes a continuum of right-wing evangelicals ranging from the relatively moderate Ralph Reed to the extremist Randall Terry. In between are fanatics such as Pat Robertson and Jerry Falwell. It is important not to paint with too broad a brush. But it is equally important not to allow some moderate trees to obscure a radical forest. The thrust of the Christian right — especially in the statements they make among themselves and not to the world in general — is a fundamental challenge to the nature of American pluralism, as I will document.

The reason I believe that the Christian right poses the most serious external danger to Jewish equality in America today is that their agenda and rhetoric undercut *all three* of the basic reasons America has been so good for the Jews.

First, many members of the Christian right claim that *they* are the *real* Americans — the old-line Americans who were here first — and that Jews are guests in *their* land, much like the Poles, the Germans, and others believed. Listen to Lou Sheldon, the founder of the "Traditional Values Coalition": "*We were here first.* . . . We are the keepers of what is right and what is wrong."

And listen to Ralph Reed, the director of the Christian Coalition: "What Christians have to do is to *take back* the country. . . . I honestly believe that in my lifetime we will see a country once again governed by Christians . . . and Christian values."

And to Jerry Falwell: "I hope to see the day when *as in the early days of our country*, we won't have any public schools. The churches will have taken them over again and Christians will be running them. . . . We must never allow our children to forget that this is a Christian nation. *We must take back what is rightfully ours.*"

And to Pat Robertson: "The Constitution of the United States . . . is a marvelous document for self-government by Christian people. But the minute you turn the document into the hands of non-Christian people and atheist people, they can use it to destroy the very foundation of our society. And that's what's been happening. . . . If Christian people work together, they can succeed . . . in *winning back* control of the institutions that have been *taken from them over the past 70 years*."[6]

Robertson goes on to claim that "our nation's spiritual *heritage* is being systematically eliminated from the *historical record*," and that the real Americans are being denied an honest look "at our nation's past." In a foul bit of immigrant bashing, he opposes "anyone running the foreign affairs of America who speaks with a foreign accent" and asks: "How can anyone who spent most of his life in Germany or Poland fully understand the family life, the shared values, the history of free enterprise and free speech and the intense patriotism of [real Americans] born in Columbus, Ohio?"[7] Pat Robertson never met my grandparents. Indeed, one is entitled to wonder whether a parochial xenophobe who rarely spends time with Americans who speak with foreign accents can "fully understand" the diversity of American life, which is its true blessing.

And then there is Pat Buchanan, who no longer speaks of our Judeo-Christian heritage, but instead rails against the "across-the-board assault on our Anglo-American heritage,"[8] and campaigns with nativist slogans and symbols.

This kind of nativist rhetoric — which is being echoed by the current resurgence of xenophobia in Poland, Germany, and Russia[9] — pits the "real" Americans, the "original" Americans, the "Christian" Americans against these newcomers who would "change" the old system. Nor do the "originalists" try to disguise the identity of the newcomers who are endangering the original Christian character of America. Listen to Billy McCormack, Director, Christian Coalition: "[It is] the Jewish element in the ACLU which is trying to drive Christianity out of the public place... because the ACLU is made up of a tremendous amount of Jewish attorneys." Jewish analogies, and comparisons with the Holocaust, are a particular favorite of Pat Robertson: "Just like what Nazi Germany did to the Jews, so liberal [does he mean Jewish?] America is now doing to the Evangelical Christians. It's no different.... More terrible than anything suffered by any minority in our history." As Robertson made this point, footage of Nazi atrocities against Jews was shown on a video monitor behind him.

More Robertson: "It is obviously one thing to insure that the horrors of the Holocaust are never repeated again.... However, it is quite another thing for a strident minority within a minority of only 5,000,000 [here, there is no doubt that he is referring to Jews] to regard the expression of the deeply held beliefs of the majority as so repugnant that it undertakes the systematic vilification, weakening and ultimate suppression of the majority point of view."

Robertson also told Larry King that the "slaughter [of] a million and a half babies [by abortionists] rivals — it exceeds — the Holocaust of Adolf Hitler." Trying to silence his critics, Robertson repeatedly invokes the Holocaust by placing *himself* in the position of the Jewish victims of the Nazis. When he was attacked by an op-ed article in the *Miami Herald*, Robertson replied that the attack reminded him of his recent visit to Dachau. He accused his critics of reeking "with the stench of Fascism" and being "the spiritual heirs of Joseph Gocbbels." Then he asked: "Do you also have a ghetto chosen to herd the pro-life Catholics and evangelicals into? Have you designed the appropriate yellow patch that Christians should wear . . . ?" He answered these questions by telling his followers that "the same thing is happening to Christians in America today." Of course he is lying through his teeth: Christians are still dominant in every aspect of American life. Indeed, that is precisely the reason civil libertarians are concerned about government entanglement with Christianity in particular; there is no realistic danger of Islam, Buddhism, or Judaism becoming the Established Church in America. Nobody is claiming that America is a Buddhist nation!

Other fanatics of the Christian right talk about a "religious cleansing" in America akin to what is occurring in the Balkans and what took place during the Holocaust: "Just as ethnic cleansing attempts to rid certain ethnic groups and their influence from public life, so religious cleansing attempts to do the same with religious groups."[10]

These analogies to men, women, and children who were physically slaughtered are incredibly insensitive, especially in a nation where Christianity is the dominant religion, where every president is Christian and proclaims his belief in God, and where the Constitution and the courts vigorously enforce the free exercise of religion. The Christian right's attempt to wrap itself in the currently voguish mantle of victimization is a transparent one. Even some conservative Christians are sick and tired of this constant complaining by the most powerful religious majority in this free country. As one critic aptly put it: "The Apostle Paul would never have done such a thing. When the whole early church was being fed to the lions, they weren't whining."[11]

In addition to invoking the Nazis as an analogy to nearly every critic of his extreme views, Robertson has himself used language to characterize his opponents that is disturbingly close to the language used by the Nazis to characterize Jews: "[T]ermites don't build things, and the great builders of our nation almost to a man have been Christians, because Christians have the desire to build something. . . . The people who have come into [our] institutions [today] are primarily termites. They are into destroying institutions that have been built by Christians. . . . The termites are in charge now, and . . . the time has arrived for a godly fumigation."[12] Compare that to this criticism of Jews by German propagandists: "[Jews are] the eternal parasite . . . that like a horrible bacillus spreads more and more."[13]

In his book *The New Millennium*, Robertson specifically accuses liberal Jews of an "ongoing attempt to undermine the public strength of Christianity" by removing Christian prayers from public schools, and he warned that "sooner or later there would be a Christian backlash of major proportions."[14]

In addition to the Christian right's claim that Christians (by which they mean Evangelical Protestants who agree with their view of religion and politics) are the "original" and "native" Americans and that Jews are invaders out to destroy Christian values, they also seek to move American politics from the center to the extreme right by "[taking] back the country, one precinct at a time, one neighborhood at a time and one state at a time." They reject centrist coalition politics and eschew democracy itself as "the great love of the failures and cowards of life," and refuse to subject their version of the gospel to a majority vote. Unless a political system produces a "Christian politics," with exclusively "Christian values," and successful "Christian candidates," it should be changed to assure that "Christians" are elected and "humanists" are "removed from office," they maintain.[15]

The particular method they have chosen to subvert secular democracy is the running of what they call "stealth" candidates, particularly in local elections with traditionally low turnouts. Ralph Reed, the major political strategist for the Christian right, has described this technique as follows: "It's like guerrilla warfare. . . . It's better to move quietly, with stealth, under cover of night." He urges his candidates to wear "camouflage" in order to "disguise [their] position and [their] truth," so that no one can "see" them and learn their position. As to his own visibility, Reed boasts: "I want to be invisible. I do guerrilla warfare. I paint my face and travel by night." He even compares his methods with those of the Viet Cong: "It comes down to whether you want to be the British army in the Revolutionary War or the Viet Cong. History tells us which tactic was more effective."[16]

Reed's stealth candidates have been known to doctor their résumés, create fictitious cover groups, disguise their religious views, and generally lie low until after they have been elected. As one defeated school board member said of the stealth candidate who beat her: "The first time anybody even laid eyes on Cheryl Jones was the day she was sworn in as a board member."[17] Other candidates as well "came out" of their religious closets only after winning the election.

Stealth candidacy may be an effective tactic, especially in off-year elections for local school boards, where the turnout is usually around 15 percent of the eligible electorate. But it undercuts the very essence of democracy. As Ken Blalack, who has established a "committee for responsible education" to expose the Christian right's tactics, put it: "It's really the collapse of the democratic process if they are able to walk into office by lying and not saying what they truly believe." Most of these candidates avoid public appearances, refuse to fill out questionnaires about their views and background, and rely on flyers distributed in church parking lots. The end result is high *name* recognition but low *position* or *affiliation* recognition.[18]

This tactic does not work in national and statewide elections, because candidates for such posts cannot successfully hide their views. In fact, candidates supported by the Christian right have not done particularly well when their views have been known, since the vast majority of American voters believe in the separation of church and state. They realize that a high wall of separation is good for both the state and the church. Most Americans understand that the relationship between church and state in this country is quite positive: Freedom of religion — any religion or no religion — is guaranteed by the state, but the state does not support any particular religion or indeed religion over nonreligion. That is left to personal conscience. It "ain't broke," so most pragmatic Americans are not interested in "fixin' it," especially by destroying the public schools — which is an acknowledged goal of the Christian right.

At a time when ethnic and religious warfare is bloodying much of the world, America should count the blessings of the religious pluralism that has made this country so great and so stable. The Christian right wants to end all of this and bring religious warfare to our shores. Listen to Randall Terry's prescription for religious bloodshed: "I want you just to let a wave of intolerance wash over you. I want you to let a wave of hatred wash over you. Yes, hate is good . . . our goal is a Christian nation. We have a Biblical duty, we are called by God, to conquer this country. We don't want equal time. We don't want pluralism." Even the somewhat more moderate Pat Robertson sounds like he is urging a latter-day Armageddon:

> If Christian people work together, they can succeed during this decade [the 1990s] in winning back control of the institutions that have been taken away from them over the past 70 years. Expect confrontations that will not only be unpleasant but at times *physically bloody*. . . . Institutions will be plunged into wrenching change. We will be living through one of the most tumultuous periods of human history. When it is over, . . . God's people will emerge victorious. But no victory ever comes without a battle.

Let there be no mistake about the ultimate goal of the Christian right: to turn the United States into a *theocracy*, ruled by Christian Evangelicals. "We are talking about Christianizing America. We are talking about simply spreading the gospel in a political context," says Paul Weyrich, founder of the Free Congress Foundation. Pat Robertson is equally frank: "I believe that [Jesus] is Lord of the government, and the church, and business and education, and hopefully, one day, Lord of the press. I see Him involved in everything. . . . I want the church to move into the world."[19]

Lowering the Wall

As part of their theocratic program, the Christian right seeks to destroy the wall of separation between church and state and to establish Christianity as the official state religion. Robertson calls separation of church and state "a lie of the left." Falwell characterizes it as "rape [of] the Constitution." And the Reverend W. A. Criswell, the man who delivered the benediction at the 1984 Republican national convention, says there is "no such thing as separation of church and state"; it is "a figment of the imagination of infidels." Others regard it as "blasphemy" and a rejection of "God's law."[20]

Never mentioned by these fundamentalists is the historical fact that Thomas Jefferson borrowed the phrase "separation of church and state" from Roger Williams, who coined it primarily as a means of protecting *churches* against state intervention. Legal historian Mark DeWolfe Howe summarized the history this way: "When the imagination of Roger Williams built the wall of separation, it was not because he was fearful that without such a barrier the arm of the church would extend its reach. It was, rather, the dread of the worldly corruptions which might consume the churches if sturdy fences against the wilderness were not maintained."[21]

As Alexis de Tocqueville recognized when he wrote about "Democracy in America" in 1835: "State religions [may] serve the interests of political power [but] they are always sooner or later fatal for the church." He further observed that "religion flourished here because it had been separated from government," in contrast to Europe, "with its history of religious warfare and dying churches." Currently, as well as historically, the separation of church and state benefits religion in America. A greater percentage of citizens attend church, believe in God, and proclaim that they are religious in this country than in any nation with an established church- or state-supported religious education: "National polls on religion report that 19 out of every 20 people affirm a faith in God, a majority say grace at mealtime and 2 out of every 5 say they regularly attend services in a church, synagogue or mosque."[22] Garry Wills has summarized the contemporary relationship as follows: "The first nation to disestablish religion remains a marvel of religiosity."[23]

But this is not enough for the Christian right. These politically ambitious preachers want the power of government at their disposal both to serve their right-wing political agenda and to help proselytize for their God. They regard the establishment of Christianity in America as a direct order from God. They want to declare the United States a "Christian nation," governed by the laws of Jesus: "a Bible-based social, political, and religious order," in which Jesus "is Lord of the government." Some members of the Christian right even reject the concept of "toleration" of other religious beliefs. They want a theocracy "which denies the religious liberty of the enemies of God."[24]

The "battle" being waged by the Christian right is *not*, therefore, a minor dispute over whether there should be silent prayer in schools or merely a moment of silent contemplation, nor is it an argument over crèches and menorahs in the town square. These divisive issues are simply the tactical stalking-horses for a much larger war plan to turn the United States into a Christian theocracy in which Jews are actively proselytized and, if they do not convert, are deemed *officially* and *legally* to be — at best — second-class citizens, as they have always been in countries where Christianity is the established state religion.

In addition to demanding prayer in the schools, an end to abortion, and the denial of equal rights to gays, the Christian right also espouses the traditional political, economic, and social agenda of the Republican right wing, including tax reduction, the end of welfare, the rollback of civil rights, isolationism in foreign policy (except in the war against Communism), and the instituting of "law and order." Indeed, the Christian right argues that there is no distinction between the *religion* of the right and the *politics* of the right, since there should be no separation between church and state.

The point man for this merger between religion and politics is, of course, Patrick Buchanan, who is the darling of both the religious and political right. In his sermon from the gutter delivered at the 1992 Republican national convention, he declared war against those who disagreed with his narrow and bigoted view of America: "There is a religious war going on in our country for the soul of America. It is a cultural war, as critical to the kind of nation we will one day be as was the Cold War itself."

Whatever one says about Pat Robertson and others on the Christian right, there is no denying that Pat Buchanan *is* an anti-Semite, in one classic sense of that term. Even the guru of conservatism, William Buckley, has affirmed the inescapable conclusion that many of Buchanan's views are anti-Semitic. After a thorough review of Buchanan's writings, Buckley stated: "I find it impossible to defend Pat Buchanan against the charges that what he said and did during the period under examination amounted to anti-Semitism."[25] Buckley was referring to Buchanan's flirtation with Holocaust denial, to his false claims that only Jews wanted us to get into the Gulf War, to his description of Congress as "Zionist Occupational Territory" (a play on the militia movement's "Zionist Occupied Government"), and other such statements. Nor has Buchanan's fling with this primitive form of bigotry been merely a one-night stand. An admirer of

the Fascist leader Francisco Franco and the demagogue Joseph Mc-
Carthy, Buchanan has gone so far as to question whether America
should have entered the Second World War. He admires Hitler's
"extraordinary gifts," "genius," "oratorical powers," and "intuitive
sense of the mushiness, the character flaws, the weakness mas-
querading as morality that was in the hearts of the statesmen who
stood in his path."[26] It was these sorts of comments that led the *New
Republic* magazine to characterize him as "in a distinct sense, fasci-
sistic,"[27] and fellow conservative William Bennett to accuse
Buchanan of "flirting with Fascism."[28] Over a great many years,
Buchanan has been the mainstream spokesman for the lunatic fringe
Jew-haters of the right.[29]

It may seem surprising that many on the *Jewish right* are working
closely with those who would deprive them of their first-class status
as full and equal Americans. But on closer analysis, it is not surprising that two groups have lent support to the Christian right: the
Jewish political right and the Jewish religious right.

Around the time Buchanan was entering the 1996 presidential
race, a cover story appeared in the *New York Times Magazine* profiling
a group of young, mostly Jewish neoconservatives who are becoming
prominent in Republican right-wing politics. I wrote a syndicated
column challenging these young Jewish men and women — some of
whom claim to be committed Jews — to disassociate themselves
from and to denounce Buchanan for his anti-Semitism, his anti-
Zionism, and his overall bigotry:

> The young neo-cons profiled in the *New York Times* claim the
> mantle of decent conservatives, eschewing bigotry. If they were
> true to their professed principles, they would speak out against
> Buchanan. But I doubt they will risk their conservative credentials
> by attacking one of the icons of the right wing. Indeed, when in-
> terviewed by the *New York Times Magazine*, these neo-cons
> seemed willing to echo and justify some of Buchanan's bigotry.
> One was quoted as asking "What's the name of our Jew from the
> West Coast?" Another characterized "the typical New York Jew-
> ish view of the world [as] that people who weren't from New York
> and Jewish were unfortunate." A third opined that "deep down I
> believe that a little anti-Semitism is good for the Jews." And an-

other fantasized that "thirty years from now . . . Harvard Square [will be] filled with Christian students . . ."[30]

These mini-cons seem too anxious to avoid alienating Pat Buchanan and the Christian right.

Some of Their Best Friends . . .

The responsibility to condemn anti-Semitism belongs to all decent people regardless of religion, as William Buckley showed. But those Jews, blacks, women, and gays who share a conservative bed with right-wing bigots bear a special responsibility. Not only have most Jewish neocons not disassociated themselves from Buchanan, Robertson, and the Christian right as a whole, some have actively participated in promoting the agenda of the Christian right. In 1995 Rabbi Daniel Lapin and the Jewish columnist Don Feder spoke at the Christian Coalition's "Road to Victory" conference on the subject "Why Jewish Conservatives Are Working with Christians." Feder has been particularly enthusiastic in his support of the Christian right. He wants "to let conservative Christians . . . know you're not alone," and he believes that "Jewish conservatives are getting more organized, more vocal and more prominent in conservative organizations, including the Religious right." When asked whether most of the evangelicals want to convert Jews, he responds, "Of course they do. That's part of their religion. . . . That bothers me much less than people with no religion."*[31]

When the Anti-Defamation League published its well-documented report on the dangers of the Christian right in 1994, Midge Decter organized an ad deploring its publication and accusing the ADL of engaging in "defamation" against the Christian right. The ad characterized the ADL's criticisms as "mainly political" — a complete misreading of the ADL report — and went on to argue that Judaism is not "coextensive with liberalism." This is a particularly lame attack on the ADL, which is among the more conservative Jewish organizations and includes a large number of wealthy conservative Republicans. But the Jews who came to the de-

---

* An Orthodox Jewish supporter of the Christian right says he is "more comfortable in a group of evangelical Christians than in the average Conservative or Reform synagogue" (*Jewish Advocate*, December 26, 1996, p. 15).

fense of the Christian right — including Herbert Zweibon, Ruth Wisse, Bruce Herschensohn, Dennis Prager, and Irving Kristol — are among our most extreme political conservatives and certainly do not speak for the mainstream of the American Jewish community, which is appropriately fearful of the politico-religious agenda of the Christian right.

Perhaps these Jews are trying to work from within to help push the Christian right away from the anti-Semitism of Pat Buchanan and some of his cohorts. Perhaps they are simply opportunists, who see their fortunes tied to those of the Christian right. Perhaps they are just naive. Either way, they are playing with fire and brimstone.

The furor produced by the ADL's report succeeded in getting some of the more moderate members of the Christian right to acknowledge that they regretted some of their remarks. Ralph Reed, for example, admitted that he had said things in "the trenches" that he wished he had not said. He specifically rejected the concept of a "Christian nation" as being "a slight to the Jews" and affirmed his belief "in the notion that church and state should be separate institutions."[32] It remains to be seen whether this reflects an actual change in the Christian right's agenda or only a tactical retreat in light of public criticism.

The safety and equality of American Jewry require the preservation of the wall of separation between church and state. The importance of this abstract wall was concretely demonstrated in 1996, when the Southern Baptist Convention adopted a resolution calling for a major campaign to convert the Jews. The reaction of some frightened older Jews made me think I was in Spain at the time of the Inquisition. Rabbi A. James Rudin of the American Jewish Committee characterized the effort as "a spiritual attempt at genocide," despite the claims of the Baptists that they were focusing on Jews "out of love" and despite the reality that conversion in today's world must be voluntary.

Most younger Jews didn't care. I agreed with them. As a committed Jew, my response to the Baptist announcement was "Go ahead and try." I have no fear of conversion efforts by any church — so long as it does not have the power of the *state* behind it.

The Jewish fear of conversion campaigns is understandable, in light of the long history of *forced* conversions by churches that had the power of the state, the law, and the army behind them. The Crusades, the Inquisition, the campaign by Martin Luther, were all examples of attempts to convert by the sword or by the threat of state-imposed consequences. Even when threats of physical violence were not used, state laws that discriminated against Jews were often the impetus behind conversion. Benjamin Disraeli could not have become the prime minister of England if he had remained a Jew, since the law of the land required officials to be Christian. And Professor Chwolson could not have become a professor in St. Petersburg.

The repeated attempts to convert Jews to Christianity throughout history were the source of many Jewish jokes, such as the one about the priest who sees an old Jew hit by a car and rushes over and asks him: "Do you believe in the Father, the Son, and the Holy Ghost?" The Jewish man looks up at the priest and answers: "I'm in pain here — why are you asking me silly riddles?" Or the one about the old Jew who is dying in the hospital and the rabbi asks whether he has any last requests. The old Jew says, "Yeah, get me a priest. I want to convert." The rabbi is incredulous. "All your life you've been a Jew and resisted conversion. Why do you want to convert now that you are about to die?" The old man says, "Better one of them should die than one of us." My favorite is about the Orthodox man who pleads with God to prevent an imminent family tragedy: "God, please help me. My son is considering becoming a Christian." God responds, "*Your* son!"

Today in America, there are no state-imposed reasons for conversion. Our Constitution forbids any religious tests for office. Our laws bar discrimination on the basis of religion. Our high wall of separation between church and state prohibits the state from helping any church to secure converts.

So what do today's Jews have to fear? We can just say no. If a Baptist can persuade a Jew that his salvation is in Jesus, so be it. If a Jew can persuade a Baptist to convert to Judaism, so be it. That is the American way. Are we, as Jews, so insecure about the power of our ideas, our faith, and our God that we are afraid of a little healthy competition? To the contrary. There is probably nothing better than a good fire-and-brimstone sermon from a born-again Baptist to solidify the determination of a wavering Jew to return to his or her tradition.

My attitude is let the contest begin — as long as it is conducted on a level playing field, without the coercion of the state. The end

result, I am confident, will be a great deal of wasted effort and resources by the Baptists or any other group that seeks to convert us,
since, historically, few Jews have ever been won over to Christianity
by pure augmentation and without coercion.* Jews have always
mocked the notion that Jews convert because of the superior claims
of Christianity. Joseph Telushkin uses the following story to illustrate this point:

> Three Jewish converts to Christianity are sitting in a country
> club, each explaining how he came to convert.
> "I fell in love with a Christian girl," the first man says. "She
> would not marry me unless I became a Christian. I loved her and
> so I did."
> "I wanted to get a promotion at my bank," the second man
> says. "I knew there was no point in even applying for a higher po-
> sition if I was Jewish. So I converted."
> "And I converted," the third man says, "because I became con-
> vinced of the greater truth of Christian theology, and of the ethi-
> cal superiority of the New Testament's teachings."
> The first two men glare at him: "What do you take us for, a
> bunch of goyim?"†[33]

---

* The December 9, 1996, issue of the *New Republic* reports that Baptist efforts in
Savannah, Georgia, have produced no converts and that at least one rabbi is fighting back by seeking to convert Baptists to Judaism.

† "The word *goy*, incidentally, is not intrinsically disparaging; it is simply the Hebrew word for 'nation.' In a famous biblical verse, Jews themselves are referred to
as a *goy:* 'And you shall be under Me a kingdom of priests and a holy nation' (*goy ka-
dosh;* Exodus 19:6). In time, however, Jews stopped using the word *goy* to refer to
themselves, and it came to denote non-Jewish nations and non-Jews. The word also
began to have pejorative connotations. (In the 1985 film *The Last Dragon*, billed as
a kung-fu comedy, some of the action takes place in a noodle factory named 'Sum
Dum Goy.') Unfortunately, as the folklorist Gene Bluestein has noted, 'there is no
neutral term in Yiddish [or Hebrew] comparable to Gentile.' Hence *goy*, with its
somewhat pejorative connotation, remains the standard Yiddish/Hebrew word for
non-Jew. Some Israelis use the term *lo-yehudi* (literally, 'not a Jew') to avoid the
problematic *goy*. Among themselves, Jews often use *goy* to describe ignorant or
nonobservant Jews. Thus, in Chaim Potok's novel *The Chosen*, a Hasidic rebbe declares: 'Why do you think I brought my people from Russia to America, and not to
[Israel]? Because it is better to live in a land of true *goyim* than to live in a land of Jewish *goyim*.' " (Gene Bluestein, *Anglish/Yiddish: Yiddish in American Life and Literature*
[Athens: University of Georgia Press, 1989], p. 45; quoted in Telushkin, pp. 136–137)

My favorite story about arguments regarding conversion takes place in Verona in the fourteenth century, when the bishop orders all the Jews to convert or die. The rabbi challenges the bishop to a public disputation, agreeing that if the bishop wins, the Jews will convert, but if the rabbi wins, they will be allowed to remain Jews. The disputation takes place in a great stadium, but the din of the crowd is so great that it must be conducted in sign language. The bishop goes first and points one finger to the sky. The rabbi responds by pointing three fingers upward. The bishop then points to his crucifix. The rabbi responds by pointing to his heart. The bishop then holds up an egg. The rabbi displays an apple. The bishop shakes his head in defeat, acknowledging that he has been bested in the argument. The Christians all surround the bishop as he explains how the rabbi defeated him. "I pointed one finger to heaven, signifying that there is only one God, and all must worship that Christian God, but the rabbi reminded me that even we believe in the triumvirate of the Father, the Son, and the Holy Ghost, thus refuting my point. I then pointed to the crucifix, signifying that Christ died for all of our sins and that we must all acknowledge that God meant for there to be only one true church, but he responded by pointing to his own heart, thus proving that sin is the product of each individual's heart. Finally, I showed him the egg, which stands for the resurrection of Christ, but he displayed the apple, which is the fruit of knowledge, thereby proving that God intended for all human beings to seek him in their own way through their own intelligence. I had no answer for that stroke of brilliance, so I had to concede." In the meantime, the rabbi was explaining to the Jews what had happened: "The bishop held up one finger to ask for the debate to last one hour. I figured we should stall for time, so I asked for three hours. He then pointed to himself, signifying that he should have the last word. I wouldn't let him get away with that, so I pointed to myself, because I wanted to get the last word. With the ground rules agreed upon, we broke for lunch and he offered me an egg, so I offered him an apple."

Even Heinrich Heine mocked the disputations that occurred throughout the Middle Ages with the following doggerel:

This is certain: That whichever
Shall at last be overthrown,
Must acknowledge the religion
Of the victor as his own.

That the Jew with holy water
Shall be sprinkled and baptized,
While the Christian, vice versa,
Shall be duly circumcised.[34]

In light of this long history of failed attempts to convert Jews by argument alone, the Christian missionary groups would be better advised to spend their money and resources educating their own members on the positive contributions Jews have made and how much poorer a world we would all live in without the diversity of religious views reflected in this great country, where all are equal before the law.

The announcement of the Baptist efforts to convert me and my coreligionists made me appreciate anew the importance of the separation of church and state. If an established church in a country with no wall of separation had announced a campaign of conversion, then there would be cause for concern. But in America there is no need to worry, precisely because we have that high wall of separation between government and religion. Here we are free to educate our children Jewishly, to teach them how to resist the importunings of other religions, and to choose for ourselves — without any pressure — what to believe. No religion that is confident in the truth of its message should need the state to promote its gospel. Let the marketplace of ideas and faiths remain open, and let the state stay entirely out of the business of competing for souls. The Christian Coalition knows that it cannot win a fair fight conducted on a level playing field. That is why it aggressively seeks the support of the state. So long as the wall remains high, American Jews will be legally secure in their status as first-class citizens.

Paradoxically, that is precisely why some on the *Jewish* religious right support the Christian right. It is important to some of these right-wing Jews that American Jews *not* be secure and equal in this country. They, like the original Lubavitch rabbi, are supporting "the czar" — out of fear that Judaism cannot survive success, equality, pluralism, and acceptance. Those are the last things they want and what they fear most. Security and equality, in their view, promote intermarriage, assimilation, and irreligion. American Jews must always remember that "we are in Gullis," as an Orthodox friend recently reminded me, using the Yiddish pronunciation of Galuth — exile from the messianic promised land. "We shouldn't be lulled into believing that this is our permanent home," he cautioned me. "It is merely another way-station on our long journey back home." This Orthodox friend, a brilliant lawyer and liberal Democrat on most issues, favors prayer in the public schools, vouchers for private schools, crèches and menorahs in public places, and much of the rest of the religious agenda of the Christian right.

He is a successful and influential American — and a deeply Orthodox Jew. Yet he worries about the effects of security, first-class status, and equality on *other* American Jews who are not deeply Orthodox. He believes that a degree of insecurity, second-class status, and inequality is necessary both to keep American Jews Jewish and to remind them that their true home — the only place where Jews are truly secure, first-class, and equal — is Israel. In this respect, my friend is a bit like President Ezer Weizman, Professor Shlomo Avineri, and other secular Israeli Zionists of the old school, who do not want Jews living outside of Israel to become too comfortable. Most American Jewish leaders disagree. They want to have it both ways: first-class status and strong Jewish identity.

Nor are ultra-Orthodox Jews who share my more moderate friend's views risking much personally by encouraging such insecurity. They want prayer in the public schools, even if it is Christian prayer, because their children don't go to public schools, and they don't want *any* Jewish children to go to public schools. They want government aid to parochial schools because *they* run Jewish parochial schools, which they would like *all* Jewish children to attend. They want crèches and menorahs in City Hall because their children don't hang around downtown and they don't want *any* Jewish children to become too comfortable downtown. They share with my modern Orthodox friend a deep fear that if life is too good for American Jews, they will stop being Jews. They seem to believe that American Jewry *needs* enemies, persecution, inequality, lack of security in order to survive. They too are praying for the czar, since they believe that unless we remain *victims*, we will no longer remain Jews.*

Some ultra-Orthodox Jews view the threats by the Christian right to Christianize America as a positive development, because it will give less-Orthodox Jews a common enemy around whom to organize. At a time when institutional anti-Semitism seems on the decline, the Christian right may fill the perceived void for those who believe that Jews *need* external threats in order to avoid internal self-destruction.

This widespread attitude raises the most profound challenge to Judaism and Jewish life. That challenge is the theme of this book. If it is true that Judaism *needs* enemies to survive — if it cannot thrive on the security, equality, and success of its people — then does Judaism *deserve* to survive? It may require an overdose of chutzpah to ask whether a religion and civilization that has endured for 3,500 years deserves to survive, but it is a question that *must* be asked. I believe that Judaism deserves to survive, but *only* if it can persuade its people to remain Jews not because of its enemies, but rather because of its virtues. With any luck, we will soon learn whether we really do need enemies and persecution to survive. The twenty-first century may be the first one in Jewish history in which external enmity and persecution will not be enough to keep us together as Jews. It may be a testing time for Judaism and Jewish life — perhaps the greatest challenge yet faced by Judaism. I think we can survive this challenge as we have survived others. But we must understand how different this challenge will be — and how ill-prepared our long history of external persecution and victimization has left us to face these new internal threats.

---

* As one Jewish neocon said: "Deep down I believe a little anti-Semitism is good for the Jews."

PART III:

PROPOSED SOLUTIONS—AND WHY

THEY WILL NOT BE ENOUGH TO

PRESERVE JEWISH LIFE

Chapter Five

Go to Shul! The Religious Solution to the Jewish Question of the Twenty-first Century

THE PROBLEM IS easily defined: the Jewish presence in America is shrinking so quickly from assimilation, intermarriage, and low birthrates that American Jewish life as we know it may cease to exist by the third quarter of the twenty-first century. The causes are not difficult to identify: We have devoted so much of our collective energy and resources to sacred survival that we have failed to extract and convey to our children a set of enduring positive Jewish values that would itself survive our victory over our external enemies. Defining the remedy is far more complex and challenging. Yet this has not deterred well-intentioned Jewish leaders and scholars from offering a variety of solutions, usually reflecting their own role in the constellation of Jewish leadership or their own parochial perspective on Judaism.

The most obvious is the one proposed by most rabbinical and religious leaders: All Jews should "return" to religious adherence, and religion should once again become the central unifying essence of Jewish life. My son Jamin calls this the ReJewvenation Movement. This is the solution of choice not only for most Orthodox Jews but also for many Conservative, Reform, Reconstructionist, Havurah, and postdenominational Jews, who define "religion" in a more open-ended and mutable manner.* Another solution, proposed by Theodor Herzl and echoed over the past century by Zionist and Israeli leaders, is: All Jews should "return" to Israel and live Jewish lives in the Jewish homeland. A third solution, offered by many secular Jews, is to distill the moral essence of Judaism from its religious sources, and transmit it to our children.

The religious solution to assimilation is, empirically, the best for those who can be persuaded to believe the theology and practice the ritual. It is a fact — indeed, it is almost a tautology — that strictly observant Jews rarely marry non-Jews, almost never assimilate, and tend to have more children. The Hasidim and the ultra-Orthodox have it absolutely right — if the *only* goal is the perpetuation of a Judaism that requires the giving up of all involvement in the outside world.

When I lecture about the Jewish future, I am always asked some variation of the following question: "How can we make sure that our children and grandchildren follow in our footsteps and marry a Jewish spouse?"

I begin my answer by telling the questioner (usually someone my age or older) to stop patting our generation of Jews on the back. We aren't *better* than our children or grandchildren, even when it comes to marrying within the faith. Of course very few Jews in our generation married non-Jews — at the time, very few non-Jews wanted to marry Jews! Furthermore, most Jews had little social contact with non-Jews. It's easy to be "virtuous" in the absence of any opportu-

---

* Orthodox Jews believe in the faithful adherence to the established practices (laws and customs) of the Torah as a divinely ordained way of life.

Conservative Jews believe that Jewish law should reflect changes in society, in order to make Halakah relevant to contemporary life.

Reform Jews emphasize the ethical and moral teachings of prophets and rabbis as taking precedence over many ritual practices.

Reconstructionist Jews apply naturalism to Judaism, stressing it as an evolving religious civilization and spiritual nationalism. They also believe the basis of Judaism to be the life of the group rather than a God-given set of doctrines and practices.

Havurah Jews seek fellowship and an enriched communal life by gathering in small groups, for study and/or worship, independently or within an institution such as a synagogue.

Postdenominational Jews believe that the entire enterprise of dividing Jews along the above bases is counterproductive.[1]

nity to do otherwise. Today everybody seems to want to marry Jews
— except, apparently, other Jews!

How to Make Sure Your Child Marries a Jew

I tell my audience that there is, of course, one near-certain way to
prevent intermarriage. Suddenly everyone in the audience pays rapt
attention. Some even take out notepads and begin to write, as I describe the preventive steps that can be taken. Here they are — the
seven-step program to guarantee that your children and grandchildren will marry a Jewish spouse:

1. Move to a totally Orthodox Jewish shtetl like New Square
in Rockland County, New York.

2. Do not teach your children any English. Teach them only
Yiddish and Hebrew.

3. Prohibit all access to television, radio, movies, newspapers,
computers, and any other gateways to the outside world.

4. Teach the boys a trade in which only other Orthodox Jews
work, such as diamond cutting. Do not teach the girls a trade,
and do not let them work outside the home.

5. Do not allow your children to go to school with non-Jews,
and certainly not to college.

6. Teach them to regard all gentiles — and non-Orthodox
Jews — with suspicion, if not contempt.

7. Arrange their marriage and have them marry by the time
they are seventeen.

I then ask my audience for a show of hands as to how many wish
to subscribe to the seven-step program. Not a single hand is raised,
of course, because what I have offered is the Hasidic way of life. (I
also offer an alternative option to the seven steps: Make aliyah to Is-

rael — which is another way of living in a mostly Jewish world. A few hands go up for this option, but hands move more quickly than feet.)

Anything short of total control over the marital (and other) options will open the door to *some* degree of intermarriage. Even among the modern Orthodox, who live in Jewish neighborhoods, attend Jewish schools and camps, eat in Jewish restaurants, and have mostly Jewish friends, there is some small percentage of marriage to non-Jews. This results from attending non-Jewish professional schools, working in mixed workplaces, and other contacts with those outside the community.

My mother understood this situation well. She insisted that I marry my Orthodox Jewish girlfriend — whom I had met at Jewish summer camp between graduating from Yeshiva University High School and starting at Brooklyn College — before I enrolled at Yale Law School, where I would be exposed, for the first time, to mostly non-Jewish men and women. I strongly believe that I would never have married a non-Jew even if I had gone to Yale unattached, but my mother was not prepared to take any chances. She could not, of course, have anticipated that my first marriage would last only a decade and that I would again be single *after* having been exposed to the entire range of dating and marital options. My second (and final) marriage is also to a Jewish woman, but this time it was entirely out of choice. I *wanted* to live a Jewish life with a Jewish wife and Jewish children. That was important to me, not because my mother wanted it but because *I* wanted it. I could not fall in love with a woman with whom I could not share my Jewish passions and commitments.

But my mother *was* right in believing that exposure to Yale Law School and the world at large would increase the *risk* that I would have met, fallen in love with, and eventually married someone who was not Jewish.

The point is that all of us who don't live in a Hasidic shtetl and who don't deny our children the options that come with living among other Americans are exposing our children and grandchildren to the risk of marriage to non-Jews. The amount of the risk is very much a matter of degree. The closer one comes to living a segregated life, the lower the risk. The further one goes toward an integrated life, the higher the risk.

It always amuses me to hear expressions of *surprise* from parents who have chosen to live in non-Jewish neighborhoods, to send their children to non-Jewish high schools and camps, to have mostly non-Jewish friends, and to minimize Jewish observances, when their children marry non-Jews. I want to emphasize that I am not being judgmental. This is an *empirical*, not a normative, judgment. It is simply true, as a matter of observable fact, that a direct statistical relationship exists between the choices we make as adults about familial lifestyle and the choices our children make as to marriage partners. This is not to say that there is one-to-one correlation in any particular case between parents' lifestyle choices and their children's marital choices. We all know of instances in which the parents did everything "right" and the child nevertheless married a non-Jew. And there are, of course, numerous instances in which the parents did everything "wrong" and the child married a Jew. But there can be little doubt that over the large range of cases, a definite correlation exists between certain actions taken by parents and the marital choices made by their children. Young men and women who are graduates of Jewish elementary and high schools and are from families who regularly participate in religious activities at home and in the synagogue have a lower rate of marriage to non-Jews than those who are not. But children of parents who live a totally Jewish religious life and do not allow them to go anyplace where they might encounter non-Jews have an even lower rate.

Several years ago, I represented a Hasidic man from a shtetl community in New York in a federal criminal case. The chief rabbi of the community, who was an elderly man, sent his son to court to pray for the Hasid. (It worked. We won.) On the drive back from court one day, the rabbi's son, who was in his twenties, started to talk to me, and I realized that he could barely speak English. My client explained that the rabbi had decided that if his son spoke no English, he could never leave the community. I have no doubt that the rabbi is correct, as a matter of fact. Whether it is right to deny his son the tools by which he could choose what kind of life to lead is another matter.

The technique used by that rabbi is rather extreme. Other ultra-Orthodox leaders employ less extreme, but nonetheless effective, methods of protecting against assimilation. When my father died several years ago, the yeshiva which he had attended, and which his father had helped to found, asked me for a contribution in my father's memory. I made one and the rabbi came to my home in Cambridge to thank me and to ask me to make it an annual gift. He was the nicest man, and I knew that the yeshiva, called Torah V'Daas, which means "Bible and wisdom," had always been considered one of the best. But it had changed considerably since my father's days there. Now, it discouraged its graduates from attending college, even Yeshiva University, because in its experience, students who went to college had a higher rate of dropping out of Orthodox Judaism than students who did not. Those few students who insisted on college were told to go to Brooklyn College at night, to study mathematics or some other subject that did not engender conflicts with their Talmudic studies, to socialize only with other students who were ultra-Orthodox, and to continue their rabbinical studies during the day.

When I asked why these restrictions were imposed, I was told "They work." The proof was that recent Torah V'Daas graduates had virtually no assimilation, got married young, to fellow Jews, and procreated often. If that is the goal, then they certainly know the right means.

But how many Jews are prepared to live that kind of life? Very few indeed — and not only because it is too difficult, but also because, for many of us, it is wrong. Perhaps, in a sense, it is even un-Jewish to remove oneself from the outside world in which we are obliged to have a positive impact. One cannot repair the world by living outside it. Jews are not supposed to be monks, we are supposed to be messengers. We are supposed to be a light unto the world.

It is no challenge to remain Jewish when there are no other options. The real challenge, and one from which we must not shrink, is to perpetuate a kind of Jewish life that will be *chosen* by our children and grandchildren from among the wide array of options they will be offered in the rich and diverse American lives they deserve to enjoy. We must create a Judaism that is not afraid of the competition of secular success — a Judaism that thrives on openness, equality, and acceptance, rather than on insularity, insecurity, persecution, and discrimination. We must teach our children a Judaism that is compatible with secular knowledge, rather than trying to hide from it.

The best of modern Orthodox Judaism does not shy away from confronting doubts, skepticism, and the apparent contradictions between religion and science. Yeshiva University president Norman Lamm, one of the great exponents of the Torah V'Madah (Bible and knowledge) school, has written extensively and perceptively on these issues. He demands of his Orthodox students that they "work on the frontiers of knowledge, both scientific and humanistic, even though the doctrines and the inner logic of [these] disciplines may cause [them] to entertain certain religious doubts." He recognizes that this is "a dangerous and risky kind of faith," but insists that the risks must be taken if Judaism is not to become unthinking fundamentalism.[2] This is the kind of Judaism that frightened Rabbi Elchanan Wasserman into remaining in Poland and facing Nazi persecution rather than confronting the "freethinking" of Yeshiva University.

Lamm himself has explored virtually every issue of modernity, from existentialism to environmentalism to privacy to psychology to leisure to the possibility of extraterrestrial life. In his essay "The Religious Implications of Extra-Terrestrial Life," he sums up his philosophy of Torah V'Madah: "No religious position is loyally served by refusing to consider annoying theories which may well turn out to be facts. . . . Judaism will then have to confront them as it has confronted what men have considered the truth throughout generations. . . . [I]f they are found to be substantially correct, we may not overlook them. We must then use newly discovered truths the better to understand our Torah — the 'torah of truth.' "* There are no questions, regardless of how challenging, that are out of bounds to Lamm. I know, since I have asked him some. As he puts it: "Jewish religious leadership must not fear honest questioning. In fact, we may consider ourselves fortunate when we find the signs of doubt. Usually we meet nothing but a spiritual vacuum in our 'Jewish intellectuals.' Where we find questions, even of a hostile variety, Judaism stands a chance. Doubt acknowledges implicitly a faith-affirmation with which it is engaged."

Rabbi Lamm, and others of his movement, categorically reject

---

* Contrast this view with that expressed by Sheik Abdel-Aziz Ibn Baaz, who issued a religious *fatwa* in 1993 declaring that the earth is flat and that whoever "claims it is round is an atheist deserving of punishment" (*Dallas Morning News*, Feb. 18, 1995, p. 4G). This is not so different from Patrick Buchanan's refusal to credit the evidence supporting evolution and his insistence that he is not descended from apes.

the frightened isolation of the current Torah V'Daas administrators, who discourage all contact with modern thought. Lamm contends: "We live in an open, pluralistic, relativist society. Modern Orthodox Judaism can no longer continue to ignore this fact of life, and act as if instruction in religious observance and education in Talmudic law will, by themselves, keep the secularist wolf from the door.... [C]ommitted Jewish teachers must face the intellectual challenges of contemporary life fearlessly, without the improvising and dissembling that have too often infected so much of modern Jewish apologetics."[3]

Lamm also understands that Judaism is not static. He recognizes that "not all Jewish doctrine is meant to be applied in all historical circumstances, and that Judaism can accommodate itself to less than ideal circumstances — as it has done successfully throughout much of its history."[4]

We must confront the challenges of the twenty-first century with confidence in what we have to offer the world. We must not retreat into ghettos or shtetls. Nor must we shed our uniqueness and melt into someone else's pot. We must offer our message in the open marketplace of ideas. As with any competition, there is the chance of failure. But the alternative will assure failure.

Modern Orthodox Jews face this challenge squarely, and I admire them enormously for their willingness to allow their children to encounter and confront secular knowledge and education, in the full awareness of the risks such exposure entails. There is some marriage to non-Jews and assimilation among the modern Orthodox precisely because they insist on living relatively full American lives while practicing Orthodox Judaism. It is a matter of degree and of cost–benefit calculus. The ultra-Orthodox strike that balance differently from the modern Orthodox, who strike it differently from Conservative, Reform, and unaffiliated Jews. The resulting differential rates of intermarriage and assimilation should surprise no one.

In the end, however, the religious solution to assimilation — especially as defined by the Orthodox — will work for some but it will necessarily exclude the vast majority of young Jews most at risk, since so many of them are simply not religious by nature and are unlikely to become religious. We must not write off such Jews, since so many of those who have contributed so much to the world and to Jewish life have come from their ranks.

What Is Judaism?

The size of the contributions made by secular Jews demonstrates that Judaism has never been *just* a religion. Although Judaism began as a religion, it is, perhaps, ironic that many of the greatest Jews in history were atheists, agnostics, skeptics, nonpracticing Jews, secular Jews, and Jews who simply did not identify with the religious or theological component of Judaism. Recently I was asked to write an introduction to a book called *The Greatest Jewish Men in History* (it was a companion volume to *The Greatest Jewish Women in History*). After reviewing the long and diverse list, I wrote:

> The extraordinary diversity among the Jewish men selected for inclusion in this volume attests to the eclectic nature of Judaism, Jewishness and the Jewish people. If "Jewish" were defined as only theological or religious, there would be no place for atheists, agnostics or secularists such as Herzl, Ben-Gurion, Anielewics, Spinoza, Freud, Spielberg and Brandeis. Yet who could deny that these were not only great men; they were also great Jews. Their Jewishness helped to form their consciences and to inform their life's work. Though these men shared little *religiously* with other greats, such as the Biblical Patriarchs, Maimonides, Schneerson, Wise, Buber, Caro, Kaplan, Rashi, Nachmanides, Baal Shem Tov, and Soloveitchik, they did share a common history, civilization and tradition. Others on the list — Wiesel, Singer, Bialek, Roth, Agnon, Chagall, Oz, Shalom Aleichem and Wouk — have written about the varieties of Jewish experience, each from a different perspective, but each uniquely Jewish.
>
> The important point is that the Jewish experience from Abraham to the end of the 20th century has transcended religion and theology and has been as diverse and eclectic as that of any of the great civilizations. That is because, as Mordechai Kaplan aptly put it, Judaism is a civilization which transcends its religious origins. A compilation of great Catholics, Protestants, Muslims or Buddhists would probably not include as many secular figures as this book does. This list celebrates the diversity that *is* Judaism.

Some of these great Jews were, in fact, simply great people who happened to be Jews, such as Albert Einstein, Louis Brandeis, Franz Kafka, George Gershwin, and Camille Pissarro. Perhaps their Jewish backgrounds contributed to their greatness, but their greatness was achieved largely outside of Jewish life. (As Einstein once quipped: "If my theory of relativity is proven successful, Germany will claim me as a German and France will declare that I am a citizen of the world. If my theory should prove to be untrue, then France will say I am a German and Germany will say I am a Jew.")

Other secular Jews were, however, indisputably great as Jews. These include Theodor Herzl, Chaim Weizmann, David Ben-Gurion, Golda Meir, and other political Zionists. They also include some of our greatest Yiddish and Hebrew writers, such as Shalom Aleichem, Ahad Ha'am, and Nobel Prize winners Isaac Bashevis Singer and S. Y. Agnon. Many Jewish community leaders, philanthropists, and political and legal advocates in America and throughout the world have been secular Jews. Yet they have made undeniably important contributions to Jewish life. They cannot be considered second-class Jews just because they did not believe the theology or practice the rituals. Their Jewishness took other forms, just as the Jewishness of many Jews today takes different forms.

The diversity of Jewish success is illustrated by the story of the Polish shtetl that decided to send someone to America at the turn of the century to observe Jewish life and report back. The observer came back to the shtetl full of enthusiasm: "I met a Jew in America who had memorized the entire Talmud by the time he was bar mitzvahed," the man gushed. "I met a young Jewish man who at twenty-one was the leader of the Communist League of New York," he continued. "I met a Jewish man who by the time he was thirty owned factories and apartment buildings. I met a Jewish man who was married to the most glamorous starlet in Hollywood." The leader of the shtetl stopped him and said, "It is not surprising you should meet such Jews in America. After all, there are a million Jews there." "You don't understand," the observer replied. "I was talking about the *same* one Jew."

Another story that illustrates the "progress" of American Jews from the synagogue to the boardroom is about Yossel, who came to America penniless but religious and applied for a job as the shammes (sexton) of a small synagogue on the Lower East Side. When the rabbi learned that Yossel was illiterate, he refused to hire him. Desperate, Yossel bought a few apples and sold them on a street corner. With his meager profit, he bought a used pushcart, then a small store, and eventually a chain of department stores, which made him a multimillionaire. He is invited to the Harvard Business School to discuss his secret of success. In introducing him, the professor refers to the fact that Yossel — now Jack — still cannot read or write and ends the introduction with the rhetorical question, "Jack, can you imagine where you would be today if you had learned how to read and write?" To which Jack responds: "Yeh, I voud be a shammes on du Lower East Side."

Although a return to religion is highly desirable for those for whom religion is meaningful, there are simply too many Jews who cannot believe in the unprovable, no matter how comforting such belief may be. Would those who believe that religion is the only solution write off every Jewish nonbeliever and skeptic? Would they insist that all Jews practice the rituals without regard to the state of their belief? Would such insistence work with highly individualistic, intelligent, and principled young men and women? Can there be a Jewish "religion" that does not require belief in the supernatural or practice of rituals that presuppose such belief? These are questions I have been struggling with all my life.

I am a deeply committed Jew. Though I am also an American, a civil libertarian, an academic, and many other things, my primary identification is as a Jew. I believe I will always be an American — and I hope I'm not like those German Jews who believed before World War II that they would always be German. I believe that I will always be a civil libertarian, an academic, and all the other things that now characterize me. But I *know* I will always be a Jew. Most of what I have become has derived from my Jewishness: my values, my drive, my chosen life's work, my charity, my family choices, my approach to academic work, and much else. Yet I am essentially a secular Jew. My religious mentors tell me that my borderline agnosticism does not disqualify me from being a theologically acceptable — even Orthodox — Jew. Some of the greatest Jewish rabbis experienced doubt about God, especially after such tragedies as the Holocaust. All that is required, I am assured, is that

I continue to struggle with my faith, that I keep open the *possibility* of God's existence, and that in the meantime — while I struggle in my *mind* — I *act* as if God existed, and obey his commandments.

But I am afraid that I do not qualify even under these exceedingly generous terms. The problem is that I think about God only infrequently, and then mostly as an intellectual conundrum. God is not central to my particular brand of Jewishness. Even if a voice came down from wherever secular voices come down from and proved conclusively that God did not exist, I would remain a Jew. Being Jewish, to me, transcends theology or deity. Harvard is no less a university today because it has abandoned its original religious mission. And the Jewish civilization is no less a great civilization because doubts have arisen in the minds of many Jews about its original theology.

I suspect that many Jews — in America, in Israel, and throughout the world — who consider themselves and who are considered by others to be very Jewish share some of my skepticism and even agnosticism. Some of these Jews guiltily regard themselves as "bad" Jews, "fallen" Jews, "incomplete" Jews, or not even Jews at all. I think they sell themselves short. They are *a different kind of Jew* in a civilization that has always been diverse, open-minded, and eclectic. Throughout Jewish history there have been different ways of being a Jew. There have been Jewish warriors, poets, philosophers, political leaders, Zionist leaders, prophets, artists, philanthropists, scholars, and, of course, religious leaders.

Would anyone but the most insular Jew refuse to count Theodor Herzl, David Ben-Gurion, and Golda Meir among the great Jews of history? Yet what do we know about their belief in God or their private level of religious observance? They and other secular Zionists built a new form of Jewish life by abandoning the wait for a Messiah in order to rescue the Jewish people from imminent peril. They learned the tragic lesson of Jewish history: that they who count on intervention from the Messiah to protect the Jewish people from their enemies will await his arrival from the grave.

They found within the diverse paths of Judaism a way to help Jews now. That way became the secular Jewish nation of Israel. The fact that Israeli governments must occasionally give in to the political pressures of the extreme Orthodox minority does not undercut the fact that Israel is an essentially secular state that is respectful of

Jewish traditions, including religious traditions. Its inhabitants are overwhelmingly secular, though most Israeli Jews — like most American Jews — observe the major rituals such as the Passover Seder, the Yom Kippur fast, and the blowing of the shofar. If Israel can be *Jewish* without being *religious*, why can't other secular Jews who share much of Israel's Jewish ideology not also be first-class Jews?

Though I am essentially a secular Jew, I have great respect for religious Jews, especially those who think critically about their faith. When I attend the weddings and bar mitzvahs of my Orthodox friends and relatives, I admire the way modern Orthodox Jews deal with the conflict between their religious duties and their desire to live full and productive modern lives. Some of my Orthodox friends and relatives, who started with nothing, have become quite successful, despite the constraints of strict Sabbath observance, kashrut, and other restrictions. Several are serious intellectuals who experience occasional doubts and who struggle to reconcile their worldviews. They decline the simpleminded temptation of fundamentalism, which rejects any "knowledge" not derived from the Torah, in favor of Torah V'Madah — Bible *and* knowledge. Had I remained Orthodox, I would be part of that school, and I know I would enjoy the intellectual search for reconcilability between faith and science. I have enormous admiration for my friends and relatives who live with equal comfort in these two worlds, which to me are difficult to reconcile. I would never try to proselytize anyone toward my doubts. I envy those who have faith and who believe in Jewish religious doctrine. My life would, in many ways, be far easier if I were a more religious person. But unlike many of my Orthodox Jewish friends, I cannot act *as if* I believe. For me, religious actions must follow, not precede, religious belief. It is entirely a personal matter. Belief is not something I can attain through practice or ritual. In my worldview, you are either a believer or a doubter. I am a skeptic by nature, by training, and in attitude. I cannot suspend my skepticism when it comes to religion. I never could do so, even as a child.

When I was a young man studying in the yeshiva and I expressed skepticism about God, theology, or the rules of Orthodox Judaism, I was told to make "the leap of faith." Sometimes a teacher would try to "prove" the existence of God or the truth of the Torah by logical or empirical arguments. Though I continued to observe the rules of Orthodox Judaism for a quarter of a century, I was never convinced by these arguments. Still, to this day, I continue to think and read about the case for and against God, Jewish theology, and religious observance. I remain fascinated by the nature of the arguments and passions on all sides. Indeed, an Orthodox Jewish rabbi once told me that so long as I continued to argue about God — or, even better, *with* God — I could still be a good Jew, regardless of how the argument came out. It was in the spirit of this observation that in May 1996, I decided to devote a class to these issues in a course I teach jointly with professors Stephen Jay Gould and Robert Nozick. The course, called "Thinking About Thinking," deals with how differently scientists, philosophers, and lawyers think about controversial issues, large and small. Why not subject religion to the same kind of scrutiny to which we subject other major institutions and phenomena in our lives? With that in mind, we took an "outsider's" perspective on a series of questions, some of which are commonly asked, others of which are not asked often enough.

The first is a modern variation on a question that goes back at least to Aristotle. Does the existence and relative orderliness of the universe prove the existence of an original creator, as distinguished from a series of random and inexplicable events like the "big bang"? Many philosophers, scientists, and theologians have debated the issues implicit in this question. Some, like Professor Paul Davies, have concluded that the case for accidental randomness is so farfetched that other, more purposive, explanations must exist. As Davies puts it:

> I belong to the group of scientists who do not subscribe to a conventional religion but nevertheless deny that the universe is a purposeless accident. Through my scientific work I have come to believe more and more strongly that the physical universe is put together with an ingenuity so astonishing that I cannot accept it merely as a brute fact. There must, it seems to me, be a deeper level of explanation. Whether one wishes to call that deeper level "God" is a matter of taste and definition. Furthermore, I have come to the point of view that mind — i.e. conscious awareness of the world — is not a meaningless and incidental quirk of nature, but an absolutely fundamental facet of reality. That is not to say

that *we* are the purpose for which the universe exists. Far from it. I do, however, believe that we human beings are built into the scheme of things in a very basic way.[5]

Let us assume, for argument's sake, that the purposive theory (which, to my mind, is quite powerful) is more persuasive than the accidental theory. Let us even assume that it is "true" (whatever that could mean in the context of a debate that can never be conclusively resolved by any scientific method). What would the truth of the conclusion that the universe was purposefully "created," rather than accidentally "formed," tell us about contemporary religion? Although it would take us a step closer to the "creation" of the universe, it would certainly not prove the existence of "God," as religious people understand and act on that concept. The universe could have been purposefully created by evil, powerful geniuses from another "universe." Robert Nozick, in his typically probative manner, puts it this way: "[S]imply being the creator of our universe is not enough alone to constitute a being as God. Consider the science fiction situation of our universe being created by a teenager living in another dimension or realm, as the equivalent of a high school science and art project."[6] (In our class discussion Nozick gives the project a B–.)

Certainly the conclusion that the universe was created tells us nothing about whether it was created by one being or several. The case for the monotheism of Judaism, Christianity, and Islam, as distinguished from the polytheism of "more primitive" religions, must be proved independently of the case for creation as distinguished from random formation. I have never even heard of a compelling argument for why one God is empirically more likely than several Gods. Further, even if the case for a single creator could be proved, this would tell us nothing about whether that creator is a good god, an evil devil, or a neutral engineer. Certainly it cannot be assumed that a creator is good just because it is powerful. To confuse power with goodness is to engage in a variation on the naturalistic fallacy that can actually be disproved empirically.

Certainly there has been no positive correlation in human history between power and goodness. Indeed, the case for a negative correlation is quite strong. Lord Acton was surely correct when he observed that power corrupts and absolute power corrupts absolutely.

Nor does the goodness of the created product prove the goodness of its creator. To the contrary, if God's goodness were to be judged by the goodness of his creatures, our creator would get a grade lower than B–. Even if we were to limit the grading to actions taken or justified in his name, there would be little improvement, because they include the Crusades, the Inquisition, the witchcraft trials, and numerous other murderous and genocidal campaigns.

The argument for God's goodness is often made by focusing on the occasional goodness of humankind, or by our relative goodness in comparison with primitive, nonreligious, or nonhuman beings. But if all of God's creatures are his creation, that is a difficult argument to sustain. It is a bit like the argument for God's selective intervention, according to which all good results are attributed to an intervening God, but all bad results are explained by a nonintervening God. Another unpersuasive variation on this theme is that we mortals simply cannot understand God's ways. He is always good, but we do not have the capacity to comprehend his goodness. Under this tautological variation, we are to assume that the Holocaust was somehow good, but not in a way that we can make sense of. Nonsense. There is no meaningful definition of goodness — in this or any other universe — that would make the Holocaust good. Indeed, any creator who considered the Holocaust good would not be entitled to a claim of goodness. Put another way, if there were a God who created the Holocaust, he would be a bad God. He would be an even worse God if he considered his handiwork to be good.

There was, of course, a creator of the Holocaust. He was the most powerful being in the universe — for a time. He exercised greater power over the Jews of Europe than any deity did. He looked upon his handiwork and declared it good. He was Adolf Hitler — a god to some, but a devil to all good people.

Let us assume that we could get past all these problems with the notion of a single, good, intervening creator. What would that tell us about religion as a concept, or the major religions? Why should anyone assume that a good, intervening God would want to be prayed to or worshiped? Good people cease to be good when they demand unquestioned obedience or worship. We condemn powerful monarchs who reward and punish on the basis of obedience, yet we follow a monarch theory of God and religion.

But even if we accept this concept of God, why should we believe that he has chosen to speak to us through self-selected intermediaries who claim to have heard his voice or seen his miracles? Logically, there could be a God, but Abraham, Moses, Jesus, Mohammed, and all the others who have claimed — or have had representatives claim for them — to be his messenger, son, prophet, or what have you, could be wrong. After all, many other people have claimed to hear God's voice, and we dismiss their claims as either insanity or mendacity. The arguments for the existence of a single, good, intervening creator tell us nothing about the authenticity of any person, document, or event that purports to be speaking in God's name. These claims must be validated — or accepted on faith — separately.

Even if we were to surmount these formidable hurdles, how would we go about deciding among the competing and mutually inconsistent claims of Judaism, Christianity, and Islam (as well as others)? Can Abraham, Moses, Jesus, and Mohammed all be truly God's messengers, or must we choose one truth and reject the others as false? A Jew cannot remain a Jew if he believes that Jesus is God's son and that Mohammed is God's messenger. A Christian cannot remain a Christian or a Muslim a Muslim if they believe that Judaism is true, because Judaism rejects Jesus and Mohammed as in any way divine. Even if you accept all the other arguments, assumptions, and leaps leading toward a belief in a single, good, intervening creator, how does that help you decide whether to believe in the Jewish God, the Christian God, or the Muslim God (or the Jewish, Christian, or Muslim approach to the same God)? It is no surprise that very few people actually pick a religion; that the vast majority simply follow the religion into which they were born. Indeed, most religions define religious affiliation initially by birth, not by ideology.

Finally, even if one could decide which approach was the true one, how does this all lead to the obscure rules and rituals of the major religions? How would one choose among Orthodox, Conservative, or Reform Judaism? How would one decide whether only the written Torah is God's word or also the oral tradition as pronounced by the rabbis? What relationship does the existence of God have to the number of hours an Orthodox Jew must wait to eat dairy after eating meat? Neither Abraham nor Moses ever heard of such a rule. But some rabbi in the Talmudic period interpreted a beautifully ethical and compassionate rule of the Bible — Thou shalt not boil a baby goat in the milk of its mother — as requiring different sets of dishes for meat and dairy and a long wait (some say six hours, some say three, others say one) between eating meat and dairy products. An entire set of complicated rules has grown up around this distinction between *milchigs* and *fleishigs* and every Orthodox Jew observes them. I certainly did for twenty-five years, without having the foggiest notion why.

Even my friend Murray, who is Orthodox and strictly observant, loves to tell an apocryphal tale that burlesques the rule. God is reading the Torah to Moses on Sinai and he comes to the part about the goat's milk. Moses stops him and asks: "Does that mean we can't have a glass of milk with a steak dinner?" God repeats the passage: "Thou shalt not boil a baby goat in the milk of its mother." Moses asks: "Does that mean we have to have separate dishes for hamburgers and sour cream?" God again repeats the passage. Moses asks: "Does that mean we have to wait six hours after a hot dog for an ice cream?" Finally God, totally exasperated with Moses, says: "All right, if you insist, have it your way."*

Despite getting a good laugh from this story, Murray continues to observe all the rules, including another one that he loves to joke about. In this one Moses comes down from Sinai holding the tablets and proclaims: "The good news is that I got him down to ten. The bad news is that the prohibition on adultery is still one of them." As another Orthodox friend, Carl, recently put it: "As I get older I seem to believe less but practice more." Unlike these religious friends of mine, many observant Jews simply never think about these matters. They just follow the rule book. The purpose of my classroom discussion of religion was to get the students to think

---

* Ibn Ezra classified the boiling prohibition as an ethical rule nearly a millennium ago: "The act implies extreme barbarism. The mitzvah is placed in the same category as that of sending away the mother bird [before catching her baby]. In both cases the quality of humanism is stressed." Originally only milk-producing animals were included in the prohibition against eating meat with milk. The great rabbi Yosi Ha-G'lili ate chicken with milk. Only later was it extended — changed — to include fowl. Irving Welfeld, *Why Kosher?* (Northvale, N.J.: Aronson, 1996), pp. 129–30.

about the relation between the rule book and broader epistemological and theological issues.

After the class on religion, a number of very religious students — some Orthodox Jews, others Catholic, Protestant, and Islamic — came up to continue the discussion. Several thanked me for challenging them and, as one put it, "finally bringing into the open some of the questions I have been thinking about." They appreciated the integration of their personal religious views into the material they were studying in school. They all told me that their faith had not been shaken, but that they had much to ponder. For weeks thereafter, students dropped by to continue the discussion. In the end, the questioning confirmed, even strengthened, their belief. I had posed the questions, but they had answered the questions in ways that were satisfying to them. For me the questions are an intellectual exercise rather than a challenge to faith. Since faith is not necessarily rational, an inability to resolve every doubt would not necessarily constitute a barrier to belief. But nor would it create belief where doubt exists. I will probably continue to confront questions like these and doubts of the kind I currently entertain until I am incapable of thinking. And for me, there is no thinking that is not "freethinking."

When I asked one of my boyhood Brooklyn friends why he thought it was important for Judaism to survive, he did not even hesitate for an instant. "Because God ordained it." For my friend — who, by the way, is no longer Orthodox but rather a very religious and spiritual Conservative Jew — Judaism without God is unthinkable. For me, a Judaism that excludes Jews who do not believe in God is unthinkable, since so many "good" Jews have serious doubts about God or almost never think about him. Nearly a century ago, the Zionist leader Max Nordau said that "Judaism had become a religious community composed of Atheists."[7] That obviously overstated the reality, but it is true that many strongly identified Jews have had doubts about God.

I do not want to challenge God-centered Judaism. For those, like my dear friend, whose Judaism requires God, there are millions of pages of God-centered Jewish books, most prominently the Torah, the Talmud, and the remarkable and never-ending commentaries. I am addressing my thoughts, however, primarily to the millions of Jews who want to remain positive Jews and yet who do not often think about God, the Messiah, the resurrection of the dead, heaven and hell, and other theological concepts. We should not be written off as un-Jewish or second-class Jews.

We must recognize what Judaism is and is not. Judaism is a 3,500-year-old, ever-changing, constantly moving phenomenon that is impossible to encapsulate in a single word or phrase. It is not "exactly like" anything else. It is not exactly like a religion, such as Christianity or Islam. It is not exactly like a geographically and temporally bound civilization, such as the ancient Greeks or Romans. It is not exactly like a race or ethnicity such as blacks, Scandinavians, or Asians. It is not exactly like a linguistic group, such as Slavs or Arabs. It is not exactly like a philosophically homogeneous people, such as Kantians, Benthamites, or hedonists. And it is not exactly like a tribe, such as the Hittus or the Navajo. But nor is it exactly *unlike* some or all of these groupings. It partakes of many, but not all, of the characteristics of other groupings, and it has some characteristics that no others share, such as a common and unique history of persecution based on its unwillingness to accept Jesus or Mohammed.

Having recognized what Judaism is not, we must recognize what Judaism is. Judaism is a culture, civilization, and religion bound together by a common and unique oral and written tradition. We are the people of the book, a community of ideas, dialogues, poetry, prayers, history, traditions, and attitudes. We share a common and quite remarkable literature that is as rich, diverse, and influential as any other literature in world history. Jewish literature — from the Five Books of Moses to the Prophets, the *megilloth*, the Talmud, the medieval tracts of Maimonides, the Responsa, the Gaonic writings, the Hasidic legacy, modern Yiddish literature, and secular Jewish writing — has had enormous influence in defining Western civilization and the two dominant religions of the world. Much of Jewish literature has been irretrievably destroyed. But even what remains contains the wisdom of the ages (and inevitably some foolishness) on virtually every issue encountered by humankind. Certainly, Jewish literature is unparalleled in a comparative sense, when one takes into account the tiny number and percentage of Jews in the earth's history. But even in an absolute sense, the influence of Jewish literature — in both the written and oral tradition — has been massive.

Though Rabbi Mordechai Kaplan was surely correct in arguing

that Judaism, in addition to being a religion, is also a civilization, it is not a *singular* civilization.[8] It is a series of ever-changing, loosely connected, and disparate civilizations. Since its geographically circumscribed tribal beginnings some 3,500 years ago, Judaism has undergone so many transformations that today's Jewish communities bear scant resemblance to their biblical forebears. Not only has the *substance* of Judaism changed, the very notion of *what kind of phenomenon* Judaism is has changed. Over the course of these transformations, many Jewish civilizations have died out, others have been born, and still others are now in the process of gestation — a process that always carries the risk of miscarriage or even abortion.

During this century alone, we have witnessed the final demise of at least two major Jewish civilizations that had existed for centuries. The Jewish communities of the Arabic nations — the Jews of Baghdad, Aleppo, and Alexandria — constituted a great civilization that began more than two thousand years ago. It shared a common religious, linguistic, geographical, and cultural heritage. But that civilization ended on Passover of 1994, when Damascus's last remnants of this Jewish community — which, according to Rabbi Ibrihim Hamra, "is as old as Damascus itself" — abandoned their ancient home. The community, which numbered 100,000 at the turn of the century, has now dwindled to a few old Jews left to fill the two dozen synagogues that are spread through the city's Jewish quarter.[9] Most are moving to Brooklyn, where they have relatives and where there are synagogues that will continue some of the Damascus traditions. But it will never be the same. The next generation will attend American schools, marry American spouses, adopt American Jewish folkways, and become part of the heterogeneous and quickly changing American Jewish community.

The Damascus Jewish community was the last of the Arabic Jewish communities to uproot itself since the establishment of Israel in 1948. The Jewish communities that used to inhabit Arabic cities and now populate Israel, France, and the United States still maintain a sense of continuity with their old civilization, but they will not be able to replicate and transmit it in the different locations and cultures in which they now live. They may sing the old songs of the old land, but they are not creating new ones. For a civilization to persist, it cannot rely on nostalgia for the past; it must be creating new folkways to the future.

The other great Jewish civilization that ended during this century was the Yiddish civilization of Eastern Europe, which went back almost a thousand years. It, too, developed its own unique dialect, religious traditions, music, and culture. It, too, survives in part through communities of descendants in Israel and the United States. Hasidic sects — Lubavitch, Bubov, Satmar, Munkatch — have made poignant and heroic efforts to re-create the past, by building communities modeled loosely on the shtetls of Eastern Europe from which they emigrated. They speak the Yiddish of Eastern Europe, wear the clothing of their ancestors, and replicate their strict religious observance. But they are not a civilization, like their forebears were. They, too, are statically replicating a part of the past rather than dynamically creating a future.

But even if the Hasidic Yiddish civilization of Eastern Europe is not dead, surely the *secular* Yiddish civilization is irretrievably gone. When Isaac Bashevis Singer died in 1991, it was widely acknowledged that he was the last of the great Yiddish literary figures. Most contemporary American Jews do not even realize that there once existed — indeed thrived — a Yiddish culture that was essentially secular. It was political, literary, musical, artistic, economic, culinary, and even military. It drew much of its inspiration from Jewish religious traditions, but many of its most eminent participants were atheists, agnostics, or simply unconcerned about religious observance or theology. There has been something of a revival of interest in the secular Yiddish civilization, including at the university level, but it is a historical and nostalgic interest, rather than a serious attempt to re-create the civilization in a contemporary context. Genuine civilizations can rarely be uprooted and transplanted from the surroundings and conditions that gave rise to their most salient characteristics.

The creation of an entirely new Jewish civilization — Israel — is a perfect example of this phenomenon. Israel's roots lie deep in Jewish religious tradition. The return to Zion was the hope of every religious Jew, expressed daily in prayers. But the dream would probably not have been realized without the demise of the European Yiddish civilization and Arabic Ladino civilizations of North Africa, Yemen, Iraq, and Syria. The population of Israel consists largely of the survivors of the Holocaust and the Jewish populations transferred from Arabic lands — and now, of course, their descendants. In recent years, the remnants of dead and dying Jewish civilizations from Ethiopia, Russia, and Persia have been ingathered to Zion, as have Jews from the former Yugoslavia and other places of conflict. An entirely new Jewish civilization — largely secular Israel — has been created and is producing its own unique language, literature, music, art, and personality.

The language is Israeli Hebrew — as close to and distant from biblical and prayer-book Hebrew as modern Italian is from the Latin of the mass. The music is largely derivative — at the moment — from the melodies of Arab lands, Eastern Europe, and contemporary popular culture, though the Israeli spirit and experience are infused throughout. The food, too, combines influences from Arabic, Polish, and other cultures.

But the personality is uniquely Israeli, with little of the European guilt or the Arabic passivity. Native-born Israelis are called Sabras, from *sabhár* (prickly pear), the desert fruit that is supposed to reflect the Israeli character: sharp on the outside, sweet on the inside. The classic joke to illustrate the abrasive Israeli personality is about the pollster who confronts four people from different countries on a street corner with: "Excuse me, what is your opinion on the meat shortage?" They all look confused by the question. The American asks, "What does *shortage* mean?" The Chinese asks, "What does *opinion* mean?" The Ethiopian asks, "What does *meat* mean?" And the Israeli asks, "What does *excuse me* mean?"

When my book *Chutzpah* was being translated into Hebrew, the editors were reluctant to use the original title, since in Israeli Hebrew — as distinguished from in "Yinglish" — *chutzpah* has an entirely negative connotation.[10] A *chutzpan* or a *baal chutzpah* is "an impossibly pushy, arrogant, and presumptuous person" in Israel, as contrasted with a *chutzpahnik*, who is a somewhat more endearing character in the Yiddish-American context. The Israeli editors thought the Hebrew slang term *baitzim* would more aptly suggest the quality of *chutzpah* — assertiveness — that I intended to convey. *Baitzim*, which literally means "eggs," is akin in colloquial Hebrew to "balls" or "ballsy." Although we eventually stuck with the original title, this vignette brought home to me the irony of the Israeli national personality, which can aptly be characterized as *chutzpahdik*, but which attaches entirely negative connotations to that term.* No one can doubt that contemporary Israel is a new Jewish civilization, built on the cultural DNA of previous Jewish civilizations that have passed through the cycle of birth, development, maturity, and death.

Is the American Jewish community a unique civilization? And if so, is it beginning its decline toward death? And if it were to die, would its cultural DNA provide the building blocks for yet another new Jewish civilization? Or will its death be an ending with no new beginnings — just a disappearance, with neither bang nor whimper nor even notice? And if the American Jewish "civilization" were to disappear, would that mark the beginning of the end for Judaism throughout the world? Could Israel survive the death of the American Jewish community? Would the world be a poorer place without the American Jewish community? Can anything be done to prevent or slow down its demise? Or do civilizations have their own internal and immutable dynamics? These are among the questions many Jews are asking these days.

The one answer that is crystal clear is that the American Jewish community of the twenty-first century will be markedly different from any other Jewish community in history. The challenge is to adapt to changing circumstances — indeed, to harness the inevitable changes in a constructively Jewish way so that we control our future instead of letting it control us. We can help make it either better or worse — by our action or inaction.

Throughout Jewish history, several central factors have given Judaism the characteristics of a civilization. Up until the nineteenth-century Enlightenment, Jews shared almost all the characteristics of a civilization. Jews lived together in shtetls or neighborhoods. Jews spoke a common dialect, either Yiddish or Ladino. Jews practiced a common religion, Orthodox Judaism of the Ashkenazic or Sephardic style. Jews shared a common destiny of persecution by the church, by the state, and by society. All that Jews lacked was a nation-state, and they aspired to a return to Zion as part of a religio-nationalistic creed.

---

* A student once told me he had heard someone use a "terrible" word about me. I asked him what the word was, and he said, "*chutzpah*dick," thinking it a reference to the male anatomy. *Chutzpahdik* is simply an action embodying the quality of chutzpah.

Now everything has changed. The shtetls are long gone, and even voluntary Jewish neighborhoods are quickly becoming a thing of the past for most non-Orthodox and secular Jews. Thus a common geography no longer characterizes most Jews who live outside Israel, and this lack of a common geography will become even more evident in the coming century as American Jews spread throughout the country.

Yiddish, which provided *all* European Jews, even the most secular, with a common medium of communication, is no longer a living language. The loss of Yiddish as the cement of the European and early-twentieth-century American Jewish civilization is often underestimated. Between the beginning of the Enlightenment and the Second World War, it was primarily the Yiddish language that maintained the Jewish civilization. Even secular Jews who left the shtetls wrote in Yiddish. Virtually every Jew could read or listen to Yiddish poetry, Yiddish revolutionary tracts, Yiddish religious books, Yiddish atheist manifestos, Yiddish theater, Yiddish music — yes, even Yiddish pornography. There were hundreds of Yiddish newspapers and magazines reflecting every conceivable point of view. Yiddish was the living dialect of a diverse and ever-changing civilization. Even non-Jews who lived in Jewish neighborhoods spoke some Yiddish, as evidenced by an encounter between my mother and General Colin Powell several years ago at an event where he and I were both being honored. My mother went over to General Powell and said "I hear you speak Yiddish." General Powell replied that although he had worked for a Yiddish-speaking store owner when he was a kid, he did not speak Yiddish himself. Then he paused, put his arm around my mother's shoulder and whispered, "Epis, a bissle," which is Yiddish for "Maybe a little." An old joke is premised on the phenomenon of non-Jews learning Yiddish. It is about the Chinese man who works as a waiter in a Jewish deli and learns to speak fluent Yiddish. A customer calls the owner over and asks, "How did you get him to learn Yiddish?" The owner says, "Shh, don't let him hear you. He thinks I'm teaching him English."

The diversity of Yiddish was brought home to me several years ago, when Isaac Bashevis Singer and I were honored at the Brooklyn College graduation. I was thrilled to be in such wonderful company, and I invited my entire family to the luncheon following the presentation of the honors. I thought that my Orthodox relatives, who spoke Yiddish, would love to meet the greatest Yiddish author then alive. I was shocked to learn that several of the most Orthodox had nothing but disdain for Singer. "He writes in Yiddish," they explained, "but he writes about Jewish prostitutes, gamblers, and apikorsim [heretics]." They wanted no part of *his* Yiddish. Having been brought up in America, I had always thought of Yiddish as a *religious* language, spoken by devoutly Orthodox older Jews like my grandparents. But it was the street language — the *Mamah loshen*, literally the mother tongue — of the Jewish people of Europe and America. Even today, Yiddish is the street language of Hasidic Jews, who regard Hebrew as *loshen Kodesh*, a holy language. This dichotomy was brought home to my wife and me a few years ago on Rosh Hashanah, when we went to Borough Park to spend the holiday with my mother. We were walking down Forty-eighth Street in front of the headquarters of the Bubov Hasidic sect about an hour before the beginning of the evening prayers which would begin the new year. Young Hasidic children, dressed in black and sporting long earlocks, were throwing a *spaldeen*, or rubber ball, just as I had done on the same street forty-five years earlier. I stopped for a nostalgic glance. Suddenly, I heard something that shocked me. One of the Hasidic kids was yelling to another: "Varf mir di fucken pilke" ("Throw me the fucking ball"). Yiddish — or Yinglish, as it has come to be — is still truly a street language for these Hasidic kids. They would never think of using the F-word in a Hebrew sentence. This, of course, is different in Israel. The street language of Israelis is Hebrew. I can recall my own sense of surprise when one of my articles appeared in the Israeli version of *Penthouse* magazine and I was sent a copy. The juxtaposition of Hebrew — which for me is still primarily the language of prayer — with naked women (Jewish ones to boot!) created a cognitive dissonance. Language is crucial as a unifier of most civilizations, and the Jewish civilization outside Israel is quickly losing its common language, except at prayer, and even at prayer most Jews are only marginally literate.

Religion, as well, is a common characteristic of many civilizations. But as Jews become increasingly secular, this common characteristic is also receding. Jews know they have a different religion, but many don't practice it, except a few days of the year, and not many know how it differs from other mainstream religions. Ultra-Orthodox Jews look different from Christians, with their *payis* (side locks), *straimals* (fur hats), *gartels* (sashes), *tzitzis* (fringes), and all-black attire. Indeed, in Israel they are called "blacks," or *shvartzes*, because of the color of their "uniforms." They also pray differently, shaking back and forth and emitting emotional sounds. But most other Jews look like Christians and even pray like many Christians, in temples that are barely distinguishable from Methodist churches. To be sure, we have our unique symbols: the shofar, the sukkah, the matzo, the menorah, and others. But these are once-a-year paraphernalia, which have analogues in other religions, and most Jews do not even understand their religious significance beyond the superficial stories attached to them in the popular culture. Indeed, for many Jews the only factor that distinguishes Judaism from Christianity is a negative one: We *reject* Jesus as the Messiah. That is why we are so appalled by "Jews for Jesus." In addition to their often misleading proselytization, they also shove in our faces the uncomfortable fact that it is *only* the rejection of Jesus as Christ that really distinguishes most Jews from many mainline Christians. A common religion is becoming decreasingly important as a characteristic of the Jewish civilization in this age of homogenized, Americanized, do-gooder religions. Indeed, it is fair to say that most American Jews, outside of the Orthodox, seem to have more in common even religiously with mainline Protestants than they do with ultra-Orthodox Hasidim. They share the commitment to "love thy neighbor" and other virtues of the "American" religion.

Nor do we still share a common destiny of persecution by the church, the state, and society. As Leonard Fein perceptively put it: "Destiny is something that happens *to* you, a course of events beyond your control, and common destiny is exactly what we may hope the Jewish people does not have, given what it is likely to be."[11] While anti-Semitism persists, it has become more marginalized. It is not a powerful enough force to keep us together as a civilization, and with any luck, it will weaken even more in the future.

What, then, do we have left? Our one *new* characteristic as a civilization is the nation-state of Israel. But most of us do not live in that nation-state, although we identify strongly with it. And even that identification is strongest during times of crises. Will the prospect of peace in the Middle East — and the divisions it has engendered within the American Jewish community — make Israel less important as a uniting characteristic of the American Jewish civilization? And even if Israel were to retain its current role as a uniting factor for Jews, can a distant land to which few Jews want to move serve as an important enough uniting factor to preserve Judaism as a civilization?

For those who believe that after all is said and done, religion must remain the common characteristic of Judaism, the question remains, Which variation on the common theme? It certainly will not be ultra-Orthodoxy, since very few Jews want to retreat so far into the past. Only if the Jewish religion becomes sufficiently eclectic, so that it can adapt to the full lives that most American Jews insist on living, will religion have any chance of remaining a unifying phenomenon in the twenty-first century. From its earliest beginnings, Judaism the religion has always changed to adapt to the changing circumstances in which Jews have found themselves, while trying hard to deny that it is changing, so that the traditions can be maintained.

During the past 1,500 or so years, one particular form of Judaism has taken hold: rabbinic Judaism, as reflected by Halakah, which in Hebrew means the *single* road. But even this single road has always had numerous byways. Traditional rabbinic Judaism — with its emphasis on insularity, rabbinic authority, ritual, and community — was adaptive to the life of the shtetl. Surrounded by hostile hosts, threatened by armed enemies, and struggling with physical survival, the Jewish religion required insularity and the promise of a messianic age, with reward in the life to come: Our tsuris will pass, and life will become better — if not in this lifetime, then in some other time and place.

Since the Jews had no state of their own, the rabbinic authorities, or their designees, became the *political* as well as religious leaders of the Jewish communities — to the extent that such a distinction even existed.[12] A wonderful literature — some written, some oral — developed from this necessity. An evolving law, called the Responsa, emerged. Rabbis were asked questions of all kinds. Their answers were collected and served as a "common law" of Jewish life. The questions were mostly practical, often concerning ritual. But some were spiritual, economic, and legal. Some of the Responsa that have survived are among the most brilliant, innovative, and insightful commentaries on the various ages and places they represent. (As might be expected of the very human rabbis who wrote them, there are also some uninspired and trivial answers reflecting the biases of that day.)*

One of my favorite stories from the Talmud reflects the double-edged nature of rabbinic Judaism. It is the account of the dispute between Rabbi Eliezer ben Hyrcanus (a brilliant, cantankerous, and thoroughly sexist rabbi who lived at the beginning of the second century A.D.) and the other members of the yeshiva over a rather arcane issue concerning an oven:

> On that day R. Eliezer brought forward every imaginable argument, but they did not accept them. Said he to them: "If the *halachah* agrees with me, let this carob-tree prove it!" Thereupon the carob-tree was torn a hundred cubits out of its place. . . . "No proof can be brought from a carob-tree," they retorted. Again he said to them: "If the *halachah* agrees with me, let the stream of water prove it!" Whereupon the stream of water flowed backwards. "No proof can be brought from a stream of water," they rejoined. Again he urged: "If the *halachah* agrees with me, let the walls of the schoolhouse prove it," whereupon the walls inclined to fall. . . . Again he said to them: "If the *halachah* agrees with me, let it be proved from Heaven!" Whereupon a Heavenly Voice cried out: "Why do ye dispute with R. Eliezer, seeing that in all matters the *halachah* agrees with him!" But R. Joshua arose and exclaimed: "It is not in heaven!" What did he mean by this? — Said R. Jeremiah: That the Torah had already been given at Mount Sinai; we pay no attention to a Heavenly Voice, because Thou hast long since written in the Torah at Mount Sinai. *After the majority must one incline* (Bava Metzia 59b).

The Talmud then recounts that a rabbi asked Elijah what God did next. According to the story, God laughed with joy and said, "My sons have defeated me [in argument]."

On the one hand, this story dramatically asserts the dominant role of man in interpreting God's Torah. On the other hand, it del-

---

* Even when the Jews of the shtetl moved to America and became more secular, they continued the Responsa tradition by writing letters seeking advice from the Yiddish newspapers. These questions and answers, called "Bintel briefs" — a bundle of letters — have been collected in Isaac Metzker, ed., *A Bintel Brief* (Garden City, N.Y.: Doubleday, 1971).

egates man's interpretive power *only* to the rabbinic authorities. (In this respect, the Talmudic story is akin to our Supreme Court's famous decision in *Marbury vs. Madison* — the case that established the power of *judges* as the final arbiter of constitutional interpretation.) Even if a man hears God's voice directly, he may not presume to interpret the Torah. He must submit to the collective decision of the rabbis, who claim the authority of the Torah as the basis for *their* power to interpret God's word.

Although this sounds very much like the Catholic church, with its hierarchical power structure, it is actually quite different, because Judaism had to adapt to its distinctive circumstances. Jews were not capable of exercising centralized authority, because they lived in separate and often isolated communities. Each community, sometimes each rabbi, exercised independent rabbinic authority. Occasionally there were chief rabbis or their equivalent in certain areas. But the realities of the time required decentralization. Perhaps that is why the concept of Halakah — the single road of rabbinic Judaism — took on so much importance. Unless rabbinic Judaism had a central core derived from the hierarchically descending influence of the Torah, the Prophets, Mishnah, Gemara, and the subsequent interpretations of rabbis in order of antiquity and perceived brilliance, there was the danger of anarchy — or at least the kind of sectarian division that had caused so many problems in the past.[13]

In order to assure the acceptance of this rabbinically controlled Halakah, the rabbis boldly asserted that the "oral law" — the Mishnah, the Gemara, and the authoritative rabbinic interpretation — was also given to the Jews at Sinai, along with the written law, the Torah. A perusal of any volume of the Talmud makes it difficult to credit this self-serving myth. Even those who believe that the Torah is God-given find it hard to believe that *everything* included in the Talmud is divinely inspired.*

The Torah — at least most of it — is elegant, dramatic, and quakes with the voice of God. The Talmud, though often infused with brilliance and cleverness, is chock full of quite ordinary argumentation, conflicting views, and trivia. And why should this be a

---

* Unless, of course, one believes that *all* human actions are divinely inspired, in which case the claim that *certain* rabbinic statements are uniquely divine becomes tautological.

surprise? The Talmud is the edited arguments, discussions, folk tales, sayings, beliefs, and biographical vignettes of a group of mostly great but all very human rabbis who happened to live in Babylon before and during the sixth century A.D.[14] How anyone can actually believe that any God wrote, inspired, or even approved of some of the statements contained in the Talmud is beyond my comprehension. Some of my favorites, from the Sefer Ha-aggadah,[15] compiled by Hayyim Nachman Bialik and Yehoshuah Hana Ravnitzky, are the following: "He who suffers from weakness of the heart should get meat from the right leg of a ram and dried cattle turd dropped during the month of Nisan. . . ." "All raw vegetables make the complexion pale, and all things not fully grown retard growth." "The night was created for no other purpose than sleep." "Women are incapable of giving legal decisions."

My favorite Talmudic story is the following one:

> If a fledgling bird is found within fifty cubits [about seventy-five feet] . . . [of a man's property], it belongs to the owner of the property. If it is found outside the limits of fifty cubits, it belongs to the person who finds it.
>
> Rabbi Jeremiah asked the question: "If one foot of the fledgling bird is within the limit of fifty cubits, and one foot is outside it, what is the law?"
>
> It was for this question that Rabbi Jeremiah was *thrown out* of the house of study (Bava Bathra 23b).

I love that story because I too would be thrown out of class at my yeshiva for asking line-drawing questions my rabbis thought were disrespectful. When we were in high school, our all-time favorite Talmudic verse was the following from Bava Metzia (84a): "Rabbi Johanan said: 'Rabbi Ishmael's penis was like a wineskin of nine kavs' capacity.' Rav Pappa said: 'Rabbi Johanan's penis was like a wineskin of five kavs' capacity.' Some report him as giving the measurement as three kavs' capacity. And what about Rav Pappa himself? His penis was like a Harpanian jug."* Nor was this macho exchange the

---

* Later rabbis tried to put a nonsexual gloss on this, claiming that it referred to "biceps," but the Maharshal, an eminent sixteenth-century sage, was clear that it referred to genitals in order to teach that "despite their passionate nature," the rabbis "always remained fully in control of their impulses" (Bava Metzia Steinsaltz edition, p. 120).

only Talmudic reference to comparative rabbinic anatomy. Two Talmudic rabbis are described as "so fat" that when they "stood talking together, a herd of oxen could have gone between them, under their bellies, and not touched either of them" (Bava Metzia 84a). Another rabbi and his wife were so portly that he was asked how he could satisfy the commandment to be fruitful and multiply. He responded, delicately, that "love overcomes the flesh" (Bava Metzia 84a). There is also rabbinic posturing about height and beauty (Bava Metzia 84a). These are the human observations of human rabbis, and it is the very human quality of the Talmud, rather than its allegedly divine inspiration, that makes it such engaging reading.

David Wolpe of the Jewish Theological Seminary reminds us that "there are angry, extremist, and even violent voices in our texts and tales." As the late Professor Louis Ginsberg used to say, "The devil can quote scripture to his purpose, and were he more learned, he could quote the Talmud too."[16] This observation was confirmed when some diabolical Jews — notably the assassin Yigal Amir — quoted the Talmud and other Jewish texts in support of murdering Prime Minister Yitzhak Rabin.

Changing Tradition

The myth that Jewish law was *always the same*, and that *all* of Halakah was handed down at Sinai, was designed to prevent Jews from recognizing the mutable nature of the very human institution that is Judaism. In that respect, it is parallel to the myth that rationalized the Anglo-American common law for several centuries. Until the advent of legal realism in the nineteenth century, legal formalists (especially judges) perpetuated the myth that the law was a fully formed "corpus," which judges merely "discovered" or "discerned." This myth, like that of Halakah, was designed to keep laypeople from understanding that secular judges, like rabbis, often *make* new law — and then simply find old authority to support their innovations.

Jewish Halakah — the methods used by rabbinic authorities to derive religious law — is a wonderful institution of which we should be very proud because it has contributed so much to the quality of our lives as Jews as well as to the lives of all humankind. But it is an ever-changing institution that must continue to change. Consider, for example, the elimination of animal sacrifices from the Jewish ritual. If you asked a Jew who lived in Jerusalem during the days of Solomon's Temple what *the* central ritual of Judaism was, he would answer without hesitation "the animal sacrifices in the Temple." He would point to verses, chapters, indeed large portions of the Torah as describing these rituals in the most minute detail and commanding them in the most unequivocal terms. Judaism without animal sacrifice would be unthinkable to a Temple Jew. Yet the unthinkable has come to pass without weakening Judaism or Jewish life. Nor will Judaism ever return to animal sacrifices. Because we need to pretend that Judaism is immutable, we have created the myth that we *will return* to animal sacrifices when the Temple is rebuilt. No we won't! Not in my religion! Jewish animal sacrifices were no more brutal than the rituals of other primitive religions — indeed, they were far less brutal than human sacrifices. But those days are over and Judaism will never return to them, even if we build another Temple. The rabbis will figure out some way to justify not returning to so primitive and anachronistic a ritual, because they know that Judaism today could not survive it. Perhaps that is why we will never have another Temple: because the rabbis would not want to be confronted with the dilemma of how to rationalize a Temple without biblically commanded animal sacrifices. In any event, this was a major change in Jewish life and in Judaism — a change that would have occurred had the Temple remained standing. (Some Orthodox scholars might well argue that God saw to it that the Temple was destroyed precisely in order to put an end to animal sacrifices, which had seen its day go by. So be it, but the result is the same: no more animal sacrifices!)

Contrast the elimination of animal sacrifices with the addition of the Kol Nidre prayer on the eve of Yom Kippur, which has become one of the central events of the Jewish calendar. Perhaps more Jews attend Kol Nidre services than any other synagogue event. Yet the Kol Nidre prayer, the earliest known version of which appears in the ninth-century prayer book *Seder Rav Amram*,[17] is a highly technical legal formulation created by the rabbis, apparently to meet a particular localized need of a small portion of the Jewish community.* But

---

* It is not entirely clear what need led to the formulation. Some believe it goes back to the Babylonian fear of curses. Others trace it to forced Jewish conversions.[18]

the Kol Nidre proved popular with Jews around the world, perhaps because of its emotionally powerful language and the haunting melody later attached to it. (Beethoven even incorporated the melody into his String Quartet no. 14.) In any event, this central ritual is the result of a change — an alteration. It did not come from Sinai.

More Jews attend the Kol Nidre service, which is non-biblical, than abide by the biblical commandment to fast during Yom Kippur. Even the concept of fasting was given a biblical meaning different from the traditional one — and perhaps one more contemporarily relevant to many views — by the prophet Isaiah.

> They ask me about the religious observances; they delight in approaching God. . . .
>
> "Why, when we fasted, did You not see? When we starved our bodies, did You pay no heed?" Because on your fast day you see to your business and oppress all your laborers. Because you fast in strife and contention, and you strike with a wicked fist! Your fasting today is not such as to make your voice heard on high. Is such the fast I desire, a day for men to starve their bodies? Is it bowing the head like a bulrush and lying in sackcloth and ashes? Do you call that a fast, a day when the Lord is favorable? No, this is the fast I desire: To unlock fetters of wickedness, and untie the cords of the yoke to let the oppressed go free; to break off every yoke. It is to share your bread with the hungry, and to take the wretched poor into your home; when you see the naked, to clothe him, and not to ignore your own kin . . .
>
> If you banish the yoke from your midst, the menacing hand and evil speech, and you offer your compassion to the hungry and satisfy the famished creature — then shall your light shine in the darkness, and your gloom shall be like noonday (Isaiah 58:2–10).

Although this portion from Isaiah is read on every Yom Kippur, its message is rarely preached. I have attended more than fifty Yom Kippur services and I don't recall a rabbi ever emphasizing that the Yom Kippur fast is a hollow gesture unless it is accompanied by a commitment to stop oppressing workers, to undo the bonds of oppression, to share your bread with the hungry, to take the outcast poor into your home, to clothe the naked and assist the less fortunate. This 2,800-

year-old Yom Kippur message speaks to today's young Jews. It is as authentically Jewish as any ritual. It may have had less relevance to a poverty-stricken Jewish community that had difficulty clothing and feeding itself, with little left over for others. But to today's affluent Jews, it gives new meaning to the Yom Kippur fast.

Judaism has changed in other fundamental ways since its origin 3,500 years ago. The Jews of Abraham's covenant, Moses's Sinai, Solomon's First Temple, Zerubabel's Second Temple, and Hillel's yeshiva would barely recognize today's Hasidim and ultra-Orthodox as coreligionists. Beyond a precious few common rituals — circumcision, some dietary restrictions, Sabbath observance, and a few of the laws of family purity — today's ultra-Orthodox practice a Judaism very different from that of their forebears. And our grandchildren will almost certainly practice a Judaism different from ours. This became clear to me recently when I had dinner with Daniel Goldin, the director of NASA, who is a traditional Jew from the Bronx and who told me he had gotten a rabbinic ruling about prayer in space. Jews are required to put on tefillin and to daven each day, when the sun rises. But for an astronaut, the sun rises many times during a day. The rabbi told Dr. Goldin that a Jewish astronaut — of whom there are several — would have to put on his tefillin only once every "earth day," as measured by twenty-four hours, rather than "tefillin on, tefillin off" every few hours. In generations past, Halakah adapted to the needs of Jewish ocean voyagers, permitting them to travel on the Sabbath, so long as they neither embarked nor disembarked on the day of rest. A literal reading of the ancient sources, which were written before transatlantic travel existed, might have made emigration to America a religious impossibility. But the rabbis adapted the rules to the necessities, just as their successors will when spaceships take Jews to Mars.

Who Is a Jew?

Another example of change is the explosive issue of intermarriage and the rule that the Jewishness of a child is determined solely by the mother — the Jewish rule of matrilineal descent. I discuss this example not to advocate adoption of the Reform position, which rejects exclusively matrilineal descent, but rather to illustrate that a principle so central to Orthodox and Conservative Judaism is the product of profound change. Matrilineal descent is *not* a biblical principle of Judaism. In fact, the Torah dictates *patrilineal* descent in all instances, and it was the practice during biblical times for the children's status to be determined by the father. As Rabbi Phillip Sigal puts it: "The Torah clearly enunciates a patrilineal principle by which offspring are classified according to the lineage of the father. There is no equivalent passage in what we consider the revealed word of God that establishes a matrilineal principle."[19] Many Jewish men married non-Jews in biblical times. Indeed, several of the most prominent Jewish men of the Bible did. According to current Halakah, their children would not have been regarded as Jews. Professor Shaye Cohen, a Jewish historian then at the Jewish Theological Seminary, now at Brown, summarized it thus:

> Numerous Israelite heroes and kings married foreign women: for example, Judah married a Canaanite, Joseph an Egyptian, Moses a Midianite and an Ethiopian, David a Philistine, and Solomon women of every description. By her marriage with an Israelite man a foreign woman joined the clan, people, and religion of her husband. It never occurred to anyone in pre-exilic times to argue that such marriages were null and void, that the foreign women must "convert" to Judaism, or that the off-spring of the marriage were not Israelite if the women did not convert.[20]

Indeed, the traditional Jewish blessing for all Jewish boys is that they should be like "Ephraim and Menasheh." But Ephraim and Menasheh were born to a non-Jewish mother. It is difficult to believe that the traditional Jewish blessing would be, "You should be non-Jews!" Everyone agrees that the rabbis made a change in the law of descent centuries after the Torah. There is dispute about exactly *when* and *why* the change was made, but there is no dispute that the biblical rule and practice were, in fact, changed.

Professor Cohen and other historians have difficulty explaining, or even dating, the adoption of matrilineal descent as *a* principle, and indeed *the* principle, of Judaism. The best Cohen can do is to put it around the second century A.D., which means that it was *not* a part of Jewish law for about as long as it *has* been a part of Jewish law. Nor can Cohen find any legitimate bases in scripture for the change. "How the Talmud derives the matrilineal principle from

[Biblical] verses is not entirely clear, for the simple reason that the matrilineal principle . . . is not Biblical." It is possible that the matrilineal principle was borrowed from Roman law.[21] Nor is the Talmudic logic that is offered in support of this apparently foreign rule particularly compelling to the modern ear. For those women who believe that the principle of matrilineal descent reflects a *favorable* view of women, the Talmudic logic is particularly disturbing. The Talmud declares that whenever a union would be valid but sinful, "[t]he offspring follows the parent of *lower* status," and that whenever the union would be invalid, there is no legal paternity at all, and thus parenthood falls by default to the mother. It is from these (and other) rather anachronistic premises that the present rule apparently derives. Why, then, has this non-biblical — and perhaps originally non-Jewish — rule survived over the past 1,800 years and become so rigid a tenet of Orthodox and Conservative Judaism that most Jews probably believe it has its basis in the Bible?

The first answer must be that until recently, it has been a relatively noncontroversial and unimportant issue. With the rare exception of an occasional Chava (Tevye's daughter in *Fiddler on the Roof*), Jewish females almost never married non-Jews. Those Jewish females who did, like the fictional Chava, were generally excluded from the insular Jewish community and became part of the non-Jewish community. Historically, Jewish parents regarded a daughter who married a non-Jew as dead and sat shiva over her. She, her Christian husband, and their children (even though the latter were "technically" regarded as Jews) were not welcome in the Jewish community. Whatever Jewish *law* may have ordained, the realities of life made the children of these rare marriages de facto non-Jews.

Until recently, many more Jewish *men* than women married out (though never in large numbers), and they too were generally excluded — or excluded themselves — from their insular Jewish communities. Their children would not likely have been brought up as Jews, regardless of what Jewish law mandated.

The only context in which the matrilineal principle realistically came into play was the frequent and tragic phenomenon of Jewish women being raped by non-Jewish men, during pogroms and other attacks, which were common from the Middle Ages through the nineteenth century. It would have been inhumane in the extreme to regard the offspring of such rapes as non-Jewish. Since the rape victim wanted to remain within the Jewish community, it would have been unfair — and self-defeating — to regard her child as a non-Jew living among Jews.[22] The same would have been true, though perhaps to a somewhat lesser degree, of a Jewish woman who had been seduced and abandoned, or married and divorced, by a non-Jew and who wanted to move back in to the Jewish community, with her child or children.

There may be other reasons as well for the survival of the matrilineal rule, such as the Roman principle of *mater certa, pater incertus* — the certainty of maternity and the relative uncertainty of paternity. But Professor Cohen persuasively demonstrates that this argument lacks historical validity, since in many other important cases where paternity is in doubt, Jewish law goes to great lengths to determine, or to presume, who the father was. And in each of these instances, the offspring's status follows the father.

We are now saddled with a rule that is neither based on the Torah nor supported by persuasive Talmudic reasoning. Although it may have served some useful purpose in days gone by, there are serious questions about its current validity. The best pragmatic argument for keeping it — made by Orthodox and Conservative defenders — is that it is important to have a *single agreed-upon rule* for defining who is a Jew, and that since the Orthodox *cannot* now change the Halakic rule, it should remain *the* rule for all Jews, even if a majority of Jews disagree with it. But that argument begs the fundamental question: Why is it so important for there to be only one definition of who is a Jew? In fact, there already are numerous *different* criteria for determining Jewishness. For example, the Orthodox do not recognize the majority of conversions to Judaism performed today and over the past several decades. Nor do they recognize the majority of divorces that Jews obtain. Over the coming decades, the number of disputes as to "who is a Jew" and "who is a legitimate Jew" will increase, as more and more "Jewish" children are born to mothers who were converted to Judaism by non-Orthodox rabbis and to parents in second marriages who were not previously divorced in accordance with Orthodox Halakah. These disputes will arise *even if* the matrilineal principle is maintained as the exclusive basis for Jewish descent.

On an even more fundamental level, there are disputes *within Orthodoxy* as to who is a Jew. Maimonides — who is recognized by Orthodox Jews as the second-greatest law codifier after Moses —

would add another criterion to the matrilineal rule. To him, the essential definition of who is a Jew is based on belief in his thirteen principles of Judaism:

> And when these fundamental principles are established by a man and he truly believes in them, he then enters into the collective unit of Israel, and it is obligatory upon us to love him and to have compassion upon him and to do all that God commanded us to do for one another, referring to acts of love and brotherhood. This is so even if he commits every possible sin by virtue of his lust or the mastery of his base nature. He will be punished according to the severity of his sins, but he has a portion in the world to come, although he is one of the transgressors of Israel. *But if a man is doubtful about one of these fundamental principles, he has removed himself from the collective unit (of Israel)* and denies an absolute truth (of Judaism). He is called a "heretic" and an "apikoros" and a "mutilator of shoots" and it is obligatory upon us to hate him and to destroy him [emphasis mine].

The thirteen principles that Maimonides says makes one a Jew are the following:

I believe with perfect faith that the Creator . . . alone has
    made, does make, and will make all things.
I believe with perfect faith that the Creator is a Unity, and
    that He alone is our God, who was, is, and will be.
I believe with perfect faith that the Creator is not a body, and
    that He has no form whatever.
I believe the Creator is the first and the last.
I believe with perfect faith that to the Creator and to Him
    alone, it is proper to pray.
I believe with perfect faith that all the words of the prophets
    are true.
I believe with perfect faith that the prophecy of Moses our
    teacher was true.
I believe with perfect faith that the entire Torah, now in our
    possession, is the same that was given to Moses our teacher.
I believe with perfect faith that this Torah will not be
    changed, and that there will never be any other Torah from
    the Creator.

I believe with perfect faith that the Creator knows every deed
of human beings, and all their thoughts.
I believe with perfect faith that the Creator rewards those
who keep His commandments, and punishes those who
transgress His commandments.
I believe with perfect faith in the coming of the Messiah; and
though he tarry, I will wait daily for his coming.
I believe with perfect faith that there will be a revival of the
dead at the time when it shall please the Creator.[23]

I am doubtful about *all* of these thirteen principles, except for the
ones that I am *certain* are untrue, such as the revival of the dead, so
according to Maimonides, I am not a Jew, even though my mother
and father are Jewish. According to other Halakic authorities, I am
still a Jew regardless of my views, even if I were to convert to another religion. Moreover, since Reform Judaism explicitly rejects
the resurrection of the dead, its adherents are not Jewish either, according to Maimonides. And since there are few Conservative or
modern Orthodox Jews who are not "doubtful about one of these
fundamental principles," the Maimonidean definition of who is a
Jew includes only a small number of never-doubting fundamentalists. So there already is more than one definition of who is a Jew,
even according to traditional Halakic sources.

One can be a deeply committed Jew and still believe that the
question of who is a Jew — for definitional purposes outside religious orthodoxy — is debatable. I am not now urging any particular
resolution of this thorny and divisive issue. What I *am* urging is that
change is inherent in Judaism and Jewish life, and that it is self-
destructive — and self-serving — for some Jews to argue that
change *was* permissible between the Torah and Talmud but that
what *used to be* a dynamic, ever-changing, adaptive religion *before* the
Talmud suddenly became a *static*, never-changing, nonadaptive religion as soon as the last of the Talmudic rabbis died. There are, of
course, ways for traditional rabbinic Judaism to change in accordance with Halakah, but in the absence of the universally acceptable
beth din (rabbinic court), these changes — if they are acknowledged
to be changes — are almost impossible to effect. Neither history
nor logic supports this selectively static view of Jewish law. There
have been important changes both before and after the Talmud, and

there must be important changes yet to come if we are to continue to adapt and survive.

The dictates of the Torah were expressly changed in numerous ways by the rabbis — some of the most important in relation to marriage. First, the Torah does not prohibit *all* intermarriage. It is very specific in prohibiting only intermarriage with the seven nations of Canaan. As if to prove that this was not meant metaphorically, the Torah specifically set a time limit on the prohibition against intermarriage with the Egyptians and Edomites: three generations. But as Rabbi Phillip Sigal put it, "Ezra acted contrary to the Torah" when in the fifth century B.C. he prohibited marriage with *all* non-Jews, even after the specific three-generation prohibition had long expired.[24]

Another major change occurred much later — after the Talmud was long completed. In the tenth century A.D., Rabbenu Gershom, a German Talmudic sage, declared that biblical polygamy was against Jewish law and that monogamy was now required. Jews had, in fact, practiced monogamy for centuries, despite the biblical rule of polygamy.* But after Rabbenu Gershom's decree, monogamy became part of Jewish law in the areas under his rabbinic jurisdiction.†

The malleability of Halakah and its adaptability to changing circumstances is aptly illustrated by the current use of Halakah by some ultra-Orthodox rabbis to transparent sexist and political ends. Consider, for example, the tragic and widespread problem of the agunah, the Jewish woman whose husband will not grant her a get — a religious divorce decree, which the husband must agree to. This has posed a tremendous problem in modern divorce proceedings, with spiteful husbands refusing to grant their wives a Jewish divorce, even after the civil divorce is completed. In this situation, the couple is still married under Jewish law, and the woman is

---

* Some argue that polygamy was only *permitted* by the Bible. But in light of the Jewish requirement to "be fruitful and multiply," polygamy — which produces more offspring by having fewer non-child-producing women — can certainly be seen as more than a permitted mode, especially since so many of the great men of the Bible were polygamous.

† One of the greatest Orthodox sages of the early twentieth century once computed the number of mitzvoth still observed by contemporary Orthodox Jewry: he put the figure at less than 300 out of the original 613 (Telushkin, *Jewish Literacy*, p. 496).

thereby prohibited from remarrying (or even dating). It has been proposed that couples include in the ketubah (marriage contract) a clause stating that if the wife ever wants a divorce, the husband will grant her a get within a certain specified period of time.[25] But despite the near-universal desire among the Orthodox to do something about this serious problem, Halakah has thus far yielded no solution to, or change in, the anachronistic get rule. Some ultra-Orthodox rabbis have, however, figured out a way to permit undivorced *men*, but not women, to date and remarry.[26] If change is *desired*, a Halakic source will almost always be found to support it. When all else fails, there is always the well-known Talmudic dictum "A restriction should not be imposed on a community unless the majority is able to stand it." (Bava Kama, 79b) If that is not a prescription for change, I don't know what is.

The point is not whether any particular change was or is good, bad, or indifferent. The point is that change has been a dominant theme running through the history of Judaism. Ultra-Orthodox Jews, like common-law judges of the old school, have created a myth *for themselves* that change never happens, that all the *current* rules were given by God to Moses at Sinai, and that only certain rabbis (the ones who wrote the rule!) are able to decode Halakah by employing certain traditionally accepted tools of interpretation. The ultra-Orthodox may well be right — for *them*. But their way is not the only authentically Jewish way, as evidenced by the many changes *they* have made from biblical Judaism, and by the flourishing of so many new flowers on the various branches of the tree called Judaism.

Amid all the current criticism of strictly Orthodox rabbinic Judaism, our enormous debt to the traditional rabbis must be acknowledged. They were largely responsible for designing a form of Judaism that was extraordinarily effective in assuring Jewish survival and continuity in the face of millennia of systematic persecution, discrimination, marginalization, hatred, forced conversion, and mass murder. Without them, and their Halakah, there would be no Jewish community today. Whatever factor or factors most contributed to our collective unwillingness to disappear — as so many others faced with far less enmity and persecution have disappeared — surely they must be found in the religious rules and religiously inspired traditions of traditional Orthodox Judaism.

We can learn much from our history of survival that is relevant to the current threats to our continuity. But we cannot assume that *exactly* the same religious and social factors that were so adaptive to our past challenges will be equally adaptive to our future ones. Our past challenges were largely from external enemies who sought to destroy us by persecution and force. We were a weak community, with little political, social, or religious power. There were some economically powerful individual Jews and Jewish families, but for the most part, Jews were poor and the Jewish community lacked usable economic leverage. Certainly it had no military or physical power, relying instead — often futilely — on others to protect it. Nor were there immediate prospects for improvement during most of Jewish history. We wandered from place to place in search of a more tolerable existence. Sometimes we found it — for a decade, a generation, a century, or even a "golden age." But it was always at risk. A change of ruler, a different pope, an unexpected war, a new ideology, a plague, an economic downturn — any of these could and did produce unanticipated disaster for Jewish communities, which rarely controlled their own destinies.

Is Judaism Messianic?

Not surprisingly, these communities turned inward, distrusted outsiders, relied on their rabbis, prayed for a messianic solution to their problems. But even messianism reflects a change in Judaism, a change that is ongoing. Judaism may be a messianic religion, but Jews (certainly contemporary Jews) are not a very messianic people, at least in the literal sense. They have rejected every claimed Messiah as a false Messiah — *and they always will!* Although my late uncle Yitchak used to keep a white garment near his front door so that he could greet the Messiah properly attired, even most modern Orthodox Jews I know think of the coming of the Messiah as a hope that they know will never be realized in their lifetime, as did some of the more practical sages of the Talmud. Rabbi Ben Zakkai taught: "If you are holding a sapling in your hand, and someone tells you the Messiah has come, plant the sapling first, then go look for the Messiah." And Rabbi Yochanan ben Torta told Rabbi Akiba: "Grass will grow out of your cheekbones, and the Messiah still will not have arrived" (Ta'anit 4:8, 68d).

One empirical proof of this reality is the attitude of most modern

Orthodox Jews toward the claim by some Lubavitch Hasidim that the late Menachem Schneerson, the Lubavitcher rebbe who died in 1993, was the Messiah. Despite the fact that Rabbi Schneerson appeared to fulfill the traditional criteria for the Jewish Messiah — he was the flesh-and-blood mortal who was the most inspirational leader, foremost scholar, and greatest moral paragon of his generation, and he suffered "pains" and "sickness" before his death, as Isaiah foretold of the Messiah[27] — almost no Orthodox Jews outside the Lubavitch sect were willing to consider even the *possibility* that Schneerson could be the Messiah. They knew that no matter how great a man he was — and he was truly great by any standard — he was a *man*, and no man is capable of performing the miracles expected of the Messiah.

Even many Lubavitch leaders were unwilling to stake the credibility of their movement on an easily disprovable claim: namely, that Rabbi Schneerson would actually arise from his grave and then raise the dead from theirs.* Their literature now speaks of "a time when the world might fulfill its purpose," rather than of a literal resurrection of the dead. If they had declared the great rabbi to be the Messiah and then no dead were raised, they would be in big trouble. Perhaps that is why some Lubavitch Hasidim have argued that Schneerson is, in fact, the Messiah but that he will not come back to earth until the Jews *merit* his return — thus turning an empirically verifiable proposition into an unprovable and hence un*dis*provable hope. Those who devised the concept of heaven and hell — of reward and punishment in the afterlife — understood the pitfalls of making religious claims provable or disprovable here on earth by empirical observations. The great virtue of an afterlife is that you don't get to experience it until after you're dead and you don't get to report about it to the living — at least, not until the Messiah comes! It cannot therefore be proved or disproved, which should be true of all good religious principles. Heaven and hell continue the narrative of justice, under which virtues are rewarded and vices punished — if not here on earth (where we can observe that it is *not* true), then in the afterlife (where we cannot observe or disprove it). As the great

---

* The joke went around the Orthodox community immediately following Rabbi Schneerson's death that the Lubavitch movement hadn't bought a gravesite for their late leader, they had merely rented one. But in fact they bought one for his eternal use.

medieval Jewish sage Saadia Goan perceptively put it a millennium ago: "In this world we see the godless prosper and the faithful suffer. There *must*, therefore, be another world in which all will be recompensed in justice and righteousness."[28]

It is not surprising that every claimant to being the Jewish Messiah, from Bar Kochba to Shabtai Tsvi, has always been rejected as false, as will any future claimant.* As Rabbi Samuel Schulman wrote in 1924: "Israel must always *await* the Messiah. It must never acknowledge any person or event as the complete fruition of its hopes. Indeed the essence of Jewish Messianism is the hope of an infinite ideal."[29] An old Jewish joke reflects the somewhat cynical Jewish attitude toward the coming of the Messiah:

> In a small Russian shtetl, the community council decides to pay a poor Jew a ruble a week to sit at the town's entrance and be the first to greet the Messiah when he arrives.
>
> The man's brother comes to see him, and is puzzled why he took such a low-paying job.
>
> "It's true," the poor man responds, "the pay is low. But it's a steady job."[30]

Very few Jews actually believe in the physical resurrection of the dead, despite the fact that all Orthodox and Conservative Jews include it in their daily and holiday prayers.[31] Indeed, the very concept of a Messiah who will revive the dead is only a *strain* of Judaism, and a relatively late strain at that. There is no reference to any Messiah or to any resurrection of the dead in the Five Books of Moses. Even the Prophets do not explicitly refer to the resurrection of the dead. There is, of course, the poetic reference in Ezekiel to the "dry bones" about which God says, "I will cause breath to enter you and you shall live again" (37:4–5).† But it was only shortly before the advent of Christianity that Jews began to believe in the resurrection of the dead. In the Book of Daniel, written around 160 B.C., the fol-

---

* Bar Kochba, a second-century Jewish warrior, was declared "King Messiah" by Rabbi Akiba but was eventually defeated in battle. Shabtai Tsvi (1626–1676) was the focus of the largest messianic movement in Jewish history, which ended ingloriously with his conversion to Islam.

† And also in Ezekiel: "Behold, I will open your graves and cause you to come up . . ." (37:12).

lowing prophecy appears: "Many of those who sleep in the dust of the earth will awake, some to everlasting life and some to the reproach of eternal abhorrence."

Despite Maimonides' assertion that to be a Jew, one must believe with complete faith in the "advent of the Messiah" and "the resurrection of the dead," most Jews through history did not. Indeed, Maimonides himself seemed to vacillate on this issue. In 1180 he wrote: "Do not imagine that King Messiah will perform signs and wonders . . . revive the dead, or do similar things. It is not so."[32] Ecclesiastics explicitly rejected the concept. For the first millennium of Jewish history, it was not even a tenet of Judaism. Thereafter, it has been the subject of ongoing disagreement. In 1589, Judah Löw, the great Talmudic scholar of Prague, declared: "A foundation of religion cannot be something that is not discernable to experience." That is why the Torah "avoided the hereafter."[33]

But the fact that the Torah did not emphasize the hereafter or the Messiah did not stop the rabbis from making them central tenets of Jewish faith during periods of Jewish history when the promise of rewards that "were not discernable to experience" were necessary to Jewish survival. The rabbis perceptively recognized that their Jews needed hope in something beyond the hopelessness of their daily existence. They created a vibrant civilization based on the reality of victimization and the hope of redemption. Their prayers, their rules, their social structures, their literature, their language, their music, their humor, all reflected their condition, their fears, and their hopes — if not for this world and this age, then for another.

Traditional Orthodox Judaism has proved its adaptability to the Jewish people during the times of external crises that have characterized much of Jewish history. With its emphasis on solidarity in the face of persecution, stiff-necked resistance to forced conversion, the promise of a messianic age, and the creation of resilient communal infrastructures, traditional Judaism has been a powerful force for survival, both of Jews as individuals and of the Jewish people. While other civilizations, cultures, nations, and religions have succumbed to external persecution, Judaism has survived some of the most vicious attempts at genocide. There must be something special — something we should make great efforts to preserve — in traditional Orthodox Judaism for it to have served the Jewish people so well, for so long, in the face of so much enmity.

But this same traditional Judaism has not yet proved its adaptability to the rather new situation currently facing Jews, especially young Jews, in America: namely, equality, openness, lack of persecution, welcomeness, choice, intermarriage, and assimilation. The options now available are as numerous as the individual Jews on the planet. We are entirely free to choose any form of Jewish identity, ranging from totalitarian Hasidism to Judaism without God, and anything in between.[34] We can also simply ignore our Judaism and give it up, not with the bang of conversion but with the whimper of inaction. Traditional Judaism must now prove its ability to compete in the open marketplace of conflicting faiths, ideologics, identities, and marriage partners.

When the Age of Enlightenment came upon Europe, and German Jews like Moses Mendelssohn began the Haskalah movement, which sought to integrate secular and Jewish learning, many Orthodox rabbis argued that Judaism was incompatible with modernism and secular enlightenment. They believed that Judaism as they knew it could survive only in isolation from secular culture, that it could not compete in the marketplace of contemporary ideas — hence the Lubavitch rabbi's prayer for the repressive czar. And in some respects, they were right. The pull of the Enlightenment tugged many young Jews out of the ghetto and into the universities, where some, inevitably, rejected traditional Judaism in favor of secularism, the newly developing Reform Judaism, agnosticism, and, for some, Christianity.

The Judaism I grew up with was a Judaism of persecution, discrimination, oppression, and victimization. The stories, the music, the folk sayings, the humor, the prayers, the hopes were all from the perspective of the victim. The stories were of pogroms, of poverty, of exile, of discrimination in schools and jobs, of exclusion, of victimization. The music was "Eli, Eli lama azavtovni" ("God, God, why have you abandoned me") and "Where Shall We Go." The folk sayings were "It is difficult to be a Jew"; "Tsuris may be blind, but it never has difficulty finding a Jew"; "Man plans and God laughs." The humor was "When a Jew eats chicken and it's not Shabbos, then either the Jew or the chicken is sick." The prayers were prayers of desperation. The hopes were of a messianic salvation from this life of misery. "Ani Maamin" — "I believe in the coming of the Messiah" — was on the lips of every Jew facing persecution and death.

The poetry reflected the desperation and poverty of most Jews, as in Shalom Aleichem's "Free":

If one has no means of livelihood, he is free to die of hunger.
If one is unemployed, he is free to knock his head against the wall.
If one breaks a leg, he is free to walk on crutches.
If one gets married and hasn't enough to support his wife,
He is free to go begging alms with her from house to house.
If one dies, he is free to get buried.

Jewish history was the accumulation of pogroms, anti-Semitic decrees, and religious persecution suffered by the Jewish people and documented by historians such as Simon Dubnow. To read Dubnow's three-volume *History of the Jews in Russia and Poland* is to participate vicariously in a millennium of uninterrupted Jewish victimization and tsuris.

It all made sense for the shtetl and ghetto world in which Jews had lived for so many centuries — for the world of my generation's grandparents and parents, who had endured the travails of immigration only to be greeted by discrimination, the Depression, and then the news of the Holocaust. It even made some sense to my generation, despite the emerging good news about Israel, an expanding economy, and a light at the end of the tunnel of discrimination. We, too, had experienced, writ small, what our parents and grandparents had experienced writ large. We met the survivors of the Holocaust. We were told not to bother to apply to certain schools or jobs. We knew about "restricted" neighborhoods and clubs. For us, our grandparents' poignant stories of victimization were history, but recent history. They had the ring of truth — a ring whose echo we could still hear in our own ears.

For my children and my students, these stories have a somewhat hollow ring. They are not within the experience of this younger generation. It is not that they don't *believe* them or sympathize with the victims. It is that this generation of Jews has never encountered anything like the kind of victimization that characterized our people in the past. They regard themselves as privileged, as part of the power structure, as the elite. To be sure, some young Jews have been victims of what they perceive as reverse discrimination. But even then, the reason they were excluded from a school or a job is generally because they are part of the white establishment, not specifically because they are Jewish.*

The Jewish world has changed so dramatically since the end of World War II, and especially over the past quarter of a century, that our children don't recognize their great-grandparents. There they sit, in sepia photographs, on mantels and pianos, bearded and bedecked in sheitels. The young search for their roots out of nostalgia and a need for connectedness to a quaint past that is unlikely to recur. Their great-grandparents didn't have to search for their roots. In their day, there was little difference between the roots, the trunk, and the branches. They all lived together in a slowly changing but largely static and narrowly circumscribed world. Judaism, too, changed slowly, almost imperceptibly, to adapt to the slow changes in Jewish life. Now the time has come for Judaism to change more quickly to adapt to the sea-change in Jewish life from victimization to equality. Our long season of external victimization is largely behind us. A new season, with unpredictable weather patterns, is upon us. And American Judaism must adapt to the new Jews of America.

If eclectic Judaism is to survive and thrive, then Jews must devise eclectic rules adaptive to the changes in Judaism and to the worlds in which Jews live today. Secular Jews have the right and the power to do what is necessary to preserve secular Jewish life. Conservative, Reform, Reconstructionist, egalitarian, Havurah, and other Jews must do what is necessary to preserve their Jewish way of life. What is adaptive for the preservation of ultra-Orthodox and Hasidic Judaism must not constrain us from finding our Halakahs — our roads. There has *never* been only one Jewish road. There have always been many. There were the diverging roads of the Pharisees and the Sadducees, of Hillel and Shammai, of the Ashkenazim and Sephardim, of the Hasidim and the Mitnagdim.

Simon Dubnow recounts the venomous conflict between the Hasidim and Mitnagdim.[35] The leader of the Mitnagdim, the more intellectual and elitist Lithuanian Jews, was Rabbi Elija of Vilna, known as the Vilna Gaon. He issued a herem against the less well

---

* Some affirmative action programs do have a greater quantitative impact on Jews than on some other groups, but that is because Jews are quantitatively "overrepresented" in various areas. Asian-Americans face a similar situation.

educated and more spiritual Hasidim. A herem was, essentially, a formal writ of excommunication, sometimes even recognized by the state. The herem was accompanied by circulars urging rabbis in other communities to wage war against the "Godless sect." Mitnagdim — who considered themselves to be the "real Jews" — were forbidden to "intermarry" with Hasidim or even allow Hasidim to be buried in Jewish cemeteries. The Mitnagdim went so far as to have several Hasidic leaders arrested for treason. The Hasidic leaders retaliated by bringing charges against the leaders of the Mitnagdim. The only matter on which these warring sects could agree was their mutual hatred for the Jews of the Enlightenment, since both the Hasidim and the Mitnagdim despised secular learning and freethinking. As Rabbi Herschel Mishkin once put it: "I pay no attention to the silly chatter of the Hasidim. Of course, I pay no attention to the prattle of the Reform and Conservative, either. I only hope and pray they will all return some day to the Jewish faith!"[36] Today's conflicts are part of a long argument over which road will best assure the survival of Jewish life. Even Hasidim cannot agree among themselves as to common rules on such basic concepts as what makes a piece of meat kosher. My mother tells me that at weddings in Borough Park there are sometimes different tables with meat certified kosher by different Hasidic sects. This kind of thinking gave rise to the story about the Hasid who died and went to heaven, where he was greeted by an angel who presented him with a beautiful arrival feast. The Hasid asked the angel who had certified that the feast was kosher. The angel responded, "God himself." The Hasid frowned and said, "Well, in that case, I'll have the salad." Sometimes the conflicts are not funny, as when a group of Hasidim in Borough Park painted a swastika on the Conservative synagogue where I taught Sunday school while I was in college. These thugs had the nerve to name their gang "T.O.R.A.H.," which they said stood for "Tough Orthodox Rabbis And Hasids."[37] There is no excuse for this kind of hooliganism, but there is plenty of room for rational disagreement over every aspect of Jewish life.

Our diversity should be seen as a blessing, a challenge, an opportunity. A single Jewish road will lead too many Jews to find nothing but a dead end. Many Jewish roads will lead some of us to destinations yet unknown. But that is the challenge of life. And that is the challenge of today's Judaism, if we are to have a tomorrow.

Chapter Six

Make Aliyah! The Israeli Solution to the Jewish Question of the Twenty-first Century

IF ALL AMERICAN JEWS were to make aliyah (emigrate) to Israel, the problems of assimilation and intermarriage would be largely solved. Just as the ultra-Orthodox are empirically correct in arguing that if all Jews were to live in insular Hasidic communities — shtetls — there would be little assimilation or intermarriage, so too the Zionists are empirically correct in saying that if all Jews were to live in a nation of Jews, there would be little assimilation or intermarriage. Jews will marry Jews if those are the only people they interact with. That is a simple reality. But another simple reality is that most American Jews want to live in a more heterogeneous world and to have contact with people of different faiths and backgrounds. That is why so few would ever consider moving into a Hasidic community. That is also an important reason — along with comfort and family ties — why so few make aliyah, though a great many love to visit Israel.

I am a committed Zionist. I believe passionately in the Jewish state. If I had several lives to live, one of them would be as an Israeli. I hope to continue to spend a considerable amount of time, even more as I approach retirement, in Israel. But I am an American, and I love America and believe in its future. I am thankful that as a Jew, I always have the Israeli option available to me and my family if the militia, the skinheads, or the Farrakhans were ever to come to power here. I know that it is unfair for American Jews to regard Israel as the provider of an insurance policy, to whom we pay premiums but with whom we refuse to share the risks and burdens of being a direct part of the Jewish state. I also know that most American Jews, and certainly those at greatest risk of assimilation, cannot be counted on to make aliyah. In this regard, emigration to Israel is like Judaism itself, in that both rely too much on external threats and enmity. Neither Israel nor Judaism seems prepared for the possibility that these external dangers may abate in the twenty-first century, and that the greatest changes may come from within. Both must anticipate this change, lest it catch them off guard.

This change was brought home to many Jews on November 4, 1995, but it should have been apparent even before that fateful date which will live in Jewish infamy forever.

On Fridays I usually work at home, writing my books and articles. But on Friday, November 3, 1995, I was having lunch with Itamar Rabinowitz, the Israeli ambassador to the United States at the time and a distinguished professor of Mideast studies at Tel Aviv University. During his tenure as ambassador, I had become friends with him, as I had with many of the Israeli diplomats in Washington, Boston, and New York. I had established a particularly warm friendship with Bibi Netanyahu when he was at the United Nations, because we had known each other since his student days at MIT and he was an "American" Israeli, as contrasted with, for example, Yitzhak Rabin, who remained a quintessentially "Israeli" Israeli when he had served as ambassador in Washington. Although I had met Rabin on numerous occasions, we had never become friends.

I was surprised, therefore, when Ambassador Rabinowitz told me: "Yitzhak and Leah saw you on television last week, and they asked whether you could put some time aside to meet with them when they come to Boston next week." I agreed, of course, but I was curious why they wanted to meet with me, since my recent interview with Israeli television had been about the O. J. Simpson case. "That's the interview they saw," Rabinowitz said. "They want to talk to me about the Simpson case?" I asked. "No, it's not about the case," he assured me, "though Israelis are fascinated by what they call the 'Simpson meshuggaas.' " (This was confirmed when, in the course of my first meeting with Prime Minister Netanyahu following his election, his initial question to me was, "So, did he do it?")

Rabinowitz reminded me that in the course of the interview, I had mentioned the fact that one of the same ultra-right-wing rabbis who had condemned Johnnie Cochran for comparing the racist ideas of officer Mark Fuhrman — he had urged the rounding up and burning of all blacks — to those of Adolf Hitler had himself once compared Prime Minister Rabin to Hitler. I had criticized this rabbi, characterizing his rhetoric as dangerous and incendiary, and I had urged a lowering of voices and an end to the name-calling among the antagonists in the always feisty Israeli dialogue. The Rabins had liked what I had said and wanted to discuss with me how to increase civility in Israeli politics.

I was very much looking forward to our scheduled meeting, which I recorded in my calendar. The next afternoon, I called my brother Nathan to tell him about the upcoming meeting. "Turn on your TV," he said immediately. "You haven't heard? He's been assassinated."

The murder of a Jewish prime minister by a Jewish zealot has become an awful symbol of the change that is occurring in Jewish life, not only in Israel but in America and in many other parts of the world today. The greatest dangers to Jewish survival come today from Jews themselves. We have become, if not our own worst enemies, certainly our own most dangerous friends. With Jewish friends like Yigal Amir, and those who encouraged and supported his murderous act, who needs anti-Semitic enemies?

This change was again brought home to me quite personally on my most recent trip to Israel, in August 1996. I was having lunch with one of my oldest and dearest Israeli friends, Aharon Barak, who is the president of the Israeli Supreme Court and one of Israel's most distinguished jurists. We and our wives met at his favorite Arab restaurant in Jerusalem, as we usually did. But this time there was a fifth person: his bodyguard. I asked Aharon whether he had received death threats from Arab extremists, many of whom he had put in prison both as attorney general and as a justice. "No," he replied. "My life has been threatened by ultra-Orthodox Jewish extremists ever since I made a ruling in favor of Reform Jews." The threat was serious and the security services insisted that he be guarded wherever he went. I was shocked that my friend — one of the most scholarly and proudly Jewish people I know — felt entirely comfortable in an Arab restaurant but needed to be protected from extremist and violent Jews. Here was a man who had survived the Nazis by hiding in a crevice in a wall in Kovno now being threatened by Jewish fundamentalists. It was heartbreaking and infuriating. When I wrote a column condemning these threats, several American Jewish fanatics wrote letters characterizing Justice Barak as "mentally unstable" and telling me to mind my own business, as if assassination threats by Jews against the president of the Israeli Supreme Court were not the business of every Jew. Several weeks later, matters became even more serious, after the Supreme Court issued a preliminary ruling requiring that a busy thoroughfare adjoining an ultra-Orthodox Jerusalem neighborhood would not be closed on the Sabbath. Several ultra-Orthodox rabbis characterized Barak as a "danger to the Jewish people" — the very term used against Prime Minister Rabin just before his assassination. The Israeli security services have increased their protection of Barak accordingly.

The great irony is that our worst internal enemies have so much in common with our worst remaining external enemies: Islamic fundamentalists. They both claim to hear God's voice, which always — quite conveniently — tells them that their politics are divinely correct. They both eschew compromise and are suspicious of peace. Though they hate each other and regard each other as subhuman and deserving of death, they need each other as badly as the preacher needs the sinner.

Jewish Fundamentalism: With Friends Like Amir . . .

Thoughtless fundamentalism — a blind acceptance of "God's word" as interpreted by certain designated "messengers" — is the real enemy of rationality, heterogeneity, compromise, and peace. If there is only one true God and he has commanded you to drive the Jews (or Muslims) out of Israel (or the West Bank), then there can be no negotiations, debate, or compromise. If that God has commanded you to kill all blasphemers (such as Salman Rushdie), women who dress indecently (as Muslim fundamentalists recently did to a mother and daughter in Turkey), abortion doctors (as Christian fundamentalists have done here in the United States), Jews or Muslims at prayer (as Islamic fundamentalists and Baruch Goldstein have done), or each other (as the followers of David Koresh and the Jonestown cult did), then there is no defying these "heavenly commands."

More people have been killed, tortured, and made to suffer in the name of fundamentalist religion than for any other human cause. The false gods of fundamentalism, or their self-proclaimed prophets, are inciters to mass murder, fomenters of intolerance, and breeders of bigotry. A God who commands you to kill your innocent neighbor — as Baruch Goldstein's, the Ayatollah Khomeini's, and Paul Hill's purportedly did — is a devil who should be disobeyed.* Even within rabbinic Judaism, there is a dispute over whether God's direct order should always be obeyed. Abraham obeyed God's command to sacrifice his son, until the angel stopped him. But Rabbi Yitchak Levi of Berdichev, an eighteenth-century Hasidic rabbi, declared: "Lord, if ever thou should issue a harsh decree against the Jews, we zaddikim [just people] will not fulfill thy commands!" There is a tradition of civil disobedience even toward God by just people.

Some of my ultra-Orthodox friends are understandably outraged by any comparison between *Jewish* fundamentalists and other fundamentalists. "The Torah *is* God's word," they assure me, and it must be obeyed. But to a Muslim fundamentalist, the Koran is God's word. And to the Christian fundamentalist, the Christian Bible is God's word.

Some of the most divisive fundamentalist interpretations of God's word are not even found in the authoritative rabbinic commentaries (or their counterparts in other religions). They are derived by contemporary rabbis, imams, and ministers from *their* selective interpretations of the commentaries. For example, the modern democratic State of Israel must decide how to deal with conflicting claims to parts of the West Bank that belonged to the biblical Jews (at least for a time), as well as to the Koranic Arabs (at least for a time). Neither the Torah nor the Talmud (nor the Koran) speaks explicitly to that complex issue, since these sources did not contemplate a secular, democratic, Jewish state born out of the ashes of the Holocaust and forced to defend itself against external armies and internal terrorists. Nor are the ultra-Orthodox rabbis experts in diplomacy, geopolitics, military options, and foreign policy. Neither were they

---

* Dr. Baruch Goldstein, an American who made aliyah and lived on the West Bank, murdered and injured dozens of Arabs at prayer in Hebron before he was killed. Paul Hill, an anti-abortion zealot, killed a Florida doctor who performed abortions. Hill has been sentenced to death.

elected by the citizens of Israel to make these difficult decisions for them. As Rabbi Yehuda Amital, a respected Orthodox Halakic authority and dean of the Har Etzion Yeshiva in Israel, put it:

> In matters pertaining to the state and its government, the Torah does not have one fixed law relevant to every situation in every generation. When it comes to the fateful questions that government deals with, the halakhist must consider the whole range of variables — spiritual, military, social, economic, and more. Only a government, calling on all its resources, can develop the broad overview that is needed. For a Torah authority to pronounce on political issues, he must be privy to the whole range of considerations that the government is taking into account.[1]

Yet some ultra-Orthodox rabbis in Israel are now claiming to speak in God's name and have told their followers whom to vote for and what secular positions they should support. In *Chutzpah*, I told the story of a group of "Gedolah Torah" — self-proclaimed rabbinic "giants" — in Borough Park who formally decreed that "according to the Torah, it is forbidden to vote for a radical/liberal like Congressman Stephen Solarz," because he favored tax increases, opposed U.S. policy in Central America, and did not support "preventive detention" of defendants before trial.[2] These crassly political rabbis are not Gedolim; they are frauds who treat their followers like golems — puppets. They are the Pat Robertsons and the Al Sharptons of Judaism, abusing their rabbinic authority in order to obtain political clout and often personal financial benefit. They are blaspheming the name of God and corrupting Judaism. As President Norman Lamm told his Yeshiva University students in the wake of the Rabin assassination: "Beware of ever lightly cloaking political views, no matter how much you believe in them, in the mantle of Halacha."[3] As Rabbi Yehuda Amital put it: "There is no such thing as the *Halachic* approach to a political issue."[4]

Now it has gotten much worse, especially in Israel. For thousands of years, Jews have prayed for the heads of state. Some Israeli (and American) rabbis have eliminated that prayer and substituted one asking God for protection *from* those leaders with whose policies they disagree.[5] Others have refused to sing the Israeli national anthem "Hatikvah" and demand that a religious song be substituted. In July 1995, more than a dozen rabbis, including a former chief rabbi, issued a religious edict forbidding the evacuation of West Bank military bases and thus forbidding Orthodox soldiers to obey military orders and government directives. A number of Orthodox rabbis repudiated this decree, while others vacillated.

The rabbis who insist that all of Judea and Samaria is holy land that Jews are forbidden to surrender as part of a peace compromise should be sent out into an empty field to do battle with Islamic fundamentalists who believe, with equal fervor, that all of Palestine (whatever that is) is "a sacred Islamic endowment" and that "any part of it is not to be surrendered," since this is a principle of Ha'asharia — the Islamic equivalent of Halakah.[6] The "true" God will surely give victory to whichever claimant truly speaks in his voice.

Some extremists have gone even further, insisting that the Torah (or the Koran) justifies — or demands — the killing of innocent civilians in today's world. According to Ehud Sprinzak, a distinguished Israeli expert on Jewish fundamentalism, one fundamentalist rabbi argued that contemporary "genocide" was approved by the Torah:

The most extreme solution, extermination, was expressed in an essay by Rabbi Israel Hess published in the official magazine of Bar-Ilan university students under the title "Genocide: A Commandment of the Torah." Hess likened the Arabs to the biblical Amalekites, who were deservedly annihilated. The Amalekites, according to Hess, were both socially and militarily treacherous and cruel. Their relation to the Jews was like the relation of darkness to light — one of total contradiction. The Arabs, who live today in the land of Israel and who are constantly waging a treacherous terrorist war against the Jews, are direct descendants of the Amalekites, and the correct solution to the problem is extermination.[7]

How can anyone distinguish this incitement to murder from similar incitements by Muslim fundamentalists who quote the Koran as authority for genocide against Jews? Rabbis, imams, or ministers who make these kinds of arguments are no better than common criminals who justify their crimes by reference to selective quotations from the holy books.

And let there be no mistake about the reality that all fundamentalism *is selective*. For every source that justifies killing, there is a source condemning it. As Rabbi Chaim Seidler-Feller of UCLA puts it:

> [T]he murder by an individual who invoked God's order as justification for his abominable act reminds us that the sacred teachings of every religion contain passages that, when read literally, constitute incitement to violence. Therefore, it is the special responsibility of religious educators in the Muslim, Christian, and Jewish communities to acknowledge the intolerance and prejudice that is embedded in some of their texts, to expose those teachings, and to denounce them as immoral in their simple form, while, at the same time, presenting layers of interpretation offered by the tradition as a filter for that particularly ignominious textual passage.[8]

Any creative rabbi, imam, or minister — even the most fundamentalist — can find a way around a biblical command or prohibition, if he wants to. It is amazing how fundamentalists always happen to find a quote, a source, an authority, or a story that just happens to support their political position. In this regard, religious fundamentalists are much like judicial literalists. Lawyers, judges, and scholars who claim to be following the literal words and original understanding of the Constitution almost always happen to find original sources that support their political or legal ideologies.

I have no quarrel with fundamentalists of any religion who wish to live their *own* lives according to what others may have written or said thousands of years ago. While I personally agree with Socrates that the unexamined life is not worth living — and with Isaiah, who quoted God as urging, "Come now, let us *reason* together" — I also agree with John Stuart Mill that adults have the right to make their own mistakes. Let foolish fundamentalists who find the answers to all of today's problems in the literal words of yesterday's texts remain free to fetter their lives in the chains of the past — just so long as they do not insist on binding others with those chains. My concern is with fundamentalists who wish to impose their selective fundamentalism on the rest of us, especially by force and violence.

In terms of the use of force, there are considerable differences between most Jewish and Islamic fundamentalists. In the first place, Jewish fundamentalists do *not* have the power of the state behind them. They have always been a small minority in Israel and have never been state-supported, as Islamic fundamentalist groups like Hamas have been and still are. Moreover, the murder of innocent civilians — whether carried out by Baruch Goldstein or advocated by Rabbi Hess — has never had widespread support among the Jewish masses, or even among the most extreme fundamentalists. Those who lionize Goldstein, Kahane, and others who participated in, organized, or advocated the murder of Arab civilians have been marginalized within Israeli society, despite their shrill voices. They have become even more marginalized since the murder of Prime Minister Rabin. In the past, Jewish terrorism was regarded as so much of an oxymoron that jokes were told about it, such as the following one:

Two Jews had a plan to assassinate Hitler. They learned that he drove by a certain corner at noon each day, and they waited for him there with their guns well hidden.

At exactly noon they were ready to shoot, but there was no sign of Hitler. Five minutes later, nothing. Another five minutes went by, but no sign of Hitler. By twelve-fifteen they had started to give up hope.

"My goodness," said one of the men. "I hope nothing's happened to him!"[9]

Jews even joked about killing the prime minister of Israel, as this one from the 1950s shows:

After an hour of standing in line at the Tel Aviv bank, Chaim was furious. "I hate all this waiting!" he shouted to his wife. "I'm leaving. I'm going to kill Ben-Gurion."

An hour later, he returned to the bank. "What happened?" asked his wife, who was still waiting in line.

"Nothing," said the unhappy man. "There was a longer line over there."[10]

No Jew would tell such a joke today. The support for Jewish terrorism, though tragically present, is very small. The same cannot be said about the level and nature of support for Islamic terrorism against Jewish civilians, which is far more widespread within the Arab world.

Moreover, Jewish fundamentalists will never become a majority or even a plurality in Israel. Because of the nature of the Israeli political system, the few Israeli fundamentalists do have disproportionate power in Israeli politics, but that power is rarely sufficient to impose their way on others. They will always remain at the fringes of the government, since most Jews are not, and will never be, fundamentalists. Questioning authority, even — perhaps especially — religious authority, is characteristic of most contemporary Jews, both in Israel and in the Diaspora. In some Islamic countries, on the other hand, fundamentalists constitute a large and growing proportion of the population. In Iran, they are in power. In Egypt, Saudi Arabia, and Turkey, they pose significant dangers to the stability of the governments.

As lethal as Islamic fundamentalism promises to be to Israel and the Jewish people, Jewish fundamentalism — religious and political — poses a far deeper and more pervasive threat to Jewish continuity and survival, despite their small numbers. Because of their refusal to obey secular law, even a few Jewish terrorists can cause enormous harm. Just as our external enemies have played too great a role in defining us as Jews, so too have they played an important role in keeping the diverse and heterogeneous Jewish people united. Even now — before our external enemies have even disappeared — the fragile cement that holds us together is beginning to crack. The religious and political Jewish fundamentalists in Israel and America who claim to speak for God and who reject all compromise in the peace process and in the balancing of the religious and secular are trying to tear Israel and the Jewish people apart. A recent novel by Tova Reich titled *The Jewish War* suggests a not too fanciful scenario under which messianic Jews reestablish the theocratic kingdom of Judea and Samaria, secede from secular Israel, and engage in a civil war. Today's headlines, both in Israel and in America, reveal the seeds of such division. The head of the Anti-Defamation League publicly resigns in protest from the Orthodox synagogue he and his family have attended for twenty years because his rabbi has been preaching "hate and vitriol toward the elected leaders of Israel." Rabbi Steven Pruzansky has urged Jews to reject "the blatherings of the Rabin *Judenrat*" — an obscene analogy to the unelected Jewish councils put in place by the Nazis to govern the Jewish ghettos and lead them to the gas chambers. Rabbi Pruzansky has substituted a new prayer for the traditional one blessing Israel's elected leaders. His new prayer calls on God to "thwart the conspiracy of those destroyers and demolishers who desire to tear apart the land of our heritage" — the land that was "a gift of God" on which Jews must build a "holy nation." But it is rabbis like him who are tearing apart the Jewish people by trying to delegitimate the elected leaders of Israel and the vast majority of American Jews who support the peace process and who reject the idea that Jews have a God-given, non-negotiable claim to all of biblical Israel.

The role of extremist rabbis in fomenting violence and lawlessness came to a head with the murder of Prime Minister Rabin. Just before the assassination, a far-right rabbi issued the following "curse" on Rabin: "And on him, Yitzhak son of Rosa, known as Rabin . . . we have permission . . . to demand from the angels of destruction that they take a sword to this wicked man . . . to kill him . . . for handing over the Land of Israel to our enemies, the sons of Ishamael."[11] The curse was to expire in early November, exactly when Rabin was murdered.

The Israeli police also looked into reports that another rabbi had issued a specific religious edict — called a "pursuer's decree" — demanding Rabin's death. Such an edict would be akin to those issued by the Iranian ayatollahs against Salman Rushdie. If the police could prove that such an edict was issued, there might be a criminal case against the rabbi. At the very least, it should result in the kind of universal condemnation that has greeted the decree against Rushdie. Rabbis, ayatollahs, or ministers who misuse their religion to call for the death of innocent people — whether they be political leaders, Jewish children, or abortion doctors — are not part of civilized society. Whether or not they are criminals in the eyes of the law, they are certainly contemptible in the eyes of humanity.

Some on the lunatic-fringe Jewish right actually tried to justify the murder of Yitzhak Rabin by citing Jewish law:

Day after day, edicts handed down by some rabbinic authorities permitted, even demanded, the assassination of the prime minister. . . . [There were posters] equating Rabin with SS storm troopers; accusations of disloyalty and betrayal; portraits of Rabin in intoxicated stupor.

A mock death certificate with Rabin's name on it was circulated around West Bank settlements. Author Moshe Shamir went on the radio to accuse Rabin of "collaborating with Nazis." A group of settlement rabbis published an opinion that "the life of anyone abandoning part of the land of Israel is forfeitable." Benjamin Kahane of Kahane Chai told an interviewer, "Many think the solution is to murder Rabin and Peres." Uzi Landau, a Likud leader, called Rabin "an ignoramus . . . who has no idea about Judaism or Zionism." Moshe Saitovitch, a thirty-seven-year-old Israeli working in New York, posted an Internet message branding Rabin a traitor whose crimes invited punishment "by death or life imprisonment." And finally, Yigal Amir called Yitzhak Rabin "a pursuer" — one who betrays his people to the enemy and must be killed.[12]

As Rabbi Chaim Seidler-Feller of UCLA put it:

The assassination made it clear that the *beit midrash*, the study hall where Talmudic learning occurs, has lost its innocence. For hundreds of years yeshiva rabbis have peppered their discourse with a range of speculative opinions, knowing that the consequences of their analyses were merely theoretical. So, for instance, when they discussed the law of the pursuer, no one imagined that the deliberations would result in action, and that the ruling would be implemented. Yigal Amir effectively changed all that, forcing the realization that in a *beit midrash* whose students are part of the military, abstract teachings can become powerfully explosive tools. The rabbinic scholars, who seem not to have been conscious of this paradigm shift, can deny the new reality no longer.*[13]

---

* Israeli secularists were stimulated by the assassination to learn Jewish sacred texts so that they did not have to "trust" the ultra-Orthodox "interpretation," which could "lead to terrible distortions, even murder" (*Jerusalem Report*, December 26, 1996, p. 16).

It is important to remember that the Talmud was written while the Jews were in exile and not responsible for actual self-governance (except in limited ways). The rabbis had the luxury of engaging in speculations that went untested in the crucible of experience. They did not have to worry that a general concept would be misapplied with lethal consequences by a thoughtless fanatic. Now that Israel is a self-governing democracy comprising all manner of people — including zealots with guns — some of these general principles may have to be narrowed or reconsidered.

Up until the Rabin murder, I had a policy of always making a small contribution to every little yeshiva in Israel that sent me a solicitation. No more! Now I scrutinize every request to assure myself that I am not helping a yeshiva that encourages murder in the name of false Talmudic teaching.

A year after the murder, the *Boston Globe* quoted Bar-Ilan University professor Nissan Rubin: "Today there is a sense in the religious community that Rabin's death was a miracle. Just as Jews have always been saved from their troubles at the last minute, so it happened this time, too. He was killed and we were saved. In the eyes of many religious Jews, the result of the election was proof of this view."[14]

This is surely an overgeneralization, even regarding the ultra-Orthodox community, but it is true that many ultra-Orthodox Jews continue to believe that Rabin's murder was justified by Halakah. As the devil can cite scripture, so, too, can some religious fundamentalists claim to cite Halakic authority for virtually any ignoble deed that serves their political ends. Had Amir feasted on a meal of ham, shrimp, and lobster on the Yom Kippur before the murder, there would be some fanatics who could find a Halakic justification for his actions — as long as he opposed the peace process. There are others who would condemn the eating of the ham, but justify the killing of Rabin. Most rabbis, of every political and religious persuasion, did, of course, condemn the murder, since killing is not the Jewish way and *pikuach nefesh* — the saving of life — is the highest of obligations. On the first anniversary of the assassination, Rabbi Shlomo Riskin — an Orthodox rabbi who had himself been unlawfully detained by the Labor government for protesting some of its policies — wrote a stinging rebuke to "such a desecration of God's name emanating from an individual who purports to speak in God's name" and to any fundamentalist "who entertains the blind conviction that he alone possess[es] the truth."[15] And one of the most distinguished Orthodox rabbis in the world, Emanuel Rackman — the chancellor of Bar-Ilan University, where Amir had been a student — wrote an article explaining how Jewish law does not authorize any individual to take the law into his own hands, except in cases when there is no time to seek intervention from the courts to *save* human life. He concluded that Amir's act was clearly in violation of Halakah.[16]

The diversity of the reactions to the murder of Yitzhak Rabin symbolized the dramatic changes that are occurring in the world today. The murder was greeted by a near-universal sadness even in the Arab world, but by joy in some Jewish quarters. Though Rabin's death united most Jews as well, his life, his politics, and his quest for peace had divided Jews as few issues in Israel's history had done.

The reactions to the surprise election of Benjamin Netanyahu in 1996 in Israel's first direct election of a prime minister demonstrated how drastically the world had changed since the 1975 UN General Assembly condemned Zionism — and hence Israel — as a form of racism. This notoriously anti-Semitic resolution energized and united the Jews of the world in support of beleaguered and embattled Israel, as had the threats by Nasser and other Arab rulers to "drive the Jews into the sea," which had precipitated the Six-Day War eight years earlier. The world's reaction to the Netanyahu victory was largely cautious and measured. There was palpable disappointment on the part of American and European leaders, who had come to know and respect Shimon Peres's commitment to the peace process and who were concerned that Netanyahu might slow it down or even end it. There was a concerned, but modulated, response from most Arab moderates, who were counting on Peres to continue the peace process Rabin had begun. Arab radicals, while secretly applauding Netanyahu's victory, continued to demonize both Peres and his victorious opponent, claiming that there was no real difference between them. The most vociferous, strident, polemical, personal, and irresponsible vilification of Israel's new prime minister came, however, from *Jews*, especially American Jews of the left. Dan Wasserman drew a cartoon showing Netanyahu's hands being raised in victory by Rabin's murderer and a Hamas terrorist. Thomas Friedman of the *New York Times* characterized the election of Netanyahu as a "disaster" and described the new prime minister as out of touch with reality.[17] There was also demonization from Israeli Jews of the left. Some of the language was reminiscent of that used by Jews of the extreme right against the late Prime Minister Rabin and his successor, Shimon Peres.[18]

This reaction demonstrated to me that what has happened to American Jewry has begun to happen to Israel. Though American Jewry still has its enemies — its Farrakhans, its Buchanans, its *Turner Diaries* crowd, its Holocaust deniers — they have become largely marginalized and we have gained general acceptance from the American mainstream. At the same time, the *internal* enmity, *within* the Jewish community, has become more open and polemical. Israel's most strident enemies have also become more marginalized, though still powerful. Since the peace process with the Palestinians began, Israel has received an increased measure of legitimacy from the international community, and even from the moderate Arab states. The massive turnout for Rabin's funeral was testimony to this development. (One of my more cynical friends commented, however, that the world has always "shown respect for dead Jews.") At the same time Israel's external enemies have become weaker and more marginalized, internal dissension has increased. Again, one symbolic act captures the change. Leah Rabin refused to shake Benjamin Netanyahu's hand at her husband's funeral, but she welcomed Yassir Arafat — a murderer of Jewish children but her husband's peace partner — into her home for a shiva visit.

Some of this change is, of course, illusory. There has always been dissension within Israel. But when external dangers threaten Israel, these differences are muted. When the external dangers abate, the internal dissension becomes more vocal. In some respects, the decibel level of internal debate reflects the degree of self-confidence within the Jewish community. A frightened community cowers together, circling the wagons, while a self-confident community is more willing to wash its dirty laundry in public.

The Two Israels

But in another, quite important sense, the recently overt divisions are all too real. While our slogans announce that "we are one," the reality is that we are deeply divided. The ultra-Orthodox are as different from modern secular Jews as Islamic fundamentalists are from secular Palestinians and secular Arabs of other nations. When a young Hasidic man told an American TV interviewer in 1996 that he would vote for whomever his rabbi told him to vote for, it brought to mind the young Islamic fundamentalists who were prepared to commit suicide if their imam told them to. Neither group has any appreciation for democracy, though the Jewish fundamentalists have quickly learned how to use it as a means to achieving their anti-democratic ends.

I am afraid that the kind of divisive rhetoric that has come to characterize much of the debate over the peace process may portend the Jewish people's future after our enemies have left us alone for a couple of generations. There may simply be too much division in worldview between Jewish fundamentalists and Jewish modernists to keep us united without common enemies. Israeli journalist Ze'ev Chafetz has advocated the division of Israel into two sovereign nations, one secular (Israel), the other theocratic (Judea).

We see this division in Arab countries that have made peace with Israel. In Egypt, for example, the civil war between Islamic fundamentalists and Egyptian modernists has intensified since Egyptians gave up their common enemy Israel. There is concern, as well, in Jordan, Saudi Arabia, and other Middle Eastern nations. The reality is that Jewish and Arab modernists have more in common with each other — at least in some respects — than they do with their fundamentalist coreligionists.

Why, after all, should we expect Jews — or Israelis — to have much in common, beyond common enemies and fears of persecution as Jews? Whether Judaism is a religion, a civilization, a nationality, or any combination of these and other characteristics, Jews are as diverse as any people can be. In the absence of common enemies, Jews have no more in common with each other than do Americans, or Catholics, or Europeans, or Slavs, or Scandinavians. In religion, we range from fundamentalists to moderates to skeptics to atheists. In politics, we cover the gamut from Communists to reactionaries. In economics, some Jews are Marxists, while others are followers of Milton Friedman's free market ideas. I was recently told the following story about Friedman: A synagogue in California called the great free market economist to seek his advice on how to invest some excess funds, but they reached another Milton Friedman, who is an adviser to charitable groups. That Friedman's advice was "Have you thought of giving it to the poor?" The synagogue treasurer incredulously asked, "Is this the real Milton Friedman?" To which Friedman replied, "Is this the real synagogue?"

If indeed we have anything in common beyond common enemies, it is our very inability to agree about anything, our contentiousness, our stubbornness, our assertiveness, our unwillingness to be subjected to hierarchy, authority, and regimentation. To expect a people such as that — a people who rejected their God in favor of a golden calf just after he freed them from slavery, a people who argue with God, a people who criticize their rabbis, their leaders, and each other — to have much in common is to harbor unrealistic expectations. The classic Jewish story reflecting this division is about the rabbi who got sick and the chairman of the synagogue's board of directors reported to him that the board had voted to wish him a full recovery — by a vote of 7 to 6. In Israel, if a prime minister got sick, the vote would probably be a tie!

But to argue requires listening and understanding one's adversary. It assumes a basic respect for him. It presupposes the possibility of being persuaded by reason. For fundamentalists, however, these conditions cannot be met. By definition, a fundamentalist does not trust in reason, in logic, or in persuasion. To a fundamentalist, argument is merely a God-approved tactic designed to prove an immutable point to a misguided disbeliever. Religious fundamentalists who argue about the existence of God don't do so because they are open to the possibility of being convinced of God's nonexistence. Indeed, even if logic and evidence all pointed to the nonexistence of God, the fundamentalist would reject logic and evidence, since the existence of God is the constant and everything else — including reason — is a variable.

Arguing with a fundamentalist — Jewish, Islamic, or Christian — is like complaining to a soda machine after it takes your money and fails to produce the bottle. Shaking it at least has the possibility, slim as it may be, of jarring the mechanism or getting out your frustration. But arguing with a machine is irrational, since a machine is incapable of responding to logic. So too with a fundamentalist. It may make you feel better to best a fundamentalist in argument, but it will not have any effect on his mechanistic thinking. It is as if an artificial-intelligence machine were programmed to hold an immutable belief and to construct all possible arguments in support of that belief and reject all arguments inconsistent with it. The most deadly combination is, of course, Jewish and Islamic fundamentalists, both determined to reject compromise, both believing that God has ordained their actions, and both unwilling to listen to voices of reason. It is a prescription for Armageddon — which, of course, pleases some Christian fundamentalists who believe that Armageddon must occur before the second coming of their Messiah. No wonder Patrick Buchanan hopes for a time "not far distant when we are all going to have to gird ourselves and take that long march up to Armageddon to do battle for the Lord."[19] Armageddon is, of course, located in Israel.

There are several different kinds of divisions among Jews and Israelis, and it matters greatly what *kinds* of divisions exist. There are tactical differences about means among Jews who essentially agree about ends. Virtually all Jews, except those messianic fanatics who believe that Armageddon must precede the coming of the Messiah, want peace. Most Jews would be prepared to trade *some* land captured during the defensive Six-Day War for a *real* peace. A small number of Jews, both Israelis and Americans, believe it to be a sin to return any land, even non-biblical land, to the Arabs. A larger number of Jews, though still a distinct minority, believe it is religiously impermissible to return the biblical Judea and Samaria, especially those cities such as Hebron, Nablus (Shechem), and Jericho that are important to Jewish history. A much larger percentage of Jews agree in principle that much of the captured land should be returned for peace, especially land with large concentrations of Arab population (which happens to be some of the same places with special biblical significance). Among these Jews, the vast majority believe that Israel should keep largely unpopulated buffer areas that enhance Israel's security. But even many of them would be prepared to surrender some such land — most particularly the strategic Golan Heights — if doing so were necessary to secure a global peace and if realistic steps could be taken to assure its demilitarization, as was done with the Sinai.

Tactical, even strategic, differences can be resolved by compromise, democratic elections, and changing realities (such as the economic boom that even a preliminary and partial peace seems to have brought). We can "reason together" about such matters. But religious differences, especially with unreasoning fundamentalists, cannot be resolved. (Ironically, when God said to "reason together," the context was religious sin.) For a Jew who believes that God gave him Hebron, there is no rational way to persuade him to give up sovereignty or leave. Nor is it possible to persuade an Islamic fundamentalist who believes just as strongly that his God gave him exclusive domain over the same land.

Increasingly, the divisions among Jews — especially but not exclusively concerning Israel — are of the kind not subject to rational resolution. This reality has made it harder for some Jews to support Israel, let alone consider moving there. It used to be much easier to be "pro-Israel" when Jews, especially American Jews, were not so divided about Israeli policies, both political and religious. Today American Jews are being asked to take sides on difficult and complex issues, some of which go right to the question of what is the nature of the Jewish state.

There is even an up side to this conflict. The irreconcilable and often passionate differences among Jews *over* Israel reflect a deep and abiding commitment by most Jews *to* Israel. People do not become so passionate over something about which they do not care deeply. So long as most Diaspora Jews continue to debate the Israeli future, they will maintain a strong connection to the Jewish state, and Israel will remain an important part of the Jewish identity of many American Jews.

American Support of Israel

Being an American Jew (or a Jew anywhere outside Israel) gives one the right to participate in the Israeli political decision-making process — but *only* if one exercises that right by becoming an Israeli citizen and moving to Israel. A Jew who does not make aliyah does not have a direct vote in Israel's future. We may support, cheer, contribute to, defend, invest in, send our children to, pray for, criticize, even love the Jewish state, but the Israeli democracy is composed of 4.5 million Jews, and nearly a million Arabs and others. The citizens of Israel must decide its future. I do not believe in American Friends of Likud, American Friends of Labor, American Friends of Peace Now, or American Friends of Gush Emunim. I believe in American Friends of Israel. Even when my dear friend and former client Natan Sharansky asked me to support his new political party, I politely declined, though I was enormously proud of what he was doing and hoped for his success.* Nor would I support Israeli Friends of the Republicans, Israeli Friends of the Democrats, or Israeli Friends of Ross Perot. All politics is local, as Tip O'Neill observed, and it should remain so. "No taxation without representation" was an important motto of the American Revolution, but its corollary does not hold. Many active Jews around the world "pay taxes" to Israel in the form of generous annual contributions to the UJA, Israel Bonds, and other Jewish philanthropic organizations that send money to the Jewish state. But these payments do not entitle us to "representation" in Israeli politics. We may vote in our own Jewish organizations and in our own nation, and these votes may have an influence on developments in the Middle East, but until we are prepared to put our bodies in harm's way by making aliyah, we should never try to dictate to a fellow democracy how it should balance the risks and benefits of different roads toward peace and security.

In the weeks before the Israeli 1996 election that brought Benjamin Netanyahu to power, I was asked to give one of the opening speeches at the American Israel Public Affairs Committee (AIPAC) conference in Washington. At the time, it looked like Peres would be elected in a close race. I urged the large crowd of influential pro-Israel activists to make a silent pledge that whatever the outcome of the election, they would continue to support Israel and lobby, in unity, on Israel's behalf. My request received a divided response. The audience expected Peres to win and most welcomed that outcome. The pro-Peres group cheered me loudly, suggesting support for my pledge. Those who favored Netanyahu but expected Peres to win remained silent. Indeed, some berated me after my talk, believing that I was suggesting a curtailment of their right to dissent. What I was suggesting was that the pro-Israel American Jewish community speak with one voice, especially when it lobbies on behalf of Israel. I disapproved of those right-wing Jews who lobbied in Congress against some of what the Rabin and Peres governments sought — just as I disapproved of those left-wing Jews who had lobbied against the Begin and Shamir governments. The small Jewish

---

* I was one of Anatoly (now Natan) Sharansky's lawyers when he was imprisoned by the Soviets. After his release, he made aliyah and eventually started his own political party, which won several seats in the 1996 election. He is now in the Israeli cabinet.

community in America can be an effective voice for Israel only if it remains united in its support of whichever government happens to be in power. I reminded the AIPAC audience how impotent we were with regard to Jonathan Pollard precisely because we did not unite and speak with a single voice.

Most American Jews seem to agree with this general principle — at least some of the time. When the Begin and Shamir governments were in power, American Jews on the right would make that speech: "Don't interfere, just support the elected government of Israel." Some American Jews on the left would invoke their right to dissent in public and even to try to influence the American government *against* supporting particular Israeli policies. When the Rabin–Peres governments came into power, the roles were reversed. Suddenly, some of the same people who had called for a united front in support of Israel and opposed dissent were now among the most vociferous dissenters, calling for the American government to oppose Israeli policies, while the previous dissenters were demanding a single voice in support of the only legitimately elected government of Israel.

As soon as the 1996 Israeli election results were final, I wrote a congratulatory note to my old friend Bibi and I enclosed a copy of my AIPAC speech. Despite my strong personal reservations about portions of the Likud platform, he could count on me to continue my staunch support for Israel. In August 1996, I spent the better part of an hour with the new prime minister in his office. When I again assured him of my support, he joked, "But you would have said the same thing to my opponent if he had won." We understand each other, and he welcomes my nonpartisan support.

I long for the days when American Jews loved, supported, and trusted Israel. The standard joke was about the two American tourists who went to a nightclub in Tel Aviv where an Israeli comedian was performing in Hebrew. Every time he came to a punch line, one of the tourists would laugh uproariously. The other said, "Wait a minute, you don't understand Hebrew. How do you know he's funny?" The first responded, "He's Israeli, I trust him." No more! Today's tourists would insist on knowing which party he belonged to before laughing.

Israel remains an important — some would argue a too important — part of Judaism and the Jewish identity. It has permitted secular Jews to feel strongly Jewish. Indeed, it has strengthened other dimensions of Jewish identification for a considerable number of Jews. I know several Jewish men and women who were well along the road to total assimilation before the Six-Day War. That epochal event transformed them into strong supporters of Israel, and their support for Israel turned them back to the synagogue, the Hebrew day school for their children, and Jewish charity.

For others, their Judaism *is* Israel. This includes many of my Israeli friends, who have absolutely no other identification with Judaism. "We don't need the Jewish house of worship," one of my Israeli friends loves to tell me, "because we live in the Jewish land where the Bible is our geography and history book." Israel is indeed a Jewish nation, with Jewish symbols, Jewish history, Jewish mannerisms, Jewish politicians, Jewish art, Jewish literature, and Jewish problems.

A Jewish State or a State of Jews?

But even the "Jewish" character of Israel is being called into question today. Ironically, the doubts are being raised by both the extreme right and the extreme left. The extreme right is threatening Israel's Jewish identity indirectly by its advocacy of continued Jewish domination over large Arab population centers, such as Hebron. An Israel with control over a quickly growing Arab population of more than 2 million would either cease to be a Jewish state or it would cease to be a democratic state. A democratic state with a majority of Arabs — which an Israel that continued to occupy the entire West Bank would eventually become, considering the unequal birthrates and the combination of low in-migrations and high out-migrations of Israeli Jews — would eventually lose its Jewish character. And a Jewish Israel that prevented a majority of its population from voting and changing the nature of the state would surrender its democratic character.

The program of some on the extreme left threatens the Jewish character of Israel more directly. Some aggressively anti-religious Israelis would eliminate the menorah and the Star of David as official symbols of Israel. They would change the national anthem to censor any reference to the "Jewish soul." Some would even abrogate the law of return, under which Jews from anywhere in the world have the right to Israeli citizenship if they make aliyah.

For Jews like me and many of my friends and students — who love Israel and Judaism but are essentially secular — the debate over the Jewish character of Israel is not only disturbing, it is in many respects a microcosm of the larger debate over what the Jewish character is and what makes something — in this case Israel — "Jewish." We refuse to accept the exclusivist definition of what is Jewish offered by those who are today in control of defining Judaism in Israel.* By relegating so many life decisions to the exclusively Orthodox, and denying authority to Conservative, Reform, Reconstructionist, and all other Jews, Israel has delegitimated the religious beliefs of the vast majority of Jews both in Israel and in the Diaspora. Like Theodor Herzl, most Jews do not want a religious Jewish state in which the ultra-Orthodox rabbis make religious policy based on their particularistic and often self-serving interpretation of Halakah. We want every rabbi, imam, minister, and priest to be free to preach and practice his (and *her*) religion. But like Herzl, we want these religious leaders to stay in their temples and not stray too far into the halls of the Knesset.

Yet most Jews want to preserve the "Jewish character" of Israel, as Herzl did, without quite knowing what that Jewish character is supposed to be. The ultra-Orthodox Jews have the advantage in this debate, since they know exactly what it is they want to preserve. They have a precise list containing 613 commandments, a series of books with rules and rituals, a methodology for interpreting these rules, and a direct mandate from God. We more secular Jews, on the other hand, are a bit like the U.S. Supreme Court justice Potter Stewart, who, when asked to define pornography, acknowledged that he could not, and then added: "But I know it when I see it." We have great difficulty defining with precision what constitutes the Jewish character of Israel, but we know it when we feel it in Israel.

Nearly every Jew I know, regardless of his or her degree of religious observance or belief, feels something special when he or she

---

* Even some Orthodox Jews are critical of the chief rabbinate for some restrictive decisions about whether certain Ethiopian Falashas meet the Halakic definition of who is a Jew for purposes of the law of return.

walks down the streets of Jerusalem, drives up the Gallil, winds through the narrow alleys of Tzefat, floats in the Dead Sea, looks down from the hills of Haifa, parasails in the Harbor of Eilat, hikes through the wadis of the Negev, or even shops in the very American malls of Tel Aviv. For a Jew — for almost any kind of Jew — being in Israel is a Jewish experience. It is an experience different from being in a Jewish neighborhood in New York, or in a synagogue in Buenos Aires, or at a Jewish wedding in Prague. Being in Israel — a nation governed by Jewish politicians, protected by a Jewish army, speaking the Jewish language — is a source of enormous pride, identity, and comfort. And yet there is ambivalence about precisely what Israel's Jewish character is — especially for those of us who refuse to identify it exclusively with a set of theological principles about which we have so much doubt and so little agreement.

The further one moves away from the strictly religious component of Judaism, the more difficult it is to define the Jewish character either of Israel or of the Jewish community. When Israel was in mortal danger of destruction from its external enemies — as it has been until recently — it was not necessary or even possible to obsess over the Jewish character of the embattled state. The Arabs wanted to destroy Israel because it was Jewish, and that was a Jewish enough reason for us to identify with it (as we identified with Soviet Jews, without debating their Jewish character). As Israel moves toward normality in the international community, it is only natural that there will be increasing debate as to precisely what the Jewish character of Israel is and should be. That debate will, in many respects, parallel the ongoing debate about the nature of Jewishness in general, as the Jews of the world begin to shed their negative identity as victims and search for an identity independent of our external enemies.

This dramatic transformation of Jewish identity — from reactive to proactive, from negative to positive, from externally imposed to internally chosen — will require change in the very theory of Zionism and will require a redefinition of the entire relationship between Israel and the Jewish communities of the Diaspora. A hundred years ago, Theodor Herzl wrote a short book titled *The Jewish State* in which he sought to answer "the Jewish question" of his era. He correctly diagnosed the central problem of the Jews on the eve of the twentieth century as persistent, endemic, and inherent anti-

Semitism in every host nation in which Jews lived in significant numbers. There is no way to end this institutional hatred, he argued, because its causes are self-reinforcing: If Jews succeed, their very success increases anti-Semitism; if Jews fail, that too contributes to the hatred; if Jews leave the places where anti-Semitism is greatest and "move to those places where we are not persecuted, our presence there produces persecution."[20]

Nor can anti-Semitism "be rejected by reasonable arguments," he claimed, since we are "disliked as much for our gifts as we are for our faults." Neither will anti-Semitism be cured by the class struggle, "because we stand in the most exposed position in the camps of both socialists and capitalists." Unless Jews take their destiny into their own hands, Herzl concluded, great dangers from their external enemies are on the horizon.

With these astute observations, Herzl summarized much of the history of Jewish victimization. As a secular, intellectual Jew living at the end of the nineteenth century, he focused more on the social, economic, and political causes of anti-Semitism than on the religious ones. Religiously inspired anti-Judaism had dominated Jewish history from the writing of the Christian Gospels until the beginning of the Age of Enlightenment, but by the end of the nineteenth century, ethnicity — "race" in the inapt language of the age — was quickly becoming a dominant factor in the prejudice against Jews. But whatever the cause du jour of anti-Semitism in the past, there could be no doubt that it was persistent, endemic, and not subject to reasoned response.

There were only two possible answers to the historic persecution of the Jews: The first, which Herzl originally considered, was complete assimilation by intermarriage. Herzl saw this solution as neither desirable nor feasible. It was not desirable because Herzl did not want to see "the distinctive nationality of Jews ... destroyed." Although he never tried to define or describe this "distinctive" Jewish character — which, for him as a secular Jew, went beyond religion — it was important for him, as for so many other Jews of all kinds, to perpetuate it. Nor would it be feasible, even if desirable, for Jews to assimilate through intermarriage in late-nineteenth-century Europe, because few gentiles wanted to intermarry with the masses of Jewish poor. For intermarriage to work, Herzl argued, the "Jews must previously acquire economic power sufficiently great to overcome the old social prejudice against them" — as the Jewish "aristocracy" demonstrated by their high "numbers of mixed marriages." But the Jewish masses would never be allowed to acquire the degree of economic power sufficient to make them desirable mates. Indeed, if they were to begin accumulating enough money to make them desirable marriage partners for Christians, that would stimulate increasing hatred toward them. Thus Herzl concluded that "the absorption of Jews by means of their prosperity is unlikely to occur."

The second answer to the Jewish question of Herzl's day — the problem of endemic anti-Semitism — was the creation of a Jewish state. The Jewish question in 1896 was "a national question, which can only be solved by making it a political world-question." The building of a Jewish nation, Herzl naively believed, would immediately end anti-Semitism: "The Jews, once settled in their own state, would probably have no more enemies."

Reflecting a paradoxical perspective that runs through Jewish history, Herzl believed that anti-Semitism was not only the *bane* of the Jewish people, it was also their *salvation*. As a secular and relatively assimilated Jew, Herzl did not have a deep appreciation for the positive aspects of Judaism. He was a Jew — he remained a Jew — largely *because* of the anti-Semitism and external hatred directed at him and his people. Herzl sought to harness the power of this hatred as the "propelling force for the creation of the Jewish state. And what is that force?" he asked. "The misery of the Jews." Tsuris!

Political Zionism was thus an answer — *the* answer, according to Herzl — to the Jewish question posed by our enemies: namely, how can we rid ourselves of the Jews?

Although Herzl occasionally alluded to the "faith of our fathers," his proposed state was entirely secular. He emphatically rejected arguments based on "divine institution" or "superior power." He eschewed any biblical notion of the Jews being a "chosen people," and instead proclaimed that "we are not a whit better than ordinary people." Indeed, he diagnosed a major cause of "the Jewish problem" as being the tragic reality that the Jewish people have never been "normalized" by nationhood. The cure was an ordinary nation-state in which Jews planted their own fields, removed their own garbage, and acted just like other people. His Jewish homeland would certainly not be a theocracy. It would be a nation in which belief and disbelief lived alongside each other, where the freethinker was welcomed, and where "our priests [shall be kept] within the confines of their temples" and "not interfere in the administration of the State."*

The Jewish question at the end of the nineteenth century was primarily an external one: How shall we respond to the hatred of our enemies? Its answer was political: By physically removing ourselves from our enemies' control and embarking on our destiny as a people with a distinct "national character." That answer addressed the most pressing challenge of Herzl's era: literal survival in the face of external threats to Jews' physical safety. The tragic history of the first half-century following the publication of *The Jewish State* — the emergence of Nazism and Communism and the anti-Semitic policies of both — certainly proved him prescient. Anti-Semitism was only exacerbated by Jewish success, by the struggle between the right and the left, and even — at least for a while — by the large influx of Jews from Eastern Europe into America, which directly resulted in anti-Semitic immigration restrictions, educational quotas, and increased social prejudice against Jews. The Holocaust, which even Herzl could not have foreseen, conclusively proved that there was no Jewish future in many parts of Europe. The creation of the State of Israel, on the ashes of the Holocaust and the pioneering efforts of the relatively small number of Jews who had earlier chosen to live the Zionist dream, fulfilled Herzl's prophecy, though not his hope that it would end anti-Semitism.

In the century since Herzl published his influential tract — which he hoped would open "a general discussion on the Jewish question" of his day — the Jewish question has changed dramatically. For the first time in the 3,500-year history of the Jewish people, individual Jews do not face significant threats to their physical survival anywhere in the world. To be sure, such threats have not abated completely — as evidenced by continuing terrorism in Israel and occasional anti-Semitic violence throughout the world — but they are not among the worst dangers posed to the Jewish people, at least as of this writing. Nor are we any longer victims of the kind of ram-

---

* This concept of a high wall of separation between church/synagogue/mosque and state has been tragically compromised in Israel, especially by the ultra-Orthodox political parties, which have used their leverage in the coalition politics of Israel to magnify the power of the ultrareligious minority.

pant discrimination — in jobs, neighborhoods, schools, clubs — from which Jews suffered in Herzl's day and even more recently. Indeed, what Theodor Herzl believed could never happen — namely, the acquisition by Jews of sufficient economic power "to overcome the old social prejudice against them" — has recently come to pass in many parts of the world. Contemporary American Jews have the full range of choices open to them, as their predecessors did not. They may choose a Jewish or non-Jewish mate, neighborhood, club, workplace, school, country — life! The Jews of the twenty-first century, except for those insular Hasidim who deliberately deny themselves and their children the opportunity to interact with others, will be Jews *by choice*. They may be the first generation of Jews entirely free to accept or reject their Jewishness, without stigma, without sanction, and even without guilt. Twenty-first-century American Jews will truly be a "chosen people": *They* will have *chosen* to remain Jewish.

In addition, we may, during the next century, experience another phenomenon that Herzl deemed unlikely. He hypothesized that if our Christian hosts "were to leave us in peace . . . for two generations," we "might well be able to merge entirely into surrounding races" by intermarriage and assimilation.

The Jewish state has, in fact, come into existence. So, too, has Jewish economic power sufficient to overcome much of the "old social prejudice." We may soon experience two generations of being allowed to live in relative peace. The new Jewish question must now be faced squarely and addressed to Israel as well as the Jews of the Diaspora: Does the perpetuation of the Jewish people and the Israeli nation require external enmity, hatred, and danger?

Negative Zionism

The Herzlian theory of Zionism, like much of nineteenth- and twentieth-century Judaism itself, is essentially negative, reactive, and based on our external enemies. According to Herzl, the "propelling force in the creation of a Jewish state" is the endemic anti-Semitism of our enemies. It is "our enemies" who have made us one and who "force us back to the parent stem." Without our external enemies — without the anti-Semites — we would disappear by merging "entirely into the surrounding races." Though Herzl was talking primarily about his kind of Jew — secular, assimilated, religiously illiterate — his point had considerable validity in an age characterized by pervasive hatred of the Jews by the church, the state, and most other elite institutions, as well as the masses.*

But the world is changing quickly. While Israel and world Jewry still have external enemies, the younger generations of Jews do not identify as strongly as my generation did with endangered Israel and embattled Judaism. Yet a hundred years after Theodor Herzl first published his reactive theory of Zionism — that endemic anti-Semitism is "the propelling force for the creation of the Jewish state" — some of Israel's leaders persist in the use of negative scare tactics to try to attract American Jews, and the Jews of other nations, to Zion. This may be understandable in light of the reality of Israel's demography. The fact is that the vast majority of Israel's Jewish population, and their forebears, emigrated to Israel for largely negative reasons. They fled Hitler's Europe; they had no place else to go after the Holocaust; they were exiled from Arab and Islamic lands; they emigrated from a hostile Soviet Union, or its post-Soviet satellites. They saw no future in apartheid or postapartheid South Africa. Only a small percentage of Jews who have made aliyah to Israel have "chosen" the Jewish state for entirely positive or ideological reasons. Among this small percentage, however, is a large percentage of past and present Israeli leaders who were a product of the pre-Holocaust aliyah movements. Most American-born Israelis — called "Anglo-Saxons" by the Sabras — also chose Israel, as did many from other free nations who made ideological or religious aliyah from places where they were generally well treated. But these "true" Zionists constitute only a small percentage of Israel's population. Many who did not originally "choose" Israel now of course feel a strong, positive, ideological identification with the country that gave them sanctuary from their enemies. Moreover, the number of Israelis who have made *yerida* — left Israel — far exceeds those who have made aliyah.

It is entirely understandable in light of the tragic history of late-nineteenth- to mid-twentieth-century European and Islamic-nation

---

* Herzl's negative Zionism was challenged at its inception by Ahad Ha'am, who viewed the Jewish homeland as a "national spiritual center" where Jews could express their culture, art, and religion. See Leon Simon, *Ahad Ha-Am* (Philadelphia: Herzl Press, 1960), pp. 157–94.

Jewry and its relationship to the establishment and population of Israel that Herzl's dreary theory of Zionism as an antidote to anti-
Semitism would persist among some of Israel's leaders. And, indeed,
these leaders have been proven correct as a matter of current reality
by the Soviet and post-Soviet experience. Most Soviet Jews who left
their "homeland" did so because of pervasive anti-Semitism. Those
who have had a choice have opted by and large for the United
States, rather than for Israel. Only when the United States shut its
doors (in part at the request of Israel's leaders) did a larger percentage "choose" Israel. This was not a perfect test, of course, because
Soviet propaganda about Israel had cast that nation in an unfairly
negative light, but even without that distortion, many Jewish émigrés from anti-Semitism select Israel not as a first choice, but rather
as an "available" one. This, of course, is also part of the theory of
Zionism and of the law of return: namely, that Israel will always be
an available sanctuary for Jewish refugees, even if no other nation
will accept them. But an understanding of the past, though necessary, is not sufficient for planning a future that will have to confront
new realities, some anticipated by Herzl, others unimaginable even
to that modern-day secular prophet.

The leaders of Israel, like the leaders of American Jewry and
world Jewry, must begin to plan for a future in which anti-Semitism
and anti-Zionism are no longer the central elements of Jewish identity. Israeli leaders responsible for encouraging aliyah must provide
the Jews of the Diaspora with *positive* reasons for uprooting themselves from wonderful countries that have helped them succeed and
that want them to stay as first-class citizens. It can no longer be said,
as Herzl said in 1896, that "anti-Semites provide the requisite impetus" for Jewish emigration to Israel. Nor can it be said that "our
presence is . . . not desired" in countries like the United States, as
Herzl observed a hundred years ago. There are, of course, bigots
who would like to see all Jews out of America,[21] but that is surely not
a widespread sentiment among average Americans.

In this respect, I am reminded of the joke about the genie who
confronts a Jew, an African-American, a Mexican-American, and Pat
Buchanan on a street corner and tells them they can each have one
wish. The Jew asks that all Jews finally be returned to Zion. The
African-American asks that Africa become a homeland for all blacks.
The Mexican-American requests that Mexico become economically

viable so that all Mexican-Americans can return home and earn a decent living. The genie then turns to Pat Buchanan, who says: "Hey, if you grant their wishes, you will have granted mine." Fortunately, Pat Buchanan is not your typical American.

Israel's leaders can no longer frighten the Jews of the modern-day Diaspora into abandoning large and successful Jewish communities by predicting pogroms and Holocausts. Indeed, there is a *danger to Israel* in attracting only those Jews who are frightened to live in contemporary America, Canada, Australia, England, France, and other hospitable countries. Those *olim* — Jews who made aliyah — often display a paranoid streak that makes them among the most radical and sometimes violent opponents of any compromise in the admittedly difficult search for peace. It is no accident that a high percentage of the Gush Emunim, the Kahane parties, and other intransigent elements on the extreme Israeli right are émigrés from the United States.* I once asked former ambassador Itamar Rabinowitz why Israel cares so much about the views of the relatively small American ultra-Orthodox community. His response: "We know *they* will always be there. Can the same be said for the more secular Jewish community?"

Israel needs more centrist, successful Jews from the Diaspora — secular, religious, and in between — who *choose* a life in Israel, whether full- or part-time, because of love of Zion and the Jewish people, not because of fear of Galuth. But this is not the current approach of many of Israel's leaders. Indeed, some are ideologically committed to the *failure* of world Jewry outside Israel — a tenet of classic Zionism. This attitude poses the danger of self-fulfilling prophecy, or at least of a conflict of interest between the Jews of the Diaspora — who want to build successful, *permanent* communities outside Israel, in which Jews can live as first-class Americans, Australians, Canadians, and so on — and some of the leaders of Israel, who count on the failures of Jewish communities abroad as the best source of new *olim*.

This conflict of interest was played out quite dramatically at a conference held in Jerusalem in June 1994 to which several dozen leaders of world Jewry, including me, were invited by the president

---

* Some of these zealots made aliyah not only because of fear of persecution but also for religious reasons.

of Israel, Ezer Weizman. The letter of invitation read, in relevant part, as follows:

> I attach great importance to the future of Jewish communities in their relationship to Israel and have come to the conclusion that a dialogue between Israel and the Diaspora is necessary. Accordingly, I have decided to convene a two-day . . . dialogue between representatives of Israel and the Jewish world . . . We will focus on basic issues affecting our lives and the relationship between Israel and the Jewish world. Among the subjects I suggest discussing are questions such as the future of Jewish communities in the face of assimilation and loss of Jewish identity, the future of Israel in an era of peace, the future of the young generation, Jewish continuity, *Aliya* to Israel, ways and means to strengthen our mutual relations. Israel's contribution to world Jewry and world Jewry's involvement in Israel will be reassessed.

During the course of the conference, President Weizman proceeded to berate the Jewish leaders from around the world for their naive belief that Jewish communities outside Israel have any real future. He paraphrased the words of the Hebrew University political theorist Shlomo Avineri, who in 1987 wrote to his American friends: "[T]he truth of the matter is simple: you, in America, are no different from French, German, Polish, Soviet and Egyptian Jews. Your exile is different — comfortable, padded with success and renown. It is exile nonetheless. . . . America, it now evidently appears, may not be your promised land."[22] Maybe not. But the "truth of the matter" is anything but "simple." Whether we are right or wrong, the vast majority of American Jews — and Canadian, Australian, British, and French Jews — do regard our adopted homes as our "promised land." We do believe that America *is* different from Poland, Germany, the former Soviet Union, Egypt, and even France.[23] Yes, we are Zionists, most of us. We believe in Israel, love it, support it, visit it, appreciate the sanctuary guaranteed us by the law of return. Some of us even fantasize about eventually owning a home in Israel and living there for a portion of our lives. But we are not afraid of America. We feel a part *of* it, not apart *from* it (at least those Jews who live *in* America, rather than *apart* from it in self-imposed ghettos). We may be as naive as the German, Polish, Russian, and North African Jews were before the Second World War. Certainly the history of the wandering Jew supports the classic Zionist perspective articulated by Herzl and repeated nearly a century later by Professor Avineri and President Weizman. Early-twentieth-century Jews also honestly believed that Germany, Poland, Russia, and North Africa were their homes; they had, after all, lived in those places for centuries. But there is an important difference: They had never lived in those nations as first-class citizens *and* Jews.

Indeed, it is likely that the very establishment of Israel has been one of the factors that have now made it possible, for the first time in our history, for Jews to be treated as truly first-class citizens in a non-Jewish nation. Now that all Jews have the realistic option of making aliyah to a strong and secure Jewish state, they need not accept the kind of mere "toleration" and second-class status that had characterized the Jews of the Diaspora for so many centuries. Moreover, Israel's success — militarily, culturally, even now politically and economically — has benefited the Jews of the Diaspora in numerous ways: by instilling pride, by reflecting positively on all Jews, by uniting Jews. Witness, for example, the effects of Israel's victory in the Six-Day War on the psyche of many Diaspora Jews. This paradox of Zionism — that the establishment of a Jewish state would elevate the status of Jews who chose not to make aliyah and thus relieve some of the pressure on them *to* make aliyah — was anticipated by Herzl, but remains misunderstood by some who now wear the mantle of Zionism. In *The Jewish State*, Herzl predicted that anti-Semitism throughout the world would "stop at once and forever" as soon as a Jewish state was established — clearly an overly optimistic assessment of the impact of Zionism on anti-Semitism.* He argued that Jews' presence in other countries will never "be desired, so long as we are a homeless people," thus implying that Jews would be more accepted by the non-Jewish nations if there were a Jewish nation. To be sure, Herzl did not contemplate the survival of thriving and vibrant Jewish communities outside the Jewish state. He predicted that those Jews who remained in non-

---

* This relationship is subtle and complex. The short-term impact of Zionism may have been to increase anti-Semitism in some quarters, but I think Herzl was generally right in the longer term.

Jewish countries would eventually become assimilated. It is, of course, possible that he will be proven right — at least in the long run. Every Jewish community outside Israel, except for those that isolate themselves in self-imposed ghettos, faces the prospect of eventual assimilation over time.

Indeed, a dominant fear that currently motivates some Jews to leave their thriving Jewish communities and make aliyah to Israel is not that they will be hated to death by their enemies at home; it is that they will be loved to death by their friends there. They are afraid that the success of Jews in becoming first-class citizens in non-Jewish states will dramatically raise the odds that their children and grandchildren will marry out, assimilate, and disappear as Jews. According to these Jews, there are two ways to avoid this danger. The first is to retreat into one of the ultra-Orthodox shtetls *within* America (and other Diaspora nations), such as the Hasidic communities, so that their children will never be presented with the option of intermarriage and assimilation. The second is to move to Israel, which is also a Jewish shtetl in the functional sense that few Israelis interact with, intermarry with, or assimilate into the Arab minority population. But because Israel is a cosmopolitan, eclectic Jewish community, it carries less of the insular disadvantages of the ultra-Orthodox shtetl while providing much of the same protection against intermarriage and assimilation.

President Weizman and some other Israeli leaders play on this fear as well. It was the combined effect of this one-two punch — the persistence of external anti-Semitism or its inevitable alternative, namely, intermarriage and assimilation — that was the dominant theme at Weizman's conference. Most of what he said in 1994 could have been said a hundred years earlier. Indeed, much of it *was* said by Herzl in *The Jewish State*: particularly, that unless all Jews move to the Jewish state, they will either be persecuted or assimilated.

Virtually any time a Jewish leader from outside Israel talked optimistically during the conference about the continuing success of his or her Galuth community, Weizman interjected his negative vision of the inevitability of Jewish failure outside Israel. He was particularly discouraging to leaders who were struggling to preserve Jewish life in countries with small Jewish populations, but he was also negative about the prospects in America, Canada, Australia, and other countries with significant Jewish communities. Finally, I rose to object, invoking the legal and moral concept of "conflict of interest," or as the Bible puts it, "Thou shalt not serve two masters at the same time." I argued that if classic Zionism in general — and President Weizman in particular — appears so committed to the failure of Jewish life outside Israel, and so dependent on such failure for Israel's continued success in attracting new Jewish immigrants (*olim chadashim* — the lifeblood of Zionist theory), then there seems to be a palpable conflict of interest between the Israeli leadership and the Jewish Diaspora. Simply put, Israel *wants* us to *fail* so that we will have no choice but to make aliyah, whereas we *want* to *succeed* so that we can have the option of choosing to make our home in Israel or in the Diaspora. The Israeli leadership recognizes that if we continue to thrive, few of us will choose Israel. Indeed, that, too, is a basic tenet of Herzlian Zionism; namely, that "the requisite impetus" for aliyah is fear of anti-Semitism.[24]

Israeli leaders understandably want new émigrés, and they believe that these new émigrés will come to Israel in order to escape the inevitable anti-Semitism and the second-class status accorded to them elsewhere. But if anti-Semitism is decreasing and first-class status is increasing in the Diaspora, fewer Jews will be emigrating to Israel. It is this conflict of interest inherent in classic Zionist theory and practice that should make Diaspora communities wary of depending too heavily on offers of assistance from the same Israeli leaders who are ideologically committed to our failure.

I am not suggesting that President Weizman and other Israeli leaders are consciously wishing, or working, for our failure. The process is much more subtle. But no matter how hard they want to try (at least consciously) to help us succeed, their ideological prediction of, and commitment to, our inevitable failure raises the real danger of the self-fulfilling prophecy. The Jewish communities of the Diaspora must depend primarily on themselves, and on one another, to assure their continuing viability as first-class Jewish communities, which support Israel but are committed to their own perpetuation outside of Israel, as a validly Jewish alternative to living in Israel.

The time has come to articulate a new, more positive Zionism, responsive not to the anachronistic realities of the late nineteenth and early twentieth centuries but to the new realities of the (hopefully) *post*-anti-Semitic era of Jewish life in the twenty-first century.

We must, of course, never forget the recent pervasiveness of anti-Semitism and the possibility of its recurrence, in either an old or a new incarnation. That is one of the reasons the law of return should never be abrogated. But we must also prepare ourselves for the prospect, admittedly unique in Jewish history, of an era without external enemies. Unless we plan for that prospect, we may find ourselves ill equipped to confront the dangers Herzl wrote of: namely, if our enemies "were to leave us in peace for two generations" we might "be able to merge entirely into surrounding races."

The challenge to twenty-first-century Jewish communities outside Israel is to create new alternatives to these limited Herzlian choices. We can no longer depend on the hatred of our enemies to keep us together. We cannot allow the love of our friends to create such fear of intermarriage and assimilation that we are driven either into the ultra-Orthodox shtetls of the Diaspora or the secular Jewish shtetls of Israel. We must create a new, more positive, Judaism that can survive not only our rejection by outsiders but also their acceptance. And we must be able to do it *in* the Diaspora as well as in Israel. Israel — like Judaism itself — must remain a positive option to be freely chosen out of love, not merely a negative response to hatred and fear, as Herzl characterized both Zionism and Judaism a century ago.

As Israel and the Jewish communities around the world strengthen and mature, a new, more symbiotic relationship must develop among them. First and foremost, Diaspora Jews must recognize that Israel, though the Jewish state, is a vibrant democracy, fully capable of governing itself. Jews in America and other nations must not try to micromanage Israel's political, economic, or religious life. These decisions must be left to Israel's voters.

As Israel grows stronger both militarily and economically, it will become less dependent on Jewish communities around the world. When I visit these Diaspora communities — I have been to nearly all of them — I always say, "There but for the grace of God, the foresight of my great-grandparents, and the luck of the draw go I and my family." There are, to be sure, significant differences among the Jews of New York, Capetown, Paris, Sydney, Haifa, Montreal, Buenos Aires, Kiev, and Marrakesh. But I am always struck by the similarities as well. As time goes on, these similarities, based largely as they are on our common origins and histories, will begin to disappear and we will become more like our fellow citizens of our country and less like our fellow Jews in faraway places. We will continue to send our children to Israel for visits from all parts of the Jewish world. Israel will continue to produce Jewish literature, Jewish music, Jewish art, and Jewish philosophy, as the rest of world Jewry gravitates more closely to the national characters of its adoptive homes.

Yes, a divided Israel may divide world Jewry in the short term, as it appears to be doing today, but as Israel becomes stronger, it will help to unite us by becoming the place where the elusive Jewish character is defined and perpetuated, especially for more secular Jews. But if life continues to be good to individual Jews in the Diaspora, then mass aliyah to Israel will not occur. Israel will continue to be a place that Jews from around the world visit and to which some retire. "Using" Israel in this way has stirred some resentment among Sabras and, inevitably, some jokes, such as the one about Sadie, who brings her beloved dog in his case to the El Al counter for a flight to Israel. Sadie is obviously nervous and concerned about her pet, and the El Al people promise to take good care of the dog and place the case in the pet section of the luggage compartment. But when the plane arrives in Israel, the dog is dead. The El Al people panic and rush immediately to a pet store and buy an identical dog, down to its unique marking. They put the replacement dog in the case and present it to Sadie as if nothing had happened. Sadie takes one look at the dog and screams, "That's not my dog." The El Al person is amazed that she can tell the difference and asks her, "How can you be so sure it's not your dog?" Sadie replies, "Because my dog was dead. I was bringing him to Israel to be buried."

The Israeli "solution" to the Jewish problem of the twenty-first century will remain only a partial answer to voluntary assimilation. American Jews will have to solve our self-imposed problems. We can do it, but it will require a massive reallocation of Jewish resources toward the building of a positive Jewish identification for all Jews, one that is based on a rich past and on the hope of a bright future.

Chapter Seven

Be a Mensch! The Ethical Solution to the Jewish Question of the Twenty-first Century

MOST CURRENTLY ACTIVE American Jews are neither very religious nor willing to move to Israel. How, then, do we define our Jewishness, other than by reference to our weakening external enemies? Many believe that Judaism — or Jewishness — is a set of ethical or political principles.[1] They believe that there is an *essence* of Judaism that they feel, though they have great difficulty defining it. For these Jews, the pressing question is "How can we transmit the 'essence' of Judaism to our children?"

Throughout the ages, Jewish scholars have claimed to know the true essence of Judaism. When Hillel was asked to transmit the core of the Torah to a skeptic in the time he could stand on one foot, the great scholar replied: "What is hateful to you, do not do to your neighbor; this is the whole Torah. The rest is commentary; go and study." Micah summarized God's demand of Jews thus: "Only to do justice, to love goodness, and to walk modestly with your God." Jeremiah quoted God as asking for "earnest devotion to Me," who delights in "kindness, justice and equity in the world." Jews constructed lists even before David Letterman made them famous. Isaiah's top six essences of Judaism were: walking in righteousness; speaking honestly; spurning profit from fraud; walking away from bribes; not listening to malicious words; and shutting one's eyes against evil. Akavya Ben Mahalalel, a first-century sage, had only three entries on his list: Torah; work; charity.

The Talmud extracted numerous essences from the rich mines of Judaism: "Do justice"; "Perform acts of righteousness"; "Study the Torah"; "Honor your father and mother"; "Make peace between a person and his neighbor." One sage even singled out circumcision as the essence of Judaism, for it is "equal in importance to all precepts of the Torah" (B. Ned. 31b-32a). David — the king, not the late-night host — had a list that included walking uprightly, working righteously, speaking the truth, using no deceit, doing no evil to neighbors, not enduring reproach against a kinsman, despising the vile, and honoring those who fear the Lord.[2]

There is, of course, nothing uniquely Jewish in these lists of essences. They are compendiums of human virtues that any group of decent and intelligent people could compile. Some preceded the advent of Judaism, others developed in parallel civilizations in far-flung parts of the world, while still others may have begun with Judaism but have become equally essential to other religions, philosophies, and civilizations. What it really boils down to is that every religion claims for itself the basic virtues of the day. That is not to denigrate these claims. It is to deny that any of them is the essence of any one religion and no others. There may be only one God, but there are as many virtues and essences as there are human beings capable of good deeds and lofty thoughts. To claim that any, or several, or all of these virtues are the essence of Judaism alone is to expropriate general human qualities to a particular worldview. It is unhistorical, self-referential, and denigrating to others. To narrow the essence of Judaism in one specific direction — for example, by focusing exclusively on human ethics, or on devotion to God, or on circumcision — is to deny the reality that Judaism encompasses the widest and most eclectic array of attitudes, philosophies, and even theologies. Asking what is "the essence" of the ever-changing and evolving Jewish civilization is as foolish as asking what is "the essence" of European, African, or American civilizations. Each of these civilizations has conflicting, contrasting, and changing essences, which are impossible to encapsulate. Even after the death of a complex civilization, good historians are unable to distill its essence. Simpleminded pop authors and crib-note writers may be able to summarize in twenty-five words or less the essence of the ancient Greek or Roman civilizations, but no historian worth his or her salt will take such oversimplifications seriously. How much more difficult, indeed impossible, it is to distill the essence of a living and changing civilization whose ultimate destiny is as yet undetermined. The essence of Judaism cannot be distilled, bottled, and passed on from generation to generation like a secret potion. Nor can it be smelted down to some core. It is not a *product*. It is a *process*. And the process is dynamic, not static. The artificial quest for the essence is a tactic of the special pleader who needs to wrap his political agenda in the mantle of scripture.

Now more than ever, special pleaders claim to know the true essence of Judaism that must be transmitted to future generations if we are to survive. This quest for the essence has taken on new urgency because my generation can no longer transmit the *totality* of Jewish life, as our great-grandparents who grew up in Jewish shtetls could easily do. They did not have to distill any essence from the totality, since the totality they did transmit obviously *included* the essence, whatever it may have been. Today, we can no longer transmit to our children a total way of life — unless, of course, we choose the totalitarian way of Hasidism. For those of us who live a largely secular, American, universal way of life that *includes* a significant Jewish component, the quest for the transmittable essence seems critical, since we must know what it is before we can pass it on to our children.

Platitudes abound. The essence of Judaism, we are told by contemporary scholars, is "love," "salvation," "idealism," "social justice," "Godliness," "social action," "community," "tradition," "repair of the world," and many other vague clichés.[3] Any "essence" that can be boiled down so as to fit on a bumper sticker or in a fortune cookie is, by definition, capable of so many definitions as to be virtually meaningless. Each of these essences is central to most contemporary religions, philosophies, and ways of life. I recently attended a meeting at the Cambridge Friends School where the essence of the Quaker philosophy was described. I could barely distinguish it from Conservative, Reform, or Reconstructionist Judaism — though I acknowledge it did not *feel* exactly the same. The words were similar, but the music was different.*

In a remarkable series of advertisements in the *New York Times* over the past several years, the American Jewish Committee asked a

---

* A friend of mine made a similar observation about another small religious sect. "They may be Amish, but they're not haimish [like home, comfortable]."

wide array of Jews, from Elie Wiesel to a prominent money manager to an astronaut to a professional football player to a university president to a senator to a Supreme Court justice to several students, what "being Jewish means" to them. The answers ranged over a diverse array of ethical, religious, and historical "essences." Most focused on doing justice, pursuing peace, repairing the world, encouraging ethical behavior, showing compassion for the downtrodden, and preserving the sanctity of life. Several pointed to the Jewish emphasis on learning for its own sake, on scholarship, and on teaching. Some identified with the Jewish tradition of questioning, doubting, and arguing. As one put it: "Being Jewish means belonging to the first human community that extolled its own critics." There was also reference to community, family, shared heritage, and tradition. Finally, a few of the people mentioned spirituality, religion, and connectedness with God.

In reading these statements, I was reminded of the extraordinary success of individual Jews and moved by the attachment of these particular Jews to their heritage. But in the end, to each of them "being Jewish" meant being good people, in the ways in which *they* were good people. Educators saw in Judaism a commitment to education. Lawyers saw a commitment to justice. Being Jewish was a Rorschach test, to be interpreted by each viewer in accordance with his or her personal bent. There were, to be sure, common themes, such as education, justice, peace, and repair of the world, but these themes were general and abstract. Is there any good person today who would not claim to be pursuing these virtues?

Virtues are, of course, somewhat in the eye of the beholder, as the story of the two older women who meet on the Miami boardwalk illustrates. Millie asks Molly how her children's marriages are doing. Molly answers: "My son has a terrible marriage. His lazy wife lies in bed all morning and doesn't even make him breakfast. Then she spends the afternoon at the beauty parlor, and as soon as my son gets home from a hard day's work, she shleps him out to a restaurant. My daughter, on the other hand, has a perfect marriage. Her husband lets her sleep late in the morning, insists that she go to the beauty parlor, and then takes her out to dinner every night."

If there is no unique historical essence of Judaism, what is it we wish to preserve and transmit to our children and grandchildren? There must be *something* positive that is characteristically Jewish and that is worth preserving. I believe that there are many Jewish virtues that can be distilled from our long heritage and from our vast library. But we should not expect them to point in any one direction or provide us with specific answers to current and future problems.

In this respect, Jewish tradition is somewhat akin to American constitutional tradition. Those who expect to find precise guidance in our eighteenth-century constitutional history for the issues that will confront and divide America in the twenty-first century are engaging in a secular form of idol worship. The framers of our Constitution, farsighted as they were, were ordinary people who did the best they could to create a document that would help a relatively homogeneous, though divided, people govern itself over the centuries. We are today a very different people, less homogeneous, and divided in different ways. Yet our Constitution, with relatively few amendments, endures and works fairly well. It contains no single essence, because America has never reflected one single essence. Special pleaders, such as the Christian right, claim that its essence lies in its invocation of God, Christianity, and natural law. Civil libertarians point to its emphasis on inalienable rights and freedoms. The reality is that the Constitution and our other foundational documents reflect substantive compromises because the framers could not agree on many basic issues, ranging from slavery to the role of religion in government. What they could and did agree on was the creation of a *structure* for governance, which distributed decision-making power widely so that a system of checks and balances would be assured and future substantive decisions could be made fairly and effectively. If prominent Americans were to be asked "What does being American mean to you?" — the analogue to the question asked of prominent Jews by the American Jewish Committee — the answers would likely be at a similar level of generality: "justice," "liberty," "compassion" — the current virtues.[4]

Just as there are cultural differences between nations, so too there are differences between various civilizations and religious groups. The United States is quite different from France, which is very different from Japan. Social observers have generalized that America is more compassionate, less selfish, less hedonistic, more religious, less cynical than France. This does not mean that *all* Americans or Frenchmen and -women share these characteristics. Nor does it mean that all the American sources and traditions point in one direction, while all the French sources and traditions point in the opposite direction. But our dominant national character points more markedly in favor of compassion and against selfishness and hedonism. Perhaps I am biased by the French reaction to Nazism and the Holocaust, but many observers have come to similar conclusions. Japan is more hierarchical and based on "interpersonal obligation."[5] Humorists have long recognized national cultural differences, as in the following description of the subtle distinction between heaven and hell. Heaven is characterized by German efficiency, Italian warmth, English manners, and French cooking. Hell is characterized by German warmth, Italian efficiency, French manners, and English cooking. (This is a variation on President John Kennedy's description of our nation's capital as combining northern charm with southern efficiency.) The British and the Yiddish (though not a nation) are also frequently contrasted, as reflected by the answer to the question, What is the difference between a British and Yiddish restaurant? In a British restaurant you see the people eating and hear them talking, whereas in a Yiddish restaurant you see the people talking and hear them eating. Or the advice to a young man: "Dress British, think Yiddish." Or the difference at the end of a dinner party: The British leave without saying goodbye; the Yiddish say goodbye without leaving.

It is also fair to say that there are certain cultural characteristics that are more prevalent among Jews than among non-Jews. Again, not all Jews share them and not all non-Jews are without them. But if you asked fair-minded Jews and non-Jews to list characteristics that they associate with Jews, most would agree on several. Among them would surely be a commitment to education and learning; active participation in social and political causes; involvement in the arts; charitable giving and compassion toward others; close familial and community ties; a high level of creativity, energy, and adaptability; a drive toward success; disproportionate success in certain fields such as medicine, law, finance, academia, and the media; and disproportionate influence in the world.

Do these characteristics grow out of the "essence" of Judaism, or are they merely adaptations Jews have made to our long history of being outsiders, victims of persecution, and statelessness? It is impossible to answer that question, since Jewish life over the millennia has always been characterized by our pariah status. Now that we may be entering an age in which we are fully accepted as equals, we will have to distill the essences of Judaism from our historical sources and separate them out from the negative social and political conditions that may have contributed to producing "the Jewish character" or "mystique."

The real question is which essences can we extract from the rich mine of Jewish tradition that will at once be true to our past and also help us to ensure our future. Put another way, what *should* the essence (or essences) of Judaism be for the coming age — an age that is unlikely to see Jews, especially American Jews, as persecuted victims of injustice but rather is likely to see us continue our economic, social, educational, political, and cultural success? Put more personally, by which Jewish values do we want our children and grandchildren to live?

"Justice, Justice Shall Thou Pursue"

I believe there are several such essences, though none speaks with a single voice. Historically, Jews have been on the forefront of the struggle *to achieve justice*. They have agreed on the *goal* of a just world, but they have never agreed on the *means* toward reaching that goal. Indeed, the Jewish dialogue — between man and God and among men (and women) — has been largely about how to pursue justice in an inherently unjust world.

To understand the remarkable contribution that Jews have made to the quest for justice, it is important to recognize that justice is not an inherent attribute of human nature. Indeed, justice is quite antithetical to basic human instincts. The need to survive, to reproduce, to protect, to gain power — these are the fundamental characteristics of the human species. Justice is a compromise with power. It requires those who have power to share it with those who do not in the interest of some higher principle, such as fairness, equality, or due process. Perhaps justice bestows some evolutionary benefits, since it entails reciprocity, but it took a long time for human beings to give up immediate power for the longer-range potential benefit of justice. The process was a gradual one, beginning with justice for the family, the clan, the tribe, and then moving slowly toward the ideal of individual justice.

The Jewish Bible is the story of this quest for justice. It begins with a tale of temptation — of Eve by the serpent and of Adam by Eve — that makes clear God's disdain for excuses: "The serpent beguiled me"; "The woman whom thou gavest to be with me, she gave me of the tree." God ordains man "to know good and evil," and then punishes Cain — quite moderately — for killing his brother out of jealousy. God also protects Cain from vigilante justice by setting a sign upon him. God then sees that "the wickedness of man was great upon the world," and decides to destroy humankind and start all over, with a righteous man and his family. God makes a covenant with Noah and imposes rules of justice that "whoso sheddeth man's blood, by man shall his blood be shed." God selects Abraham to become the father of a great nation "to the end that he may command his children and his household after him that they may keep the way of the Lord, to do righteousness and justice." Thus, the very purpose ("end") for which God chose the Jewish people was "to do righteousness and justice." Immediately upon telling Abraham that he and his people must do justice, God informs him of his plan to destroy all the residents of Sodom and Gomorrah because "their sin is exceedingly great." Abraham protests this divine notion of collective guilt and asks God: "Wilt Thou indeed sweep away the righteous with the wicked?" Then, in one of the most remarkable passages in all of literature, Abraham rebukes his newfound God and demands of him that he, too, be just. The power of the biblical sentence is hardly captured in the standard translations, which render the original Hebrew as: "Far be it from Thee ... to slay the righteous with the wicked; that be far from Thee; shall not the judge of all the earth do justly?" In the original, Abraham uses the word *chalilah*, which is far stronger than "far be it from Thee," or even from translator Everett Fox's more modern "Heaven forbid." The word *chalilah* has as its root "profane": Abraham's rebuke borders on the disrespectful. If a lawyer were ever to use a comparable word to a judge in a courtroom, he would be held in contempt and disciplined. This is how Abraham addresses God in demanding justice for the people of Sodom and Gomorrah. Yet Abraham demurs when God commands him to sacrifice his innocent son, raising profound questions about justice which have been debated for millennia.

Indeed, the justice of the Bible is not always one of compassion or individual guilt. The terrible story of how Jacob's sons "slew all the males" in the clan of Hamor the Hivite because one of them had seduced their sister Dinah and "humbled her" suggests that the concept of collective guilt remained acceptable when applied to certain actions. The theme of collective punishment and individual justice recurs throughout the Bible, with no definitive resolution. Moses and Aaron ask of God: "Shall one man sin and You grow angry at the whole congregation?" But there is little objection when God ordains genocide against the nation of Amalek for its grievous sins. Nor is Jonah as sensitive about the innocent of Ninevah as Abraham was about the righteous of Sodom and Gomorrah.

Neither God nor man speaks with one voice about the *content* of justice, though they do speak consistently about the quest for this elusive quality. Job is treated unjustly, as are his children. Ecclesiastes sees injustice as part of the natural order. David, on the other hand, sees justice as essential to God's order.

The Bible includes some fairly specific rules regarding distributive justice for the less fortunate, such as the command that fallen fruit and the corner of the field be left for the poor and the stranger, that wages not be withheld even overnight, and that no stumbling block be placed before the blind. But it also requires that neither the poor nor the rich be favored in judgment and that justice be the guiding principle.

The biblical concept of "cities of refuge" is a remarkable innovation reflecting a sophisticated response to the basic human instinct for revenge. God orders the Jews to build cities of refuge to which a person who kills another by accident may flee. This concept recognizes that to the relatives of the victim, there is little difference between a negligent and deliberate killing. But a just system must draw a distinction, and so a kind of protective imprisonment is mandated in order to keep the "avenger of blood" from committing a retaliatory injustice against the accidental killer. If the avenger finds the accidental killer outside the city of refuge, however, and slays him, "there shall be no blood-guiltiness on him" because he has acted in accordance with his understandable need for revenge. The layers of sophistication reflected in this approach to vengeance is amazing for a people who had so little experience in governance.

The Prophets demand justice. Amos rails against those who "trample upon the poor" and "turn justice to wormwood." He rejects burnt offerings and solemn songs, insisting instead that "justice well up as waters and righteousness as a mighty stream." Isaiah too rejects empty prayers and "vain oblations," admonishing the Jewish people to "seek justice, relieve the oppressed, judge the fatherless, plead for the widow." Zion will be "redeemed with justice," he prophesies. Jeremiah preaches primarily against religious sins, but he includes injustice between man and his brother — "woe unto him who builds his house by . . . injustice" — and he cries out to God, "Wherefore does the way of the wicked prosper?" The psalmist sings, "Happy are they that keep justice, that do righteousness at all times."

The Talmud continues this dialogue about justice, without specific resolution. Indeed, in the Mishnah it is stated that "to explain the relative peace for the wicked and suffering of the righteous is beyond us," and one rabbi speculates that "in this world we see the godless prosper and the faithful suffer; there must therefore be another world in which all will be recompensed in justice and righteousness."[6] Rabbi Simeon Ben Gamliel believed that the world stands on three pillars: truth, justice, and peace. He cautioned to "take care not to subvert justice, for if you subvert justice, you shake the world."

The Jewish emphasis on justice led to the creation of the first system of criminal trials, which placed a heavy burden both procedurally and evidentially on the prosecution. In the rabbinic structure, for example, an accused *could not* abdicate his right against self-incrimination; any testimony he offered that incriminated himself would be ignored by the court (Sanhedrin 96). In capital crimes, the court went out of its way to afford every possible defense to the accused: The trial could not be consummated in a day; rather, the members of the court were compelled to consider the case overnight, that they might diligently search for ways to exonerate the accused. On the second day, only those members who had discovered new arguments for the accused's innocence were allowed to speak; members who had become convinced of his guilt were permitted merely to vote without stating their reasons (Sanhedrin 34a). Finally, if after the preliminary vote on the first day of the trial all members of the court thought him *guilty*, the accused was *set free!* (Sanhedrin 17a). The reason: If it seemed so clear to all that the accused was guilty, no one would have seriously explored avenues in his defense — and he had thus been deprived of a fair trial.

There is much academic debate as to whether the Talmudic criminal construct would have been workable, and even as to whether it was ever instituted as an operative system.[7] What is more significant is the intense scrutiny employed by the Talmudists in establishing principles of criminal justice and their preoccupation with the establishment of a fair system.

In the civil realm as well as the criminal, the Talmudic sages demanded a strict adherence to just principles. Judges could not allow one litigant to sit while requiring the other to stand. Nor could they permit one to speak at length while requiring the other to keep his remarks to a minimum (Shvuot 30a). In the business world, weights and measures were standardized, and practices that distorted a fair measuring were banned. Land was generally measured by rope lengths, and it was forbidden to apportion parcels of land to equal purchasers by measuring one parcel while the rope was wet and slightly elongated and the other while the rope was dry and contracted. Of course, weights and scales could not be physically altered to change the outcome of the weighing, and even when measuring a liquid for purchase, one could not pour the liquid hastily, causing it to froth and occupy a larger volume (Bava Metzia 61b). Specific rabbis were criticized by their peers for not attending to the litigation of the downtrodden (Shabbat 55a). The message that issues forth from the pages of the Talmud is unanimous: In all areas, civil and criminal, just laws must be strictly adhered to. In fact, out of the seven laws the Talmud cites as incumbent upon non-Jews, the only positive ordinance is the establishment of a justice system (Sanhedrin 56a).

The rabbis of the Talmud occupied yet another role besides that of lawgivers and judges. They saw themselves as the philosophers and ideologues of a developing civilization, and published a second genre of literature to transmit their thoughts and philosophies on matters other than law to their pupils and to the nation as a whole. This material, interspersed throughout the Talmud and other works, is known as the Haggadah, the legends. Through the literary media of allegory, hyperbole, parable, and legend, the sages constructed a moral and ethical philosophical framework for a nation without borders. The sages depict Justice as one of ten ingredients with which the world was created (Hagiga 12a). According to the Haggadah, Justice played a crucial role in the creation of man as well. God's decision to make man engendered the opposition of many of the angels, who thought man to be unworthy. Then Justice spoke, urging: "Let him be created, for he will perform acts of justice" (Genesis Rabbah 8). Rabbinic legend thus propounds the notion that man was created, quite literally, to the task of justice. The Haggadah ascribes to Sodom and Gomorrah the sins of lawlessness and *perversions of justice*, although the Bible is silent as to the nature of their sins (Sanhedrin 108b–109a; Genesis, Leviticus, and Bamidbar Rabbah). It describes Moses — who in rabbinic lore attained the greatest spiritual heights accessible to a human being — as the embodiment of justice.

Pursuit of justice continued to play an important role in the philosophies of the medieval Jewish thinkers. Maimonides, in expounding his belief that God cannot properly be depicted because he is not a being but can only be described through his actions, maintained that biblical passages referring to God's aspects instruct us to mimic these actions in reality. Thus, when Jeremiah mentions that God exercises and delights in justice, he intends that justice issue forth from man through an attempt to imitate this aspect of God.[8] An old Yiddish saying sums up the Jewish concern for justice: "Rather suffer an injustice than commit one." Gerson Cohen describes this unique preoccupation during the Talmudic age and throughout Jewish history as "obsessive concern of the Jew with justice and fair play."[9]

Ultimately, in the eighteenth and nineteenth centuries this immense ideological richness and this passion were translated into action as men and women of Jewish heritage agitated not only for their own emancipation, but for the emancipation of the oppressed all over the world. In the pre-Revolution Germany of the early nineteenth century, Karl Marx and Moses Hess advocated changes in the political structure. Two Jewish physicians, Adolf Fischhof and Joseph Goldmark, were chief architects of the Revolution of 1848. From 1865 to 1876, Ferdinand LaSalle, a political theorist, organized the German Labor Party. The historian Salo Baron explains that because of a long history saturated with the ideal of social justice, many Jews were naturally drawn by the call of socialism.[10] In America, too, Jewish workers from Eastern Europe were pioneers in forming labor unions, and many Jewish labor leaders continued to work for the unions even when presented with more attractive economic alternatives.

The forms of justice have even influenced Jewish prayer. The Kol

Nidre service is set before heavenly and earthly courts. Rabbi Levi Isaac of Berdichev wrote a famous prelude to the Kaddish that takes the form of a lawsuit (a *din Torah*) against God for unjustly abandoning the Jewish people, and Elie Wiesel recounts the trial of God by the doomed rabbis of Birkenau in which God lost and then everyone prayed.[11]

It is not surprising, therefore, that most contemporary commentators — both Jewish and non-Jewish — view the Jewish tradition as the bedrock of modern justice. "The passion to shape the forms of justice has been one of the dominant forces in the life of the Jewish people from the time of the tablets to the days in which we now live," wrote Professor Arthur Goodhart of Oxford University in 1949. "The whole Bible is a hymn to justice — that is, in the Hebrew style, to charity, to kindness to the weak on the part of the strong, to voluntary renunciation of the privilege of power," wrote Pierre-Joseph Proudhon a century earlier. "The Jews were in the beginning the most unstable; they submitted to their law and came out the most stable of nations," observed Walter Bagehot in 1872. "The fundamental principle of the Hebraic Commonwealth was that there are great moral laws," observed Lyman Abbott in 1901. And Lord Acton credited the Hebrew nation with having laid down the basis for "all freedom" through its doctrine of "higher law." No wonder Rabbi Solomon Goldman wrote in 1927 that any Jew "who fails to understand the importance of law misses the very essence of his people's contribution to humanity."[12]

The quest for justice, then, is an important essence of Judaism, but there is no uniquely Jewish way to define justice. Judaism is inherently neither "liberal" nor "conservative" on issues of justice, but it is inherently active in its pursuit.* A balance is obviously required. The rabbis say that God has two names, one representing justice, the other mercy. At different times and places, one is emphasized more than the other, but over time a balance must be struck. God sometimes berates his people for lacking compassion, as in the case of Jonah, while at other times he berates them for being too merciful, as he did when Saul delayed in taking the life of Agag, the king of Amalek. Hillel reminded us of the need to strike a balance when he said: "If I am not for myself, who will be for me? But if I am for

---

* Even here, there is the dissenting voice of Ecclesiastes.

myself alone, what am I?" That balance between self-preservation and justice must be struck differently in every generation. In times of persecution and victimization, the emphasis must be on self-protection and preservation — "If I am not for myself." In times of success and empowerment, the emphasis must be on helping others less fortunate — "If I am for myself alone."

Until recently, most Jews actively pursued justice and tried to repair the world by what could be characterized as "liberal" or "progressive" means. Jews have been at the forefront of nearly every movement for redistribution of power and wealth. This should not be surprising, since most Jews were powerless, poverty-stricken, and persecuted. As an old Yiddish expression goes: "The poor are always liberal." Since they had little power, Jews benefited from redistributive justice. Now that Jews — as individuals — are far more powerful than they have ever been, it is also natural that many will pursue justice by more conservative means. This phenomenon is illustrated by the story of Yankel and his friend Moishe, who follows him to America from a Polish shtetl. When Yankel greets him at the dock, he tells Moishe that he has discovered something wonderful in America: Communism. Moishe asks him to explain. "Communism means that if I have two buildings, you get one. If I have two cars, you get one." Moishe is thrilled: "Let me understand. Communism means that if you have two shirts, I get one?" "No," Yankel shouts, "you don't understand nothing. It doesn't apply to shirts." "Why not?" Moishe asks. "Because two shirts I actually have." What is surprising is that so many wealthy and powerful Jews who have many shirts, cars, and buildings still seek redistributive justice for others, though they will not benefit, at least not directly, from the redistribution of power, money, and other resources. As Milton Himmelfarb, former research director of the American Jewish Committee, once observed: "Jews earn like Episcopalians, but they still vote like Puerto Ricans."[13]

Repair the World

A related Jewish imperative has been to *repair the world*. We Jews may not be very good at repairing our cars or our homes — at least that's what Jackie Mason tells us — but throughout history, Jews have been on the forefront of trying to repair people, countries, and the world. It is difficult to think of any movement in which Jews have not been in the vanguard of either support or opposition. It is widely known that Jews were at the forefront of the Bolshevik Revolution (for understandable reasons, considering the anti-Semitism of the czar). But few know that "Italian Jews were . . . disproportionately overrepresented in the Fascist Party," before Mussolini allied himself with Hitler.[14] Jews have been active in gay rights, but the recent neo-conservative movement in America has also been dominated by Jews, many of whom had been leaders in the socialist movement of the past.[15] The biblical imperative not to stand idly by has been fulfilled by Jews of the right, left, and center. We are never satisfied with the status quo. We must always demand improvement. We constantly complain. My favorite story about this quintessential Jewish trait takes place in Boston, where old man Schwartz gets sick and is taken to Massachusetts General Hospital, reputed to be the best in the world. Because he is a wealthy and charitable businessman, he is given the finest room in the fanciest pavilion. But after only one day, Schwartz insists on being transferred to Beth Israel Hospital. The intern at Beth Israel, who was turned down for a more prestigious internship at Massachusetts General, says to Schwartz, "I see you agree with me that the medical care at Massachusetts General is not as good as people think." Schwartz responds, "No, it was very good. I can't complain." "So it must have been the nurses: they were too cold?" "No," says Schwartz, "the nurses were fine. I can't complain." "Was it the food? All that watercress salad?" "No, the food was fine. I can't complain." "Then why did you switch hospitals?" the intern asks in frustration. Schwartz answers, "*Here*, I can complain." Jews always complain, not only about their own condition but about the state of the world. A friend who teaches in Canada — where only "visible minorities" are eligible for affirmative action — was asked whether Jews qualified. He responded that we are an "audible minority." We do tend to speak up on every issue. But again, this imperative to act, to repair, to participate, to lead contains little specific substantive context. Jews are activists, leaders, innovators in many different types of causes all through the political spectrum.

Give

Charity — tzedakah — is surely another important essence of Judaism harking back to earlier days. Indeed, the root of the Hebrew word for charity, *tzedek*, means justice, and hence the concepts have always been related in the Jewish mind. Several years ago, I was asked to make the appeal for funds at Harvard Hillel on Kol Nidre night. I brought along an old tzedakah box — my grandmother called it a "pushka" — to illustrate my point that excavations of ancient Jewish communities almost always turn up charity boxes. I put the pushka in my tallith bag, ready to pull it out to make my point. That particular Kol Nidre night was also the night of the final game of the American League championship series in which the Boston Red Sox were involved, so I also took with me a tiny television set, hoping to watch the final inning before services began. Just before I was to give my talk, my nephew Adam — an MIT student, adept at pranks — switched the TV for the charity box, hoping that when I came to the dramatic moment and pulled out the item that proved Jews were always involved with charity, I would be displaying a TV set. Fortunately for both of us, I felt the TV and replaced it with the pushka and all went well with the appeal for charity.

The Jewish tradition of giving, though ancient and pervasive, is also content-neutral. Obviously, the recipients of charity should be the poor. But beyond that truism, Jews contribute to the arts, to politics, to Jewish causes, to secular causes. Jews not only give more money per capita than any other group, but in one recent year gave the most in absolute terms, a remarkable achievement for a group representing just over 2 percent of this nation's population. Jews have been among the largest contributors to black causes, gay causes, human rights causes, civil liberties causes, even Palestinian causes.[16] In 1996, Tom Lee, a Jewish alumnus of Harvard, contributed $22 million to his alma mater. Among the other major gifts to Harvard that year, nearly all of them had come from individuals of Jewish background: A Harvard fund-raiser told me that in recent years, "Harvard has been virtually supported by Jews."[17]

Even when we were a relatively poor community, our charitable giving was high. Jokes abound concerning the legendary power of the Jewish fund-raiser, such as the one about O'Brien, Johnson, and Cohen, shipwrecked on a desert island. O'Brien prays, Johnson writes his last will, but Cohen seems unconcerned. O'Brien and Johnson ask him why he isn't worried. Cohen replies: "I made my pledge to the United Jewish Appeal but I haven't paid it yet. They'll find me." Or the one about the circus strongman who challenges anyone to squeeze more juice out of a lemon than the twenty drops he has just struggled to produce. A small Jewish man from the UJA squeezes out twice as many drops without breaking a sweat. Charitable giving and the compassion it reflects are surely important essences of Judaism.

Learn

Another essence of Judaism has been *education, scholarship,* and *learning.* There is no people in history that has valued the oral and written word as greatly as the Jews have. The poorest and least well educated Jew always learned. A colleague of mine told me of his discovery of an old Talmud, whose inscription read: "The daily Talmud class of the woodcutters of Berdichev." But the imperative to learn did not stop with the Torah and the Talmud. Jews have refused to be constrained by their holy books. The Haskalah — the Jewish Enlightenment — broke the chains by which traditional religion had bound so many Jews. The great secular books were translated into Yiddish. Many Jews learned other languages — French, German, English — in addition to their local and regional ones. The imperative to learn drove some Jews not only out of the shtetl, but out of Judaism as well, since some Jews were limited in their choice of schools by the notorious *numerus clausus* (restricted number) system, which extended throughout Europe and came even to the United States, including to Harvard, Columbia, Yale, and other universities, which today have large numbers of Jewish students.

Argue — Two Jews, Three Opinions

Perhaps the essence most characteristic of Judaism and one found in no other religion, culture, or civilization is its *argumentative nature.* We are a civilization of arguers. We argue with God, about God, with each other, about each other, and about everything that matters. Abraham and Moses argued with God. The Prophets argued with God, kings, and priests. The Berdichev rabbi *sued* God. Elie Wiesel put God on trial. An entire book has been written on the subject: *Arguing with God: A Jewish Tradition.* It recounts dozens of such arguments throughout history. The Talmud is a collection of arguments, in which even the losing side is given great status. We "extol" our critics so long as their arguments are sound. We praise the tough question more than the facile answer. How could anyone expect so dialogic a people to have one *substantive* essence or even one *substantive* answer to fundamental questions? A Jew answers a question with a question. I once represented a Jewish insurance broker who sold life insurance policies to alleged members of organized crime. He was called before a grand jury and when asked "Do you know 'Fat Tony' Salerno?" he responded: "Do *I know* 'Fat Tony'?" The prosecutor pressed him: "Well, *do* you know 'Fat Tony'?" His answer: "How would I know a man like *that?*" Again he was pressed: "Just answer yes or no. Do you know him?" Again he answered with a question: "What do you mean by 'know'? I know him, but I don't *know* him. Does that answer your question?" It went on and on until the prosecutor finally gave up. The classic Jewish joke about answering a question with a question is set in Nazi Germany, where a Gestapo officer stops a Jew and asks him who is the cause of all of Germany's problems. "Why, it is the Jews and the bicycle riders, of course." The Gestapo man asks, "Why the bicycle riders?" The Jew responds, "Why the Jews?"

Such a people refuses to accept any given answer as definitive, at least not for long. An answer begets a new question — and on and on. We cannot even agree on a single process for arriving at answers. We have no pope, chief rabbi, or other authoritative source for resolving disputes. As David Gordis, the president of Hebrew College in Boston, puts it:

> The Talmud itself is the "in process" text par excellence. It preserves all sides of argumentation, it insists that minority views be preserved along with prevailing views, and it exposes its readers to a range of possibilities even where a simple monochromatic response might be welcome. Attempts to shortcut the Talmudic process, even by so distinguished an interpreter [and codifier] as Maimonides, were doomed to failure, because the core style of reasoned reflection, of respectful consideration of alternatives, is fundamental to the mindset of classical Judaism.[18]

The Talmud itself declares that "there are seventy facets to Torah" (Bamidbar Rabbah 13), and even refuses to ascribe to God a monolithic view: "*These and these* are the words of the living God" (Eruvin 136). The rabbis even went so far as to remove the Ten Commandments from the communal prayer service for fear that

Jews would come to regard that list of ten as the essence of Judaism
(Mishna Brurah 1:16).

Jews even argue about the right approach to teaching the Talmud, as in the following seventeenth-century debate, which strikingly parallels the current debate in American law schools over the
Socratic method of law teaching. Rabbi Nathan Hannover lauds the
traditional Polish method of teaching the Talmud:

> In no country . . . was the study of the Torah so widespread among
> the Jews as in the Kingdom of Poland. The scholars and young
> students of the community as well as all interested in the study of
> the Law assembled daily at the yeshibah, where the president
> alone occupied a chair, while the scholars and college students
> stood around him. Before the appearance of the rosh-yeshibah
> they would discuss questions of Jewish law, and when he arrived
> every one laid his difficulties before him, and received an explana-
> tion. Thereupon silence was restored, and the rosh-yeshibah de-
> livered his lecture, presenting the new results of his study. At the
> conclusion of the lecture he arranged a scientific argumentation
> (*hilluk*), proceeding in the following way: Various contradictions
> in the Talmud and the commentaries were pointed out, and solu-
> tions were proposed. These solutions were, in turn, shown to be
> contradictory, and other solutions were offered, this process being
> continued until the subject of discussion was completely eluci-
> dated. The boy who knew nothing or who did not answer ade-
> quately was by order of the trustee turned over to the inspector,
> who subjected him, in the presence of his fellow-pupils, to severe
> physical punishment and other painful degradations, that he
> might firmly resolve to improve in his studies during the follow-
> ing week. On Fridays the heder [younger] pupils presented them-
> selves in a body before the rosh-yeshibah himself, to undergo a
> similar examination. This had a strong deterrent effect upon the
> boys, and they devoted themselves energetically to their stud-
> ies. . . . The scholars, seeing this . . . studied assiduously in conse-
> quence. Prompted originally by self-interest, they gradually came
> to devote themselves to the Torah from pure, unselfish motives.

Rabbi Solomon Ephraim criticizes this manner of teaching the
Talmud:

The whole instruction at the yeshibah . . . reduces itself to mental equilibristics and empty argumentations called hilluk. It is dreadful to contemplate that some venerable rabbi, presiding over a yeshibah, in his anxiety to discover and communicate to others some new interpretation, should offer a perverted explanation of the Talmud, though he himself and every one else be fully aware that the true meaning is different. Can it be God's will that we sharpen our minds by fallacies and sophistries, spending our time in vain and teaching the listeners to do likewise? And all this for the mere ambition of passing for a great scholar! . . . These empty quibbles have a particularly pernicious effect on our bahurs [young students] for the reason that the bahur who does not shine in the discussion is looked down upon as incapable, and is practically forced to lay aside his studies, though he might prove to be one of the best, if Bible, Mishnah, Talmud, and the Codes were studied in a regular fashion. I myself have known capable young men who, not having distinguished themselves in pilpul, forfeited the respect of their fellow-students, and stopped studying altogether after their marriage.[19]

There is an old joke about the Talmudic method for resolving apparent textual contradictions. Two of the greatest rabbis arrive in heaven and God asks them to conduct a dialogue over a conflict between two statements made by Maimonides. They debate, quite brilliantly, for hours without resolution. Finally God orders his angel to bring forth Maimonides himself to resolve the dispute. When Maimonides is shown the conflicting texts, he immediately says: "It is a transcription error. There is no conflict." The rabbis respond in disappointment: "What an uninteresting resolution to a great intellectual puzzle." Jews not only argue about everything, they also joke about everything. The Talmud is full of humor, as is the entire history of Jewish life. And it is humor with an edge. From Sigmund Freud to Joseph Telushkin, writers have understood the important role humor has played in Jewish argumentation. Rodger Kamenetz combined the two themes of argumentation and humor when he observed that the secret of Jewish survival is that we *had* to last forever "because there wasn't enough time in the universe to finish our arguments."[20]

In the 1996 public television series on Genesis, Rabbi Burton Vistozky of the Jewish Theological Seminary argues that the Bible

is "a covenental document — we have give and take . . . There has to
be argument." The Bible, he says, cannot be put on a pedestal. It
must be challenged, just as God must be challenged. In the seminars
leading up to the series, it was observed that "the Christians were so
quiet and the Jews were so verbal. [T]he Christians were exhilarated
by the Jewish freedom of reading" — by the willingness to argue
about everything, even whether God is just.[21]

Yes, we are committed to pursuing justice. But even the word *pursue* — in Hebrew *tirdof*, literally, "chase after" — suggests an eternal
quest for an elusive concept. So, too, the imperative to repair the
world suggests a never-ending process akin to painting the George
Washington Bridge: by the time the painters have finished at the
New Jersey side, the New York side needs to be repainted. Charity
never ends, and Jews have argued for millennia over the best way to
be charitable. Certainly education is an eternal task. The more we
learn, the more we realize how little we know. So, at bottom, Judaism does have essences, but they are not static substantive verities.
They are all continuing quests, which may be undertaken from different perspectives and which will likely produce different answers.
The essences of Judaism are not programmatic. Nor are they either
liberal or conservative. Beyond generalities such as basic fairness,
the substance of justice is left to each generation, indeed each individual, to define. There is no one Jewish approach to justice. There
is certainly no one right way to balance justice with compassion.
Nor is there one right way to repair the world, to give charity, or to
learn. The imperative is to be active, to be engaged, not to stand idly
by. But a Jew may satisfy these imperatives by conservative as well as
liberal means — by finding racial justice, for example, in color-
blindness or in race-conscious affirmative action. Milton Friedman
is no less a Jew because he believes that economic justice is best
achieved by leaving the market alone than is Michael Walzer, who
believes that the government can best redistribute wealth justly.
The Jewish tradition demands that justice be pursued, but it leaves
it to each individual Jew to pursue it by his or her own lights. It
should come as no surprise, therefore, that Jews continue to argue
about how best to achieve the essences of Judaism. Indeed, Jews
even argue about why Jews argue. Some friends and I once had a big
fight over whether the Jewish people argue so much because our

holy books are so argumentative or whether our books are so argumentative because we are inherently an argumentative people. Needless to say, the dispute remained unresolved.

The futility of the quest for the transmittable essence of Judaism was played out in dueling advertisements in the *New York Times* following the 1994 congressional election. Soon after it became clear that Newt Gingrich would be the new Speaker of the House, a group of politically conservative Jews took out an ad headlined "Mazel Tov, Speaker Gingrich" that claimed to understand "the true nature of Judaism." Not surprisingly, that "true nature" matched the Republican political agenda perfectly. The "timeless Torah values" that constitute the true essence of Judaism, according to these special pleaders, include "fewer government regulations, lower taxes, effective crime fighting," as well as "capital punishment," support for "the military," "personal responsibility," and regarding "wealth as a blessing." The Torah, they assure us, explicitly rejects "modern American liberalism whose policies have failed," because "Judaism is a conservative and traditional religion."[22] I guess the Eleventh Commandment reads, "Thou shalt have no other party but the Grand Old Party."[23]

Not to be outdone, a group of politically liberal Jews took out an ad in which they argued that "Judaism's core political commitment" — its essence — "is to the pursuit of justice." Judaism, these special pleaders said, is at odds with the Republican Party's Contract With America and instead supports an "active" government and "a more equitable society," with — I suppose — higher taxes.*[24]

While my politics correspond with the second ad, that special plea is as misleading and historically inaccurate as the first: Judaism does not dictate whether to vote Republican or Democrat, conservative or liberal, capitalist or socialist. One can find within the Jewish tradition support for virtually any political, economic, or social agenda, because Jews throughout history have expressed every conceivable point of view on every conceivable issue with

---

* This debate was played out again on the eve of the 1996 elections in the November 1 issue of the *Jewish Journal*, which ran an op-ed piece by a liberal named Michael Goldman, who argued that "the heart and soul of today's Gingrich-driven conservatism is 'me-ism,' which is the antithesis of Judaism's basic core values." A conservative named Steven Glovsky argued that a good Jew can be a conservative.

equal authoritativeness and passion. Rabbi Richard L. Rubenstein once said that "Judaism has much to say about justice but very little about politics."[25] I respectfully dissent. Judaism has much to say about both — but so much, in fact, that it cannot be simplified into one-sided slogans, platforms, or ads.

The author of the "liberal" ad, Leonard Fein, has written a thoughtful essay in which he claims to have found the essence of Judaism. He argues that it is *tikkun olam*, repair of the world. I wish he were right, since it is an essence my fellow liberals and I could be proud of. But he is as wrong as those who claim that the essence of Judaism can be found in Newt Gingrich's Contract With America. Fein, like other special pleaders with political agendas, begs the critical question. He asks what the essence of Judaism is, and then he simply asserts his chosen answer: "The essence, the specific genius of the Jews, is the proposition that this world is not working the way it was meant, that it is a broken, fractured world, and that we are implicated in its repair."[26]

That is fine. Actually, that is *Fein*. But it is not necessarily Judaism. It is Fein's take on Judaism. It is Feinism. There are, of course, sources that support Fein's claim. For example, the Kabalistic text *Zohar* speaks of *tikkun olam*, and there is even a contemporary movement and magazine called *Tikkun*, which is premised on this approach to Judaism. But the most that can be said for "repair of the world" is that it is a strain that runs through parts of the Jewish tradition, a small tributary of a mighty river with shifting and raging currents. Moreover, to the extent that "repair of the world" is to be found in the Jewish sources, it is too general, too broad, too ambiguous to be a guide to action. It is another cliché, another fortune cookie, another bumper sticker. Everyone wants to repair the world, to bring it social justice. Read *Mein Kampf*, or Mao's *Little Red Book*, or Marx's *Kapital*, or Jesus' Sermon on the Mount, or Mohammed's Koran, or the Code of Hammurabi, or Confucius's aphorisms, or the Dalai Lama's Five-Point Peace Plan, or the Contract With America. The argument is not over *whether* to repair the broken world, but in what *direction* and by which *means*. The world is broken, some say, because of too many abortions, too little prayer in the schools, too much homosexuality, too progressive a tax system, too many rights for criminals, too much free speech, too much affirmative action, too many liberals like Leonard Fein and Alan

Dershowitz. What is my answer to those who want to repair — in the name of Judaism — *these* perceived breaks in the world, and who want to do it by means that I believe undercut *my* notion of Jewish justice? Do I do the mirror image of what the phony rabbis of Borough Park and the West Bank have done: demand in the name of Judaism that all Jews must accept *my* liberal political agenda or not be deemed Jews?

Even Fein acknowledges that he is stretching the sources to make them fit his political agenda. He writes about mending the world "somehow" as being "one marker common to all" forms of Judaism, claiming that this is "at least, one fair reading of the tradition." He admits that his concept of *tikkun olam* is not as important a part of *Orthodox* Judaism, thus confirming the paradox that some of the best of Jewish values seem to need some distance from the source. But Fein ultimately falls into the trap of all special pleaders when he asserts that "Judaism is inherently a political religion" and that Jewish interests, as he defines them, "are all more likely to be pursued by the left than by the right."

Fein is more convincing when he sticks to relatively uncontroversial forms of social action with unimpeachable traditional sources: feeding the hungry, not placing obstacles before the blind, caring for the widowed and orphaned. Fein's own "Operation Mazon" is a wonderful example of an uncontroversial activity conducted in a Jewish manner. According to Fein, "The Mazon idea is disarmingly simple: Whenever Jews celebrate a bar or bat mitzvah, a wedding, non-ritual occasions as well, let them add 3 percent to the cost of their celebration and forward it to Mazon for distribution to soup kitchens and food pantries and agencies that work to put an end to hunger."[27] Though not *uniquely* Jewish (indeed, Fein quotes Catholic sources in support of these actions), such virtues are certainly *part* of being Jewish. But when he moves to depositing Jewish Federation funds in "community banks" and other specific items in his liberal agenda, he is preaching Feinism, not necessarily Judaism.

But what harm is there, one may ask, in Feinism? Leonard Fein is a wise and decent man whom many of us would like to see have more influence on the social actions of our community, our friends, and our children. I would vote for him as mayor of Cambridge, or Newton, or Boston. His policies of repairing the world are good ones, even including depositing funds in community banks. But he risks considerable damage to Judaism and to the Jewish future when he tells the next generation of Jews that they *must* support his liberal political agenda to be authentic Jews. He threatens to drive away thousands of youngsters who want to be Jewish and act Jewishly but who vehemently disagree with his political agenda. Much as I dislike it, one can be an authentic Jew and live in a Hasidic enclave in Monsey, New York, and do nothing to repair the outside world. One can be an authentic Jew and oppose just about everything Leonard Fein and Alan Dershowitz hold dear. One can also be an authentic Jew and support the entire Fein agenda.

Fein's special pleading would be more persuasive if he admitted that he is an advocate and that his mission is to persuade Jews to become more liberal, and to find sources for their liberalism within the Jewish tradition. That is a noble mission. Indeed, I think Fein is probably right in suggesting that for Jews of the coming century, *tikkun olam* is an aspect of Judaism that should be emphasized and advocated. Fein is surely right that liberalism is *consistent* with Jewish sources — but so is conservatism. He may also be correct in arguing that, quantitatively, more American Jews seem to be attracted to liberalism than to conservatism. But that is more a function of our recent history than our distant traditions, and it may be changing. We should not tie the destiny of our millennia-old civilization to the political flavor of the week, to the ideology du jour, or to the agenda of any special pleaders. We must recognize the eclectic and encompassing nature of Judaism and welcome all to sit under our tent as brothers and sisters without regard to their politics.

Just as one can discern a liberal call for *tikkun olam* in some Jewish sources, so too can one discern a conservative caution against change in other, equally authentic Jewish sources. The Book of Proverbs "counsels submission to political authority": "Fear, my son, God and King, and meddle not with those who seek change." Ecclesiastes sends a similar message: "If you observe the despoiling of the poor and the perversion of Justice and right in the state, do not be astonished. . . . Keep the King's command . . . since the King's word is law, who can say to him 'What are you doing?' " — an undoubtedly docile approach for a Jew.[28] The Talmudic edict that "the law of the Kingdom is Jewish law" presents a similarly conservative approach to law-abidingness.[29]

When I was a yeshiva student, we were always taught that every word of the Bible was the word of God and could be reconciled with every other one. Creative arguments were advanced to reconcile apparently inconsistent words, ideas, concepts, attitudes, and approaches. But it was not deemed religiously correct to argue, "Of course they are irreconcilable, because they were written by very different people, with different experiences, attitudes, and beliefs." To be sure, sophisticated religious scholars — even modern Orthodox ones — accept the reality of multiple authorship, arguing that the individual writers were all inspired by God. But ultra-Orthodox students even today are taught that every word of the Bible is ultimately reconcilable with every other, if we just work hard enough at it.

To deny that there are real — and often irreconcilable — differences among the Bible's authors denigrates the rich diversity of Jewish thought in favor of the myth that there is a single religiously correct "Jewish view" on a wide array of issues, ranging from life after death to reward and punishment to the meaning of life itself to the nature of God.

Compare, for example, two books of the Bible attributed to father and son. Psalm 37, attributed to David, beautifully describes a narrative of justice in which righteousness is rewarded and unrighteousness is punished. In this psalm, on which much of Jesus' Sermon on the Mount is based, we are promised that the "humble [or meek] shall inherit the earth," while "the evil doers shall be cut off." We are also assured that "the Lord loveth justice and forsakes not his saints ['Hasidim']; they are preserved forever; but the seed [and the future] of the wicked shall be cut off." Perhaps the most powerful line in the narrative is King David's personal observation that "I have been young, and now am old; yet I have not seen the righteous forsaken, nor his offspring begging for bread."

The deepest and most profound poem in the Bible, Ecclesiastes (Kohelet), presents a dramatically opposite narrative, detailing the injustice and futility of life and the absence of a hereafter in which the righteous are rewarded and the unrighteous punished. The author of Ecclesiastes — whether King Solomon, a "female-gatherer" (which is what Koheleth literally means),[30] or anyone else — is a very different person from the author of Psalm 37, with a very different religious worldview. He (or she) believes that "man is mere chance, and the beast is mere chance and they are both subject to the same chance." Nor is man more likely than beast to achieve a heavenly reward: "As is the death of one, so is the death of the other . . . both go to the same place, both were made of dust, and both turn into dust again." Nor are the righteous more likely to be rewarded than the unrighteous: "The same fate happens to the righteous and the wicked; to the good and pure and to the impure . . . This is the greatest evil of all that is done under the sun, that there is the same fate for all." As if to directly contradict the claimed observation of the psalmist, the author of Ecclesiastes provides his own personal testimony: "I have seen wicked men buried and come again, and those who did right depart from the place of the holy, and be forgotten in the city." No wonder he believes that "all is *hevel*" — the Hebrew word for steam or vapor, which has been translated poetically as "vanity," but can more aptly be interpreted as "in vain" ("all is in vain") or as "futility."

Rabbi Leon Harrison once cynically commented that if Ecclesiastes was not part of the Bible, "it would certainly be an extremely popular book," because "it is so modern, it is so skeptical, it is so blasé, it is so fashionably free from enthusiasm, from all fervor of deep conviction."[31] Scholars have long wondered how such a work found its way into the Jewish Bible.

Heroic efforts can be and have been made to reconcile the very different worldviews found in the different books of the Bible. But the obvious reality is that these worldviews simply do not reflect a single approach to these large issues. I cannot quarrel with those who believe that all the views reflected in the Bible were inspired by God, any more than I could quarrel with those who believe that all views represented on earth, no matter how diverse, reflect God's inspiration.* But I can and do quarrel with those who deny the diversity of Jewish views, whether in the Bible, the Talmud, the Responsa, or the wide array of Jewish secular literature. There is no one Jewish view, or approach, or set of beliefs, any more than there is one American perspective. Hamilton's approach to governance was incompatible with Jefferson's, though they eventually agreed on a series of compromises that gave rise to our Constitution. So, too,

* I do quarrel with the view that divine inspiration stopped at a particular moment in Jewish history.

with the Bible and the Talmud, which are compilations of diverse and inconsistent Jewish worldviews brought together brilliantly by canonizers and editors. It trivializes the rich diversity of the 3,500-year-old Jewish civilization to reduce it all to a singular, consistent, and always-reconcilable view.

When I read the Bible now as an independent adult, I appreciate its brilliance even more than when I read it as God's word. As the writing of a single infallible God, it isn't so great, since it occasionally has mistakes, inconsistencies, bigotry, and mean-spiritedness. As the writings of fallible Jewish humans, the Bible is an awe-inspiring work of unsurpassed beauty, timelessness, and virtue — especially considering the attitudes of most other human beings who lived in the days of its composition. I learn new things every time I open the Bible, and I admire its writers more deeply with each reading. Now that I understand that different people with different worldviews wrote different parts — and I no longer make artificial efforts at reconciliation — I feel closer to them as people. I identify strongly with Ecclesiastes' description of injustice, but I am more comfortable with Isaiah's prescription for justice: "To deal thy bread to the hungry," "to let the oppressed go free," and to welcome "the poor that are cast out."

Just as Ecclesiastes declares that there is no single essence to life, so too there is no one substantive essence to Judaism.* Requiring Jews, especially young Jews, to choose between their politics and their Judaism sends the wrong message. I have heard ultra-Orthodox Jews argue that one cannot be a Jew and a feminist. Nonsense. There are, to be sure, Jewish sources that argue against feminism. For example, certain rabbis in the Talmud speak terribly about women: women should not be taught the Torah; "one is not to rely on what they say" (Num. R. 10:5); they are "lightheaded" (B. Shea. 336); they are "gluttonous, eavesdropping, slothful and envious" (Gen. R. 45:5); "haughty," "jealous," "deceitful." Other rabbis characterize women as endowed with "more understanding than men,"

---

* The "editors" of Ecclesiastes added a postscript, in the form of a commercial for God: "In sum, having heard everything, fear God and keep his commandments, for that is man's whole duty." This crude attempt to reduce the complex views of Ecclesiastes into an essence trivializes the depth of this multifaceted poem.

"merciful," energetic, scholarly, and "equal to a man." This is typical of the diversity of Jewish attitudes. The Talmud describes one woman named Beruriah as equal to the most brilliant rabbis and contemptuous of those sexist sages who characterized all women as lightheaded.[32] As with virtually every political or social issue, there are conflicting sources because our traditions were written by men (and occasionally women) with very different worldviews. There is no one Jewish attitude toward women, equality, feminism, or sexism. What is unique about the Jewish tradition is that it has preserved these conflicting views in its authoritative texts, so that future generations have available to them a wide array of approaches to any one issue.

The Prophets, the Talmud, the Responsa speak in many voices about every subject, ranging from the afterlife to taxation to the environment to sexuality. Even the Five Books of Moses were written, edited, and compiled by different people over different times. Why should we expect to find a single voice, a one-way road, a holy grail, a monolithic approach, a simple answer in such a divergence of authority and human existence?

The essence of Judaism is not *substantive* so much as it is *procedural* — a *process* for arriving at changing truths for changing times. Our essential procedural approach to life is our very unwillingness to accept any one static substantive essence, our need to continue the dialogue — among ourselves, with others, and even with God — until the end of time.

A Story

I end this chapter with a vignette that illustrates the elusiveness of defining the essence of Judaism in any substantive way.

A secular Jewish couple in their forties brings their thirteen-year-old son to each of his grandparents on the eve of his bar mitzvah to ask the following question: "What is the essence of Judaism?"

Grandpa Moishe, a rabbi from the old country, replies: "God is the essence of Judaism. His Torah, his commandments, his having chosen the Jewish people — that is the essence of Judaism."

The young man is puzzled. "Then my parents aren't Jewish and neither am I. God and his commandments are not at the center of our lives, as they are of yours. We go to synagogue on the High Holidays. We have a Passover Seder. We fast on Yom Kippur. But we aren't Jews because of God."

"Then why are you Jews?" Grandpa Moishe asks.

"I don't know. That's why I am asking you and my other grandparents my question."

Grandma Yetta, who works for the Anti-Defamation League of B'nai B'rith, joins in. "You should be a Jew because we have been persecuted for thousands of years, and we share a common history and destiny."

"But so have blacks and Armenians. Even more important, Grandma, *I* don't feel persecuted. It's not part of my experience."

"That's what the German Jews said in 1920," Grandma Yetta replies. "We must stick together and fight our common enemies, the anti-Semites."

"But there has to be a better reason for being Jews than our common enemies."

"That's good enough for me," says Grandma Yetta.

"It's not good enough for me," replies the young man politely.

The next day, they go to visit Grandpa Justin, a lawyer, and Grandma Esther, a schoolteacher.

"Justice is the essence of Judaism," says Grandpa Justin. "We have been on the forefront of the struggle for justice from Abraham's demand that God treat the people of Sodom justly, to the civil rights movement, to the prevalence of so many Jews on today's courts, in today's law schools, and in the vanguard of every good cause."

"But Jews are not alone in their quest for justice," the young man replies. "Many persecuted people seek justice, as a way of resisting power. As Jews become more powerful, the test of time will be whether they continue to be at the forefront of justice."

"I'm certain they will be," Grandpa Justin says. "Even wealthy Jews tend to vote with the poor and to support civil liberties. *We* remember."

"That's true. But it's also true that the more ultra-Orthodox Jews — those who claim to be closer to the core — are less involved in justice for others. Doesn't that prove that justice is not at the essence of Judaism?"

"No. It only proves that those ultra-Orthodox Jews who reject justice are not necessarily more Jewish than secular Jews who are more committed to the Jewish concept of justice."

"What do you think, Grandma Esther?" the young bar mitzvah boy asks his schoolteacher grandmother.

"Well, it shouldn't surprise you that I believe that the essence of Judaism is education. In my forty years of teaching, I've observed that Jewish families have a deep commitment to the education of their children — secular education, Jewish education, musical education."

"But so do many Asian families."

"That's true. My fellow teachers refer to the Asian children as 'the new Jews.' "

"What has happened to the old Jews, Grandma?"

"They no longer attend public schools — at least not in large numbers. They're in the private schools now. I guess that proves my point. They outgrew the public schools and want to better themselves."

"No, Grandma. It only proves that education was the way out for poor Jews. Let's see how committed Jews remain to education as they become more wealthy."

"It's true that Jews are becoming more like WASPs in many ways, as they attend their schools, go into their businesses and country clubs. They even play lacrosse and row on the crew along with the WASPs."

"And marry them."

"I hope you won't do that."

"Why not, Grandma? Why should a Jew marry only another Jew, if we're becoming so much like other people?"

"Because we need to preserve Judaism."

"But why? Unless there is something special about Judaism, what would be lost if more Jews married out and there were fewer Jews in the next century?"

"That would be a real tragedy. Both we and the world would lose so much," Grandma Esther says, a tear forming in her eye.

"But if Judaism really has an essence, why can't that essence be transmitted even without Jews?"

"Because I don't really know what the essence of Judaism is. For me it's education, for Grandpa Justin it's justice. For your other grandparents, it's religion and a common history of persecution."

"I think I know what it is, Grandma," the young man interjects with a smile.

"What is it?" Grandma Esther asks eagerly.

"It's our willingness to argue about issues like this. It's your willingness to treat my ideas as deserving of respect even though I'm only thirteen years old. It's my willingness to learn from my grandparents and your willingness to allow me to argue with you. From Abraham's argument with God to the Birkenau rabbis' trial of God, Jews have always argued with God, about God, about justice — even about the essence of Judaism. That's for me!"

But is it enough? In the next chapter, I will suggest that it may be enough — provided that the continuing dialogue be based on *educated* and *informed* argument steeped in 3,500 years of unparalleled wisdom, of which most secular Jews today are abysmally ignorant.

PART IV:

A WORKABLE ANSWER TO THE

JEWISH QUESTION

Chapter Eight

Filling the Yiddisher Cup: The Competitive Solution to the Jewish Future

I AM CONVINCED that we *can* find a promising answer to the Jewish question of the twenty-first century — how can we endure in the face of our success? — but we must first learn where to look for it. We have been called the people of the book. Our collective library, both religious and secular, is unparalleled. We have been the teachers of humankind. In every nation in which we have lived, we have taught, written, created, invented, and left an intellectual legacy. Maimonides listed "the advancement of learning" as "the highest commandment." Zechariah Frankel, the nineteenth-century German Talmudic scholar, said that without learning, Jewish life will end. Ahad Ha'am, one of the greatest nonreligious Jewish thinkers in modern history, declared in 1910 that "the secret of Jewish survival" is "learning, learning, learning."*[1]

In light of this long commitment to teaching and learning, it is sadly remarkable that no group in America is less knowledgeable about its traditions, less literate in its language, less familiar with its own library than the Jews. We are the most ignorant, uneducated, illiterate Americans when it comes to knowledge of the

---

* Ahad Ha'am, which means "one of the nation," was the pen name of Asher Ginzberg (1856–1927), who wrote some of the most probing essays on Zionism, Jewish tradition and philosophy, and Jewish survival.

Bible, the history of our people, Jewish philosophy, religious rituals, and traditions. More Jews can tell you the name of Jesus' mother than Abraham's father. More Christians than Jews can recite the Ten Commandments. More Muslims than Jews know the story of Abraham. There is nothing more traumatic for most Jews than to be called up to the Torah for an "aliyah."* I have seen famous lawyers — at ease before the Supreme Court or on television — quake with fear and turn red with embarrassment as they try to read the transliteration of the simple blessing over the Torah.† American Jews, who are the most highly educated group in this country when it comes to general knowledge, are the least educated group when it comes to knowledge of their own heritage. We get our history from *Fiddler on the Roof*, our traditions from canned gefilte fish, our Bible stories from television, our culture from Jackie Mason, and our Jewish morality from the once-a-year synagogue sermon most of us sleep through. (The rabbinic sermon as a sleeping aid is the subject of many jokes, such as the one about the American rabbi and the Israeli cab driver who get to heaven at the same time. God gives the cab driver a large cloud and the rabbi a small one. The rabbi complains, "God, I have been preaching your message for forty years. Why is the cab driver treated better than me?" God replies: "When you preached, everyone in your congregation slept, but when he drove, everyone in his cab prayed.")

The typical non-Orthodox Jew today has no idea what is contained in the Jewish library beyond a children's-storybook summary of the Bible, has little familiarity with Jewish history before the Holocaust and the establishment of Israel, and has virtually no knowledge about the diversity of Jewish tradition. Even most Orthodox Jews are unaware of the vast array of Jewish writing that is not specifically religious in nature. Much of the Jewish library is unavailable in English or other languages commonly spoken by today's Jews. Just as virtually all of Jewish learning was translated into the vernacular of yesteryear, Yiddish, so too all of Jewish learning must be translated into today's vernacular, English. And the translations

---

* Making aliyah means "going up" to Israel. Getting an aliyah means being called "up" to bless the Torah.
† These quaking lawyers are in good company. Theodor Herzl complained that reading the blessing in Hebrew caused him "more sweat than an entire speech."[2]

must be accessible, understandable, and usable. There is a wonderful theater poster of the 1930s advertising a new Yiddish production of *King Lear*, which has been "translated, updated and improved upon!" Perhaps we cannot meet those demanding criteria, but we can do a lot better than we are currently doing. Jews have always excelled at nearly everything they do — except Jewish education.

Is the Yiddisher Cup Half Full or Half Empty?

The famed Yiddisher cup — the Jewish mind — is only half full: it is overflowing with general knowledge, but it is almost completely empty when it comes to Jewish knowledge. It is this ignorance as much as assimilation, intermarriage, and low birthrates that threatens the survival of Jewish life in America today. If learning is indeed the secret of Jewish survival, then unless we can reverse the trend toward Jewish ignorance, we are doomed. We are a dialogic people whose essence is the continuing *quest* for such elusive ideals as justice, repair of the world, and godliness. Intelligent dialogue about these issues can continue only as long as those engaged in it are knowledgeable about the diverse literature and learning of our people over time.

Currently, only religious Jews (primarily those who received an Orthodox or Conservative day school education) and university-trained professionals in Jewish studies (many of whom are also religious) are capable of continuing the dialogue. This skews the debate heavily in favor of the religious component of Judaism. Today, very few secular Jews possess the knowledge essential to entering the dialogue, as contrasted with the period between the Jewish Enlightenment (Haskalah) and the Second World War, when many secular Jews were literate in Jewish sources. The great secular institutions of Jewish learning that developed between the Enlightenment and the end of Yiddish culture are gone. This is not to criticize those religious leaders who have built religious Jewish houses of learning. To the contrary: They are to be congratulated for at least trying. Some, in fact, have done a fairly good job. It is to criticize secular Jews for abandoning Jewish learning, especially at the elementary and high school levels, where they have the greatest impact.

There are many reasons for the current disparity between the high level of Jewish involvement in general education and the low level of involvement in Jewish education. The most obvious reason is that general knowledge is rewarded with good jobs and other indices of success, while no one includes Hebrew school honors on his or her résumé. In fact, Jewish learning, if done right, can contribute considerably to secular success, as I will show. Moreover, we are supposed to be a people that believes in education for education's sake; many Jews are involved in activities that are not immediately rewarded in the job market, such as music and art lessons, athletics, and chess clubs. Why not Jewish learning? For anyone who has attended after-school Hebrew classes, the answer is obvious. For the most part, these classes today are boring and poorly taught. They simply aren't fun. More important, it isn't good education. No upwardly mobile American Jew would ever accept the quality of today's *Jewish* education in *secular* elementary, high school, or college classes to which they send their children. There are, of course, some very poor secular schools. *But we do not send our children to these schools!* We scrimp and save, if we have to, in order to send them to the best private schools, or we move to neighborhoods with the best public schools. But we continue to tolerate mediocrity in the Jewish schools to which we send our children.

Forward-looking Jewish leaders are beginning to recognize our collective failure in educating Jews. They realize that Jewish learning must *compete* with other learning in the marketplace of ideas. To make Jewish learning truly competitive in a very crowded market, we must take advantage of every Jewish talent, experience, success, and resource. If there is any enterprise at which Jews should excel, it is teaching. And we do excel at *secular* teaching: the universities of America are dominated by Jewish professors who regularly win awards for their teaching skills and dedication. There are also many extraordinary Jewish elementary and secondary school teachers, principals, and administrators. Jews excel as well in other areas of communication, from advertising to publishing to public relations to the media. But we have not harnessed these talents toward the single most important mechanism for assuring Jewish continuity: namely, Jewish education in the broadest sense of that term.

Our library remains closed, our teachers remain silent, and our students remain deaf, mute, and blind to the wonders of our tradition. The reasons for this collective failure, though varied, can be encapsulated in one word: *monopoly*. For the past several genera-tions, rabbis have held monopolistic control over teaching Jewish children. This religious control has led most Jews to believe that Jewish literature deals exclusively with theology and ritual. Indeed, much of it does, and that part is largely irrelevant to many contem-porary Jews, who aren't interested in the prohibition against mixing wool and linen, or how many hours one is supposed to wait between eating a hamburger and drinking a milkshake. During my twelve years of yeshiva, I never learned anything but the Bible and the Tal-mud in my Jewish studies, and that was taught by rote in a most un-interesting and irrelevant way. I was never exposed to the writings of the Hasidic masters, the Responsa, the early Zionists, the Yid-dishists, the Jewish political pamphleteers, the Kabalists, the Skep-tics, or the Bundists. I was taught that the *only* way to lead a Jewish life was to obey the 613 commandments, wear a yarmulke, live in a Jewish neighborhood, have only Jewish friends, and pray three times a day. It is not surprising, therefore, that so many young Jews remember their Judaism as "an old man saying no" — or as Rabbi Moshe Waldoks puts it, too much of Judaism emphasizes the "oy" over the joy.

Parents have had little choice but to send their children to the lo-cal synagogue for bar and bat mitzvah preparation. Since these ritu-als are religious in nature, they have been performed by rabbis under the auspices of synagogues. Preparation has been done in a religious context. There has been no real competition. The result-ing "education" has been generally mediocre, with some inspiring exceptions. The kids typically hate it, but they want to be bar or bat mitzvahed, because it is a rite of passage and it comes with a party and presents. The "deal" usually made between the parents and their children is that in exchange for "giving up" several afternoons or Sunday mornings, the children would get the party *and* a promise of no more Hebrew school. For this reason, Jewish education gen-erally ends at the bar or bat mitzvah. The moment that event takes place, the education stops, because it has served its limited purpose.[3] This phenomenon is illustrated by the joke about the Reform syna-gogue that became rat infested. The board of directors called a con-ventional exterminator who sprayed, but to no avail. Then they called a high-tech company that sent sound waves through the walls, but still the rats returned. When the rabbi learned of the problem, he proposed a simple solution: "I'll bar mitzvah all the rats; then we'll never see them anywhere near the synagogue again."

Jewish religious education geared exclusively toward the bar or bat mitzvah has been largely a failure. For many young Jews, it has engendered negative feelings about Jewish learning rather than positive appreciation for the wisdom of our sages. It has been neither educational nor uplifting. As one perceptive expert has put it: "We have no one to fault but ourselves. We have failed to properly educate our children. What we do teach is so negative that it's been said, only half in jest, that if the Jews for Jesus were smart they would send every Jewish child to Hebrew school because, in most instances, it's proved to be the greatest turn-off to Jewish life."[4]

When young Jewish boys and girls drop out of Hebrew school in the seventh or eighth grade, they go through life with a seventh- or eighth-grade understanding of Judaism. None of us would permit our children to go through life with a seventh- or eighth-grade understanding of science, math, or literature. Yet we are satisfied when our children have mastered (usually by memorizing a tape) their quickly forgettable Haftorah reading and a few blessings.

We know from long experience with business that monopolies are generally bad for customers. Monopolists get lazy. They take the path of least resistance. In education, this brings about a vicious cycle of uninspiring teachers, uninspired students, and a general sense of Hebrew school as bitter medicine that may be good for you in some nonspecific way, but is awfully hard to swallow. This must change if the Jewish future is to have any chance. This does not mean denigrating the rabbis who currently teach our children. They must retain a central role, but they will become better educators with a little healthy competition. The American Jewish community has both the talent and the wealth to create the very best Jewish education in the world. We boast some of the most talented and innovative educators in the world. The subject matter is inherently fascinating — if it is taught in the spirit of free and open inquiry. It is a scandal that it took Bill Moyers to bring the Book of Genesis to life for millions of Jews (and others). It is *our* Bible and we have neglected it and desecrated it by the deadly dull manner in which we have taught it.

The Jewish community must demand of its educators that they be judged like the CEOs of competitive businesses. (They should also be paid a salary that reflects the importance of their work.) The bottom line is making after-school Jewish education competitive with other attractive options, such as soccer practice, drum lessons, and hanging around the mall. My friend Rabbi Moshe Waldoks asks his audiences how many want their children to become professional soccer players. No hands go up. Then he asks them how many want their children to remain Jews. All the hands go up. "Nu?" he asks. "Isn't something wrong if you put more energy into soccer practice than into Jewish education?"

Jewish day schools must be every bit as good as Choate, Exeter, Dalton, Friends, and Horace Mann. We must remember that most of these elite schools began as Christian religious schools and are now attended by large numbers of Jews, not *because* they were Christian but because they are excellent. Even when the Jewish community was not nearly as affluent as it is today, we built Jewish hospitals — nearly every major city has a great hospital with a Jewish name like Mount Sinai, Beth Israel, or simply Jewish Hospital. We built these hospitals because we believed that we needed them to train Jewish doctors and treat Jewish patients in an age of discrimination. We did not build second-rate hospitals. We insisted that they be among the best. But we have settled for second-rate schools and fifth-rate after-school programs. Why? Because we regarded health as of more immediate concern than Jewish education. Now that we are far more affluent, we can afford both, and the need for Jewish hospitals has waned as discrimination has. The time has come for a major commitment of resources to Jewish education so that it can become competitive.

Our Competitive Advantage

We must use what my friend Michael Porter, the Christenson Professor of business administration at Harvard, calls our "competitive advantage." Professor Porter, in describing the competitive advantage of nations, writes that "differences in national values, culture, economic structures, institutions, and histories all contribute to competitive success."[5] Nations and corporations succeed if they can harness their unique advantages and thereby gain an edge over the competition. When it comes to teaching and communicating, there is no group that has a greater competitive advantage than Jews. Moreover, as the most affluent and charitable group in America, we could easily harness that advantage toward Jewish survival. It would not even require that Jews contribute more to Jewish charities. A simple reallocation of resources toward Jewish education would do the trick. The problem is that Jewish fund-raising today is geared primarily toward "sacred survival." The money pours in only when Jews are endangered by *external* enemies. We have raised enormous amounts for the defense of Israel, for the rescue of Soviet, Ethiopian, and other endangered Jews.[6] We must, of course, continue to regard defense against external enemies as our highest priority *when it is needed*. But now that Israel is economically and militarily more secure, now that the Jews of the former Soviet Union are free to leave, now that most Ethiopian and other endangered Jews have been rescued, the time has come to turn our charitable giving toward defense against our *internal* dangers: Jewish ignorance and the resulting assimilation. Reallocating resources toward Jewish education is helping ourselves and our children reap the benefits of our 3,500-year-old civilization.

For Judaism to become a transmittable civilization in an integrated, secular world where Jews do not experience isolation, discrimination, and victimization, Jewish learning must become *accessible* to integrated and secular Jews. It must become *usable* to them in their daily lives, much the way it was usable in a different way to their ancestors in the shtetls of Eastern Europe and elsewhere. In those days, no Jew would open a business without first consulting the diverse Jewish sources on business practices. He would then be obliged to follow these sources. Today, we have the advantage of *including* the Jewish sources among many others we consult and picking and choosing the most useful. But to ignore millennia of accumulated wisdom on an issue of importance is just plain foolish.

Ahad Ha'am, who devoted his life to Jewish learning, was a thoroughly secular Jew who abandoned the religious aspects of Judaism as a youth. His goals were the creation of a great Jewish university and the writing of a great Jewish encyclopedia, modeled on the French encyclopedia of Diderot that transformed French culture and removed it from the dominance of the church. Ha'am saw his first goal accomplished with the establishment of Hebrew University in Jerusalem in 1918. Although the encyclopedia, as Ahad Ha'am envisioned it, was never compiled, many secular Zionists viewed the creation of a Jewish state in Palestine as a living encyclopedia, where Jewish learning could continue and Jewish spirituality and culture could thrive in a Jewish setting.

We must make Jewish education important not only to the survival of *Jewish* life but also to success in life in *general*. We must devise curricula that use Jewish sources to provide all students with competitive advantages in their business, professional, and personal lives. We must persuade our children that studying Jewish sources will make them not only better Jews, but also better lawyers, doctors, corporate executives, teachers, literary critics, husbands, wives, mothers, fathers, and citizens. Best-selling books have been written about how the teachings of Confucius, Jesus, Machiavelli — even Genghis Khan — can lead to success. Why not the writings of the Prophets, Maimonides, Rabbi Akiba, Israel Salanter, Joseph Soloveichik, and Ahad Ha'am? Jewish scholarship has always balanced the practical with the theoretical. The traditional rabbi was as much a dispenser of pragmatic business advice as of ritual guidance. The modern rabbi and teacher must bring the Jewish sources alive and make them relevant to the current generation of students. It should come as no surprise that among the primary religious obligations a father owes to his children is to teach them how to swim — that is, how to survive in an often dangerous world. An old story tells of God announcing to the leaders of Catholicism, Protestantism, and Judaism that he has changed his mind and has decided to flood the world again in seven days, but this time with no ark. The pope calls on all Catholics to confess their sins over the coming week. Protestant leaders ask their followers to engage in a week of prayer. The chief rabbi tells the Jews, "We have seven days to figure out how to live under water."

I am absolutely convinced that my own immersion in Jewish sources has made me a better lawyer and teacher. My exposure to two very different worldviews — one with a 3,500-year-old library — has given me a competitive edge over those with a single worldview. I feel it every day as I work through problems of every kind. I see it every day in my classroom. Students who have rigorously studied the Talmud and other Jewish sources come to law school with a competitive advantage.* I know I certainly did. At law school, the yeshiva alumni tend to be more familiar with modes of argumentation and with other ways of thinking like a lawyer. When I explain to my law students the role of hierarchical precedent in American law — the Constitution, statutes, regulations, practices — the ones who have studied Talmud immediately see the analogy to Jewish hierarchical precedent — the Bible, Mishnah, Gemara, and so on. The nature of Talmudic argumentation, developed over centuries, parallels legal reasoning in many important respects.

I have been told by friends in other disciplines that they have had similar experiences. For example, students of literary criticism who have studied the four types of Jewish biblical exegesis have found that they have a significant head start in textual analysis. Since the Middle Ages, Jewish scholars have employed *peshat* (literal interpretation), *remez* (veiled allusions), *derash* (homiletical interpretation), and *sod* (more esoteric speculations) to elucidate traditional texts. The Jewish scholar Emmanuel L'evinas's deconstruction of Talmudic texts helped pave the way for Jacques Derrida and other deconstructionists. As one scholar has written: "Levinas is . . . one of the thinkers who made Derrida and deconstruction possible."[7] Yet most literary scholars who are Jews have neglected the Jewish sources of literary interpretation. Exposure to these and other ancient hermeneutical techniques gives a contemporary student a competitive edge. Daniel Goldin, the head of the National Aeronautics and Space Administration, credits Jewish education with his success: "The training I received as a young boy, thinking about my ancestors . . . , about the constant study of Torah, was to be inquisitive, to prove, to understand" (*Jerusalem Report*, September 19, 1996).

If we are to compete for the minds and hearts of Jewish children and adults, we will have to shift our resources toward Jewish education. By Jewish education, I do not mean only religious education. Nor do I mean only elementary or secondary school education. I recently attended a class in Jewish learning sponsored by Aish Hatorah, an Orthodox outreach group that has had considerable success with college-age Jewish students. Although they have an ex-

---

* Students with a good Jesuit education also have an advantage.

plicitly religious *goal*, they employ *means* that are not overtly religious. They emphasize the intellectual aspects of Jewish learning. The rabbi started the class by exclaiming, "All right, let's have some fun!" I do not recall the word *fun* ever being used in my twelve years of yeshiva education, except as a put-down. And the Aish Hatorah class *was* fun. It was also intellectually stimulating. It began by posing a problem from the Talmud about a man in the desert with a bottle of water, who comes upon another man with no water. If they share the water, both will die of thirst. If one drinks all the water, he will survive but the other will die. What should be done? Every answer was greeted with a slight shifting of the facts: for example, one of the men is very old, or one is the child of the other, or the bottle is found by both at the same time. Eventually we got to the decision made by Jewish leaders during the Holocaust, when Nazi officials demanded that they turn over a certain number of Jews so that others would be spared. Generations of Jews have debated this and other "tragic choice" dilemmas over the millennia. In a wonderful book, *Collaboration with Tyranny in Rabbinic Law*, Professor David Daube of Oxford explores the diverse rabbinic approaches to the tragic choice with which Jews were often confronted by tyrants: Surrender one Jew for execution or all will be killed.[8] Variations on this theme have occurred in numerous contexts throughout Jewish history: A Roman general demands the production of any one Jew for execution within a walled city or else the entire city will be destroyed; the authorities demand the surrender and execution of a named Jew — who is innocent — or else all the Jews will be killed; a group of "heathens" walking on a road demands of a smaller group of Jews, "Give us one of you that we may kill him, otherwise we shall kill you all." The Talmudic discourse over these cases is as informed, intelligent, and compelling as any contemporary debate on comparable issues. The rabbis raise every possible argument in support of every conceivable position. Their approaches are varied, and there is no one *right* answer or *Jewish* answer. But to ignore these hundreds of approaches suggested over thousands of years would be like ignoring Aristotle, Plato, Kant, Bentham, and Wittgenstein in approaching contemporary philosophical issues. A Jew who is ignorant of his or her great intellectual heritage is an ignorant and uneducated *person* — to say nothing of an ignorant and uneducated Jew!

I always use Jewish sources in my law school and college teaching. Indeed, in my thirty-two years of teaching criminal law, legal ethics, Thinking About Thinking, and other courses at Harvard, I have rarely come upon an important intellectual or moral issue that was not debated, in one form or another, by the Jewish sages. That's not to say that the precise question was always posed exactly as we would debate it today. But the underlying concerns were addressed. Indeed, I plan to teach a course at Harvard Law School in 1997 titled "Concepts of Justice in the Bible." It will explore how our ideas concerning justice grew out of biblical accounts. It will be taught from an eclectic perspective that includes, but is not limited to, religious views of the Bible. I constantly employ biblical and Talmudic references in teaching criminal law, just as I do literary and historical references. In my office, I have pictures of some of my heroes: Justice Arthur Goldberg, Judge David Bazelon, Thomas Jefferson, Elie Wiesel, and others. I also have a painting of bearded Talmudic scholars sitting around a table in Poland discussing Jewish law. It is there to remind me, and my students, of the enormous debt we owe to these Jewish scholars for their devotion to law, justice, and ethics. The author of Ecclesiastes was certainly correct when he observed: "What has been will be again, what has been done will be done again; there is nothing new under the sun." There is no civilization in the history of the world that has a richer library of knowledge, spanning the millennia, dealing with every issue under the sun and presenting so many alternative approaches to life's dilemmas. Yet we are ignorant of our past, and that makes us less able to defend our future. Again Ecclesiastes: "Is there anything of which one can say, 'Look, this is something new.' It was like this already, long ago; it was here before our time. There is no remembrance of men of old and even those who are yet to come will not be remembered by those who follow." We cannot confront the future intelligently without remembering the men and women of old. To paraphrase Rabbi Mordechai Kaplan, the past may not have a veto, but it certainly deserves a vote — especially when the past is as rich and diverse as the Jewish past has been. As Rabbi Charles A. Annes put it: "When American Jews become thoroughly familiar with their own literature, history, and faith and become aware of its awe-inspiring glory, its all-embracing scope, its sharp reasoning, and its beautiful emotions, then they will proudly present all this to the world rather than have the world present it to them. On that day they will have learned to live comfortably and meaningfully in two cultures and find that they are able to accept the new with no fear of total assimilation."[9]

In Boston, a model Jewish education program is having considerable success. It focuses on adults, because as one of its proponents put it: "What we've discovered is something that should have been quite obvious: if you want to transform lives, you can't simply educate children. It's as families that people make decisions about religious involvement. You can have the best Hebrew School in the world, but if there is no involvement in the home, then it doesn't mean a hell of a lot."[10] With that in mind, classes have been offered to adults pursuant to the philosophy of Jewish learning as an end in itself. Indeed, one of the programs is called "Learning for the Sake of Learning." The center of these programs is the classroom, not the temple, and the classes are taught by Jewish scholars as well as rabbis.

A new Jewish high school is opening adjacent to the Brandeis University campus, which will emphasize the intellectual, moral, and spiritual aspects of Jewish learning over its ritual requirements. "It will be an innovative curriculum . . . , rigorous, with a lot of integration of Jewish and general studies material." Making full use of our "competitive advantage," the new school will emphasize the "progressive models" of Professor Howard Gardner of Harvard, recognized for his work on how children think, and Ted Sizer, former headmaster of Phillips Exeter Academy and dean of the Harvard School of Education.[11] The school's location near Brandeis is designed to encourage use of the university's facilities, including library and faculty. Like Brandeis, the school will be Jewishly interdenominational, equally open to Orthodox, Conservative, Reform, Reconstructionist, and unaffiliated Jews. Unlike Brandeis, it will be limited to Jews, though the criteria for who is a Jew will probably be a matter of self-definition. The goal will be to provide a total education — both Jewish and general — that is competitive with the very best prep schools in the country. There is no reason why it cannot succeed, since it has received start-up grants and gifts of close to a million dollars. This is the kind of model for other Jewish communities around the country that has a real chance of reversing our collective drift toward Jewish illiteracy.

Programs of this kind were not available when I was growing up. Fortunately, I have been able to define for myself a positive Jewish identity and to live a meaningful Jewish life. I feel part of the Jewish civilization, a link in the "sacred chain" that goes back thousands of years. I *think* Jewishly about virtually every secular issue that is part of my diverse life. I *teach* Jewishly. I *practice law* Jewishly. I conduct my *business* and *personal life* Jewishly. My *family* life is Jewish. I surround myself with Jewish *music* and Jewish *art*. My *politics* are Jewishly inspired. Even my *agnosticism* is Jewish, since the God whose existence I wonder about is the *Jewish* God.

When I confront a problem in my life, whether it be professional or personal, I consult Jewish sources in addition to contemporary American sources. I do not necessarily feel compelled to obey the Jewish answers, as a Halakic Jew might feel. I consult the Jewish sources not because I regard them as binding, but because I value their wisdom. They provide a different worldview, a worldview reflecting an ancient tradition of which I am a part. My Jewish views help me challenge the current conventional wisdom, just as modern learning allows me to challenge traditional Jewish views. To ignore the wisdom of our sages is both arrogant and ignorant. It is comparable to deciding a complex constitutional issue without even bothering to find out what the framers of our Constitution had in mind.

I have benefited enormously from looking back at Jewish sources to help resolve contemporary legal and ethical issues. For example, I represent criminal defendants whom I often suspect are guilty of the crimes they are charged with. I rarely know for certain, because they all tell me they are innocent. But as a scholar of criminal law, I realize that the vast majority of defendants brought to trial on criminal charges in America are, in fact, guilty. Thank God for that! Would anyone want to live in a country where the majority of people charged with crimes were innocent? That may be true in Iraq, Iran, China, and the former Soviet Union, but it is not true in America. My professional obligation as a lawyer requires me to defend my clients without regard to my personal belief in their possible or even probable guilt. But my moral obligations as a human being and as a Jew require me to question whether I am doing the right thing by helping some guilty people get acquitted. I have participated in several cases — I cannot be more specific — over the past thirty years in which I have helped to free people I believed to be guilty of horrendous crimes. In each case I felt terrible personally, though I believe that I performed an important professional duty.

The first time I experienced this feeling was back in the early 1970s, when I represented on a pro bono basis a young member of the Jewish Defense League, now deceased, who had made the bomb that had been placed in the office of Sol Hurok, the famous impresario who brought Soviet talent to the United States. The JDL disapproved of cultural exchanges between our nation and a nation that was oppressing Jews, and it showed its disapproval by a series of escalating acts of violence, culminating in the bombing, which took the life of a young secretary who happened to be Jewish. In an effort to solve the horrible crime and to prevent others, the police engaged in unconstitutional conduct, including unlawful wiretaps and improper physical threats against my client. The wiretaps and confessions proved beyond any doubt that my client had made the bomb. But I won the case and everyone went free. I refused to participate in the victory celebration, because even though I knew my legal efforts had vindicated the constitutional rights of all Americans, I also knew that I had helped free a guilty killer.

I couldn't sleep for weeks. I read everything I could get my hands on relating to a lawyer's obligation to defend the guilty. I found British sources, such as the noted barrister Henry Brougham, who in 1820 said:

> An advocate, by the sacred duty which he owes his client, knows, in the discharge of that office, but one person in the world, that client and none other. To save that client by all expedient means — to protect that client at all hazards and costs to all others, and among others to himself — is the highest and most unquestioned of his duties; and he must not regard the alarm, the suffering, the torment, the destruction which he may bring upon any other. Nay, separating even the duties of a patriot from those of an advocate, and casting them, if need be, to the wind, he must go on reckless of the consequences, if his fate it should unhappily be, to involve his country in confusion for his client's protection.[12]

I found a justice of the United States Supreme Court who said:

> Defense counsel has no . . . obligation to ascertain or present the truth. Our system assigns him a different mission. He must be and

is interested in preventing the conviction of the innocent, but, absent a voluntary plea of guilty, we also insist that he defend his client whether he is innocent or guilty . . . Defense counsel need present nothing, even if he knows what the truth is. He need not furnish any witnesses to the police, or reveal any confidences of his client, or furnish any other information to help the prosecution's case. If he can confuse a witness, even a truthful one, or make him appear at a disadvantage, unsure or indecisive, that will be his normal course. Our interest in not convicting the innocent permits counsel to put the state to its proof, to put the state's case in the worst possible light, regardless of what he thinks or knows to be the truth.[13]

But I also found sources in the Talmud and other Jewish writing, such as Norman Lamm's seminal article "The Fifth Amendment and Its Equivalent in the Halakah."[14] Lamm cites the Halakic principle that a person "cannot declare himself to be an evil doer." Two independent witnesses must so testify. He then explores the political, legal, and psychological roots of this principle, juxtaposing Maimonides with Freud and concluding that the Halakic principle is based on considerations somewhat different from those underlying the Fifth Amendment. But both share a preference for acquitting the possibly guilty over convicting the possibly innocent. Lamm's writings were cited by the Supreme Court in the *Miranda* decision as well as in other decisions. I always find his discussions of similarities and differences between our Bill of Rights and traditional Jewish sources enlightening.

When I arrived at the synagogue on the eve of Yom Kippur in 1995 for the Kol Nidre service, these Jewish sources jumped into my consciousness. Six hours earlier, a Los Angeles jury had acquitted O. J. Simpson of murdering his former wife Nicole Brown and her friend Ron Goldman. I was a member of the defense team, and the only reason I had not been in court for the verdict was that I wanted to be with my family for Yom Kippur. The acquittal had shocked white America, including most Jews, who were outraged at what they believed was an injustice brought about by racial considerations. Many Jews were reminded of the acquittal in 1991 of the Arab man who was believed to have murdered Rabbi Meir Kahane in Manhattan and of the black youth who was thought to have killed rabbinic student Yankel Rosenbaum in Crown Heights, Brooklyn, in 1992. In the Simpson case as well, there was a Jewish victim and an acquittal by a predominantly black jury of a black man who was widely believed to be guilty.

When I walked into the synagogue that night, no one looked at me or greeted me. Only when the rabbi made mention of the injustice of the Simpson verdict did all eyes peek in my direction to see how I would react. A few people looked at me during the recitation of the "Al Chet" prayer — the ritual admission of sins — to see whether they could discern any sign of remorse, perhaps a harder pounding of my heart, when I came to the sin of having "given evil counsel" ("*Ya'atznu ra*").* It was a very different experience from the one I'd had when I attended High Holiday services in the Moscow Great Synagogue during the time I was representing Jewish refuseniks in the 1970s. There, the congregants turned to smile at me and several passed me notes about their problems. It was the KGB agents who gave me dirty looks.

All through the Yom Kippur service following the Simpson acquittal, I thought about Shimon, the son of Shetah, and how he understood the biblical imperative to do justice. I had told the story of Shimon in my novel *The Advocate's Devil* in the context of a difficult contemporary ethical dilemma:

> "Believe it or not, this old judge — his name was Shimon, the son of Shetah — actually confronted a situation a bit like ours."
>
> "How so?"
>
> "Well, he had presided over a case in which a guilty murderer was let off because there was only one witness. The Bible expressly requires at least two witnesses — in capital cases. The acquitted murderer then goes out and kills again, and the judge sees him with 'the sword in his hand, the blood dripping, and the dead man still twitching.' "
>
> "Quite graphic."
>
> "Yeah, these guys knew how to write some gut-wrenching stuff."

---

* Jews joke about everything, even the most solemn occasions. An Orthodox friend sent a Jewish New Year card that listed each of the sins for which we seek forgiveness. Underneath this list was the greeting: "Better luck next year!"

"So what does the judge do?" Abe asked.

"Nothing. That's the point. He asks the murderer the same question we've been asking ourselves."

"What?"

"Here, let me read it to you, straight from the Talmud: 'Wicked one, who killed this man? You or I?' "

"So what does the judge answer?"

"He answers that *he*, the judge, is surely *not* responsible, because he followed the biblical rule, requiring two witnesses."

"Well, that seems right, doesn't it?"

"Maybe for a judge, certainly not for a lawyer," Justin said.

"To the contrary. It seems to me more justified for a lawyer than for a judge."

"Why so?"

"Well," Abe explained, "both have to obey the law. A lawyer's primary responsibility is to his client, while a judge's is to society in general. If a judge does the right thing by occasionally letting a guilty person go free — perhaps even to murder again — it would seem to follow that an advocate can't be blamed for doing the same thing."[15]

I also thought about the portion of the Torah that I had chanted at my bar mitzvah, which included that ringing imperative, "Justice, justice, shall thou pursue." I will always remember the interpretation that our rabbi, Samuel Mirsky — who had been educated as a lawyer in Palestine before the Holocaust — had given to these words. He asked why God found it necessary to repeat the word *justice*. His answer: Because without the *means* of justice being satisfied, we can never be certain that the *ends* of justice will be served. I comforted myself with the knowledge that Jewish tradition had long understood the role of the zealous defender of the innocent, the guilty, and the probably guilty about whom there might still be reasonable doubt. Indeed, one of God's attributes is that he is *"moser asirim,"* redeemer of the imprisoned. I remembered with fondness that Natan Sharansky had greeted me with that blessing after I had helped to secure his 1986 release from the Soviet Gulag. When a talk show host asked me who had paid me my "biggest fee," I had no hesitation in answering "Sharansky." The host said, "I didn't know he had any money." I said, "He didn't. I received no money for representing him. But I never received more gratification than when he was released from the Gulag and thanked me with the Hebrew blessing."

None of this made me feel less bad for the Brown and Goldman families, who had lost loved ones to a brutal murder. But it helped me to place my role as a defense lawyer in the broader context of both the Anglo-American and Jewish traditions of justice.

I am certainly not suggesting that there is only one Jewish way to think about these and other issues. What I am suggesting is exactly the opposite. The Jewish sources are so diverse, so heterogeneous, so contentious, so dynamic, that there is something for (and against) almost anybody and any attitude. A zealous Jewish prosecutor can find solace in the Jewish sources, even if he succeeds in having a murderer executed. Nor am I suggesting that I think about important issues *only* Jewishly. My guides to ethical questions include the Bible, Maimonides, Kant, Bentham, Israel Salanter, Spinoza, the psalmists, Nozick, the Baal Shem Tov, Aristotle, the Vilna Gaon, Jefferson, Brandeis, my parents and grandparents, my teachers, Wiesel, Holmes, Madison, Burke, Soloveichik, Babel, Kafka, Rawles, and many others. I do not believe, as some fundamentalists do, that the Jewish sources have all the answers or are God's literal words. But they help me frame the questions and work out tentative and ever-changing answers. The Jewish sources give me an additional worldview — or really views — to juxtapose against the dominant Western canon. I recall the great lunch-hour debates while I was a yeshiva student in which we challenged our afternoon secular learning — about evolution, the age of the earth, attitudes toward sexuality and liberty — by invoking the religious doctrines we had been taught in the morning, and vice versa. The tragedy is that we did this *only* during the lunch hour and never in class. But we were fortunate to have two sets of worldviews to juxtapose. If there is any one secret to Jewish intellectual success over time, I suspect that it has something to do with the fact that we have always lived as a persecuted religious minority that has been required to try to reconcile its worldview with that of the majority culture. As Dean Daniel Gordes of the University of Judaism recently put it:

We need a new and expanded *beit midrash* [house of Jewish learning], one in which the tractate Sanhedrin is studied along with

Jean Jacques Rousseau, in which Maimonides's *Mishneh Torah* is in dialogue with John Locke. This notion will sound strange to those used to the traditional *beit midrash*. No matter. This is a house of study that could bind the Jewish people, in which the secular would learn from the religious, in which right might glean from left, in which we could search together for new definitions of our peoplehood.[16]

Having been raised as a patriotic American who loves his secular culture and also as a proud Jew who loves his Jewish heritage, I have always struggled to reconcile — or choose among — those overlapping but often irreconcilable views. These struggles have strengthened both my American and Jewish identities and have enhanced the complexity of my thought processes.

But to think Jewishly, one must be Jewishly educated. I was fortunate to have attended yeshiva for twelve years. Despite the mediocrity of my Jewish education, I was at least given the tools for subsequent self-education. I learned Hebrew and I studied much of the Bible and some of the Talmud. I know my way around Jewish sources, and I read a great deal on my own. I also know how to look things up and search them out, so that when I want to know what the Jewish sources say on a given subject, I can find out.

Many books and articles have been written on "the Jewish approach" to such contemporary issues. The true works of objective scholarship — as distinguished from agenda-driven tracts designed to prove that Jewish "law" supports a particular answer — generally produce conflicting views over time, rather than a singular static answer. Jews have tended to be codifiers, simplifiers, and summarizers over our long and complex history. The resulting codes and summaries of Jewish law and tradition have created the false impression of a single road or point of view. There is no singular Jewish position on abortion, euthanasia, or homosexuality, because these issues are different today than in biblical, Talmudic, and medieval times. The same is true of virtually every contemporary issue. Asking what is *the* "Jewish view" of in vitro fertilization is like asking what is *the* American constitutional view of that late-twentieth-century subject. There may be Jewish ways to frame the question, just as there are constitutional ways to frame the question. There may be Jewish sources (as well as constitutional sources) that appear relevant to any answer, such as the importance of procreation, the acceptance of technological assistance to nature, the sanctity of human life, and the centrality of the family to Jewish life. But there is no *one* correct Jewish answer.

Most Jews would be surprised to learn about the diversity of Jewish thought on issues of concern to them. If they would read but one good compendium of Judaism — for example, Joseph Telushkin's *Jewish Literacy* — they would immediately witness the extraordinary diversity, indeed incompatibility, of Jewish thinking. They would read of the Vilna Gaon excommunicating Hasidim, of Hasidim dancing joyously upon learning of the death of the Vilna Gaon, of Mordechai Kaplan ridiculing the mysticism of his colleague Abraham Joshua Heschel, of Heschel condemning the isolation of many of his colleagues, and of the numerous battles royal that make the conflicts between Christian denominations seem trivial by comparison.

Jewish Spirituality: You Don't Have to Become a Buddhist

Nor are the disputes only over intellectual and ritual issues. Some of the most heated arguments have been over how to balance the intellectual component of Judaism with its more spiritual side. The early Hasidim rebelled against the rigorous intellectualism of the Lithuanian Mitnagdim, taking spiritualism too far, in the opinion of many Jews. Subsequent generations tried to strike more of a balance. Many of today's Jews complain that Judaism isn't "spiritual" enough for them. They are simply unfamiliar with the spiritual *side* of Judaism. They are correct that *much* of contemporary Judaism lacks the kind of spirituality they are searching for, and often find in Quakerism, Buddhism, and other religions. Jews joke about the large numbers of their children who have joined Eastern religions. My favorite is about Sadie Goldberg, who travels all the way to the Himalayas to visit a small mountain sect. She asks to see its leader, but the sexton says that she will have to fast and be purified for five days and even then she can utter only five words to His Sublime Holiness. Finally, she is ready. Entering the sanctuary, she sees a saffron-robed young man levitating and emitting strange mantras. The sexton invites her to utter her allotted five words. She turns to His Sublime Holiness and demands, "Sheldon, enough already! Come home."

Jokes aside, there are significant components of Judaism that are essentially spiritual. The writings of Martin Buber, the Baal Shem Tov, Gershom Scholem, the Lubavitcher rabbis, and the Kabalists are highly spiritual. Nor must a Jew accept all the ritual that accompanies the spirituality of *most* Jews who emphasize the spiritual side of Judaism. It is *our* tradition, *our* religion, *our* civilization, and *we* may pick and choose among its diverse sources and then create our own Jewish way of being spiritual at this point in our history. As I was editing this chapter, I came across an advertisement in Boston's *Jewish Advocate* of October 31, 1996, for "a month of learning" about "Jewish spirituality," with ten classes ranging from "Jewish Mysticism, Philosophy and Law" to "Parents, Children and God: A Philosophical and Kabalistic Perspective." Similar classes are offered in many large cities. For those Jews who prefer to combine Jewish and non-Jewish sources, there is the wonderful book by Rodger Kamenetz, *The Jew in the Lotus*, which recounts the meeting between the Dalai Lama and several Jewish scholars in 1990.

The Dalai Lama, who is in exile from Tibet, which has long been the national homeland of his people, turned to Jews for guidance on how to maintain a diaspora that does not give up on regaining its homeland. "Tell me your secret," he asked, "the secret of spiritual survival in exile." Here was someone whom many regard as the most spiritual man in the world, seeking advice from Jews on "spiritual survival." The author of *The Jew in the Lotus* was himself quite skeptical of what Jews could offer in the area of spirituality: "After all, as a child I didn't know many spiritually minded Jews. I knew Rabbis, of course, but they were affable, or highly intellectual. Few of them struck me as full of religious enthusiasm. That would have been embarrassing."[17] But the eclectic group of Jewish men and women who met with the Dalai Lama — it included an Orthodox rabbi, a Reconstructionist woman rabbi, a former Hasidic rabbi, a secular Zionist, a Havurah leader, and an Orthodox feminist — conveyed the deeply spiritual side of Judaism in the Kabala, in Hasidic tradition, and in the modern Havurah movement.[18]

As American Jews continue to move beyond the basic material requirement for survival — protection against persecution and poverty — many are looking to their Judaism for a different kind of spirituality. As an evolutionary matter, spirituality is something of a luxury, since it is not necessary for mere physical survival. When human beings must devote most of their time, energy, and resources to physical survival, there is often little room for spirituality. Ironically, when matters become so desperate that little can be done to assure physical survival, some people turn to spirituality, in a desperate search for meaning. At the opposite extreme, when persecution and poverty pose no perceptible threats, there is time to transcend the material and contemplate the spiritual. The one period when spirituality often takes a back seat is during the transition between these two extremes, when hard work and long hours are necessary to survive and thrive.

It should come as no surprise, therefore, that as many contemporary American Jews move beyond persecution and poverty and toward acceptance, equality, and affluence, they find something missing from their lives. As usual, Rabbi Harold Kushner captured this need perceptively in the title of one of his books, *When All You've Ever Wanted Isn't Enough*. During the immigration, Depression, Holocaust, and immediate post-Holocaust periods, Jews were busy "making it" (to quote the title of yet another book). The spiritual side of Judaism was less important than the success-oriented side. We built beautiful temples, created effective organizations, moved into nice neighborhoods, saved our money to pay for the colleges and professional schools our children could now attend, became politically active and succeeded — as individuals and as a community. Now we have made it. We have everything material we ever wanted (not *all* of us and not quite *everything* for the rest of us, but the point is made). For many Jews, however, it isn't enough. Something is missing — from their lives, from their souls, and from their Judaism. They aren't spiritual enough. (I have heard the same complaint from some Catholic friends.)

The concept of spirituality is a complex one. To many, it means little more than the absence of the rational. To some, it is a need to address something in their relationships, with their spouses, parents, children, and friends. To some, it is a search for God or for a more meaningful religious ritual. To others, it has something to do with nature and the environment. And to still others, it is as simple as introducing music, art, and beauty into their lives. To most everyone, it is a sense that we must somehow transcend the day-to-day banality of our existence and try to find our place in the larger scheme of things.

Those who believe that Judaism is not sufficiently spiritual are missing the point. As a diverse and heterogeneous civilization, Judaism has the capacity to satisfy different needs for different people at different times. There is a deeply spiritual component to Judaism, which complements its ritualistic, intellectual, and practical components. It is available in Havurah and other movements in many places around the country. To everything there is a season, and this may be the season for Judaism's more spiritual side to resurface.

Nor does spirituality necessarily require a belief in God, as some have argued. If anything, doing good for its own sake is more elevated, more spiritual, than doing good because God has commanded it and will punish you if you don't and reward you if you do. What I once argued in an essay on Saint Thomas More is equally applicable to Jewish mitzvoth — commandments:

Why is it more noble for a firm believer to do something because God has commanded it than because the king has, if to that person God is more powerful than a king? In general, submission to the will of a powerful person has not been regarded as especially praiseworthy, except, of course, by the powerful person. Would Thomas More have joined the genocidal Crusades in the eleventh century just because God and the pope commanded it? If he did, would he justly be regarded as a hero? Nor is this question only applicable to Christian believers. I have wondered why Jews praise Abraham for his willingness to murder his own son when God commanded. A true hero who believed in a God who rewards and punishes would have resisted that unjust command and risked God's wrath, just as a true hero would have refused God's order to murder "heathen" women and children during the barbaric Crusades.

This then is the conundrum of religious martyrdom. Those religious leaders who select martyrs and saints cannot have it both ways. They cannot declare someone to be both a hero and a believer, since the two honors are logically inconsistent. The undoubting believer is less of a hero for choosing death over eternal damnation. The real hero is necessarily less of an undoubting believer. Real heroes are those who face death for a principle — say, to save the lives of others — without any promise of reward.[19]

For those who need God for their spirituality, there is much to be found in Jewish sources. For those who find spirituality in all things, that too has Jewish sources.

Rabbi Jeffrey K. Salkin argues that "spirituality is about God," and that "it is simply not enough to speak of inwardness. The inward must be connected to God."[20] This is true for Rabbi Salkin, perhaps, but certainly not for all Jews. He argues that a Jew who works in a soup kitchen because it "is ordained by God" is more "spiritual" than a Jew who works in that same kitchen because it is right or because it is the Jewish way. I respectfully disagree. In human development we recognize the moral progress from doing something right because an authority figure commands it to doing it simply because it is right. Doing it because God commands it connotes a lack of choice; doing it because you believe it to be right connotes a moral choice.

The point is that Judaism embraces all of these variations, as any diverse civilization does. A Jew can act Jewishly and spiritually under any of these variations, so long as he or she tries to ground those actions in Jewish sources, Jewish traditions, and Jewish values. There are no 13 or 23 or 613 immutable principles, rules, or commandments of Judaism *as a civilization*, any more than there are numbered check-offs for the American, Greek, or Roman civilizations.

Ultra-Orthodox Jews who pray and sway under their prayer shawls manifest one kind of Jewish spirituality that is wonderful to behold. Reform Jews who work in soup kitchens — either because God ordained it or because it reflects *rachmones*, Jewish compassion — manifest another kind of Jewish spirituality. Secular Jews who work to preserve the environment because they want to leave something better for their progeny are acting in accord with Jewish spirituality.

Jewish Ethics

For Jews who seek a higher sense of morality through their Judaism, there is the Musar movement initiated by the great Lithuanian rabbi Israel Salanter (Lipkin) during the nineteenth century. He argued that ethics was central to Judaism and preached more about the relationships among people than between people and God. In a famous letter, he railed against Jews who are more scrupulous about the ritual commands of Jewish law than its ethical imperatives:

Praise God that in our districts injunctions against consuming [unkosher food] have become innate in the Jewish soul. . . . Indeed, it would not dawn upon a single butcher to be lax in consulting the local rabbinic authority . . . , though the butcher sometimes suffers a major loss by consulting the authority [who may disqualify the ritual fitness of the animal], the fear of Heaven rests on the butcher by nature and habit; far be it from him to do evil, to mislead a Jew [by supplying non-kosher meat].

But in our great iniquity the contrary is true in commercial relations. When their business dealings possibly entail thievery and extortion, most men will not be concerned prior to being sued, and there are some among them who, even after being sued, will employ deceitful devices [to evade the charges] or will be arrogant [in outright denial]. But in the Torah all are equal — "thou shalt not eat [unkosher]"; "thou shalt not extort thy neighbor"; "thou shalt not steal" — this is a negative commandment and that is a negative commandment, in the way of Torah and her judgments.

Just as it is ingrained in the Jewish soul that all types of [unkosher] are equal . . . so should it be in monetary matters. For indeed, any possession which, according to Torah, belongs to one's fellow [but which is not turned over to him] is stolen property; "thou shalt not steal" has been violated. We observe that, in our great iniquity, even the scholars and almost also the God-fearing are not so scrupulous as they should be about this negative commandment, whose transgression neither Yom Kippur nor death itself can cleanse.[21]

There is, of course, no evidence that Jews, as a group, are less ethical than others, but Jews have always joked about their perceived lack of business ethics, as with the story of Abe and Jake, who owned a shirt store. A customer bought a shirt for ten dollars but inadvertently gave Abe two ten-dollar bills which got stuck together. When Abe discovered the customer's mistake, he was confronted with an ethical dilemma: Should he tell his partner, Jake? A variation has

Abe and Jake eating lunch at the deli, when Abe suddenly remembers he forgot to lock the safe. Jake says, "Nu? So what's to worry about? We're both here, aren't we?" For Rabbi Salanter, Jewish ethics was no joke. He told his students that Jewish businessmen must be even more scrupulous with non-Jews than with Jews, because there is more social pressure on Jews to be honest with their coreligionists. Always controversial, this Orthodox rabbi ate food and drank wine on one Yom Kippur in front of his entire congregation during a cholera epidemic in order to persuade his sick congregants to eat and drink in order to preserve their health. His hallmark was the following statement (often quoted, for obvious reasons, by embattled rabbis): "A Rabbi they don't want to drive out of town is no Rabbi, and a Rabbi who lets himself be driven out of town is no man." Rabbi Salanter's congregants often wanted to drive him out of town when he preached of equality, justice, compassion, charity, and self-denial. But they never did, and his writings, and those of his followers, are available to those who wish to emphasize the moral aspects of Judaism.

Jewish Environmentalism

For those Jews who want social justice — *tikkun olam* — there are numerous Jewish sources as well, such as the new Jewish environmental movement, which finds its inspiration in Jewish tradition. In an article titled "Ecology and the Judaic Tradition," Robert Gordis reviews the diverse Jewish sources and makes a powerful case for environmental responsibility:

> The rabbis of the Talmud built on the laws of the Bible and with their genius for discerning a general principle in a specific law, they enunciated a universal doctrine. . . . They then proceeded to develop a comprehensive code on ecology by extending the biblical law in three directions:
>
> 1. The biblical passage forbade wielding an axe against a tree during a siege. The rabbis extended the prohibition to any other means of wanton destruction in war, direct or indirect, including shifting the course of a stream so that the tree would dry up. They condemned the stopping of wells, a tactic King Hezekiah had

adopted in wartime. They forbade the killing of animals or giving them possibly polluted water to drink.

2. Even more far-reaching was the extension of these prohibitions to apply not only to war tactics but to all situations, including the more usual conditions of peace. Under all circumstances, the wanton or thoughtless destruction of natural objects was prohibited. In addition, the pollution of the air by various enterprises, like a threshing floor operation, or the establishment of tanneries, furnaces, or cemeteries in proximity to cities, was forbidden.

3. Going beyond ecological concerns was the extension of the doctrine "You shall not destroy" from objects of nature to human artifacts. The biblical passage deals with a tree, which is a product of nature. The rabbis of the Talmud applied the principle to all the artifacts of man: "Whoever breaks vessels, or tears garments, or destroys a building, or clogs up a fountain, or does away with food in a destructive manner, violates the prohibition of [do not destroy].

The general principle was clearly formulated: "It is forbidden to destroy or to injure anything capable of being useful to men."[22]

A "Coalition on the Environment and Jewish Life" has developed specific programs based on these and other Jewish sources.[23]

Jewish Feminism

For Jewish feminists, there are great Jewish women — from Deborah, Ruth, and Esther to Golda Meir and Blu Greenberg — to inspire them, along with women of other religions and ethnicities. Blu Greenberg, an Orthodox woman married to a rabbi, has written critically but optimistically of Jewish Halakic treatment of women:

> I am not arguing here whether *halakhic* Judaism deems a woman inferior, although there are more than a few sources in the tradition that lend themselves to such a conclusion; nor will I accept at face value those statements that place women on a separate but higher pedestal. What I am saying is that *halakhah*, contrary to . . .

feminist values . . . continues to delimit women. In some very real ways, *halakhic* parameters inhibit women's growth, both as Jews and as human beings.

I do not speak here of all *halakhah*. One must be careful not to generalize from certain critical comments and apply them to the system as a whole. In fact, my critique could grow only out of a profound appreciation for the system in its entirety — its ability to preserve the essence of an ancient revelation as a fresh experience each day; its power to generate an abiding sense of kinship, past and present; its intimate relatedness to concerns both immediate and otherworldly; its psychological soundness; its ethical and moral integrity. On the whole, I believe that a Jew has a better chance of living a worthwhile life if he or she lives a life according to *halakhah*. Therefore, I do not feel threatened when addressing the question of the new needs of women in Judaism or in admitting the limitations of *halakhah* in this area. Indeed, it is my very faith in *halakhic* Judaism that makes me believe we can search within it for a new level of perfection, as Jews have been doing for three thousand years.

From this understanding one is moved perforce to ask the next question: If the new feminist categories are perceived to be of a higher order of definition of woman than those that limit her, how are we to explain the gap between the feminist model and the *halakhic* model? This becomes even more problematic when one considers the sheer abundance of ethical and moral constructs in Judaism (e.g., the injunctions not to insult another, to lift up one's brother before he falls, not to lead another into temptation, not to judge unless one has been faced with the same situation).

How is it possible that a tradition with so highly developed a sensitivity to human beings could allow even one law or value judgment that demeans women, much less a host of such laws?[24]

As with all Jewish issues, the role of women is the subject of significant disagreement. Some sources see the primary obligation of woman as serving man:

And the reason women are exempt from positive time-bound commandments is because a woman is obligated to fulfill the needs of her husband. Were she mandated to perform the positive commandments fixed by time, it is possible that while performing this mitzvah, her husband will insist that she fulfill mitzvah of listening to him . . . Therefore the Creator relieved her of performing these mitzvot, so that she would be at peace with her husband.[25]

Other sources view women as superior to men:

It appears from Genesis, that whatever is superior is created later . . . The human being was created after all other animals. But in the human species the male gender came first and then the female gender. This proves the proposition that women have innate spiritual superiority as compared with man . . . Woman's character was molded by God in accordance with the eschatological goals that Almighty God reserved for the world.[26]

Every "ism" — from Communism to capitalism to feminism to environmentalism to legalism — has sources in Judaism. Jewish lawyers and doctors have much to search for in Jewish sources, as do Jewish businesspeople, teachers, psychologists, farmers, mothers who work at home, scholars, and politicians. Any Jew who wants to live a full and diverse life can live it Jewishly, with or without ritual, prayer, synagogue attendance, or even God. But to live a Jewish life requires some knowledge — or at least some willingness to learn — of the rich and diverse array of Jewish sources. If the secret of Jewish survival is "learning, learning, learning," then there are concrete steps we can take to increase the odds of survival. It is in our hands, and we have no excuse for not buying the ticket.

Conclusion: Choosing Our Future

The reality is that American Judaism in the twenty-first century will be very different — smaller, less influential in group terms, more assimilated — than it was a century ago and is today.[27] The number of ultra-Orthodox Jews will grow dramatically in proportion to the otherwise shrinking Jewish population. They will also increase their political clout, but they will remain on the periphery of American intellectual and cultural life. Mainstream Jews can improve their survival prospects by working toward preserving enough of Judaism and Jewish life, in its many forms, so that a hundred years from now Jews will still be writing about the "Jewish question" and the Jewish future.

To ensure that Jewish future, we must make some changes that will increase the likelihood that Jewish life will survive the unprecedented demographic and lifestyle challenges it is likely to face in the coming century.

1. Judaism must become less tribal, less ethnocentric, less exclusive, less closed off, less defensive, less xenophobic, less clannish. We jokingly call ourselves "members of the tribe" (MOTs), as if to remind us of our tribal origins. But we are not a tribe, or a clan, or even an ethnicity. Jews comprise many ethnicities, as a visit to Israel or even to the Sephardic neighborhoods of Brooklyn should make plain. This persistent tribalism makes us less welcoming of Jewish converts than we ought to be. It also explains why we make conversion so difficult, and why we — unlike other religions — do not seek converts from outside, though we actively proselytize within our own ranks.

These tribal traits are entirely understandable in light of our long history of persecution and our tried-and-true manner of resisting it by circling the wagons and relying on each other. We were brought up to be distrustful of non-Jews — and for sound historical reasons. But these reasons are misunderstood by our current non-Jewish friends. *We* remember how our parents and grandparents were persecuted by those friends' parents and grandparents, but — quite understandably — our friends do not remember. Victims tell their children; persecutors don't. Even the victims' stories begin to lose their impact after several generations free of persecution. The time has come to open up Judaism, to end our clannishness and tribalism, and to welcome the reality that we are now accepted in America. Tribalism may be easy to justify when others treat us as a tribe, as they long have. But it becomes anachronistic — and antagonistic — to behave like a tribe when others treat us like part of the mainstream.

We have two basic options for the future. If we keep to ourselves, the way the ultra-Orthodox do, we will become like the Amish of Pennsylvania — a quaint sect whom tourists come to gape at and who have no influence on the outside world. If we open up our minds and our schools, we will become more like the Quakers, whose schools are among the best in the world and whose message has enormous influence beyond their small numbers. We will never be exactly like any other group, but I would prefer to see the future of mainstream American Jews modeled more closely after the Quakers than the Amish. The Quakers are less tribal than the Jews, less concerned about mixed marriages, more willing to share their message without conditions or conversions, more confident that they have something positive to offer in the marketplace of ideas. Though their community is small in number, and rife with intermarriage, their influence is pervasive and generally positive. We have much to learn from them, and also much to teach them and others. Whatever we do, we will do with our unique Jewish attitude, energy, and chutzpah.

2. Jews must adopt a different approach to the increasing reality of intermarriage. We must become much more welcoming of the non-Jewish spouse. Refusal to permit intermarriage has failed as a deterrent mechanism. We must try another way. If a non-Jew wants to marry a Jew and is prepared to have a rabbi participate in the ceremony, a rabbi should be willing to lend his or her Jewish participation to so important an event.* The unwillingness of most rabbis to sanctify a mixed marriage simply drives both parties further away from Jewish life. In every way, Jews must become more welcoming of anyone who wants to be part of our heritage.

During a recent Yom Kippur service, I watched several of my non-Jewish friends who were sitting next to their Jewish

---

* In December 1996, the Reform Movement rejected a resolution that would have abrogated its official stance against Reform rabbis officiating at interfaith marriages. Many Reform rabbis do officiate at such marriages, citing data that 63 percent of the children of mixed marriages performed by rabbis were raised as Jews. (*New York Times*, December 14, 1996)

spouses and children. They wanted to be in the synagogue on their family's holiest religious day, but they were uncomfortable and did not know what to do. Some read the prayers in English. Others sat at attention, showing respect but little understanding. It occurred to me that a prayer should be written specifically for the non-Jewish family members of Jews who attend High Holiday services. It should not be a Christian (or other religious) prayer; that would not be appropriate in a synagogue. But it could be a prayer that non-Jews recite for their families. There is a long Jewish tradition of prayers tailored for specific people: children, parents, widows, widowers, those who have overcome adversity and danger. We Jews pray for non-Jews, such as the president and vice president of the United States. There is no reason why non-Jews should not be encouraged to pray for their family members. A prayer specifically written for non-Jewish relatives of Jews would recognize the reality of their status, would demonstrate that they are welcome, and would make them feel included in the service. I intend to include such a prayer in our next Seder, to which several non-Jewish spouses of Jews are always invited. Our rabbi has told me that she will consider including such a prayer in next year's High Holiday services.

But Jewish parents should not feel defensive about their desire to have their children marry other Jews, remain Jewish, and not assimilate. Judaism is a wonderful civilization, and we should try hard to preserve it for our families and for humankind. The only way to maximize the likelihood of a Jewish marriage is to make Judaism and Jewish identity so central to the lives of Jewish children that it becomes unthinkable to give up something so important. Threats, guilt, and other traditional mechanisms for discouraging intermarriage and assimilation do not work. Indeed, they tend to backfire and turn the children away from Judaism. Intermarriage will continue; it will probably increase. We must learn how to deal with that reality in the most constructive manner possible. A *half*-Jewish grandchild who is proud of his or her Jewish heritage is preferable, from a Jewish perspective, to a grandchild who completely rejects it. A non-Jewish son-in-law or daughter-in-law who loves Judaism and Jewish life is better than one who resents it. If we cannot *fight* our children's mixed marriages, we must try to get these children to *join* us. We must reject the current all-or-nothing approach to Judaism, under which a person is either *all* Jewish, in which case we accept him or her, or not Jewish at all, in which case we reject that person as an outsider. Orthodox and Conservative Jews have the right to decide that only the child of a Jewish mother is an *Orthodox* or *Conservative* Jew for *religious* purposes, but they do not have the power — at least not in America — to decide whether the child of a Jewish father and a non-Jewish mother is a part of the Jewish civilization. In America, and in other nations that separate church from state, one's Jewishness is a matter of self-definition, and anyone who wants to be considered a Jew, or a half-Jew, or a partial Jew, or a person of Jewish heritage, has a right to be so considered.* As Isaiah Berlin once put it: A Jew is anyone who wishes to share in the Jewish future.

Such an open-ended approach to Judaism will not create conflict; it will recognize — in a positive, constructive, and inclusive way — our current reality and our future situation.

3. Recognize the validity of secular Judaism, which does not require belief in the supernatural, which is devoted to Jewish learning, and which regards Judaism as an evolving civilization. In many respects, such secular Judaism already exists in the minds and hearts of many committed Jews. It is different from ethical culturalism or other secular movements that may have developed from Jewish roots, in that secular Judaism is an authentic form of Judaism based on Jewish sources and committed to Jewish learning.

Secular Judaism would not compete with God-centered Judaism. It would seek no converts. Indeed, it would encourage those who believe in God to act on that belief. The issue of secular Judaism was brought to a head in 1994, when the Union of American Hebrew Congregations, the religious arm of Reform Judaism, voted 115–13 to deny membership to a

---

* I do not mean to include former Jews who practice Christianity under the deliberately misleading name of Jews for Jesus. A Jew for Jesus already has a name: a Christian.

Cincinnati synagogue that had removed all references to God from its liturgy. Its rabbi, Robert Barr, argued that the congregation did not necessarily "disbelieve" in God: "We are not an atheistic congregation, but a Jewish one. Our goal is to create a liturgy that clearly reflects our common values, while providing all members the opportunity to infuse that liturgy with their personal beliefs regarding the nature of the deity."[28]

The president of the Reform movement, Rabbi Alexander Schindler, defended the decision to exclude this synagogue: "I believe that the concept of God is the very foundation of Judaism," he said. But the Orthodox believe that Halakah — the rules and methodology largely rejected by Reform Judaism, including matrilineal descent — is "the very foundation of Judaism." That is why some ultra-Orthodox Jews would exclude Reform Jews from *their* Jewish tent. Indeed, one Orthodox leader in Israel recently proposed that Israel officially recognize Reform Judaism as a *separate* religion.

I have no quarrel with the decision of Reform Judaism to exclude a congregation that has eliminated God from its ritual. Nor would I have a problem with Orthodox Judaism excluding a congregation that allowed men and women to pray together. The Reform and Orthodox authorities have the right to decide who is a Reform or Orthodox Jew — who is entitled to membership in their club. But neither they nor anyone else has the right to decide who is a Jew for other than religious purposes. Rabbi Schindler may be correct in believing that "the concept of God" is essential to Reform Judaism (though I doubt that all Reform rabbis believe in God), but he is wrong when he claims that the concept of God is the very foundation of all Judaism. Judaism encompasses more than God, as evidenced by the centrality of political Zionism to Jewish life over the past century, the importance of the secular Yiddish culture to Judaism for a century and a half, and the continuing contributions to Jewish life of many Jews for whom God is not central to Judaism.

God is an important part of Judaism and is central to religious Judaism, as to all theistic religions.[29] Most Jews probably believe in God (as most non-Jews probably do). Few Jews agree as to the nature of the God in whom they believe, beyond the standard clichés. But there must be room in Judaism and in Jewish life for the skeptic and the disbeliever, just as there is room for all manner of Jews in the Jewish nation of Israel. If God is important to Judaism, so is skepticism, argumentation, disagreement, dissent, and diversity. The Jewish tent must be open to all who wish to participate in the Jewish dialogue, without litmus tests about belief in the supernatural.

There already exists the beginning of such a secular Jewish branch of the menorah. The Society for Humanistic Judaism, which describes itself as "a non-theistic alternative in contemporary Jewish life," has a presence in about twenty American and a dozen other cities. It offers schools, Sabbath and High Holiday services, bar and bat mitzvahs, and other "life cycle" celebrations. One of its leaders, Yehuda Bauer, is a world-renowned Holocaust scholar. They study the Torah, Talmud, and other Jewish sources in order to "understand the beliefs and behavior of their ancestors without feeling compelled to agree with the beliefs of the past. They seek to explore the entire range of Jewish experience, past and present, and to choose what is reasonable and useful."[30] Are such nontheistic Jews authentic Jews? Of course they are. In a diverse Jewish world that has always changed and adapted to new realities, there has to be room for those who wish to explore Judaism from a human-centered perspective. The cover story in the *Jerusalem Report* of December 1996 describes extensive Jewish learning in which many Israeli secularists are engaging.

Though I am a doubting Jew, who identifies primarily with the secular aspects of Judaism, I love attending traditional Jewish religious services — and not only because I enjoy the music or because it brings back positive memories of my youth. Participating in a Jewish minyan — a communal prayer service — moves me in ways that I cannot fully explain. It connects me to the Jewish people over time and also throughout the world today. When I read prayers that have been recited for hundreds, in some cases thousands, of years, I feel a deep connection to the generations of Jews that preceded mine. I marvel at the poetry and beauty of the language, the depths of despair and the heights of passion in the sentiments — even the differences in worldviews reflected in the approach to God and to prayer. I think of all the people, now long gone, who chanted the same words and the same melodies. I wonder what they were thinking when they acknowledged the sins *they* had committed, or when they asked God for forgiveness. I recall my grandmother crying uncontrollably in the synagogue when the cantor uttered the words "who will live and who will die over the coming year."

On the eve of Rosh Hashanah 5757 (1996), I decided to recite the Kiddush from an old prayer book I had found in a small town in Eastern Europe several years earlier. It had been published in Przemysl, Poland — on the eve of Hitler's invasion. The beautiful leather-bound volume was in pristine condition and I had always assumed that it had never been used. I imagined that it was in a bookstore when the Nazis killed the town's Jewish inhabitants in 1941. When I turned to the page on which the Kiddush appears, I saw a wine stain in the shape of a *bechah* — a silver wine cup used for Kiddush. Suddenly, I welled up with emotion as I pictured the family who had used the prayer book, spilled the wine, and then perished in the Holocaust. The prayer book was no longer an item of Judaica. It was a living reminder of a family, connected over time, with my family. As I chanted the Kiddush, I imagined a mother and child — much like my own wife and daughter — listening to the father chant the Kiddush. I saw the child put the Kiddush cup on the prayer book, causing the stain. Did the father smile at her? Did he get angry? Did the mother try to clean it up? My mind kept alternating between images of that family and mine. Up until that moment, I had not told my six-and-a-half-year-old daughter about the Holocaust, but when I completed the Kiddush I could see that she had noticed my emotional reaction to the wine stain, and I decided that this was the right moment to begin what will be a several-year project of explaining the Holocaust to my child. I made up a story about the family who may have used the prayer book, and the little girl who may have spilled the wine. Then I said I would tell her the rest of the story of what happened to them later, perhaps on future Rosh Hashanahs. It was a way to begin to discharge the difficult responsibility that every Jewish parent bears: to explain the Holocaust so that our children will never allow the memory of those who perished to be forgotten, but to explain, as well, that there is more to Judaism than remembering our terrible history of victimization. Reciting that prayer from that prayer book — even the words that go down hard, such as "you selected us over all other nations"* — provided me and my wife with the right setting for beginning our family dialogue about this painful issue. It gave us a connection to the past that was personal, rather than merely abstract.

After Kiddush, when we sat down for the Rosh Hashanah meal, my wife and I told our daughter that in millions of Jewish homes around the world — from Israel to Russia to Australia to South Africa to Argentina to Siberia — mothers, fathers, and children were celebrating the Jewish New Year in roughly the same way, by dining together, reciting prayers, listening to the shofar, and throwing away the sins of the past. The realization gave us all a feeling of close connection with Jews around the world. It was particularly relevant for our daughter, since we had traveled during the past year to South Africa, Israel, and the Caribbean and had met Jews and participated in Jewish services in each place. Our daughter could visualize the Jewish children she had met in these places doing what she was doing.

The next day in the synagogue, we were approached by a man, his wife, and their child. They simply said, "Thank you," reminding me that I had helped them emigrate from the former Soviet Union eighteen years earlier. Now we were praying in the same synagogue on Rosh Hashanah. It did not matter whether they or I believed in God or in the power of prayer. It felt right to be praying together with a family I had helped become part of a thriving and eclectic Jewish community.

Some congregants were praying intensely, rocking back and forth like Hasidim. Other congregants were reading the text with an academic eye. There was even an alternative reading for agnostics, though the rabbi and most of the congregants believe in God. The alternative prayer was an invitation for agnostics and skeptics to join in the communal prayer on their

---

* Interestingly, those words appear in small print and in parentheses in the Polish Siddur (prayer book), published in 1936.

own terms. The "contemplation for those who do not define their belief as a belief in God" included the following:

I know that the world is a place of contradiction. If I did not, why would I, one who does not define myself as a believer in God, come here today to pray with my fellow people?

It is to be with them that I have come, it is because I believe in them, in us, and in what we can create and in what we can destroy that I am driven here out of a feeling of need to be with and worship with them. If it were merely out of habit or out of guilt, I should quickly abandon this practice. Although every day is a day for appreciating the wonder of the world, although every day is a day for fighting the good fight to perfect the world, although every day is a day to meditate and to struggle, we also need times set aside to come together as a community and to pause and celebrate our struggles and meditations. At this moment, I am gathered here with others saying prayers apparently addressed to a transcendent God. Every day of my life I employ traditions of speech which at the same time reflect and yet do not reflect the reality I understand before me. In the morning I say, "the sun rises," and at evening I say, "the sun sets," knowing very well that the sun neither sets nor rises, and that it is the earth which is rotating. I use these words nevertheless, because they describe the feelings of dawn and dusk. In the same way, I can still pray to the Eternal Power of our parents in the Amidah . . . Even though I do not define my belief as they do, that does not mean that what I do believe in is any more probable and requires any less a leap of faith. That is because I may be making an even greater leap of faith than they are.

After all, I believe in people, and I act as if we have a hope for the future; and during a time of possible nuclear annihilation, such a belief may have even less foundation than a belief in God.

And so this day I will allow myself to say that the sun sets and rises and allow myself to say "Y — H" and "Shechinah" not because they are the real things of the universe, but because they are real symbols of eternal powers in which the universe is one, and because these names reflect the feelings of awe generated by the contemplation of the infinite and of the infinitesimal, feelings generated in contemplation of, and interaction with, the cosmos, with people, with art, and with history which is yet ours to make or to end.

I did not feel less a Jew to read this; indeed, reading it made me more comfortable when I also recited the traditional prayers to God.

Participating in Jewish prayer services also makes me feel like a participant in the millennia-long dialogue between Jews and God — and among Jewish men and women about God. Reciting the prayers, even while wondering why I am reciting them, makes me rethink my own doubts, makes me ask myself why I have so much difficulty making the leap of faith, and makes me ponder how this glorious world could have come about without divine intervention. When I participate in prayer, a part of me hopes that some event will occur that will shake my faithlessness, or more accurately my pervasive doubts. So far, it hasn't happened, and I do not believe it ever will . . . but who knows?

The important point is that doubting Jews must not be alienated from Judaism because of their doubts. They should not be given an ultimatum: Believe or leave. Belief, disbelief, doubt, and certainty are lifelong processes, at least for any thinking person. Everyone should be welcome at a Jewish prayer service — on their own terms, at least as far as belief is concerned. As I read the prayers declaring unwavering faith in God, I know that they have been recited by generations of believers, doubters, skeptics, agnostics, and atheists. This reality is reflected by the old Jewish joke abut the Jewish youth who declares to his father that he is an atheist. Without a moment's pause, the father responds, "Atheist, shmatheist, it doesn't matter as long as you go to shul." This is not a *new* joke. It, and its numerous variations, go back generations. A great Hasidic rabbi once observed that "even atheism can be uplifted through charity. If someone seeks your aid, act as if there were no God, as if you alone could help."[31] And Rabbi Zalman Schechter-Shalomi has quipped that God himself must be an atheist because "God has no God."[32]

One more point about Jewish participation in prayer services. Many synagogues will not allow a Jew to attend High Holiday services without buying a ticket. The price can range between several hundred to more than a thousand dollars. I understand the need to use the attraction of Rosh Hashanah and Yom Kippur services to support the year-round expenses of the synagogue. But there is absolutely no justification for ever turning away a Jew who wants to pray but cannot afford to pay. I am reminded of the story of the man who tries to walk past the ticket-taker on Rosh Hashanah and is stopped. He explains that he must deliver an important family message to one of the congregants. The ticket-taker lets him pass, but only after warning him, "I better not catch you praying." The wealthiest community in America cannot afford to lose any Jews — especially young Jews — because they lack the money to buy tickets.

4. A new Jewish leadership must emerge to supplement the traditional rabbinic and political leadership of the Jewish people. When Judaism was primarily a nation, Jews were led by kings. When Judaism was primarily a religion centered in the Temple, Jews were led by priests. When Diaspora Judaism became embattled by a Christianity determined to convert the Jews, Jews were led by rabbis. When Judaism became more political, Jews were led by political leaders. When Judaism became philanthropic, Jews were led by philanthropic leaders.

Today, a new leadership must be added to this great and diverse pantheon of heroes. We need a leadership of Jewish *educators* who can address the pressing issue of Jewish illiteracy and ignorance. We need teachers who can inspire, without necessarily proselytizing. We need educators who believe in Jewish education for education's sake — as an end, not only as a means toward returning Jews to God.

Some of the greatest scholars and teachers of Jewish learning have been skeptics, agnostics, or disbelievers, such as Ahad Ha'am, Chayim Zhitlofsky, Simon Dubnow, Theodor Herzl, Eliezer Ben-Yehuda, and Chayim Cohen. This should not be surprising, since the enterprise of objective scholarship requires a suspension of belief and dogma. But these great scholars and teachers would be largely disqualified from Jewish leadership roles today for the reason given by one of the most open and liberal of Jews, Rabbi Alexander Schindler: "God is the very foundation of Judaism." Although Jewish leadership has a "don't ask, don't tell" policy when it comes to belief, a prospective leader who admits to disbelief will likely be disqualified.

The time has come to broaden Jewish leadership beyond the religious, political, and philanthropic. Tomorrow's Jewish crisis will center around Jewish *education*, rather than sacred survival, religion, politics, and philanthropy. Our motto will no longer be "Let my people go." It will be "Let my people know." We must develop a cadre of educational leaders — great teachers, scholars, and innovators — capable of addressing this crisis.

5. There should be Jewish schools which, like Quaker schools, are open to all who wish to learn about the Jewish way of life. These schools, like Quaker schools, should be excellent educationally — why not the best? Today, Jewish parents who send their children to Jewish schools often feel that they are compromising their secular education. They argue, defensively, that the Jewish schools are "every bit as good," or "just as good," or "almost as good" as the best non-Jewish schools. But they know that they are making a trade-off. Some Jewish schools are, in fact, very good, but none — at least in America — is at the very top of the academic rankings. The schools that *are* at the very top are highly attended by Jewish students, but they are not Jewish schools. In Australia, on the other hand, the Jewish schools are so good that a majority of Jewish students attend them and so do non-Jews, though in small numbers. Such schools would be open to all who wish to explore Jewish sources, Jewish tradition, Jewish history, Jewish philosophy, Jewish music, and anything else Jewish, without necessarily accepting the theology. In this respect, it would be like the best of the Jewish studies programs that currently flourish in some of our major universities, but it would not be limited to university students. Such programs do not require belief, nor do they proselytize. They are open to non-Jews,

atheists, agnostics, Orthodox Jews — anyone with an interest in Jewish learning. Some of their professors are not Jewish. Indeed, in 1996 a non-Jew was originally appointed to head the Department of Jewish Studies at Queens College but was forced to resign by misguided chauvinism and a misunderstanding of the proper role of Jewish studies in a secular, public college. (He has now been made codirector of the program along with two Jewish colleagues.)[33] If 3,500 years of Jewish learning have contributed something unique to offer to the world, why keep it to ourselves? A light unto the nations can only shine in an open arena.

6. But first and foremost, we must educate *ourselves* in the most eclectic and welcoming manner. Every city and town with a Jewish population must plant many trees of Jewish knowledge with branches extending into every Jewish home, school, synagogue, community center, Havurah, and other institutions. There must be classes, discussion groups, study groups, lectures, videotapes, computer programs, books, book clubs, newsletters, and other mechanisms of Jewish learning. If the key to Jewish survival is "learning, learning, learning," then we must use that key to open up our minds — our Yiddisher cups — to the neglected wonders of Jewish learning.

Currently, there are available two general paths to learning about these sources. The first, which I call "Judaism Lite," is assorted quotations from Jewish sources, collected in such books as Rabbi Joseph Telushkin's *Jewish Wisdom* and *Jewish Literacy*. Like all compendiums, these volumes allow you to skim the surface of Jewish knowledge and familiarize yourself with the diversity and range of Jewish thinking over time. They are a good beginning.

At the other extreme is what I call "Judaism Heavy," that is, the original unedited sources as taught in yeshivas and in graduate courses at the Jewish Theological Seminary, Hebrew Union College, and other religious institutions of higher education. This sort of learning requires the kind of extensive commitment that few busy, secular Jews will be willing to make. It also requires a religious commitment that many will be unable to make honestly.

What is needed is an intermediate curriculum, perhaps "low-fat Judaism." Such a curriculum would require the translation and publication of a library of several hundred books, each containing *substantial* portions of the original sources in context. They should be edited not to reflect a particular point of view — for example, a pro-Orthodox or pro-Reform bias or even pro-religious — but rather to make them accessible for classroom or home study. Learning for learning's sake, not only as a means toward more religiosity! They should reflect the diversity of the Jewish civilization over time and place and provide a rich array of source material from which Jews who want to live their own kind of Jewish life may creatively draw. Many of these books are already available, such as the writings of Buber, Wiesel, the Lubavitcher rabbi, Rabbi Soloveichik, and selected volumes of the Talmud. But much more is needed, both for home study and for eclectic classes, *havurah* study groups, and the new secular Jewish learning that my plan envisions. The experiments that are currently under way in Boston, both for adults and schoolchildren, are a good model for other communities to emulate. In the Appendix, I provide a listing of books for a good beginning Jewish library.

In every generation, Jews have redefined themselves to adapt to the ever-changing world. This ability to change to keep Judaism relevant, to give the past a vote but not a veto, has been a key ingredient in our long and mysterious survival against all odds.

In the end, my proposals for a more open Judaism, adaptive to the new realities of Jewish first-class status, acceptance, and marginalization of anti-Semitism, will not save the kind of Judaism that is God-centered, rule-bound, ritual-driven, and clannish. That kind of Judaism will be saved by those who believe in and practice Halakic Judaism. They are doing a fine job and need no help from me or others who are not members of their club. The Judaism I am trying to defend and enhance is a Judaism of ideas, of attitudes, of skepticism, of justice, of compassion, of argumentation, and of inclusiveness. That kind of Judaism can survive, indeed thrive, in an open and welcoming world into which Jewish ideas can cast a beacon light. That kind of Judaism does not depend on numbers, or on religious definitions of who is a Jew, or on whether one's mother or father was a Jew, or on whether one is a "whole" Jew or a "half" Jew. That kind of Judaism depends on the power of Jewish ideas to educate, influence, and repair the world. Every Jew who cares about our future must join in building the foundation for this new Judaism, so that it will reflect the collective intelligence, experience, spirituality, wisdom, attitude, and determination of our remarkably diverse civilization.

Elchanan Wasserman, the Polish rabbi who preferred to face physical annihilation rather than risk the spiritual challenge of assimilation, feared something that is in *our* control, even more than he feared the physical threat of Nazism, which was not in our control. The Judaism of that rabbi — like the Judaism of the founder of the Lubavitch movement who feared Napoleon's victory because it would be *good* for individual Jews — was a Judaism based on persecution, fear, and victimization. It was a Judaism of tsuris — of "oy." It is easy to keep people together during bad times, during periods of collective victimization. That is a challenge traditional Judaism has met well. It will be far more difficult to keep Jews Jewish during good times. That is a challenge we should all relish, because we have fought so long, so hard, and so successfully to create these good times. We must insist on a Judaism that does not depend on the czar winning, on the Nazis killing, or on the new anti-Semites multiplying. We have the right to a Judaism that thrives when individual Jews succeed and that gets stronger when times are good. If we cannot create such a Judaism, we will be unable to ensure the future of the Jewish people.

American Jewish life in the mid-twenty-first century, if it exists, will not look like American Jewish life today. Except for the Orthodox, Jews will be far more assimilated into the American mainstream in every way: in neighborhoods, in lifestyles, and in marriages. Jewish ideas too will become even more assimilated into the mainstream, as many already have been for generations. We will be a less identifiable community — by geography, by appearance, by names, and by political ideology. It will be much harder to ensure our collective future under these changing conditions. But the Jewish condition has always been a changing one. Usually it has changed for the worse, as a result of external forces largely beyond our control.

Now it is changing for the better, and this has caused us to lose some control over our own future as a people. We must find ways — our own unique ways — of ensuring the Jewish future in good times as we have in bad.

Yes, we will look different in 2076 than we look today. But we look different today than we did in 1876, and in 1896, and in 1916, and in 1926, and in 1946. Our future does not depend on how we look, but rather on what we do. And we can do much — in good times as in bad — to increase the odds that Jewish life will survive our success.

Judaism is embarking on a new phase in its history as an evolving civilization. It is no longer a civilization characterized by persecution, ghettoization, and anti-Semitism. It must now define itself anew, develop a new state of mind more adaptive to its contemporary condition, and move beyond its long history of victimization and into its post-persecution era of Jewish life. It must recognize its newfound acceptance, power, and success — without ever forgetting its millennia-long history as pariah, outsider, scapegoat, and victim, and without lowering its guard against the possibility of recurrence. It must write new literature, create new philosophies, sing new songs, and paint new pictures reflective of its changing outlook — of its new Jewish state of mind. It must prove to itself and to the world that it can survive, indeed thrive, without external enemies; that it can compete in the open marketplace of ideas and ideologies; that it is as adaptive to acceptance as it was to rejection.

As with all evolving civilizations, this new Jewish civilization must be built on a foundation of the past. The treasures of our past must not, however, blind us to the needs of our future. Our new state of mind must be adaptive to the present and it must look to the future.

Creating a new Jewish civilization will be a daunting task, especially for those of us who cannot look to God or his messenger Moses to bring us out of our old slavery and into a new promised land. But there are traditional sources even for us. The Passover Haggadah — the story of the Exodus from the bonds of slavery — never mentions the name of Moses. The Megillah of Esther — which recounts the Jewish triumph over yet another enemy, Haman — never mentions God. And the Book of Job — the Bible's most sublime story of man's suffering — never refers to Jews or persecution by our external enemies. These old books have endured because they transcend any particular theology, person, time, location, group, or even God, and speak to humankind's eternal conditions and transitions. In writing our new books, we must look to old books, but we must give them new meanings, contemporary interpretations, current relevance. The past must have "a vote but not a veto."[34]

When the biblical Jews left Egypt, they sang a "new song." When the halutzim built Israel, they danced new horas. Jews have always written new music as they entered new ages, but they have always remembered the old melodies. A civilization can live only by moving forward. Like the enslaved Jews of ancient Egypt, we must make an exodus — from the Judaism of victimization to a new Judaism of freedom, of success, and of acceptance. We will wander through spiritual deserts for at least forty years, where we will encounter false prophets urging us to return to familiar victimization, we will encounter illusory golden calves promising quick salvation, and we will encounter as yet unanticipated barriers to our entrance into our new home. But this time, the land that awaits us is neither promised nor geographic. The new Jewish state is neither a secular nation, as it was with Herzl's Zionism, nor a messianic age, as was promised by Isaiah. It is nothing more nor less than a new, more positive Jewish state of mind.

Epilogue

A Call to Action

A CENTURY AGO a worldwide conference on Zionism was convened at Basel, Switzerland, by Theodor Herzl to consider the Jewish question of the twentieth century — the need for Jews to be able to live as first-class citizens in a Jewish state, free from persecution and discrimination.

This conference brought together Jews from around the world — Russia, Palestine, Algeria, England, Poland, Austria, Germany, the United States — to debate the Jewish future. It was "the first Jewish worldwide congress" in history.[1] Some two hundred Jews, representing a wide array of viewpoints, participated. There were Orthodox rabbis, atheist revolutionaries, bankers, lawyers, journalists, doctors, scholars, politicians, and even some ordinary laypeople who had been active in Zionist causes.

Following this remarkable "Jewish parliament," Herzl predicted that a Jewish state would come into existence "no later than fifty years hence." On November 29, 1947, the United Nations voted to end the British mandate in Palestine, thus making possible Israel's declaration of an independent Jewish nation, in May of 1948.

It is now a century since the Basel conference and half a century since Israel's creation. The time is ripe for another worldwide Jewish congress to consider the Jewish future. This conference would debate the Jewish question of the twenty-first century: How can

Jewish life endure in a post-persecution age of widespread inter-marriage and assimilation?

The actual conference could take place in a convenient and safe location, such as New York or Jerusalem,* but it should be telecast live by satellite so that Jews throughout the world could participate via the Internet and e-mail. The conference could extend over several days and would consider the widest range of issues relevant to Jews — all Jews, from the most religious to the most secular — in the coming century.

This is a time of Jewish ferment, creativity, and concern. Despite, perhaps because of, the growing threats of assimilation, intermarriage, and low birthrates, many Jews are writing about the Jewish future. Many more are thinking and speaking about it. The time is ripe for bringing our disparate ideas together in a collective enterprise devoted to devising a plan — or plans — of action to preserve the Jewish future. The widest array of Jewish intelligence, experience, knowledge, and chutzpah is needed to respond to the Jewish question of the twenty-first century.

Among the proposals that might be considered is the creation of a worldwide twenty-four-hour-a-day Jewish television educational network, which would transmit a diverse array of Jewish courses, discussion groups, religious programming, and news of concern to the Jewish people. This could be accompanied by Jewish websites (there are many already) geared into the programs, Jewish book clubs, computer networks, data bases, translation services, religious and secular Responsa, and other innovative uses of modern technology.

The great Jewish library — which is today dispersed from Vilna to Riga to Jerusalem to Brooklyn and beyond — can never be brought together physically in one place. But it can be put online for every Jew to be able to access. Discussion groups, perhaps even prayer groups, could be convened over the Internet. Jews could learn Hebrew, Yiddish, Ladino, prayers, rituals, songs, traditions, philosophy, theology, archaeology — and everything else contained in our vast library. If contemporary Jews from around the world cannot be joined together by a common theology, a common ideol-

---

* Switzerland has disqualified itself by its disgraceful role during the Holocaust and its current attempt at covering it up.

ogy, a common language, or a common enemy, they can at least be wired together by a common technology.

To succeed, this worldwide Jewish network would have to be eclectic, inclusive, and tolerant. It must recognize that there is no single way to be Jewish in today's world. It must be willing to enlist all concerned Jews, from every occupation and background, so that we may benefit from the competitive advantage we have in communications, education, and other disciplines. Unlike most current religious and ethnic programming — which is amateurish and inadequately produced on low budgets — the Jewish network must be competitive with the most professionally produced commercial network programming. It must attract viewers not only because it is Jewish but also because it is great television and teaching. The goals of this Jewish network are simple and should not be controversial: maximize Jewish learning, so that we can make up in quality what we will inevitably lose in quantity; make Jewish learning so fascinating that it will capture the imagination of today's drifting Jews; make Judaism competitive with other current "isms"; and submit the various strands of this wonderful tapestry called Jewish life to the open marketplace of ideas.

There is no reason why one of the oldest continuing human civilizations cannot turn to the newest of technologies to enhance its prospects for continuity. For the first time in our long history, our survival is in our own hands, and not in those of our enemies. We owe it to our children, our grandchildren, our parents, our grandparents, ourselves, and the world at large to do everything in our power to prove once and for all that Jews can thrive without persecution and in an open, welcoming, and pluralistic society. A worldwide conference, connecting all interested Jews electronically, would be a good beginning. I look forward to saying "Shalom" to you on the information superhighway!

Notes

Introduction: The "Jewish Question" for the Twenty-first Century

1. Yehuda Rosenman, "Research on the Jewish Family and Jewish Education," in *Facing the Future: Essays on Contemporary Jewish Life*, ed. Steven Bayme (New York: Ktav, 1989), p. 156. According to Seymour Martin Lipset, in *American Exceptionalism: A Double-Edged Sword* (New York: W. W. Norton, 1996), the average American Jewish woman bears 1.1 children (p. 175).

2. There is significant dispute over this figure because it depends on the definition of who is counted as a Jew. If one included only Jews as defined by Orthodox and Conservative religious laws, the number would be lower. J. J. Goldberg, in *Jewish Power* (Reading, Mass.: Addison-Wesley, 1996), puts the percentage at 2.5. He also cites one expert who says that there are 8 million members of the "Jewish political community," in which he includes non-Jewish spouses and children of Jews (p. 57).

3. A 1992 survey by Martilla & Kiley for the Anti-Defamation League found the median estimate by gentiles of the size of the U.S. Jewish population to be slightly lower, but still whopping, at 18 percent. The study also found that only 10 percent of gentile Americans believe that Jews constitute less than 5 percent of the U.S. population. See Lipset, p. 151; see also Goldberg. Mark Twain noticed the disparity between the tiny number of actual Jews and their enormous perceived influence in a remarkable essay in *Harper's Monthly*, September 1899.

4. Elihu Bergman, "The American Jewish Population Erosion," *Midstream*, October 1977, pp. 9 – 19.

5. As a deliberate survival strategy, America's ultra-Orthodox Jews attempt "to recreate the world that had existed in pre-war Europe" (Jerome R. Mintz, *Hasidic People: A Place in the New World* [Cambridge, Mass.: Harvard University Press, 1992], p. 29). To this end, they take pains to keep secular American influences at

bay. Rabbi Elliot Kohn of Kiryas Joel, a Hasidic village in the foothills of upstate New York, explains, "We want isolation. That's why we have no TV's or radios," and that is why such communities use the Yiddish tongue rather than English, dress distinctively, and eschew secular studies (quoted in Don Lattin, "Church-State Conflict in a Jewish Town," *San Francisco Chronicle*, March 25, 1994, p. A1). See also Marc D. Stern, "Orthodoxy in America: The Trend Toward Separatism," *Congress Monthly* (New York: American Jewish Congress), January 1992, pp. 10 – 12; Egon Mayer, *From Suburb to Shtetl: The Jews of Boro Park* (Philadelphia: Temple University Press, 1979).

6. Simon Dubnow, *History of the Jews in Russia and Poland*, trans. I. Friedlander (1916; reprint, New York: Ktav, 1975), pp. 356 – 57.

7. Theodor Herzl, *The Jewish State*, trans. Jacob M. Alkow (1896; reprint, New York: Dover, 1988), p. 92.

8. Ibid., p. 91.

9. Albert Einstein, *About Zionism: Speeches and Letters*, trans. Leo Simon (New York: Macmillan, 1931), p. 33.

10. Jean-Paul Sartre, *Anti-Semite and Jew: An Exploration of the Etiology of Hate*, trans. George J. Becker (1948; reprint, New York: Schocken Books, 1995), pp. 69, 91. It should be noted that Christian theological anti-Semites had long espoused a version of this argument. The Apostle Paul was the first to enunciate a doctrine that Jews survive not because of the strength of their faith, their culture, or their ethnic cohesiveness, but rather because God preserves them in a wretched state, by reason of what one might term divine anti-Semitism. Saint Augustine elaborated that God maintains the Jews as wretches and *as* Jews in order to bear out scriptural prophecies about punishing the Jews for rejecting Jesus (see Augustine, *The City of God*, trans. Marcus Dods [New York: Random House, 1950], pp. 656 – 58). Similarly, the very devout Pascal wrote in *Pensées* that Jesus preserves Jews in such impossibly abject conditions in order to prove his omnipotence generation after generation.

11. Today, 4.6 million Jews live in Israel, a number that is growing thanks to immigration by former Soviet Jews and the positive Jewish birthrate in Israel, which contrasts with the negative birthrate of every Diaspora Jewish community in the world. Israel is thus well on its way to surpassing America in its Jewish population. (To get a sense of Israel's dynamic growth rate, consider that only 600,000 Jews lived there in 1948.) Demographers predict that in the near future, the majority of the world's Jews will reside in Israel, for the first time since the destruction of the Second Temple nearly two thousand years ago (see Herb Keinon, "In 10 Years, Most Jews Will Be Living in Israel," *Jerusalem Post*, Jan. 7, 1991).

12. Dubnow, passim.

13. Spain distinguished in practice, though perhaps not in theory. The forced conversions attendant upon the Christian "reconquest" of Iberia involved massive Jewish populations, and many converts practiced Judaism in secret — the Spanish called them Marranos, meaning "swine." As a result, Spanish clergy came to view *all* Jewish converts with suspicion. In 1449, the *estatuto de limpieza de sangre* ("the statute of purity of blood") was enacted, which barred converts and their progeny from holding positions in the church hierarchy. This was Europe's first "racial"

anti-Semitic legislation: even Christians in good faith, generations removed from ancestors who converted from Judaism, were denied certain rights on the basis of their "blood." A Spanish pope, Alexander VI, decreed the *limpieza* law to be in force in all Christendom in 1495. His successor, the Italian pope Julius II, quickly abolished the "purity of blood" sanctions against Christians of Jewish descent, decrying distinctions based on race rather than religion as "detestable customs and real corruption." Nevertheless, the "purity of blood" policy became even more widespread in Spain, "until it dominated all Spanish ecclesiastical organizations — and, through them, also a major part of Spain's public opinion" (Benzion Netanyahu, *The Origins of the Inquisition in Fifteenth Century Spain* [New York: Random House, 1995], p. 1063. See also Bernard Lewis, *Semites and Anti-Semites: An Inquiry into Conflict and Prejudice* [New York: W. W. Norton, 1986], pp. 82 – 84).

14. *Forbes*, Oct. 14, 1996, pp. 100 – 295. A perusal of the 1996 *Forbes* list of the four hundred richest people in America makes it clear how difficult it will soon be to identify people by their Jewish background. But by any standard, the number of Jews on the list is highly disproportionate to their percentage in the population. Even if one were to count only Jews who strongly identify with their heritage — such as Wexner, Soros, Spielberg, Milken, Fisher, Taubman, Pritzker, Bronfman, Lauder, Perlman, Tisch, Le Frak, Lee, Geffen, Lauren, Stern, Rich, Green, Heyman, Peltz, Wasserman, Redstone, and others too numerous to list here — the percentage is amazing.

15. Seymour Martin Lipset and Earl Raab, *Jews and the New American Scene* (Cambridge, Mass.: Harvard University Press, 1995), p. 26. The study was conducted in 1971 – 72. The percentage is higher now.

16. Steven Cohen, *The Dimensions of American Jewish Liberalism* (New York: American Jewish Congress, 1989), pp. 28 – 29.

17. Barry A. Kosmin, *The Dimensions of Contemporary Jewish Philanthropy* (New York: Council of Jewish Federations), p. 28. See also *Los Angeles Times*, Nov. 2, 1992. The UJA replaced the Salvation Army at the top of the Philanthropy 400, an annual ranking of nonprofit groups by the *Chronicle of Philanthropy*. The UJA raised $668.1 million in 1991, up 57 percent from the preceding year. Most of the money helped resettle Soviet Jews.

18. This finding by the National Jewish Population Survey of 1990 reflects the widespread Jewish distaste for nonuniversalist Jewish charities. A 1989 survey of American Jewish attitudes toward Jewish identity revealed that 31 percent of American Jews believe that "Jewish charities and organizations place too much emphasis on helping only Jews and not enough on helping all people in need whether they're Jewish or not" (Steven M. Cohen, *Content or Continuity? The 1989 National Survey of American Jews* [New York: American Jewish Committee, 1991], p. 59).

19. Richard L. Zweigenhaft and G. William Domhoff, in *Jews in the Protestant Establishment* (New York: Praeger, 1982), credit the term "J.A.S.P." to Peter I. Rose (p. 107). See also Robert C. Christopher, *Crashing the Gates: The De-WASPing of America's Power Elite* (New York: Simon & Schuster, 1989), pp. 43 – 44.

20. See Charles Silberman, *A Certain People: American Jews and Their Lives Today* (New York: Summit Books, 1985), p. 145. Silberman has updated the statistics

originally presented in Harriet Zuckerman, *Scientific Elite: Nobel Laureates in the United States* (New York: Columbia University Press, 1977), p. 68.

21. David Brion Davis, review of Edward S. Shapiro, *The Jewish People in America*, vol. 5: *A Time for Healing: American Jewry Since World War II*, in *New Republic*, April 12, 1993. (Shapiro summarized several sociological surveys.) Moreover, the 1986 edition of the *World Almanac and Book of Facts* ranked eight Jewish women, whose occupations range from historian to syndicated columnist to women's rights leader to novelist, as among "America's 25 Most Influential Women" — fully 32 percent of the total. Cited in Jacob Rader Marcus, ed., *The Jew in the American World: A Source Book* (Detroit: Wayne State University Press, 1996), p. 519.

22. Depending on the year, somewhere between 25 and 40 percent of the students at Ivy League schools are Jewish (Norman F. Cantor, *The Sacred Chain: The History of the Jews* [New York: HarperCollins, 1994], p. 400). If we use a low figure of 30 percent, and then take a high estimate of Jews as 2.5 percent of the general U.S. population, we can calculate the rate of disproportional Jewish representation in the Ivies as twelve times greater than Jewish presence in the overall population.

23. Lipset and Raab, p. 75. The poll was conducted in 1985. As of 1996, both of California's U.S. senators are Jewish, as are eight other members of Congress from the state.

24. Goldberg, p. 6.

25. Ibid.

26. Quoted in Goldberg, p. 147.

27. Quoted in Rodger Kamenetz, *The Jew in the Lotus* (San Francisco: Harper-San Francisco, 1994), p. 48.

28. Ibid.

Chapter One: An America Without Jews

1. Elihu Bergman, assistant director of the Harvard Center for Population Studies, shocked the Jewish world in 1977 when he published his forecast in *Midstream*. Already, the American Jewish population has shrunk from a high of perhaps 6 million to a current figure of 5.5 or 4.4 million — despite substantial Soviet/Russian Jewish immigration — depending on whether one counts 1.1 million people of Jewish parentage who deny any connection to Judaism. In the Council of Jewish Federations' 1990 National Jewish Population Survey, only 4.4 million Americans identified themselves as Jews by religion (*Highlights of the CJF 1990 National Jewish Population Survey* [New York: CJF, 1991], p. 5). The findings made the front page of the *New York Times*, which quoted a variety of Jewish leaders giving their spin as to why the figure was distorted. Most argued that there were over a million other "Jews by birth" who should be added to the aggregate, even if they did not actively identify as Jews. The counterargument is that Jewishness is more than a Jewish surname; it involves certain actions, at least a minimal way of life or thought. Without that, Jews are, for most intents and purposes, assimilated. Rabbi Max Schenk reasoned in a 1964 *Look* magazine article titled "The Vanishing American Jew" (May 5, 1964) that " 'Judaism is a history, a civilization, a way of life, a martyred people, a language, a custom. Above all, it is a Jewish *home*' " (emphasis in

original). By "Jewish home," Rabbi Schenk meant "a marriage committed to Judaism." Only such a home could produce children grounded enough in Jewish learning and customs to prevent assimilation. Any classification of identifying secular Jews as "Jews" is largely meaningless — or so goes the argument.

2. Nathan Glazer, "New Perspectives in American Jewish Sociology," in *American Jewish Yearbook* (New York: American Jewish Committee, 1987), p. 8.

3. The Wannsee Conference, convened by Reinhard Heydrich in 1942, detailed the Nazi plan to destroy European Jewry. John Mendelsohn, ed., *The Holocaust: Selected Documents in Eighteen Volumes* (New York: Garland, 1982), vol. 11, p. 23. Had the Nazis' aggression gone further, they would have produced a similar chart and solution for the rest of the world's Jews as well. This is evident from the chart's inclusion of Ireland — a country they never managed to attack — and Switzerland and Sweden — two nations that were neutral during the war. Had the Jews of the Soviet Union, North Africa, and the Middle East as well as America been murdered, the number of Jewish deaths would have reached 15 million. This hypothetical figure naturally assumes that the European Jewish survivors — of whom there were between 1 and 2 million — would also have been wiped out. For figures on European Jewish survivors, see Martin Gilbert, *The Holocaust: A History of the Jews of Europe During the Second World War* (New York: Holt, 1985), p. 18, and *Atlas of the Holocaust* (New York: Da Capo, 1982), p. 243.

4. See, for example, Ephraim Buchwald, "The Holocaust Is Killing America's Jews: An Obsession with Victimization Leaves No Room for the Joy of the Faith and Is Driving Many Away," *Los Angeles Times*, April 28, 1992, p. A11. See also the quotation from Rabbi Ari Korenblit in Philip Weiss, "Letting Go," *New York* magazine, Jan. 29, 1996, p. 28; and Sheldon Engelmayer, "American Jewry in Midst of Spiritual Holocaust," *Cleveland Jewish News*, June 14, 1991; Jonathan Sacks, the Chief Rabbi of England, has written, "Not since the ten tribes were lost ha[s] there been such a flight from tradition." See his article "Only Orthodox Judaism Will Enable the Jewish People to Survive," *Moment*, April 1992, p. 44. See also Goldberg, *Jewish Power*, for a quotation from Rabbi Pinchas Stolper about intermarriage: "It's another Holocaust" (p. 66).

5. Several leaders of the Christian Coalition identify themselves as "Christian Jews" or "Jewish Christians." See *Reform Judaism*, Winter 1996, pp. 14–25.

6. Peter Stothard, "The Loudest Whisper in Washington," *New York Times*, Aug. 31, 1990.

7. In 1991, when the Council of Jewish Federations published the results of its 1990 National Jewish Population Survey, they identified six subgroups of the Jewish population: religious Jews, Jews by choice, agnostic Jews, born/raised Jewish–converted out, adults of Jewish parentage raised with other religion, Jewish children being raised with other religion. The use of such categories by professionals is only a sign of further divisions and groupings in the future of American Jewry.

8. "The major sources of higher fertility ideals and larger family size are among the self-segregated religious Jews in a few metropolitan areas of the United States." See Samuel C. Heilman, *Portrait of American Jews: The Last Half of the Twentieth Century* (Seattle: University of Washington Press, 1995), pp. 114–15, and Egon

Mayer, *From Suburb to Shtetl: The Jews of Boro Park* (Philadelphia: Temple University Press, 1979), p. 101. Besides having more children than non-Orthodox couples, Orthodox Jews also marry at a younger age and divorce less often (at a rate of one in ten, as opposed to one in four among the non-Orthodox) (Nechamia Meyers, "Divorce Rates Rise among Ultra-Orthodox," *Los Angeles Jewish Times,* July 12, 1996, p. 23). There is disagreement about the fertility figure (see n. 1 ch. 1), but there is agreement that it is low.

9. There is considerable debate about the accuracy of the figures, with some demographers putting the figure at "more like 40 percent." See Goldberg, pp. 67 – 68.

10. Recent statistics suggest — on these issues they can never be more than suggestive — that approximately 68 percent of all currently married Jews are married to fellow Jews. The percentage among recently married is lower. This larger number for all married Jews — regardless of how long ago they were married — reflects, of course, the trend toward mixed marriages among younger Jews and older Jews who have recently married.

11. Peter Steinfels, "Debating Intermarriage and Jewish Survival," *New York Times,* Oct. 18, 1992.

12. See Egon Mayer, cited in Steinfels.

13. Estimates of the Orthodox representation among American Jews vary from 6.8 percent (the 1990 Council of Jewish Federations survey) to 15 percent (various Orthodox sources). Most studies, however, place the number at 10 percent or 11 percent (e.g., Steven M. Cohen, *Ties and Tensions: The 1986 Survey of American Jewish Attitudes Toward Israel and Israelis* [New York: American Jewish Committee, 1987]).

14. Lawrence Frankel, "Intermarriage: Can We Survive This Challenge to Our Identity?" *Jewish Star,* December 1992.

15. Stuart E. Eizenstat, guest column in *Moment,* April 1992, p. 16.

16. Goldberg, p. 301.

17. Egon Mayer, *A Demographic Revolution in American Jewry* (Ann Arbor, Mich.: Frankel Center for Judaic Studies, 1992), p. 17.

18. The chasm widened when, in 1985, the Reform movement validated patrilineal descent. For Reform Jews, children born to Jewish fathers in a mixed marriage are Jewish if they live a Jewish life. Orthodox and Conservative Jews disagree. As the Orthodox rabbi Marc D. Angel writes, "The decisions of the Reform movement have created a sizeable body of people who consider themselves Jewish by the Reform definition but who are not Jewish according to *halachah.* Consequently, it will become increasingly difficult, if not impossible, for marriages to take place between Jews who follow *halachah* and those who do not." Rabbi Angel sees this as leading "to the total splinterization of the Jewish people" with "two (or more) distinct groups . . . [following] separate religions" (see Albert Vorspan, "Is American Jewry Unraveling?" *Reform Judaism,* Summer 1995, pp. 10 – 13, and Rabbi Angel's "Response," p. 14).

19. Of these children, 28 percent are raised Jewish, 31 percent are raised with no religion, and a full 41 percent are raised in a non-Jewish faith. See *Highlights of the CJF 1990 National Jewish Population Survey,* p. 16.

20. Kamenetz, *The Jew in the Lotus*, p. 111. Brown University sociologist Calvin Goldscheider says that for many Jews today, "They're Jewish because they're not Christian" (quoted in Goldberg, p. 73).

21. *New York Times*, July 20, 1996; *New York Times Magazine*, Sept. 29, 1996, p. 170.

22. Simon Rawidowicz, "Israel: The Ever-Dying People," in *Israel: The Ever-Dying People and Other Essays* (Cranbury, N.J.: Associated University Presses, 1986), pp. 53 – 54, 61, 66.

23. Cantor, *The Sacred Chain*, pp. 433 – 34.

24. Ibid., p. 425.

25. Rawidowicz, p. 61. This paragraph is particularly remarkable in its optimism, in light of the date when it was originally published: just three years after the end of the Holocaust. Surely the Jewish people were "taken by surprise," "put off balance," and nearly obliterated, despite their historical preparation for disaster.

26. Lipset and Raab, *Jews and the New American Scene*, p. 203.

27. Cantor, *The Sacred Chain*, p. 425. Cantor predicts that "as for the [secular] eighty-five percent of the Jews in America, they are on a one-way ticket to disappearance" (p. 426).

28. See Cantor, *The Sacred Chain*, p. 426.

29. Ernest van den Haag, *The Jewish Mystique* (New York: Stein and Day, 1969), p. 35.

30. Quoted in Ernest van den Haag, *The Jewish Mystique*, pp. 35 – 36.

31. Jacob R. Marcus, *The Jew in the Medieval World* (Cincinnati: Sinai Press, 1938), pp. 166 – 67. Much of Luther's good will toward the Jews hinged on his conviction that if Christians would "deal kindly with the Jews and instruct them in the Scriptures . . . we could expect them to come over to us" (Marcus, p. 167). When Luther's attempts to convert the Jews failed, he became a rabid anti-Semite. In his later writings, such as his 1543 monograph "Concerning the Jews and Their Lies," Luther urged Germans to destroy all synagogues, forbid rabbis to teach on pain of death, confiscate all Jewish holy books, impoverish all Jews, turn them into forced laborers, raze their homes, force them to live in stables, and expel them all from Germany if they resisted (see Marcus, pp. 167 – 69).

32. *New York Times*, April 14, 1968.

33. *Jewish Week*, Nov. 1, 1996, p. 30.

34. Mark Twain, "Concerning the Jews," *Harper's Monthly*, September 1899.

35. Charles S. Liebman, *The Ambivalent American Jew: Politics, Religion and Family in American Jewish Life* (Philadelphia: Jewish Publication Society of America, 1973), p. 177.

36. Maimonides, *Commentary on the Mishna: Tractate Sanhedrin*, trans. Fred Rosner (1168; reprint, New York: Feldheim, 1981), p. 156.

37. For a survey of the theological innovations by these movements, see Jack Wertheimer, *A People Divided: Judaism in Contemporary America* (New York: Basic Books, 1993); and Jacob Neusner, *American Judaism: What the Books Say, What the People Do* (Minneapolis: Fortress Press, 1994).

38. Many other contemporary Jewish theologians have influenced Christian theological discourse, such as Franz Rosenzweig, Emil Fackenheim, Richard Rubinstein, and David Hartman, but their influence has not been noted by broad Christian publics. Though Wiesel is not, strictly speaking, a theologian, his writings have had a profound impact on non-Jewish religious thinking.

39. See Goldberg, p. 59.

40. Quoted in Paul Mendes-Flohr and Yehuda Reinharz, eds., *The Jew in the Modern World* (New York: Oxford University Press, 1980), p. 104.

41. *Jewish Week*, Nov. 1, 1996, p. 36. For a discussion of changing political views, see Goldberg. "A slight moderation in enthusiasm for the liberal side of the political spectrum" is evident among younger Jews, according to leading pollster Steven Cohen, but young Jews remain decidedly, disproportionately, left of their gentile peers. Jews in general vote Democratic over Republican by a 4 – 1 margin, whereas gentile Caucasians are split equally in party affiliation. Jews even prefer to uphold liberal political values, like church-state separation, over rights to Jewish self-expression in cases in which non-Jews would actually favor Jewish religious expression: only 37 percent of Jews support the idea of erecting a Hanukkah menorah in a public space, while 60 percent of African-Americans and 81 percent of white gentiles approve of the idea! Such a preference for liberal values over Jewish particularity is corroborated in a *Los Angeles Times* poll in which half the Jews surveyed cited "a commitment to social equality" as the quintessence of their identity as Jews, while only 17 percent cited Judaism as the core of their Jewish identity (Peter Steinfels, "American Jews Stand Firmly to the Left," *New York Times*, Jan. 8, 1989, section 4, p. 7).

42. Van den Haag, p. 30.

43. Cantor, p. 57.

44. Ibid., p. 424. See also Richard J. Herrnstein and Charles Murray, *The Bell Curve: Intelligence and Class Structure in American Life* (New York: Free Press, 1994), p. 275.

45. Van den Haag, p. 14.

46. Ibid., p. 17.

47. See G. Gordon Liddy, *Will* (New York: St. Martin, 1980), p. 38.

48. Memorandum, May 1, 1978, reprinted in Bernard Schwartz, *Behind Bakke: Affirmative Action and the Supreme Court* (New York: Notable Trials Library, Gryphon, 1995), p. 135.

49. Don Feder, "The Kosher Majority: Orthodox Jews as Political Conservatives," *National Review*, April 10, 1987, p. 40. In 1984, for example, while Ronald Reagan carried only 34 percent of the Jewish vote, he carried 66 percent of the mostly Hasidic vote in Borough Park.

50. Ibid. In 1986, leaders of New York City's ultra-Orthodox community were among the leading opponents of the city's gay rights ordinance, Agudath Israel supports anti-abortion legislation, Lubavitch supported prayer in the public schools. All supported government aid to their parochial schools, while urging reduction in welfare benefits to others. See Goldberg, pp. 61; 45 – 46.

51. Emil Fackenheim, *The Jewish Return into History* (New York: Schocken Books, 1978), pp. 22 – 24.

52. Michael Wyschogrod, "Faith and the Holocaust: A Review Essay of Emil Fackenheim's *God's Presence in History*," *Judaism*, Summer 1971, p. 289.

53. Cited in S. Liptzin, *Peretz* (New York: Y.I.V.O., 1947), p. 378.

Chapter Two: Will the End of Institutional Anti-Semitism Mean the End of the Jews?

1. Jonathan S. Woocher, *Sacred Survival: The Civil Religion of American Jews* (Bloomington: Indiana University Press, 1986), pp. 72 – 73.

2. Quoted in Sara Bershtel and Allen Graubard, *Saving Remnants: Feeling Jewish in America* (New York: Free Press, 1992), p. 14. Emphasis in the original.

3. Arthur Hertzberg, "The Emancipation: A Reassessment After Two Centuries," *Modern Judaism*, May 1981, p. 48. The three-generation schema was first formulated as the third generation after Jewish emancipation in France came of age.

4. Quoted in Annie Kriegel, "Generational Difference: The History of an Idea," *Daedalus*, Fall 1978, p. 34. One concrete example of how the third generation marries out at a rate of one-third is sociologist Erich Rosenthal's early-1960s study of intermarriage patterns in Washington, D.C., which revealed that Jewish immigrants married non-Jews at a rate of 1.4 percent, their American-born children at a rate of 10.2 percent, and their American-born grandchildren attending college (comprising the vast majority of them) at a rate of 37 percent (Thomas B. Morgan, "The Vanishing American Jew," *Look*, May 5, 1964, p. 43).

5. Joseph Telushkin, *Jewish Humor* (New York: Morrow, 1992), p. 131.

6. Several recent works have explored the sensitive issue of North American Jewish inaction during the Holocaust, among them Irving Abella and Harold Troper, *None Is Too Many: Canada and the Jews of Europe, 1933 – 1948* (New York: Random House, 1983); Yehuda Bauer, *American Jewry and the Holocaust: The American Jewish Joint Distribution Committee, 1939 – 1945* (Jerusalem: Institute of Contemporary Jewry, Hebrew University, 1981); Richard Breitman and Alan M. Kraut, *American Refugee Policy and European Jewry, 1933 – 1945* (Bloomington: Indiana University Press, 1987); Henry L. Feingold, *Did American Jewry Do Enough During the Holocaust?* (Syracuse, N.Y.: Syracuse University Press, 1985); Walter Laqueur, *The Terrible Secret: An Investigation into the Suppression of Information About Hitler's Final Solution* (London: Weidenfeld and Nicolson, 1980); Haskel Lookstein, *Were We Our Brothers' Keepers?: The Public Response of American Jews to the Holocaust, 1938 – 1944* (New York: Hartmore House, 1985); David S. Wyman, *The Abandonment of the Jews: America and the Holocaust, 1941 – 1945* (New York: Pantheon Books, 1984); see also *America and the Holocaust: Deceit and Indifference*, a film produced by public television station WGBH of Boston, 1993. Goldberg, *Jewish Power*, takes a somewhat different point of view: see pp. 113 – 19.

7. See Jacob Katz, *Out of the Ghetto: The Social Background of Jewish Emancipation, 1770 – 1870* (New York: Schocken Books, 1978).

8. Norman Cantor, "Is This the Final Chapter in the Jews' Glorious History?" *New York Times Magazine,* Aug. 20, 1995.

9. "Polish anti-Semitism remains substantial, although ... [o]nly a few thousand Jews still live in Poland" (Associated Press, "Walesa Condemned for Silence After Hearing Anti-Semitic Views in Sermon," *Baltimore Sun,* June 18, 1995). Japanese anti-Semitism has been traced to the czarist secret police's supplying Japanese soldiers with copies of the forged *Protocols of the Elders of Zion* when Japan participated in the West's post–World War I effort to oust the Bolsheviks. Negative attitudes toward Jews were, perhaps, bolstered by Japan's contacts with its Axis partners in World War II (despite some Japanese wartime officials who rescued East European Jews and brought them to Japan and China, perhaps as part of the "Fugu Plan" to colonize and develop Manchuria). A spate of books and articles in recent decades reveals the extent to which classic Western anti-Semitic notions have taken root in Japan. Eisaburo Saito, director of Japan's Agency for Science and Technology, penned *The Secret of Jewish Power That Moves the World* (arguing that Franklin Roosevelt was a Jewish spy, that the Jews began World War I to activate the process of global Armageddon, and that Japan's postwar constitution was imposed by Jews). Other works in this vein include Masami Uno's *If You Understand the Jews You Will Understand the World* and *If You Understand the Jews You Will Understand Japan* (rehashing old anti-Semitic conspiracy theories, adapted to explain the latest downward trends in Japan's economy); a series of books with the collective title *Shoot Japan: The Last Strong Enemy* (more anti-Semitic conspiracy theories); and several recent articles in major Japanese magazines blaming "Jewish pressure" for President Clinton's inflexibility in trade talks with Japan. While it is astounding that the Japanese have imported the West's former obsession with scapegoating Jews, which at least serves a "practical" need for evading responsibility, some Japanese are now flirting with Holocaust denial and other forms of contemporary anti-Semitism. Masanori Nishioka authored "There Were No Nazi Gas Chambers" for the popular *Marco Polo* magazine, a glossy publication with a circulation of 200,000 that normally covers fashion, culture, and consumer news. See Kunio Tanabe, "Reflections and Distortions," *Washington Post,* Feb. 19, 1995; T. R. Reid, "Tokyo Magazine Shut for Denying Holocaust," *Washington Post,* Jan. 31, 1995; and Quentin Hardy, "Japan's Top Economic Daily Runs Advertising for Antisemitic Book," *Asian Wall Street Journal,* July 29, 1993.

10. Irving Greenberg, "Jewish Survival and the College Campus," *Judaism,* Summer 1968, p. 260.

11. Researchers who study anti-Semitism design surveys so as to catch and distinguish both of these types of Judeophobia. "Abstract," "attitudinal," or "ideological" anti-Semitism is measured by having survey respondents answer questions about their views of Jews' religion, financial clout, political power, patriotism, intelligence, and concern for others. "Personal" or "behavioral" anti-Semitism is gauged with reference to how respondents feel about the prospect of Jewish neighbors, a Jewish candidate for president, overt acts of anti-Semitism, interfaith marriage, or a Jewish business partner. Such polling criteria, suggested by organizations like the National Jewish Community Relations Advisory Council, have been used in recent

surveys such as those conducted by the National Opinion Research Center (1994) and the Roper Organization (1992). See Jerome A. Chanes, ed., *Antisemitism in America Today: Outspoken Experts Explode the Myths* (New York: Birch Lane, 1995), pp. 26 – 30, 79 – 83.

12. This was not always true. In the Visigoth kingdom, for example, King Erwig enacted his "Leges Wisigoth" at a church synod in the year 681, which stipulated, inter alia, that Jewish converts to Christianity "not emigrate so as to apostate again." Nonconverts were free to leave (and presumably were encouraged to do so), yet converts became virtual prisoners within the kingdom (Carl Joseph von Hefels, *A History of the Councils of the Church*, trans. William Clark [Edinburgh: T. and T. Clark, 1896], p. 318).

13. See Edward H. Flannery, *The Anguish of the Jews: Twenty-three Centuries of Anti-Semitism* (New York: Paulist Press, 1985), p. 198. A variation on this theme is a simultaneous charge by two enemy countries that their own Jewish populations collaborate with the enemy. Such was the case in the interwar period, as both Germany and Russia blamed their Jews for sabotaging their military campaigns in World War I.

14. Allan Gould, ed., *What Did They Think of the Jews?* (Northvale, N.J.: Jason Aronson, 1991), pp. 369 – 71.

15. *Los Angeles Times*, Feb. 14, 1996; *Houston Post*, Feb. 16, 1995; *Newsday*, Oct. 30, 1992; *New York Times*, Dec. 13, 1992. See also "Hate Crimes Against Jews in State Rise, Study Says," *Los Angeles Times*, Feb. 16, 1995, and "Reports of Anti-Semitism Hit Record High in 1991," *Chicago Tribune*, Feb. 6, 1992. Since the ADL audits break incidents down by category, headlines really should differentiate between different types of incidents. Examples of headlines that have done that: "Slight Increase in Anti-Semitism; Survey Finds Rise in Harassment, Drop in Vandalism," *Chicago Tribune*, Jan. 25, 1994; "Anti-Semitic Incidents Up Statewide; Downward Trend in U.S. and Northern California," *San Francisco Chronicle*, Feb. 15, 1996; "Anti-Semitic Actions Decline, but Personal Threats Increase," *Atlanta Journal and Constitution*, Feb. 3, 1993; and "Anti-Semitism in NYC; Report Shows 28% Jump in Vandalism, Assaults," *Newsday*, Feb. 13, 1993.

16. *1994 Audit of Anti-Semitic Incidents* (New York: Anti-Defamation League, 1995), p. 8.

17. *1995 Audit of Anti-Semitic Incidents* (New York: Anti-Defamation League, 1996), pp. 1, 16.

18. Goldberg provides some such examples in *Jewish Power*, such as Secretary of State James Baker's alleged statement about the Jews: "Fuck 'em. They don't vote for us anyway" (p. xxiii); President Jimmy Carter's calculated effort to blame his firing of United Nations Ambassador Andrew Young on the Jews (p. 323); and President George Bush's attack on the power of the Jewish lobby (p. xvi).

19. Most surveys hover around the figure cited by B'nai B'rith, which counts 20 percent of gentile Americans as anti-Semitic (Alison Carper, "Survey: 1 in 5 Anti-Semitic," *Newsday*, Nov. 17, 1992. See also Christine Wicker, "Keeping the Faith: American Jews Set to Tackle Fears of Assimilation," *Dallas Morning News*, Sept. 5, 1994).

20. See, e.g., Joel Carmichael, *The Satanizing of the Jews: Origin and Development of Mystical Anti-Semitism* (New York: Fromm International, 1992).

21. On Jan. 10, 1944, Josiah DuBois, chief counsel for the Treasury Department's Foreign Funds Control Division, issued a "Report to the Secretary [of the Treasury, Henry Morgenthau, Jr.] on the Acquiescence of This Government in the Murder of the Jews," in which DuBois and his staff wrote that the State Department was "guilty not only of gross procrastination and wilful failure to act, but even of wilful attempts to prevent action from being taken to rescue Jews from Hitler." Randolph Paul, also of the Treasury Department, came to the conclusion during the war that the State Department was behaving like an "underground movement . . . to let the Jews be killed." Both are cited in Wyman, *The Abandonment of the Jews*, pp. 187, 191.

22. Henry Adams, T. S. Eliot, and Ezra Pound were the avant-garde of an intellectual culture in which expressing anti-Semitism was not just acceptable, but de rigueur. See Gould, n. 14 above.

23. Goldberg, pp. 112, 116, 111.

24. Robert S. Wistrich, *Antisemitism: The Longest Hatred* (London: Thames Methuen, 1991), p. 120.

25. The influx of East European Jews was stemmed by the 1921 Immigration Quota Act and the even more restrictive 1924 Act, laws "passed largely out of fear that America would be 'Judaized' in the near future" (Berel Wein, *Triumph of Survival: The Story of the Jews in the Modern Era, 1650 – 1990* [Monsey, N.Y.: Shaar Press, 1990], p. 332). These laws were occasioned by a groundswell of popular opposition to large-scale Jewish immigration, typified in popular works like *The Passing of the Great Race* (1918; reprint ed. New York: Arno, 1970) by Madison Grant, in which the author argued that Jews mongrelized America's gene pool, debased American culture, and had instigated World War I.

26. Whereas in 1940, 63 percent of Americans surveyed said they thought that Jews possessed "objectionable traits," by 1980, a Gallup Poll revealed that fully 81 percent of gentile Americans surveyed had favorable attitudes toward Jews and only 8 percent expressed an opinion to the contrary (Charles Herbert Stember et al., *Jews in the Mind of America* [New York: Basic Books, 1966], p. 54; Gallup Poll, April 16, 1981).

27. John Paul II, *Crossing the Threshold of Hope*, ed. Vittorio Messori (New York: Random House, 1994), p. 97.

28. *Boston Globe*, July 8, 1996, p. 4.

29. Cardinal Hlond, an old-fashioned anti-Semite, also blamed anti-Semitism "to a great degree on the Jews" (*New York Times*, July 12, 1946, p. 1).

30. Even before the Ecumenical Council of the Catholic church issued *Nostra Aetete* in 1965, the umbrella organization of all Protestant, Eastern Orthodox, and other non-Catholic denominations, the World Council of Churches, promulgated its own condemnation of anti-Semitism in Christian theology at its Third Assembly in New Delhi, India, held Nov. 19 – Dec. 14, 1961. While the Protestant and Eastern Orthodox denunciation of theological anti-Semitism is less well known than that made by the Catholic church several years later, it is nevertheless epochal

in importance, and maintains, inter alia: "We call upon all the churches we represent to denounce anti-Semitism, no matter what its origin, as absolutely irreconcilable with the profession and the practice of the Christian faith. Anti-Semitism is a sin against God and man" (quoted in Gerhard Falk, *The Jew in Christian Theology* [Jefferson, N.C.: McFarland, 1992], p. 117). Consequently, various "Protestant denominations issued declarations regarding the Jews upon the recommendations of the World Council of Churches" (ibid., p. 133).

31. Antoine Halff, "Lutherans Rebuke Luther for Anti-Jewish Diatribes: Church Repudiates Writings of Its Founder," *Forward*, May 20, 1994, p. 1.

32. See Franklin Littell, "American Protestantism and Antisemitism," in Naomi Cohen, ed., *Essential Papers on Jewish-Christian Relations* (New York: New York University Press, 1990); Robert Andrew Everett, "Judaism in Nineteenth Century American Transcendentalist and Liberal Protestant Thought," *Journal of Ecumenical Studies*, Summer 1983, p. 397; Rosemary Radford Ruether, "Anti-Semitism and Christian Theology," in Eva Fleischner, ed., *Auschwitz: Beginning of a New Era?: Reflections on the Holocaust* (New York: Ktav, 1977). Also see works by Krister Stendahl, Paul M. Van Buren, Walter Burghardt, and Robert Evans.

33. Years before the establishment of the State of Israel, Muslim clerics in Iraq, Egypt, India, Morocco, and Syria issued *fatwas* declaring the "illegality" of Jewish territorial acquisitions in the Holy Land: "accepting [any such acquisition is] an act of apostasy and rejection of Islam." Palestinian clerics issued their own *fatwa* to this effect on Jan. 26, 1935, thirteen years before the establishment of the State of Israel, forbidding "the Zionists to turn this holy Muslim land into Jewish land." This *"fatwa*, declaring [it] illegal to forgo any part of Palestine," was signed by no fewer than 249 Palestinian religious leaders. When the UN voted to partition Palestine in November 1947, the foremost religious institution in the Muslim world — the al-Azhar seminary in Cairo — issued a *fatwa* declaring the UN action null and void, urging an economic blockade of Jewish Palestine, and calling on Muslims to "prepare the requisites of *Jihad* . . . Fulfill what Allah has required of you." (All the above quotes are from "Palestine: History, Case and Solution," *Nida'ul Islam*, January–February 1996, n.p.) At the outbreak of hostilities in 1948, Haj Amin el-Husseini, the Grand Mufti of Jerusalem and the father of Palestinian nationalism, issued this bloodcurdling *fatwa*: "I declare a holy war, my Muslim brothers! Murder the Jews! Murder them all!" (cited in Mitchell Bard and Joel Himmelfarb, *Myths and Facts: A Concise Record of the Arab-Israeli Conflict* [Washington, D.C.: Near East Reports, 1992], pp. 295 – 96). From then on, anti-Israel *fatwas* were a commonplace in the Arab and broader Muslim world. Typical was a *fatwa* issued by al-Azhar in 1956 "forbidding a truce with the new Jewish government," which read as follows: "It is not permitted for Muslims to reconcile with these Jews . . . in any manner which will allow the Jews to remain on these holy Islamic lands as a nation. In fact, it is required of [Muslims] . . . to exert all they can to cleanse the land from any trace of these transgressors. Whoever falls short in this or neglects it . . . is — according to the law of Islam — one who left the Muslims and committed the gravest of sins." The imam of al-Azhar, Hasan Ma'moun, later issued another *fatwa* demanding holy war: "The land of Islam must remain in the hands of its people. What is required of the Muslims in the situation of trans-

gression . . . is *Jihad* against the enemy with force, and this is an individual obligation upon all its people" ("Palestine: History, Case and Solution"). The doctrinal basis for *fatwas* concerning the impermissibility of Jewish sovereignty in the Jewish Holy Land is the Islamic legal precept, formulated here by al-Mawardi, that "[a] land which the Muslims conquer by force [as they conquered Palestine in A.D. 636] . . . becomes 'Dar Islam' [Islamic territory] whether Muslims live there or pagans are allowed back to it" (Dr. Abd al-Fattah el-Awaisi, "The Significance of Jerusalem in Islam," Islamic Society home page, last updated April 1, 1996).

Today, *fatwas* are used by Islamic revolutionaries to "weave an ideological fabric that justifies suicide bombings in Israel, hostage-taking in Lebanon, and the killing of foreigners in Algeria and tourists in Egypt" (Youssef M. Ibrahim, "Religious Edicts Sow Divisions in Islamic World," *Dallas Morning News*, Feb. 18, 1995, p. 4G). In May 1996, leaders of Hamas, the Palestinian terrorist organization that opposes peace with Israel, issued a *fatwa* from London, published in the Hamas magazine *Filisteen al-Muslima*, declaring that all Muslims are compelled by religious law to engage in suicide bombings against Israeli civilians and Jews. The *fatwa* said, in part: "[I]t is possible that as a result some children may be killed unintentionally and this is permitted by religious law" ("London Fatwa Backs Suicide Bombers," *Sunday Telegraph*, May 26, 1996, p. 24).

34. Marilise Simons, "Chirac Affirms France's Guilt in Fate of Jews," *New York Times*, July 17, 1995, p. 1.

35. Reuters, "UN Commission Formally Condemns Antisemitism," *Jerusalem Post*, March 10, 1994, p. 1.

36. Despite conciliatory pronouncements toward Israel by Arab leaders before the international media and world diplomatic forums, some of these leaders continue to reassure their constituencies at home that their overtures to Israel are merely tactical, and that their strategic, long-term goal of Israel's politicide remains. Examples include Yassir Arafat's speech in South Africa comparing the Oslo accords to Mohammed's peace pact with the Qureish tribe of Mecca and Medina, which Mohammed abrogated as soon as he had sufficient power to destroy the tribe; Arafat's speech early in 1996 in Norway in which he pledged to "make life unbearable for the Jews by psychological warfare and population explosion"; speeches by Syria's President Assad before Syria's parliament in which he compares any possible deal with Israel over the Golan to the ploy-truces Arabs made a thousand years ago with the Crusaders to gain themselves time to build up their forces enough to evict the Crusaders from the Holy Land; PLO Foreign Minister Farouk al-Kadumi's 1994 statement that Israel "is a state that was established through coercion and it must be destroyed"; Arafat's declaration over the PLO's Radio Monte Carlo in 1993 that his gestures toward peace are "in accordance with the Palestine National Council Resolution of 1974," which is termed "The Phased [*marhali*] Political Program," Articles 2 and 4 of which propose a purely *provisional* mini-state for Palestinians in Gaza and the West Bank, should liberation of all Palestine in one fell swoop prove impractical; the 1994 statement by PLO executive committee member and nominee to head the Palestinian police force Abbas Zaki that the Oslo accords are "only a cease-fire until the next stage"; the claim by former chief of the

Palestinian delegation to the Washington peace talks Dr. Haidar Abdel-Shafi that "the PLO Agreement is not binding on the Palestinian people"; leading moderate Faisal al-Husseini's 1992 interview to the Jordanian paper *Al-Rai* in which he remarked, "Sooner or later, we will force the Israeli society to cooperate with the larger society — that is, our Arab society — and ultimately lead to the dissolution of the 'Zionist entity' gradually"; PLO refugee camp director Abu al-Aynan's assertion that "We have to accept the deal and wait for a change in the circumstances that could lead to the elimination of Israel," and so on.

37. As a result of the 1967 war, the left in America followed the Soviet lead in turning against Israel. An exodus of Jews from the more rabid anti-Zionist leftist organizations began, and thus the moderating influence these Jews might have exercised on their colleagues was lost. For example, the Socialist Workers Party in the United States issued a statement in 1971 that "the major task confronting American revolutionaries [regarding the Middle East] remains that of educating the radicalizing youth . . . for destruction of the state of Israel" (cited in Dennis Prager and Joseph Telushkin, *Why the Jews?: The Reason for Antisemitism* [New York: Simon & Schuster, 1983], p. 147). The U.S. Communist Party has consistently published articles describing Zionism as racism, although unlike the Socialist Workers Party, it does not call for Israel's politicide. Such pronouncements received scholarly support from radical academics like Maxime Rodinson, whose tract *Israel: A Colonial-Settler State?*, trans. David Thorstad (New York: Monad Press, 1973), influences Western leftists up to the present. Noam Chomsky remains the most outspoken and prolific anti-Israel academic, while left-wing journalists like Alexander Cockburn, Christopher Hitchens, and Gore Vidal follow close behind. On the political front, anti-Zionism and overt anti-Semitism are most evident today among the leftist parties led by African-Americans, such as Lenora Fulani's New Alliance Party and Kwame Ture's All-African People's Revolutionary Party. Ture's case clearly shows the nexus between the radicalism of the 1960s and today: Ture, the former Stokely Carmichael, was a leader of the Black Panthers.

38. Leonard Dinnerstein, *Antisemitism in America* (New York: Oxford University Press, 1994), p. 239.

39. The problem of date rape on college campuses has been treated similarly. Though by every reliable account, there has been a dramatic decrease in date rapes on campus — due largely to the innovative work of feminists, rape crisis centers, and education — many feminists and professional rape counselors whose identity and occupation are dependent on the persistence of date rape, continue to pretend that there has been no improvement — and according to some, there has been a worsening — in the date rape "crisis" on campus. See Wendy Kaminer, "Feminism's Identity Crisis," *Atlantic Monthly*, October 1993.

40. Goldberg, p. 279.

Chapter Three: Anti-Semitism in the Twenty-first Century

1. *Time*, June 17, 1996, pp. 52 – 54.

2. Hannah Arendt, *The Jew as Pariah: Jewish Identity and Politics in the Modern Age*, ed. Ron H. Feldman (New York: Grove Press, 1978), p. 68.

3. David Usborne, "Jews Pay the Price of an American Success in the U.S.," *The Independent*, May 25, 1996.

4. Goldberg, *Jewish Power*, p. 281.

5. Chip Berlet, ed., *Eyes Right* (Boston: South End Press, 1995), p. 41.

6. The announcement that Barricade Books would be reissuing *The Turner Diaries* in midsummer 1996 sparked outrage among human rights activists who contend that the book inspired violence by Timothy McVeigh, the chief suspect in the Oklahoma City bombing, as well as by other white supremacists. In response to those who attempted to halt publication of the book, Lyle Stuart, Barricade's publisher, conceded that the novel is an "incendiary volume" filled with anti-Semitic and racist concepts. However, he insisted that it was important to rush ahead with publication in order to "alert the average American to what these people advocate" ("Group Tries to Halt Selling of Racist Novel," *New York Times*, April 20, 1996, p. 8).

7. Anti-Defamation League, *Paranoia as Patriotism: Far-Right Influences on the Militia Movement*, 1995. This report can be accessed via the Internet (pub/orgs/american/adl/paranoia-as-patriotism/covenant-sword-arm-lord). In it, Bill Thomas, seminar organizer for The Covenant, the Sword, and the Arm of the Lord (CSA), is also quoted as describing the Jews as "the seed of Satan, not the seed of God"; Kerry Noble, an elder and "ordained minister" of the CSA, states that "nonwhites and Jews are a threat to our Christian, white race" and that "Jews are financing the training of Blacks to take over most of our major cities."

8. "U.S. Indicts 23 in White Supremacist Organization," *New York Times*, April 16, 1985, p. 16A.

9. Chip Berlet, "Armed Militias," Cambridge, Mass., June 30, 1995, p. 3.

10. *Jewish Journal*, Salem, Mass., July 1996.

11. Kenneth Stern, *A Force Upon the Plain* (New York: Simon & Schuster, 1996), pp. 30, 69.

12. Ibid., pp. 52 – 54.

13. Ibid., pp. 247, 120.

14. Berlet.

15. Chomsky made these statements in the 1980s in support of a Holocaust denier in France named Robert Faurisson. Nor can Chomsky fall back on the excuse that his defense of Faurisson was merely a defense of his right to speak, in the spirit of civil liberties. Chomsky has gone well beyond a defense of free speech in the tradition of the ACLU's (correct, in my view) defense of the rights of neo-Nazis to march through Skokie, Illinois. Chomsky signed a petition that characterized Faurisson's falsifications as "findings" based on "extensive historical research," which they plainly were not (see *Chutzpah*, pp. 174 – 75). Moreover, Chomsky *substantively* defended Faurisson against charges that he was an anti-Semite, claiming that Faurisson was "a sort of relatively apolitical liberal." In any event, Chomsky has no credentials as a civil libertarian defender of freedom of speech for those with whom he disagrees (see *Chutzpah*, p. 177).

16. As G. E. Moore explained in criticizing the social Darwinism of Herbert Spencer, "To argue that a thing is good *because* it is 'natural,' or bad *because* it is 'un-

natural' ... is ... certainly fallacious" (Moore, *Principia Ethica* [London: Cambridge University Press, 1903], p. 45).

17. Quoted in Deborah Lipstadt, *Denying the Holocaust: The Growing Assault on Truth and Memory* (New York: Free Press, 1993), p. 1. Original source: Marvin Perry, "Denying the Holocaust: History as Myth and Delusion," *Encore American and Worldwide News*, September 1981, pp. 28 – 33.

18. Jean-Paul Sartre, *Anti-Semite and Jew*, p. 148.

19. According to Dr. Shmuel Krakowsky, head of Israel's Yad Vashem Memorial for Jewish Victims of the Holocaust, "5,860,000 perished during the Holocaust" ("Auschwitz Deaths Reduced to a Million," *Daily Telegraph*, July 17, 1990, p. 1). According to recent estimates generated after the opening of previously inaccessible Soviet archives, as many as "6.25 million [Jews] died at the hands of the Nazis" ("List Read to Recall the Dead," *Charleston Gazette*, April 11, 1994, p.1A).

20. Tom Gross, "False Figures," *Jerusalem Post*, April 16, 1996. Gross, who is an expert on the Romanies and is sympathetic to their plight, demonstrates how certain Holocaust "revisionists" are trying to "inflate" Romany deaths in order "to minimize the Jewish 'share' of ... death in the Holocaust."

21. Newsletter, June 30, 1996. One of the anti-Semitic letters I recently received acknowledged that Poles killed Jews at Kielce and declared that my correspondent was proud of that fact: "You have missed the whole point about Kielce. It was Polish Catholics who killed the Jews but don't make it look like something negative but rather a moment of glory. After all that Poland had been through, they were not going to let the perfidious Jews rob her again. While the Poles were doing this act of glory, they were shouting 'NEVER AGAIN' and in later years the Jews would even steal this saying."

22. Recently, a new form of Holocaust-related bigotry has emerged, which seeks to explain, and even justify, the actions of those who participated in the genocide. Its most pernicious manifestation took the form of a "historical" novel that became a best-seller in Australia and won several prestigious awards. See my United Feature Syndicate column "Ultimate Abuse Excuse Justifies Holocaust," July 14, 1995.

23. In an investigative report documenting and analyzing the relationship between the deniers and Buchanan, the *New Republic* magazine concluded that "much of the material on which Buchanan bases his columns [on the Holocaust] is sent to him by pro-Nazi, anti-Semitic cranks" (Jacob Weisberg, "The Heresies of Pat Buchanan," October 22, 1990, p. 22). When the reporter asked Buchanan where he got the crackpot idea he had published that Jews could not have been gassed at Treblinka, he replied: "Somebody sent it to me." As the article concluded, these haters and deniers know "they can expect a hearing from Buchanan," who has defended virtually every accused Nazi war criminal, even those against whom the evidence has been overwhelming. Buchanan also neatly fits the profile of the deniers and minimizers: he is not a historian; he was a bigot before he was a denier; he has written for hate publications (such as *Spotlight*); he admires Fascists such as Franco; and he is an equal opportunity hater (gays, feminists, Jews, and others).

24. *Newsweek*, March 4, 1996.

25. Lipstadt, p. 209.

26. Ibid., p. 208.

27. Recent statutes, regulations, and university "speech codes" have made some inroads on this important principle in the context of sexual harassment, and there are efforts afoot to expand that to social or religious vilification, but thus far, the courts have required that the harassment or vilification be directed at a specific individual.

28. Lipstadt, p. 158.

29. Alan M. Dershowitz, "The Holocaust on Trial," *Boston Herald*, April 29, 1985, p. 5.

30. Alan M. Dershowitz, *The Abuse Excuse* (Boston: Little, Brown, 1994), p. 328.

31. ADL, *Uncommon Ground* (Research Report, 1994).

32. Ibid.

33. Ibid.

34. Ibid. See also Alan M. Dershowitz, "Farrakhan's Politics of Division," *Boston Herald*, Jan. 31, 1994, p. 21.

35. ADL, *Uncommon Ground.*

36. Ibid.

37. ADL, *Uncommon Ground,* p. 13.

38. Ibid., pp. 9 – 11.

39. ADL, *Jew Hatred as History* (Research Report, 1993), p. 45. See also Murray Friedman, *What Went Wrong* (New York: Free Press, 1995), p. 348.

40. ADL, *Jew Hatred,* p. 46. These figures are "striking, considering Jews made up by then less than three percent of the American population" (Paul Berman, ed., *Blacks and Jews: Alliances and Arguments,* New York: Delacorte, 1994, pp. 13 – 14). Indeed, Jewish support of African-American organizations and of liberal causes is "disproportionate not only to their numbers but also even to their proportion of the wealthy" (Kosmin, *The Dimensions of Contemporary Jewish Philanthropy,* p. 16).

41. Martin Luther King Jr., *A Testament of Hope* (New York: Harper and Row, 1996).

42. "In the 1920s, the 'buy-black' campaign of the black-nationalist leader Marcus Garvey was explicitly targeted at Jews, and Garvey later spoke admiringly of Adolf Hitler" ("Facing Up to Black Anti-Semitism," *Commentary,* December 1995, p. 26). "Many of Garveyism's specific tenets foreshadowed Farrakhan's black Muslimism . . . Garvey on the cunning, cosmopolitan Jews: 'Their particular method of living is inconsistent with the broader human principles that make all people homogeneous'" ("Echoes of Marcus Garvey," *New Republic,* Nov. 6, 1995, p. 16).

43. Murray Friedman, *What Went Wrong: The Creation and Collapse of the Black-Jewish Alliance* (New York: Free Press, 1995), p. 28.

44. "A Yarmulke for Farrakhan," *Jerusalem Post,* Aug. 8, 1996, p. 5. See also "A Message of Distrust; Media Are Enemies and Agents for Farrakhan, Muhammad," *Cleveland Plain Dealer,* May 8, 1994, p. 1C. The Nation of Islam has published a book titled *The Secret Relationship Between Blacks and Jews,* which details the alleged Jewish involvement in slave owning and slave trading.

45. "Muslims, Arab and black, were the principal slave raiders and sellers of black slaves," not Jews. While Farrakhan contends that Jews were primary movers in the slave trade, the truth is that "in the old South, Jews constituted three-tenths of one percent of slaveholders, not 75%. The entire slave population of the South was a little over 3.5 million in 1865. Few Jews owned plantations. Plantations required slaves. Most Jews were small merchants who would have little advantage in slave labor" ("Farrakhan Should Speak the Truth," *Cleveland Plain Dealer,* Jan. 29, 1996, p. 11B).

46. Quoted in Friedman, p. 18.

47. Ibid.

48. See Alan M. Dershowitz, "Farrakhan's Politics of Division," p. 21.

49. Alan M. Dershowitz, *The Abuse Excuse,* pp. 97 – 99.

50. See Sylvester Monroe "The Risky Association: A Bold Strategy to Revitalize the NAACP; Could Lead to Disaster for the Civil Rights Group and Its Leader," *Time,* June 27, 1994, p. 39.

51. See also Henry Louis Gates, *New York Times,* July 20, 1992, p. 15; April 14, 1993, p. 21; *Boston Globe,* July 28, 1992, p. 15. Even fewer college students have read the following words of the eminent historian C. Vann Woodward of Yale: "The Nation of Islam undertakes to prove that Jews 'used kidnaped Black Africans disproportionately more than any other ethnic or religious group in New World history.' It is curious that an organization of Black Muslims should have overlooked the vital role of African chiefs in capturing and providing slaves for the trade, as well as the pioneer work of Muslims, black and white, in trading and exploiting slaves from sub-Saharan Africa." (ADL, *Jew Hatred as History,* p. iii)

52. *Reform Judaism,* Fall 1994, p. 12.

53. Massimo Calabresi, "Dispatches: Skin Deep 101," *Time,* Feb. 14, 1994, p. 16.

54. Martin quotes letters of support from Michael Williams, director of African-American studies at Simmons College (who writes of "Zionist machinations"); a black professor from the State University of New York; a citizen who refused to give his name because of "Jewish terrorist activity in the U.S."; and a prisoner who asks Martin to send him a copy of *The Protocols of the Elders of Zion.* Martin never tells his readers whether he sent the prisoner this anti-Semitic forgery.

55. Tony Martin, *The Jewish Onslaught* (Dover, Mass.: Majority Press, 1993).

56. In a July 1994 report compiled by CAMERA (Committee for Accuracy in Middle East Reporting in America), Alex Safian, senior researcher for CAMERA, argued that "over the last 17 years the Public Broadcasting Service has presented more than 20 documentaries bearing on the Arab-Israeli dispute, most of them levelling distorted or false charges damning Israel. *Journey to the Occupied Lands,* a recent *Frontline* documentary focusing on Israel's alleged oppression of the Palestinians, extends and reinforces this regrettable pattern of publicly-funded misinformation" ("PBS and Israel: A Pattern of Bias," a CAMERA monograph, July 1994, p. 1). Michael Hoffman, director of CAMERA, said that "whatever violence happens in Israel or the territories seems to be put under a press microscope, whereas much worse violence happening elsewhere is barely covered at all." Furthermore,

it has been charged that ABC *World News Tonight* anchor Peter Jennings displays an anti-Israel bias in his broadcasts. Hoffman stated that Jennings "doesn't even seem to care that he's not making an attempt at being fair and impartial." These charges against Jennings have been supported by Jim Lederman, author of *Battle Lines* (a critical assessment of the media) and a reporter who covered Israel for over twenty years for National Public Radio — "a media outlet regarded by pro-Israelis as a mother lode of misinformation and distortion" ("News Bias on Israel Is in Eye of Beholder," *Washington Times*, May 7, 1992, p. E1).

57. Martin, *The Jewish Onslaught*, p. 35.

58. See Sunday *New York Times* Education Supplement, Nov. 3, 1996, sec. 4A, p. 24.

59. See my book *Reasonable Doubts* (New York: Simon and Schuster, 1996), pp. 161 – 63, for my assessment of some Jewish anti-black bigotry that accompanied the O. J. Simpson case.

60. Martin Kramer, "The Jihad Against the Jews," *Commentary*, October 1994, p. 38.

61. Interview with Husayn al-Musani, *Stern*, July 5, Aug. 21, 1990.

62. Kramer, p. 38.

63. Quoted in ADL, *The Struggle Is Now Worldwide* (1995), p. 26.

64. Quoted in Will Maslow, *Radical Islamic Fundamentalism Update*, September 1995, p. 6.

65. Ibid., p. 7. See also Federal News Service, April 6, 1995.

66. Maslow, p. 7.

67. U.S. State Department, "Patterns of Global Terrorism, 1995," April 1996.

68. See also Will Maslow, *Radical Islamic Fundamentalist Update*, July 1995, p. 5.

69. The anti-Semitic attacks in the campaign were mainly directed at Kwasniewski and his post-Communist colleagues in the Alliance of the Democratic Left (SLD), which controls parliament. Right-wingers and right-leaning newspapers have claimed to have researched candidates' origins. Kwasniewski, put on the defensive, said his family has had the same name for generations and is from eastern Poland. *The Warsaw Voice*, July 9, 1995 (Lexis News Library, CURNWS File).

70. "Poland's Right Stokes Fires of Anti-Semitism But Power of Slurs in Campaigns Slips," *Christian Science Monitor*, Nov. 13, 1995, p. 6.

71. Ibid.

72. Ibid.; see also Agence France-Presse, "Anti-Semitism Plays a Role in Polish Election Campaign," Nov. 2, 1995.

73. "The Essential Zyuganov," *Newsweek*, June 17, 1996.

74. "New Yeltsin Aide Rails at Foreign Religions; Lebed Calls Mormonism 'Mold and Scum,' " *Washington Post*, June 28, 1996, p. A23. The number of Jews in Russia is difficult to estimate and there are no definitive figures.

75. "Zhirinovsky Cult Grows: All Power to the Leader," *New York Times*, April 5, 1994, p. A1.

76. "Politics: View from Abroad; from Japan to Britain, Foreign Leaders and Press Look Askance at Buchanan Fever," *New York Times*, Feb. 28, 1996, p. B6.

77. See "Freedom Betrays Hungary's Jews; Anti-Semitism Has Risen from Communism's Ashes," *The Independent*, Oct. 7, 1990, p. 13.

78. "Hate Survives a Holocaust: Anti-Semitism Resurfaces; Immigration Fears the Intifada and East Europe's Revolutions Have Unleashed an Ugly, Anti-Jewish Deja Vu," *Los Angeles Times*, June 12, 1990, p. H1.

79. "Hungarian Campaign Uses Anti-Semitic Art," *Chicago Tribune*, March 27, 1994, p. C6. See also "Hungary and the Jews: Looking at 1944 Is Difficult," *New York Times*, April 18, 1994, p. A3.

80. "Anti-Semitism Rears Its Head Once Again," *St. Louis Post-Dispatch*, June 24, 1991, p. 3B.

81. *Boston Globe*, Nov. 2, 1996, p. B3.

82. Tom Tugent, "Moscow Judge Calls 'Protocols of Zion' an Antisemitic Forgery," *Jerusalem Post*, Nov. 28, 1993, p. 1.

83. See Shepard Nevel, "Second Thoughts About Third Parties," *Denver Post*, Aug. 27, 1995.

Chapter Four: The Dangers of the Christian Right — and Their Jewish Allies

1. *1990 Detailed Ancestry Groups for States*, Ethnic and Hispanic Branch Population Division, U.S. Bureau of the Census, Washington, D.C., 1990.

2. Oscar L. Arnal, "Between the Red and the Black: Catholic Politics from Dreyfus to Pétain" in *Ambivalent Alliance: The Catholic Church and the Action Française 1899–1939* (Pittsburgh: University of Pittsburg Press, 1985).

3. Herzl, *The Jewish State*, pp. 86 – 87.

4. Guinier's proposals included cumulative voting, whereby a voter would have as many votes as positions being filled, and "supermajorities," whereby 51 percent is not considered a majority, but rather an arbitrary 60 or 70 percent is (William Raspberry, "Clinton's Cold Feet," *Washington Post*, June 4, 1993, p. A25, and "Guinier for the Defense," editorial, *Richmond Times Dispatch*, June 7, 1996, p. A16).

5. In 1994, the Anti-Defamation League issued a controversial report, *The Religious Right: The Assault on Tolerance and Pluralism in America*, which painted with a broad brush and made some factual errors. The Christian Coalition issued a rebuttal. To the extent I rely on quotations from the ADL report, I have checked them against the Christian Coalition rebuttal. I include no disputed quotations or facts unless I have confirmed them independently.

6. ADL, *The Religious Right* (1994), pp. 4 – 6.

7. Ibid., pp. 12, 24. He was referring, of course, to Henry Kissinger. Does he also include the chairman of the Joint Chiefs of Staff, General John M. Shalikashvili?

8. Ibid., p. 40.

9. "Hostility toward foreigners has been on the rise in Germany since the country was reunified in 1990. Right-wing and neo-Nazi movements have contributed to hundreds of violent crimes" (" 'Germany for Germans': Xenophobia and Racist Violence in Germany," *Human Rights Watch/Helsinki*, 485 Fifth Ave., New York [ISBN 1-56432-149-5], 1995).

"This is our tragedy," said Stanislaw Sankiewicz, a vice president of the International Romani Union. "With the new democracy — in the new Europe — the xenophobia has started, the racism" (Linnet Myers, "New Europe Brings Back Old Anti-Gypsy Prejudice," dateline Warsaw, *Chicago Tribune*, Feb. 21, 1993).

"But the recent upsurge in fraternity activity and membership is definitely also symptomatic of [the former East Germany's] conservative mood. Never since the end of the war have so many young Germans expressed a predilection for nationalistic and chauvinistic ideas as during the past few years. According to a 1992 survey by Leipzig's Center for Social Research Analysis, 43 percent of apprentices (age 16 to 19) in East Germany want 'annexation' of Germany's former eastern territories, now part of Poland. Eleven percent favor a takeover by a Nazi-style party. Some 30 percent are overtly racist and call for 'Germanic purity and expulsion of other ethnic groups from Germany.' " There are similar trends in West Germany. According to Bielefield University sociologist Klaus Hurrelmann, 40 percent of seventeen-year-olds decline to reveal their political preferences. "This is a vacuum which radical rightists are trying to fill" (John Dornberg, "The Real Menace in Germany — The 'Intellectual' Far Right," *Ethnic NewsWatch*, March 31, 1995, p. 20).

10. ADL, *Religious Right*, pp. 4 – 5, 26, 43, 48.

11. Quoted in Stephen Bates, "Political Christians: How the Fundamentalist Right Plays the Victim Game," *Washington Post*, July 17, 1994, p. C3.

12. ADL, *Religious Right*, p. 26.

13. Quoted in Carmichael, *The Satanizing of the Jews*, p. 153.

14. ADL, *Religious Right*, pp. 21 – 22.

15. Ralph Reed, executive director of the Christian Coalition, quoted in ibid., p. 5. Robert Simonds, founder and president of Citizens for Excellence in Education, has been quoted as saying "America is now groaning! Atheistic secular humanist's [sic] should be removed from office and Christians should be elected. We can all then rejoice continually as our children and our nation will be more safe. Government and true Christianity are inseparable!" (ibid., p. 6)

16. "Christian Political Soldier Helps Revive Movement; Ralph Reed Broadens Agenda to Appeal to More Voters — and Presidential Contenders," *Washington Post*, Sept. 10, 1993, p. A4.

17. ADL, *Religious Right*, p. 29.

18. Ibid. The Christian Coalition now claims that it does not engage in stealth technique. But the record belies such denials.

19. ADL, *Religious Right*, pp. 6, 12 – 13.

20. Ibid. See also *New York Times*, Sept. 8, 1984, p. 21. Although the Christian Coalition now claims that there is "a lively debate" within its ranks over the separation of church and state, an analysis of statements made by its leaders *to* its members makes it clear that it is a one-sided debate.

21. Mark DeWolfe Howe, *The Garden and the Wilderness* (Chicago: University of Chicago Press, 1965), p. 6.

22. *New York Times*, Sept. 28, 1996, p. 12.

23. Garry Wills, *Under God: Religion and American Politics* (New York: Simon & Schuster, 1990), p. 25.

24. ADL, *Religious Right*, p. 4.

25. William F. Buckley, *In Search of Anti-Semitism* (New York: Continuum, 1994), p. 44.

26. Patrick Buchanan, syndicated column, Aug. 25, 1977.

27. Quoted in *Reform Judaism*, Winter 1996, p. 30.

28. ABC News, *This Week with David Brinkley*, March 1, 1992.

29. See *Chutzpah*, p. 350.

30. Alan M. Dershowitz, "Will Neo-Cons Condemn Buchanan's Bigotry?" United Feature Syndicate, March 3, 1995.

31. Steve Rabey, "Some Conservative Jews Join Hands with Religious Right," *Dallas Morning News*, Feb. 18, 1995, p. 1G.

32. Quoted in Peter Steinfels, "Beliefs," *New York Times*, July 23, 1994, pp. 26, C3.

33. Telushkin, *Jewish Humor*, pp. 136–37.

34. From "The Disputation" by Heinrich Heine, trans. reprinted in *The Big Book of Jewish Humor*, ed. William Novak and Moshe Waldoks (New York: Harper & Row, 1981), p. 88.

Chapter Five: Go to Shul!

1. Definitions from Geoffrey Wigoder, ed., *The Encyclopedia of Judaism* (New York: Macmillan, 1989). Rabbi Moshe Waldoks represents the emergence of post-denominational Judaism. "Waldoks considers himself a non-denominational Jew, neither Orthodox nor Conservative nor Reform." Waldoks was ordained by three rabbis: Rabbi Zalman Schechter-Shalomi, leader of the "Jewish renewal movement"; Rabbi Arthur Green, father of the Havurah movement; and Rabbi Everett Gendler, retired chaplain of Phillips Exeter Academy in Andover, Massachusetts ("A Most Unorthodox Rabbi: Moshe Waldoks Turns to Buddhism and Humor to Wake Jews Up," *Boston Globe*, Oct. 22, 1996, p. 1D).

2. Norman Lamm, *Faith and Doubt: Studies in Traditional Jewish Thought* (New York: Ktav, 1972), pp. 13–16.

3. Ibid., pp. 124–25; pp. 30–31.

4. Norman Lamm, in *Rebuilding Jewish Peoplehood* (New York: American Jewish Committee, 1996), p. 62.

5. Paul Davies, *The Mind of God* (New York: Simon and Schuster, 1991), p. 16.

6. Robert Nozick, *The Examined Life* (New York: Simon and Schuster, 1989), p. 47.

7. Nordau, *The Tragedy of Assimilation*, quoted in Joseph L. Baron, ed., *A Treasury of Jewish Quotations* (New York: Crown, 1956), p. 249.

8. Rabbi Mordecai M. Kaplan, *Judaism as a Civilization: Toward a Reconstruction of American-Jewish Life* (1934, reprint, Philadelphia: Jewish Publication Society of America, 1981).

9. *New York Times*, Jan. 15, 1994; *Ottowa Citizen*, March 31, 1994, p. G4.

10. See Leo Rosten, *The Joys of Yiddish* (New York: Pocket Books, 1968), p. ix. Rosten defines Yinglish as "Yiddish words that are used in colloquial English in both the United States and the United Kingdom."

11. Leonard Fein, in *Rebuilding Jewish Peoplehood*, p. 36.

12. Professor Michael Walzer of Princeton is working on a book about the political structures of Diaspora Judaism.

13. See Dubnow, *History of the Jews in Russia and Poland*.

14. Actually, there is both a *Talmud Yerushalmi* and a *Talmud Bavli*. In the *Yerushalmi*, which was compiled around A.D. 400, the rabbis of Palestine included their own discussions of and commentaries on the Mishnah. However, it is the *Bavli* that is referred to most often as "the Talmud" (Telushkin, *Jewish Literacy* [New York: Morrow, 1991], p. 152).

15. The Talmud is divided into Halakah (rules) and Aggadah (stories). The Aggadah holds a special status in Jewish life: "Our Sages teach: If you wish to know the One Who Created the World, learn *aggadah* (the nonlegal sections of the Talmud). In *aggadah* there is historic narrative at a deeper level, perspectives on Providence, human character, Exile and Redemption, the secrets of God's relation to His world, and the character and destiny of Israel. For a variety of reasons, the Sages often presented their views through veils of metaphor and parable, not only as protection from unfriendly eyes but also to simultaneously instruct the learned and saintly as well as the ignorant and simple" (quoted in *Jewish Book News*, Oct. 10, 1996, p. 18).

16. Louis Ginsberg, quoted in *Rebuilding Jewish Peoplehood*, p. 197.

17. Stuart Weinberg Gershon, *Kol Nidrei: Its Origin, Development and Significance* (Northvale, N.J., Jason Aronson, 1994), p. 29.

18. See *Encyclopedia Judaica*, vol. 10, p. 1167.

19. Phillip Sigal, "Halakhic Perspectives on the Matrilineal–Patrilineal Principles," *Judaism*, Winter 1985, p. 89. Orthodox rabbis believe that the Talmud is also the "revealed word of God," so any Talmudic change from the Torah has divine authority.

20. Shaye J. D. Cohen, "The Matrilinear Principle in Historical Perspective," *Judaism*, vol. 34, no. 133, Winter 1985, p. 7.

21. "Although it is generally very difficult to prove the influence of one legal system upon another, here the evidence is rather strong. The Roman law, whose principles are clearly attested in republican times, antedates the earliest attestation of the rabbinic law. This suggestion accounts for the phraseology of the Mishnah as well as its dominant ideas. It takes seriously the Mishnah's explanation of itself, since the Mishnah's notion of 'potential to contract a valid marriage' seems to reflect the Roman notion of *conubium*. It also is economical, since it accounts at once for both halves of the matrilineal principle. Perhaps, then, the matrilineal principle entered rabbinic Judaism from Roman law" (Shaye J. D. Cohen, "The Matrilineal Principle in Historical Perspective," *Judaism*, Winter 1985).

22. Indeed, yet another example of change in Jewish law to adapt to new realities was in the status of a child born to a Jewish mother who was raped by a non-Jew. Originally, the child of such an involuntary union was declared a mamzer — a status akin to, but worse than, a bastard. Later, such a child was declared to be a Jew fully entitled to marry another Jew. See Menachim Elon, *The Principles of Jewish Law* (Jerusalem: Keter, 1975), p. 436.

23. Adapted from Maimonides, *Commentary on the Mishna: Tractate* Sanhedrin, chapter 10, paragraph 1.

24. Sigal, pp. 89, 88.

25. Rabbi Wayne Dosick, *Living Judaism* (San Francisco: HarperSan Francisco, 1995), p. 302.

26. "Jewish First Wives Club," *Los Angeles Jewish Times*, Oct. 25, 1996, p. 10.

27. *Chabad-Lubavitch in Cyberspace*. The Lubavitch movement issued several papers enumerating the traditional criteria, which demonstrated that their rebbe fulfilled them.

28. Emunot Ve Deot, 933, 9.1.

29. *Menorah Journal*, 1924 x, p. 318.

30. Telushkin, *Jewish Humor*, p. 147.

31. Simcha Paull Raphael argues that traditional Judaism has an extensive literature on the afterlife and resurrection of the dead because "Jews have always believed in life after death," yet twentieth-century rabbis and theologians have systematically played down this dimension of the faith. As a result, many Jews no longer believe in resurrection because they are taught that Judaism does not sanction such a belief: "Somehow, in the twentieth century, Judaism has been proclaimed as a 'here and now' religion. As an inadvertent result, both Jews and non-Jews have come to believe that Judaism does not have any conception of a life after death." Raphael cites poll data charting the progressive decline in Jewish faith in resurrection: from a near-universal belief in the previous century, only 35 percent of Jews in 1952 believed in resurrection (in contrast to the 85 percent of Catholics and 80 percent of Protestants), and a mere 17 percent of Jews in 1965 continued to believe in resurrection (as opposed to 83 percent of Catholics and 78 percent of Protestants) (Raphael, *Jewish Views of the Afterlife* [Northvale, N.J.: Jason Aronson, 1994], pp. 13, 29). Only 41 percent of Jews polled in 1989 believe in a God who regularly intervenes in human events, and 47 percent believe in a God who answers prayers (Goldberg, *Jewish Power*, p. 58).

32. Yad (Muhna Torah): Melakim, 11.3, xiv 239.

33. Derech Hachaim, 126 – 49.

34. See *New York Times*, June 13, 1994.

35. Dubnow, pp. 222 – 61.

36. Quoted in *Why Is a Joke Jewish*.

37. Kamenetz, *The Jew in the Lotus*, p. 20.

Chapter Six: Make Aliyah!

1. Yehuda Amital, *Rebuilding Jewish Peoplehood*, p. 9.

2. *Chutzpah*, p. 335.

3. *Rebuilding Jewish Peoplehood*, p. 12.

4. Ibid., p. 9.

5. Yossi Klein Halevi, "Torn Between God and Country: Is the Alliance Between Orthodoxy and the Modern State Unraveling?" *Jerusalem Report*, Aug. 10, 1995, p. 16.

6. Hamas Covenant, Aug. 18, 1988.

7. Ehud Sprinzak, *The Ascendance of Israel's Radical Right* (New York: Oxford University Press, 1991).

8. Chaim Seidler-Feller, *Rebuilding Jewish Peoplehood*, p. 92.

9. *Big Book of Jewish Humor*, p. 81.

10. Ibid., p. 137.

11. *Jerusalem Report*, Nov. 16, 1995, p. 17.

12. *Rebuilding Jewish Peoplehood*, pp. 53, 70.

13. Ibid., p. 91.

14. "Rifts Still Not Healed a Year After Rabin Assassination," *Boston Globe*, Oct. 24, 1996, p. A12.

15. *Jewish Advocate*, Nov. 1 – 7, 1996, p. 38.

16. *Jewish Week*, Nov. 1, 1996, p. 31.

17. *New York Times*, June 2, 1996; May 12, 1996.

18. The language used by the right in Israel before the assassination is by now familiar: Rabin was targeted with such epithets as "traitor," "murderer," and "Nazi." As Israeli philosopher and theologian David Hartman has said, "We don't talk to one another here. We scream" (quoted in Richard Z. Chesnoff and David Makovsky, "The Struggle for Israel's Soul," *U.S. News and World Report*, Nov. 20, 1995, p. 64).

19. Quoted in *Reform Judaism*, Winter 1996, p. 17. In *The Late Great Planet Earth*, the evangelical Hal Lindsey argued that the return of Jews to the Holy Land and Israel's 1967 conquest of biblical territory including Jerusalem were signs that "the prophetic countdown" to Tribulation had begun. Recall the 1984 presidential debate in which Ronald Reagan admitted that as a result of consultations with evangelical ministers, he believed that nuclear war might be inevitable as part of God's plan, especially since other prophecies seemed to be coming true. The liberal Christic Institute then issued a statement warning that evangelicals used such prophecy "to justify nuclear war as a divine instrument to punish the wicked and complete God's plan for history" (cited in Ed Dobson and Ed Hindson, "Apocalypse Now? What Fundamentalists Believe About the End of the World," Policy Review of the Heritage Foundation No. 38, Fall 1986, p. 16).

20. All quotations are from Herzl's *The Jewish State*. I focus on Herzl's Zionism not because he was the only theoretician of Zionism — he was not — but because he was an influential innovator whose approach has many parallels today.

21. My mail certainly attests to this continuing but localized cancer. See *Chutzpah*, pp. 94 – 97.

22. Shlomo Avineri, "Letter to an American Friend: Soured Promise," *Jerusalem Post*, March 10, 1987, p. 10. Avineri repeated this point at a Harvard conference in October 1996.

23. See *Chutzpah*, passim.

24. See *The Tribes of Israel Together* (Jerusalem, 1996).

Chapter Seven: Be a Mensch!

1. According to a poll conducted in 1990, while 80 percent of "secular" American Jews believe that "to be a Jew in America" means being a member of a "cultural group," only 35 percent believe that it also means being a member of a "religious group." Indeed, even for "religious," while 70 percent believe it means being a

member of a "cultural group," only 49 percent believe it means being a member of a "religious group" (*Highlights of the Council of Jewish Federations 1990 National Jewish Population Survey*, p. 28).

2. Sefer Ha-aggadah, p. 462.

3. Gustav Karpeles, quoted in Ben Shia, p. 43. Kaplan, pp. 45, 205.

4. A 1988 *Los Angeles Times* survey asked Jews to name "the quality most important to their Jewish identity." Half selected "a commitment to social equality" (Goldberg, *Jewish Power*, p. 71).

5. *Encyclopedia of Cultural Anthropology*, vol. 3 (New York: Holt, 1996), p. 841.

6. Saadia, Emunot Ve Deot, 933, 9.1.

7. Both historian Salo Baron and Heinrich Graetz greatly limit the time frame for an autonomously functioning Talmudic penal system by noting the frequent and lengthy periods of foreign dominion over the Judean state. During most of these periods, the Sanhedrin, with its laws of criminal justice, was either proscribed from functioning or needed the assent of the foreign governor or procurator to mete out capital punishment. Additionally, the foreign ruler meted out his own justice as well — often cruel — but did not leave the policing of society wholly in the hands of the Jewish courts.

Even in times of Jewish autonomy, however, Talmudist Myer Galinsky (*Pursue Justice* [London: Nechdim Press, 1983], pp. 48 – 49) stresses that there was a dual system of justice at work: the technical, sometimes esoteric, and often feeble justice of the rabbinic courts, and the much more pervasive, stern, and societally effective rule of the Jewish monarch. The laws of the monarch and not the courts, Galinsky notes, really controlled the criminal system in ancient Israel.

Finally, Talmudic sources themselves view the leniency of the proposed criminal system with skepticism and apprehension. R. Shimon b. Gamliel in Makkot 7b notes that the bias against punishment shown by some of his contemporaries would have had disastrous societal results if they had been judges on a capital court, encouraging lawlessness and murder in Israel.

8. *Guide for the Perplexed*, 3:54.

9. Gerson Cohen, "The Talmudic Age," in *Great Ages and Ideas of the Jewish People*, p. 198. Cohen was a professor of Semitic languages at Columbia University.

10. Salo Baron, "The Modern Age," in *Great Ages and Ideas of the Jewish People*. Baron was a professor of Jewish history, literature, and institutions at Columbia University and authored *A Social and Religious History of the Jews*.

11. See Anson Laytner, *Arguing with God: A Jewish Tradition* (Northvale, N.J.: Jason Aronson, 1990), pp. 221 – 22 (quoting Elie Wiesel, *Gates of the Forest*, trans. Frances Frenaye [New York: Holt, Rinehart & Winston, 1966], pp. 197 – 99).

12. Pierre-Joseph Proudhon, *System of Economical Contradictions, or the Philosophy of Misery*, trans. Benjamin R. Tucker (1846; reprint, Boston: 1887). Walter Bagehot, *Physics and Politics iii Works & Life viii 19*. Lyman Abbott, *Life and Literature of Ancient Hebrews*, p. 111. Lord Acton, *Freedom in Antiquity*, Feb. 26, 1877, p. 4. Solomon Goldman, *Reflex*, Dec. 1927, p. 19. Arthur L. Goodhart, *Five Jewish Lawyers of the Common Law* (New York: Oxford, 1949); all quoted in *A Treasury of Jewish Quotations*.

13. Quoted in Goldberg, p. xxi.

14. Stanley Payne, *Fascism* (Madison, Wisc.: University of Wisconsin Press, 1980), p. 53.

15. One leading Jewish neoconservative, Irving Kristol, has spoken about his roots as a Communist, a neo-Marxist, a neo-Trotskyist, and a neo-socialist. See Mathew Robinson, "Author, Editor Irving Kristol," *Investor's Business Daily*, May 2, 1996, p. A1 (quoting Kristol's book *Neoconservatism: The Autobiography of an Idea*). For more on the Kristol family and their ideological roots, see Jacob Weisberg, "The Family Way," *New Yorker*, Oct. 21 and 28, 1996, p. 180. See also Goldberg, p. 159.

16. American Jews have donated to Palestinians in a two-pronged effort. On a grassroots level, Jews have worked with local Palestinian groups and charities in the United States to funnel individual contributions to Palestinians in the West Bank, Gaza Strip, and East Jerusalem. An example of this kind of giving is the Jewish contingent in the Jewish-Palestinian Living Room Dialogue Group of San Mateo, California, which "raised $21,000 in cash and medical equipment to give to two hospitals, one in the Gaza Strip and another in western Jerusalem" ("Jews and Palestinians Cooperate for Peace," *Timeline*, May/June 1996). On an institutional level, Israel has encouraged American Jewish organizations to lobby for congressional approval of aid to the Palestinian Authority. As a result, Congress funneled $75 million in aid to the P.A. in 1995 and "extend[ed] for 12 months the Middle East Peace Facilitation Act, which allows U.S. aid to flow to the Palestinians" (Matthew Dorf, "Senate OK's Aid to Palestinians," *Jewish Telegraphic Agency*, Nov. 10, 1995). American Jewish supporters of Israel's Peace Now put out an urgent plea on the World Wide Web asking its members to "phone, fax or email" congressmen to provide "financial support for the Palestinian Authority" (at http://www.peacenow.org/Cando/Docs/mepfanov.html).

17. Leonard Goldensohn, the founder of ABC, gave $40 million to the Harvard Medical School; the Loeb family contributed $70 million to the university; Gus and Rita Hauser contributed $13 million to the law school. See *New York Times*, Sept. 15, 1996, p. 40; *Boston Herald*, April 26, 1994, p. 24, and Oct. 8, 1994, p. 8.

18. David Gordis, in *Rebuilding Jewish Peoplehood*, p. 43.

19. Quoted in Dubnow, *History of the Jews in Russia and Poland*, pp. 117 – 20.

20. Kamenetz, *The Jew in the Lotus*, p. 60.

21. *New York Times Magazine*, Oct. 20, 1996, pp. 64 – 66.

22. *New York Times*, Dec. 16, 1994. A rightward trend in U.S. Jewish political temperament has been under way since the left began to savage Israel in 1967 (Jerold S. Auerbach, "Liberalism, Judaism, and American Jews," in Seltzer and Cohen, eds., *The Americanization of the Jews* [New York: New York University Press, 1995]); others discern Jewish disenchantment with liberalism in a gradual shift in Jewish voting patterns; Roosevelt gleaned 90 percent of the Jewish vote to Dewey's 10 percent, Kennedy enjoyed a greater percentage of the Jewish than the Catholic vote in 1960, and Lyndon Johnson beat out Barry Goldwater for the Jewish vote by a 90 – 10 margin; then an adjustment set in, as Nixon received 19 percent of the Jewish vote in 1968 and 35 percent of it in 1972, and Reagan received 39 percent of the Jewish vote in 1980 and 34 percent in 1984. Some observers, however, notably Leonard Fein, dispute this voting trend as a sign of rightward political drift among

U.S. Jewry. See his *Where Are We?: The Inner Life of America's Jews* (New York: Harper & Row, 1988), pp. 228 – 29. See also Goldberg, p. 299.

23. This commandment is often attributed to President Ronald Reagan (see Mark A. Dupuis, "Hart Supporters Hesitant," United Press International, Dec. 15, 1987). The late Republican strategist Lee Atwater rephrased it as: "Speak no ill of Republican candidates" (Bernard Weinraub, "Bush's Rivals Resent His Advantages," *New York Times*, June 10, 1987, p. 24).

24. *New York Times*, Jan. 3, 1995.

25. Samuel Silver, *American Rabbis* (1967), p. 154.

26. Fein, *Smashing Idols*, p. 18.

27. Fein, *Where Are We?*, p. 296.

28. In *Koheleth: The Man and His World* (1951; reprint, Northvale, N.J.: Jason Aronson, 1995), Robert Gordis characterizes this as "the most conservative passage in the Bible" (p. 37).

29. The original Aramaic dictum, *"dina d'malchuta dina"* — which literally means "the law of the land is the law" — can be found in four different Talmudic texts: Nedarim 28a, Bava Kama 113a, Bava Bathra 54b, Gittin 10b.

30. It is extremely unlikely that the author of Ecclesiastes was a woman, since the book reflects quite negative attitudes toward most women.

31. Leon Harrison, *Religion of a Modern Liberal* (New York: Bloch, 1931), p. 1.

32. Telushkin, *Jewish Literacy*, p. 148.

Chapter Eight: Filling the Yiddisher Cup

1. Frankel, quoted in *A Treasury of Jewish Quotations*. Ahad Ha'am, letter to Judah Magnes, Sept. 18, 1910 (in Ahad Ha'am, *Essays, Letters, Memories*, Tel Aviv: Bet Ahad Ha'am, 1931, p. 269).

2. Quoted in Ernst Pawel, *The Labyrinth of Exile* (New York: Farrar, Straus & Giroux, 1989), p. 330.

3. Professor Geoffrey Bock of the Harvard School of Education found that "unless you have 3,000 hours of formal Jewish studies, there is not much impact on the formation of a positive sense of Jewish identity" (*Dov Aharoni Fisch, Jews for Nothing: On Cults, Intermarriage, and Assimilation* [New York: Feldheim, 1984], p. 253). A 1988 study found that children enrolled in after-school Jewish studies programs achieved only a 10 percent increase in their Jewish knowledge between grades 1 and 6. Even more startling, between grades 4 and 5 the children actually showed a *decline* in Jewish learning in every subject area they were tested in! It is, then, hard to say who is in worse shape in terms of Jewish learning: the children suffering though afternoon Hebrew school or the "60 percent of the 1 million Jewish children of school age in North America [who] do not receive any form of formal Jewish education whatsoever" (Sheldon Engelmayer, "American Jewry in Midst of Spiritual Holocaust," *Cleveland Jewish News*, June 14, 1991, p. 8). See also Steven M. Cohen, "Jewish Continuity over Judaic Content: The Moderately Affiliated American Jew," in *The Americanization of the Jews*, Robert M. Seltzer and Norman J. Cohen, eds. (New York: New York University Press, 1995), p. 403.

4. Ephraim Buchwald, *Los Angeles Times*, April 28, 1992, p. A11.

5. Michael E. Porter, *The Competitive Advantage of Nations* (New York: Free Press, 1990).

6. An article in the *St. Louis Post-Dispatch* (Nov. 26, 1992, p. 16D) suggests that the fund-raising success of the United Jewish Appeal (UJA) in 1991 was due largely to the fight for Jewish survival: "Americans gave more money to the UJA last year than to any other nonprofit organization, mainly to help Soviet Jews emigrate to Israel." In fact, much of the $668.1 million raised by the organization in 1991 did go to Operation Exodus, a $1 billion drive to help resettle thousands of Soviet Jews. Since then, however, the UJA has slipped from its first-place ranking on the *Chronicle of Philanthropy*'s list of top charities. An article in the *New York Times* (Dec. 27, 1995, p. 10A) attributes the UJA's current financial woes to the fact that its foundations have been weakened "by its donors' lessening interest in a Jewish state that is increasingly more secure and by their own secure standing in the United States." Therefore, it seems that the absence of any formidable external enemies has given American Jews a sense of security that makes them less inclined to donate money to the UJA. Gershon Kekst, an active donor to Jewish causes, was quoted in the *Times* as saying "the history of Jewish philanthropy is that the Jews put up a lot of money when they are motivated to do so by a sense of urgency about the mission they are financing, like anti-Semitism, Hitler or Israel. Now there is no impetus to put up the money, and that is the threat to U.J.A.-Federation."

7. Susan A. Handelman, *Fragments of Redemption* (Bloomington: Indiana University Press, 1991), p. 179. Derrida wrote an entire essay on Emmanuel L'evinas, "Violence and Metaphysics: An Essay on the Thought of Emmanuel L'evinas," in *Writing and Difference*, trans. Alan Bass (Chicago: University of Chicago Press, 1978).

8. David Daube, *Collaboration with Tyranny in Rabbinic Law* (New York: Oxford University Press, 1965).

9. Quoted in Samuel Silver, comp. and ed., *The Quotable American Rabbis* (Anderson, S.C.: Drake House, 1967), pp. 8 – 9.

10. Quoted in *Boston Globe*, Sept. 13, 1996, pp. 1, A16.

11. *Boston Globe*, Oct. 27, 1996, pp. B12 – 14.

12. Quoted in Alan Dershowitz, *The Best Defense* (New York: Random House, 1982), p. xv.

13. *U.S. v. Wade*, 388 U.S. 218.

14. Rabbi Norman Lamm's article first appeared in *Judaism*, Winter 1956, p. 53. It has since been revised and republished several times. It most recently appeared in his *Faith and Doubt*, 2nd ed. (New York: Ktav, 1986).

15. Alan M. Dershowitz, *The Advocate's Devil* (New York: Warner Books, 1994), p. 326.

16. Daniel Gordis, *Rebuilding Jewish Peoplehood*, p. 40.

17. Kamenetz, p. 112.

18. The Havurah movement, which began in Somerville, Massachusetts, in the 1960s, seeks spirituality through small groups of "like-minded *chevra*, or friends, who worship together, usually in private homes" (Kamenetz, p. 24).

19. Introduction, E. E. Reynolds, *The Trial of Sir Thomas More* (New York: Newbridge Communications, 1993).

20. Jeffrey K. Salkin, "How to Be a Truly Spiritual Jew," *Reform Judaism*, Fall 1995, p. 22.

21. Quoted in Hillel Goldberg, *Israel Salanter* (New York: Ktav, 1982), pp. 78 – 79.

22. Robert Gordis, "Ecology and the Judaic Tradition," in *Contemporary Jewish Ethics and Morality*, ed. Elliot N. Dorff and Louis E. Newman (New York: Oxford University Press, 1995), pp. 327 – 35.

23. For more information about COEJL, contact Mark Jacobs, 443 Park Ave. South, 11th floor, New York, NY 10016-7322. E-mail: coejl@aol.com.

24. Blu Greenberg, *On Women and Judaism* (Philadelphia: Jewish Publication Society, 1981), pp. 40 – 41.

25. Avraham Weiss, *Women at Prayer: A Halachic Analysis of Women's Prayer Groups* (Hoboken, N.J.: Ktav, 1990), p. 6, quoting *"Sefer Abudarham ha-Shalem."*

26. Ibid., pp. 2 – 3, quoting "Rav Aharon Soloveichik."

27. Goldberg suggests that Jewish influence does not rest on numbers alone (see pp. 110 – 11, 366). But there may come a point when the numbers become so relatively small that they will matter.

28. Thomas J. Billitteri, "God's Not Dead Here," *St. Petersburg Times*, June 25, 1994, p. 10.

29. See *A New Dictionary of Religions* (Blackwell, 1995), for a discussion of Buddhist and Shinto beliefs regarding divinity (pp. 83 – 84, 472 – 73).

30. Society for Humanistic Judaism, "What Do Humanistic Jews Do?"

31. Martin Buber, *Tales of the Chasidim*, trans. Olga Marx (London: Thames and Hudson, 1956), vol. 2, p. 89.

32. Quoted in Kamenetz, p. 25.

33. See *Jewish Week*, Oct. 25, 1996, p. 11.

34. Mordechai Kaplan, *Not So Random Thoughts* (New York: Reconstructionist Press, 1966), Introduction.

Epilogue: A Call to Action

1. Ernst Pawel, *The Labyrinth of Exile*, p. 331.

Appendix

The $500 Beginning Jewish Home Library

If the secret to Jewish survival is "learning, learning, learning," then every Jewish home should be equipped with the tools necessary for this task. Since two Jews produce three opinions on any subject, no one should expect consensus on the contents of a library. I have asked a wide variety of Jewish experts for their views on this issue, and they are reflected in this list, but in the end this is *my* list, based on my eclectic approach to Judaism. I have tried to include only easily available books, some in paperback, but some are not in bookstores and may have to be ordered from the Jewish Book Club (P.O. Box 618, Holmes, Pennsylvania 19043-0618. Phone: 610-534-2884; Fax: 610-532-9001) or other specialized sources, such as local Jewish bookstores.

Every Jewish home library should start with a good translation of the Jewish Bible. Everett Fox's poetic translation is highly readable: *The Schocken Bible: Volume One — The Five Books of Moses: Genesis, Exodus, Leviticus, Numbers, and Deuteronomy*, translation and commentary by Everett Fox (Schocken, 1995). Thus far Fox has translated only the Five Books of Moses. The remainder of the Jewish Bible is available in several excellent editions published by Soncino, Artscroll, and the Jewish Publications Society.

The best introduction to the Talmud is by Rabbi Adin Steinsaltz. I recommend starting with *Steinsaltz's The Talmud: A Reference*

Guide, which is available from Random House either in hard or soft cover, and his first substantive volume, *The Talmud: The Steinsaltz Edition, Volume 1, Tractate Bava Metzia*, translation and commentary by Rabbi Adin Steinsaltz.

My favorite books of the Bible are Ecclesiastes and Job, and an excellent work on Ecclesiastes is *Koheleth: The Man and His World*, by Robert Gordis (Jason Aronson, 1995). An interesting contemporary interpretation of Job is *The First Dissident: The Book of Job in Today's Politics*, by William Safire (Random House, 1993).

For an understanding of the Midrash and Aggadah, there are *What Is Midrash?* and *A Midrash Reader* (Jacob Neusner, ed.; Scholars Press, 1994); *Sofer Ha-Aggadah: The Book of Legends* (Bialik & Ravnitzky, eds.; Schocken, 1992); and *The Legends of the Rabbis* (Judah Nadich, ed.; Jason Aronson, 1994).

The Sayings of the Fathers (Pirkei Avot) is available in *Ethics of the Fathers Treasury with an Anthologized Commentary* (Nosson Scherman, ed.; Mesorah/Artscroll, 1995).

A good introduction to the Responsa literature is *The Responsa Anthology* (Avraham Finkel, ed.; Jason Aronson, 1990).

Medieval Jewish philosophy is diverse, but a good introduction might include *Mishne Torah: Maimonides' Code of Law and Ethics* (Philip Birnbaum, ed.; Hebrew Publishing Co., 1974); *The Essential Maimonides: Translations of the Rambam* (A. Y. Finkel, ed.; Jason Aronson, 1996); *A Maimonides Reader* (Isadore Twersky, ed.); *Zohar: The Book of Enlightenment* (Paulist Press/The Classics of Western Spirituality, 1983); and *The Essential Kabbalah: The Heart of Jewish Mysticism* (Daniel C. Matt, ed.; Harper San Francisco, 1995).

The best books on Jewish mysticism are by Gershom Scholem: *Major Trends in Jewish Mysticism* (Schocken, 1995) and *On the Kabbalah and Its Symbolism* (Schocken, 1996).

A good introduction to the schism between Hasidim and Mitnagdim is *The Hasidic Movement and the Gaon of Vilna*, by Elijah Judah Schochet (Jason Aronson, 1994).

An excellent introduction to biblical criticism is Richard Elliot Friedman's *Who Wrote the Bible?* (HarperCollins, 1989).

It is difficult to find one definitive and accessible Jewish history, but I have found H. H. Ben-Sasson's *A History of the Jewish People*

(Harvard, 1976) valuable. Also important is Jehuda Reinhartz and Paul Mendes-Flohr, *The Jew in the Modern World: A Documentary History* (Oxford, 1995).

Several books on the Holocaust deserve inclusion in any library. These include two by Elie Wiesel: the classic *Night* (Bantam, 1982) and the memoir *All Rivers Run into the Sea* (Knopf, 1995). Raul Hilberg's *The Destruction of the European Jews* (Holmes and Meier, 1985) is also a must. *The Golden Tradition*, edited by Lucy S. Dawidowicz (Syracuse University Press, 1996), is important to an understanding of what was destroyed. David Wyman's *Abandonment of the Jews* (Pantheon, 1985) is valuable, as is Debra Lipstadt's *Beyond Belief* (Free Press, 1993).

A good survey of the history of anti-Semitism can be found in Edward Flannery's *The Anguish of the Jews: Twenty-three Centuries of Anti-Semitism* (Paulist Press, 1985) or in Dan Cohn-Shirbok's *The Crucified Jew: Twenty Centuries of Christian Anti-Semitism* (Harper-Collins, 1992).

An interesting introduction to the land of Israel is James Michener's novel *The Source* (Random House, 1965). Arthur Hertzberg's anthology, *The Zionist Idea* (Greenwood Press, 1971), is a useful compendium. David Hartman's *Conflicting Visions: Spiritual Possibilities of Modern Israel* (Schocken, 1990) is a good contemporary analysis. Theodore Herzl's *The Jewish State* (Dover, 1988) is short, a bit dense, but invaluable.

Contemporary Jewish philosophers and theologians who should be read include Martin Buber, *I and Thou* (Touchstone, 1996); Emil L. Fackenheim, *The Jewish Thought of Emil Fackenheim: A Reader* (Wayne State University Press, 1987); David Hartman, *Living Covenant: The Innovative Spirit in Traditional Judaism* (Free Press, 1985); Lawrence J. Kaplan, ed., *Abraham Isaac Kook and Jewish Spirituality* (New York University Press, 1995); Jonathan Sacks, *One People?: Tradition, Modernity, and Jewish Unity* (B'nai B'rith, 1993); Abraham Joshua Heschel, *God in Search of Man: A Philosophy of Judaism* (Jason Aronson, 1987); Joseph B. Soloveitchik, *Halachic Man* (Jewish Publication Society of America, 1991); Stephen T. Katz, ed., *Interpreters of Judaism in the Late Twentieth Century* (B'nai B'rith, 1993); Mordechai Kaplan, *Judaism as a Civilization* (JPS Philadelphia, 1994); Arthur Cohen and Paul Mendes-Flohr, eds., *Contempo-*

rary Jewish Religious Thought (Free Press, 1988); and Nahum Glatzer, ed., *Judaic Tradition* (Behrman, 1982).

I will not venture into religious practices, since one's library is dependent on one's Jewish denominational preference. But every Jewish home should have an excellent prayer book in Hebrew, with translation and, if necessary, some transliteration. Among the useful books on Jewish ritual are Blu Greenberg's *How to Run a Traditional Jewish Household* (Simon and Schuster, 1983), and her husband Rabbi Irving Greenberg's *The Jewish Way: Living the Holidays* (Simon and Schuster, 1993). Also, Hayim Helevy Dowin's *To Be a Jew: A Guide to Jewish Observance in Contemporary Life* (Basic Books, 1991).

Finally, I offer a miscellaneous list of books I have found particularly valuable: *Ahad Ha-Am Asher Ginzberg: A Biography*, by Leon Simon (Herzl Press, 1960); *Israel Salanter: Text, Structure, Idea*, by Hillel Goldberg (KTAV Publishing House, New York); *Jewish Literacy* (Morrow, 1991) and *Jewish Wisdom* (Morrow, 1994), by Joseph Telushkin; *Women and Jewish Law: The Essential Texts, Their History, and Their Relevance for Today*, by Rachel Biale (Pantheon, 1995); *On Being a Jewish Feminist: A Reader*, edited by Susannah Heschel (Schocken, 1995); *Fear No Evil*, by Natan Sharansky (Random House, 1989); *Tevye the Dairyman* and *The Railroad Stories*, by Sholom Aleichem (Schocken, 1988); *The Penguin Book of Modern Yiddish Verse*, edited by Howe and Wisse (Viking, 1987); *My Mother's Sabbath Days*, by Chaim Grade (Knopf, 1986); *In My Father's Court*, by Isaac Bashevis Singer (Farrar, Straus and Giroux, 1996); *Against the Apocalypse: Responses to Catastrophe in Modern Jewish Culture*, by David Roskies (Harvard University Press, 1984); *The Penguin Book of Hebrew Verse*, edited by Carmi (Viking, 1981); *The Oxford Book of Hebrew Short Stories*, edited by Abramson (Oxford University Press, 1996); *The Complete Short Stories of Franz Kafka*, by Franz Kafka (Penguin, 1983); *A Book That Was Lost and Other Stories*, by S. Y. Agnon (Schocken, 1995); *Great Jewish Short Stories*, edited by Saul Bellow (Dell, 1978); *The Collected Stories of A. B. Yehoshua*, by A. B. Yehoshua (Penguin, 1991); *This Is My God*, by Herman Wouk (Little, Brown, 1992); *The Chosen*, by Chaim Potok (Buccaneer Books, 1994); *Exodus*, by Leon Uris (Bantam, 1983); *In the Land of Israel*, by Amos Oz (Harcourt Brace Jovanovich, 1993); *Jewish Law: History, Sources, Principles*, by Menachem Elon (JPS Philadelphia, 1994); *Days of Awe*, by S. Y. Agnon (Schocken, 1995); and *Hebrew-*

English English-Hebrew Dictionary, by Reuben Alcalay (Shalom, 1987).

The Schocken Guide to Jewish Books (Pantheon, 1993) contains a much more extensive library. *The Encyclopedia Judaica*, which was published in 1972 by KTAV in Jerusalem, is out of date on current issues, but it is an unparalleled source of information on classic Judaism. Because it is not current, it can be bought at a bargain price, and I recommend it.

INDEX

Waldoks, Rabbi Moshe, 12, 295, 297,
    365n.1
Walesa, Lech, 86n, 138, 144
Walzer, Michael, 276
Wannsee Conference, 24, 116, 347n.3
Washington, George, 144–45
Washington Post, 111
Wasserman, Dan, 232
Wasserman, Rabbi Elchanan, 3, 175, 335
Wealth, 10
Weber, Max, 54
Weil, Simone, 54
Weizman, Ezer, 164, 250, 251, 252–53
Weizmann, Chaim, 178
Wellesley College, 130
Wells, H. G., 83
West, Cornel, 126, 131
West Bank, 223, 225, 236, 240
Western civilization, 50–51, 53, 188
Western Europe, 71
Weyrich, Paul, 154
When All You've Ever Wanted Isn't Enough
    (Kushner), 313
Who's Who in the Zionist Conspiracy, 101
Wiesel, Elie, 54, 258–59, 268, 272, 302, 334
Will, George, 110
Williams, Patricia, 126
Williams, Roger, 155
Wills, Garry, 155
Wilson, Woodrow, 78–79
Wisse, Ruth, 159
Witchcraft trials, 184
Wittgenstein, Ludwig, 54
Wolpe, David, 200
Women, 11–12, 346n.21
    discrimination against, 88
    and divorce, 209–10
    Halakah and feminism, 318–20
    and intermarriage, 28–29, 31, 43, 44,
        205
    Islamic fundamentalism and, 222
    matrilineal descent, 31, 203–6, 366n.21
    Talmud and, 283–84
Woocher, Jonathan S., 71

Woodward, C. Vann, 361n.51
World Council of Churches, 354–55n.30
World Trade Center bombing, 136
World War I, 74, 353n.13
World War II, 23–24, 84, 157, 352n.9
Wright, Richard, 121
Wyschogrod, Michael, 64

Xenophobia, 363–64n.9

Yale Law School, 172
Yemenite Jews, 60
Yerida, 247
Yeshiva College, 3
Yeshiva University, 175
Yiddish culture, 17, 190, 193–94, 325
"Yiddisher cup," 18, 59, 293
Yinglish, 194, 365n.10
Yom Kippur, 35, 201, 202–3
Yom Kippur War, 90
York, Sarah Ferguson, Duchess of, 87
Yosi Ha-G'lili, Rabbi, 186n

Zakkai, Rabbi Ben, 211
Zalman, Rabbi Shneur, 2–3
Zhirinovsky, Vladimir V., 138, 139
Zhitlofsky, Chayim, 331
Zionism, 15
    anti-Zionism, 74, 82, 88–89, 90, 105, 145,
        357n.37
    Basel conference on, 339
    and Diaspora Jewry, 248, 249–50, 251–53
    Herzl's theory of, 170, 242–43, 244–45,
        246–48, 251–52, 253
    and Jewish survival, 17, 219, 245
    Palestinians and, 355–56n.33
    and secularism, 17, 244–45, 325
    UN resolution on, 87, 88, 232
"Zionist occupation governments" (ZOG),
    101–2, 156
Zohar, 278
Zundel, Ernst, 114–15
Zweibon, Herbert, 159
Zyuganov, Gennady A., 138–39